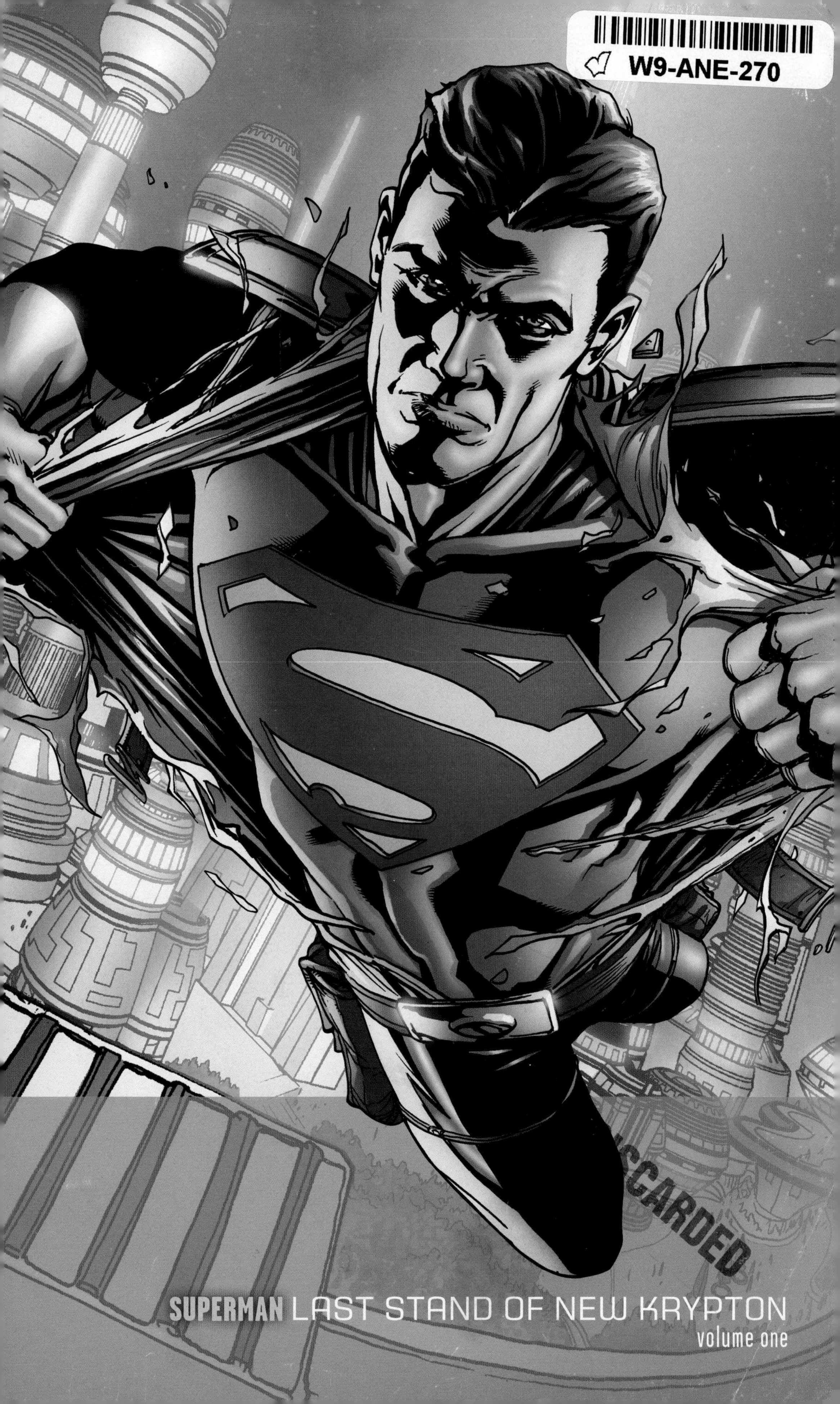

SUPERMAN LAST STAND OF NEW KRYPTON

volume one

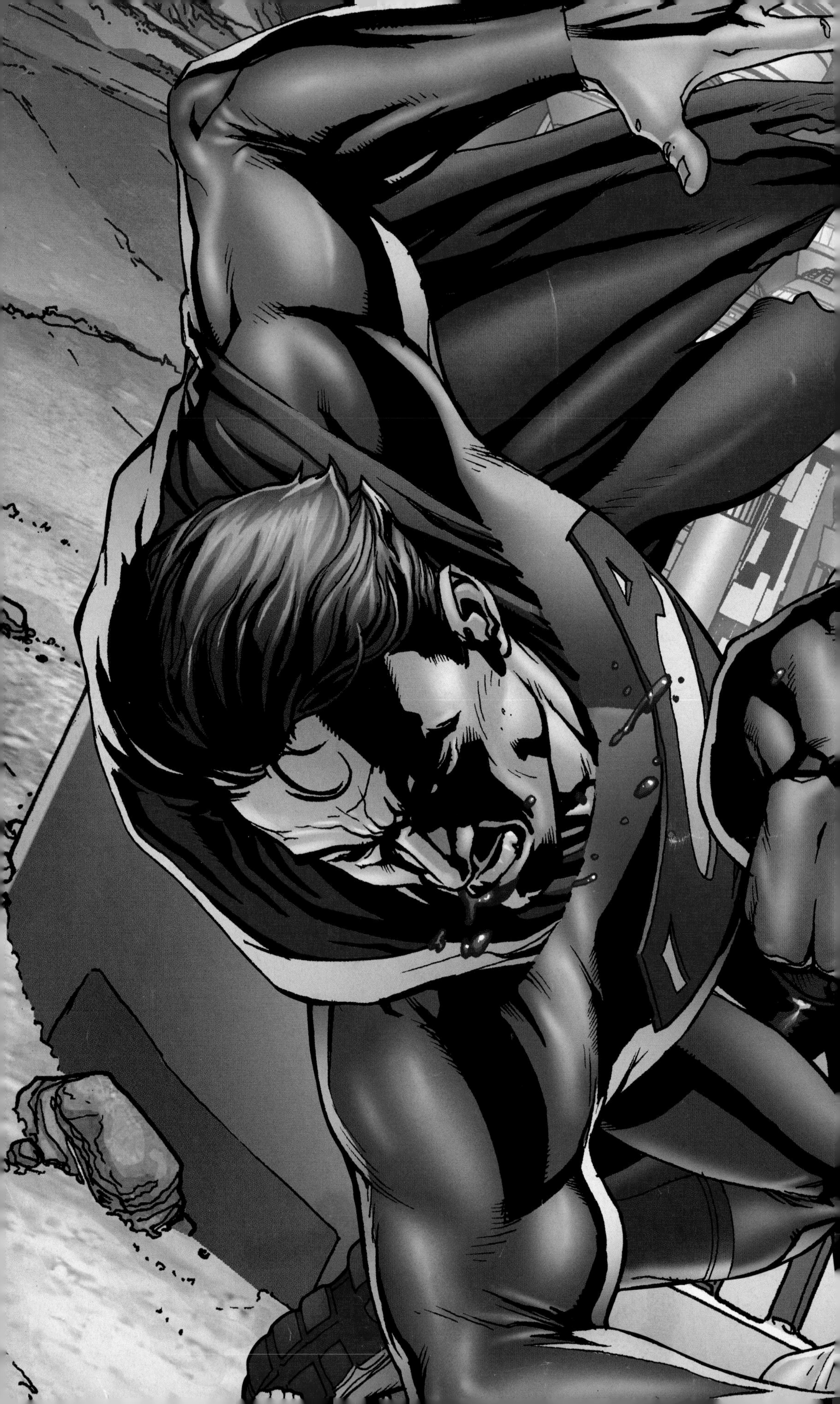

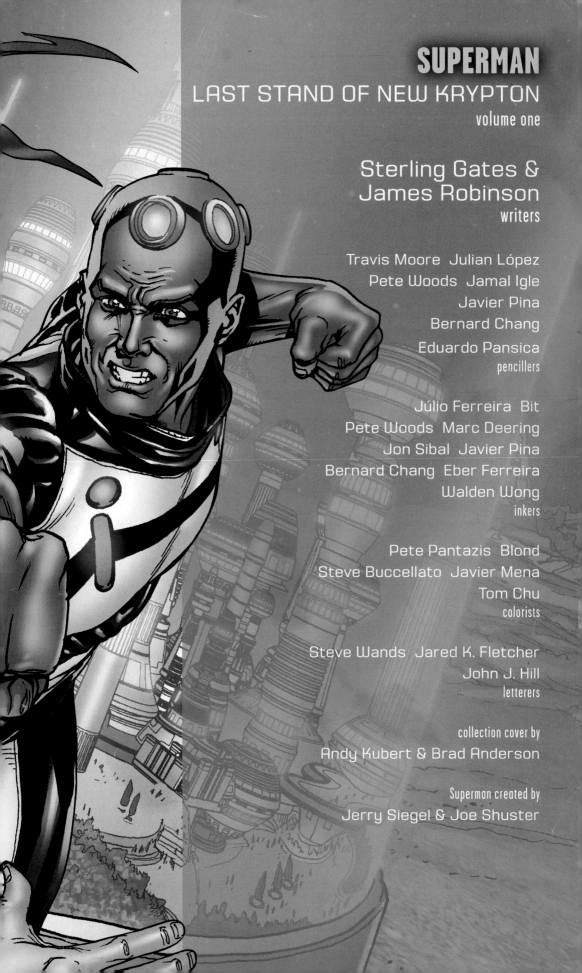

SUPERMAN
LAST STAND OF NEW KRYPTON
volume one

Sterling Gates & James Robinson
writers

Travis Moore Julian López
Pete Woods Jamal Igle
Javier Pina
Bernard Chang
Eduardo Pansica
pencillers

Júlio Ferreira Bit
Pete Woods Marc Deering
Jon Sibal Javier Pina
Bernard Chang Eber Ferreira
Walden Wong
inkers

Pete Pantazis Blond
Steve Buccellato Javier Mena
Tom Chu
colorists

Steve Wands Jared K. Fletcher
John J. Hill
letterers

collection cover by
Andy Kubert & Brad Anderson

Superman created by
Jerry Siegel & Joe Shuster

MATT IDELSON Editor-original series WIL MOSS Assistant Editor-original series BOB HARRAS Group Editor-Collected Editions SEAN MACKIEWICZ Editor ROBBIN BROSTERMAN Design Director-Books

DC COMICS

DIANE NELSON President DAN DIDIO and JIM LEE Co-Publishers GEOFF JOHNS Chief Creative Officer PATRICK CALDON EVP-Finance and Administration

JOHN ROOD EVP-Sales, Marketing and Business Development AMY GENKINS SVP-Business and Legal Affairs STEVE ROTTERDAM SVP-Sales and Marketing JOHN CUNNINGHAM VP-Marketing

TERRI CUNNINGHAM VP-Managing Editor ALISON GILL VP-Manufacturing DAVID HYDE VP-Publicity SUE POHJA VP-Book Trade Sales ALYSSE SOLL VP-Advertising and Custom Publishing

BOB WAYNE VP-Sales MARK CHIARELLO Art Director

SUPERMAN: LAST STAND OF NEW KRYPTON Volume 1

DC Comics, 1700 Broadway, New York, NY 10019

A Warner Bros. Entertainment Company

Printed by RR Donnelley, Salem, VA, USA. 10/7/11. First Printing.

ISBN:978-1-4012-2933-7

SUSTAINABLE FORESTRY INITIATIVE

Certified Chain of Custody
Promoting Sustainable Forest Management
www.sfiprogram.org

Fiber used in this product line meets the sourcing requirements of the SFI program. www.sfiprogram.org SGS-SFI/COC-US10/81072

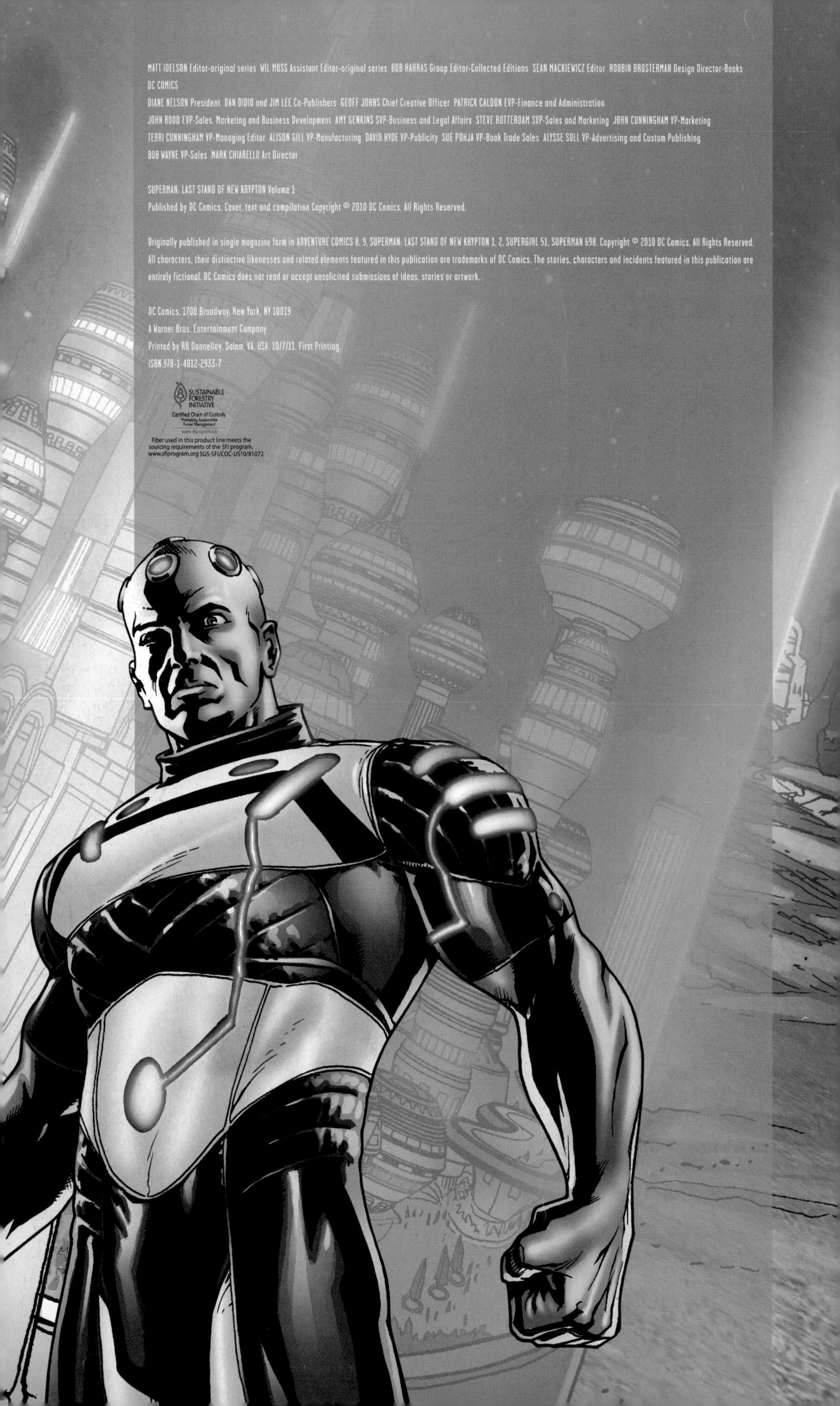

cover by **FRANCIS MANAPUL & BRIAN BUCCELLATO**

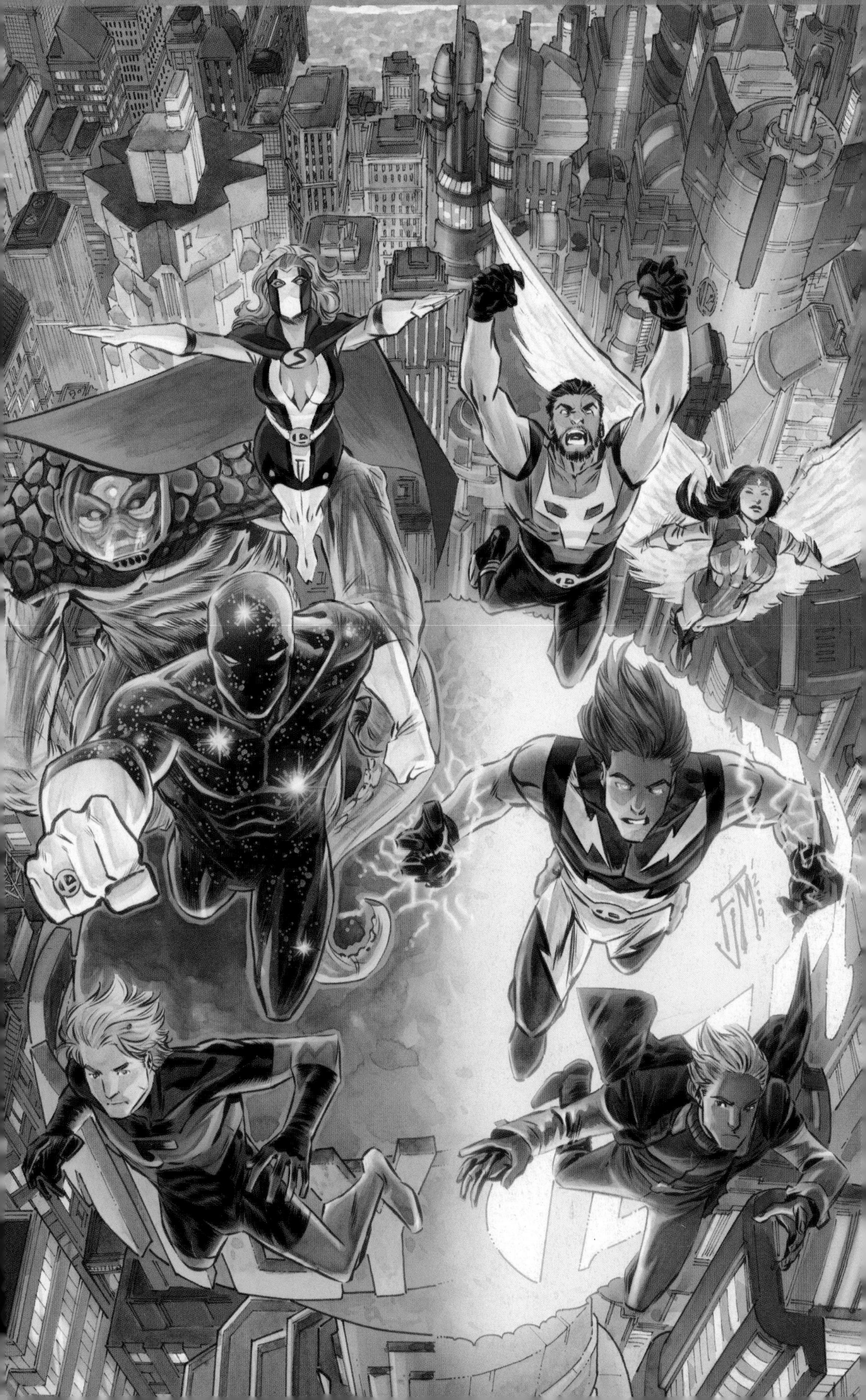

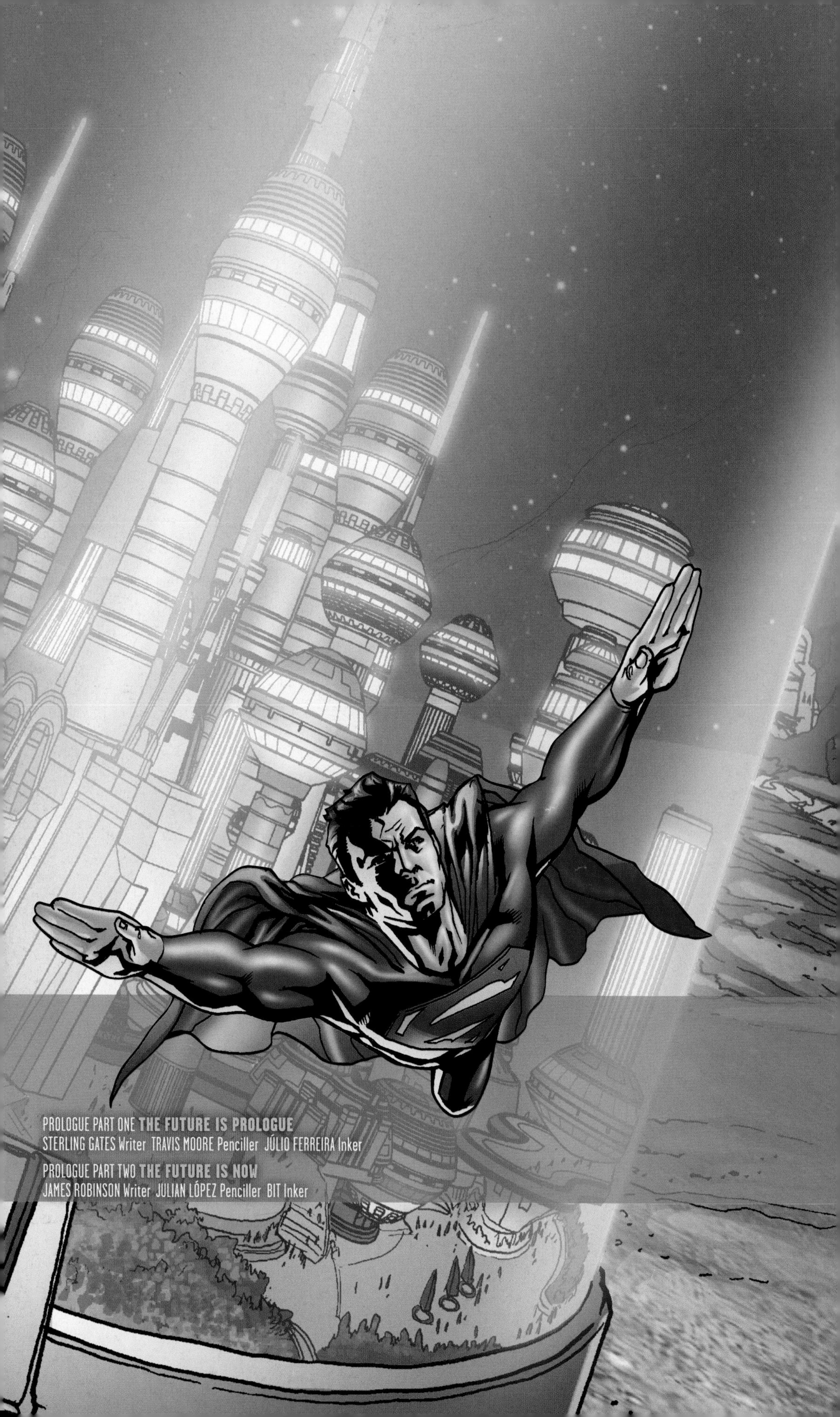
PROLOGUE PART ONE THE FUTURE IS PROLOGUE
STERLING GATES Writer TRAVIS MOORE Penciller JÚLIO FERREIRA Inker
PROLOGUE PART TWO THE FUTURE IS NOW
JAMES ROBINSON Writer JULIAN LÓPEZ Penciller BIT Inker

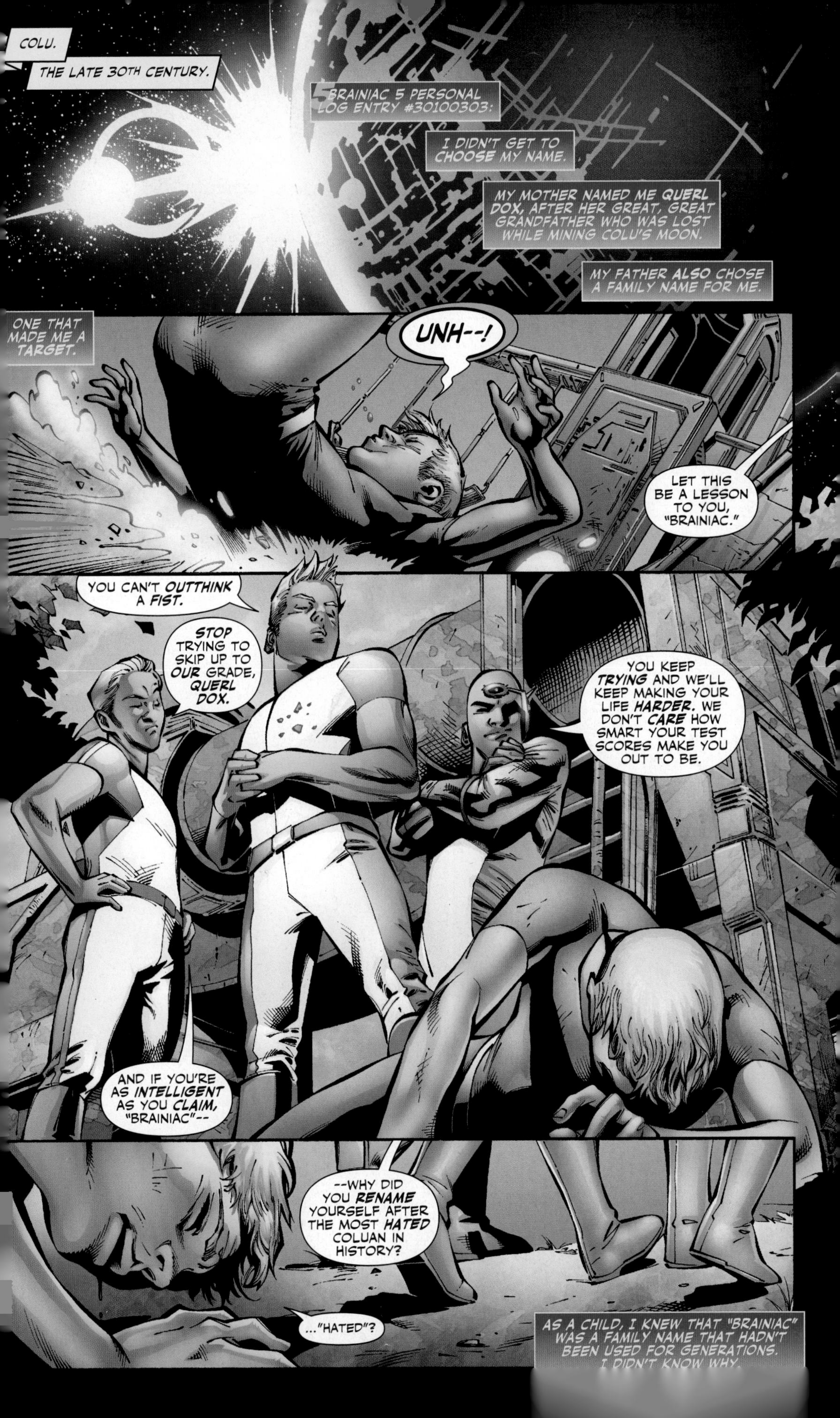
COLU.
THE LATE 30TH CENTURY.
BRAINIAC 5 PERSONAL LOG ENTRY #30100303:
I DIDN'T GET TO CHOOSE MY NAME.
MY MOTHER NAMED ME QUERL DOX, AFTER HER GREAT, GREAT GRANDFATHER WHO WAS LOST WHILE MINING COLU'S MOON.
MY FATHER ALSO CHOSE A FAMILY NAME FOR ME.
ONE THAT MADE ME A TARGET.
UNH--!
LET THIS BE A LESSON TO YOU, "BRAINIAC."
YOU CAN'T OUTTHINK A FIST.
STOP TRYING TO SKIP UP TO OUR GRADE, QUERL DOX.
YOU KEEP TRYING AND WE'LL KEEP MAKING YOUR LIFE HARDER. WE DON'T CARE HOW SMART YOUR TEST SCORES MAKE YOU OUT TO BE.
AND IF YOU'RE AS INTELLIGENT AS YOU CLAIM, "BRAINIAC"--
--WHY DID YOU RENAME YOURSELF AFTER THE MOST HATED COLUAN IN HISTORY?
..."HATED"?
AS A CHILD, I KNEW THAT "BRAINIAC" WAS A FAMILY NAME THAT HADN'T BEEN USED FOR GENERATIONS. I DIDN'T KNOW WHY.

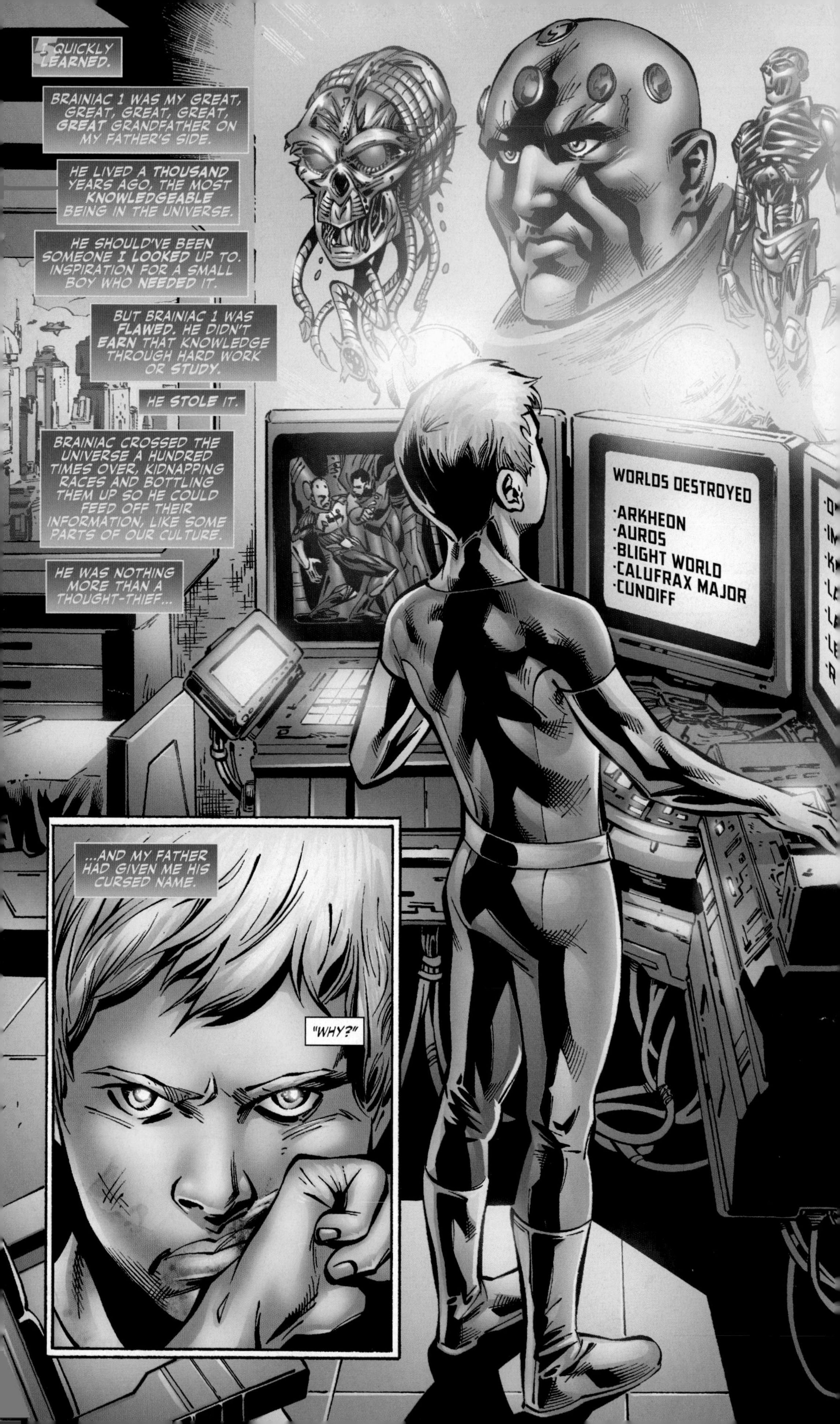
I QUICKLY LEARNED.
BRAINIAC 1 WAS MY GREAT, GREAT, GREAT, GREAT, GREAT GRANDFATHER ON MY FATHER'S SIDE.
HE LIVED A THOUSAND YEARS AGO, THE MOST KNOWLEDGEABLE BEING IN THE UNIVERSE.
HE SHOULD'VE BEEN SOMEONE I LOOKED UP TO. INSPIRATION FOR A SMALL BOY WHO NEEDED IT.
BUT BRAINIAC 1 WAS FLAWED. HE DIDN'T EARN THAT KNOWLEDGE THROUGH HARD WORK OR STUDY.
HE STOLE IT.
BRAINIAC CROSSED THE UNIVERSE A HUNDRED TIMES OVER, KIDNAPPING RACES AND BOTTLING THEM UP SO HE COULD FEED OFF THEIR INFORMATION, LIKE SOME PARTS OF OUR CULTURE.
HE WAS NOTHING MORE THAN A THOUGHT-THIEF...
WORLDS DESTROYED
·ARKHEON
·AUROS
·BLIGHT WORLD
·CALUFRAX MAJOR
·CUNDIFF
...AND MY FATHER HAD GIVEN ME HIS CURSED NAME.
"WHY?"

WHY WOULD YOU GIVE ME THAT *NAME!?*

BRAINIAC WAS A *CRIMINAL!* ONE OF THE *THOUGHT-TYRANTS* OF THE 21ST CENTURY! HE WAS RESPONSIBLE FOR THE EXTINCTION OF *HUNDREDS* OF RACES!

HE WAS SO HATED THAT COLU OUTLAWED THE USE OF THE TITLE "BRAINIAC" FOR ALMOST A *THOUSAND* YEARS! UNTIL--

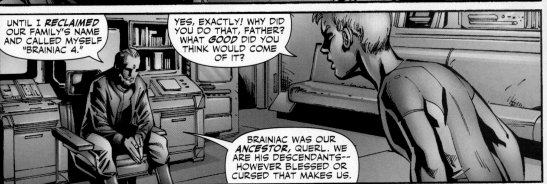

UNTIL I *RECLAIMED* OUR FAMILY'S NAME AND CALLED MYSELF "BRAINIAC 4."

YES, EXACTLY! WHY DID YOU DO THAT, FATHER? WHAT *GOOD* DID YOU THINK WOULD COME OF IT?

BRAINIAC WAS OUR *ANCESTOR*, QUERL. WE ARE HIS DESCENDANTS-- HOWEVER BLESSED OR CURSED THAT MAKES US.

IT'S UP TO *US*--YOU AND I--TO *RETAKE* THAT NAME AND MAKE OUR FAMILY TITLE SOMETHING COLU IS *PROUD* OF.

SOMETHING THE UNIVERSE WILL *ADMIRE*, NOT FEAR.

I *TRIED*, BUT NOW IT'S YOUR TURN. *YOUR* TIME. SOON, THE ENTIRE UNIVERSE WILL KNOW YOU'RE THE *SMARTEST* BEING IN IT.

UNIVERSE? WHAT DO YOU MEAN?

I RECEIVED A HOLOCALL TODAY FROM A MAN NAMED R.J. BRANDE.

TELL ME, BRAINIAC 5. HAVE YOU EVER HEARD OF THE *LEGION OF SUPER-HEROES?*

5 AFTER STUDYING AT THE TIME INSTITUTE, I BEGRUDGINGLY JOINED THE TEAM, TRYING TO DO RIGHT BY THE NAME "BRAINIAC." I'VE COME TO ACCEPT MY *NAME*--EVEN ENJOY ITS IMPLICATION.

IT SAYS EXACTLY WHAT I *WANT* IT TO SAY--

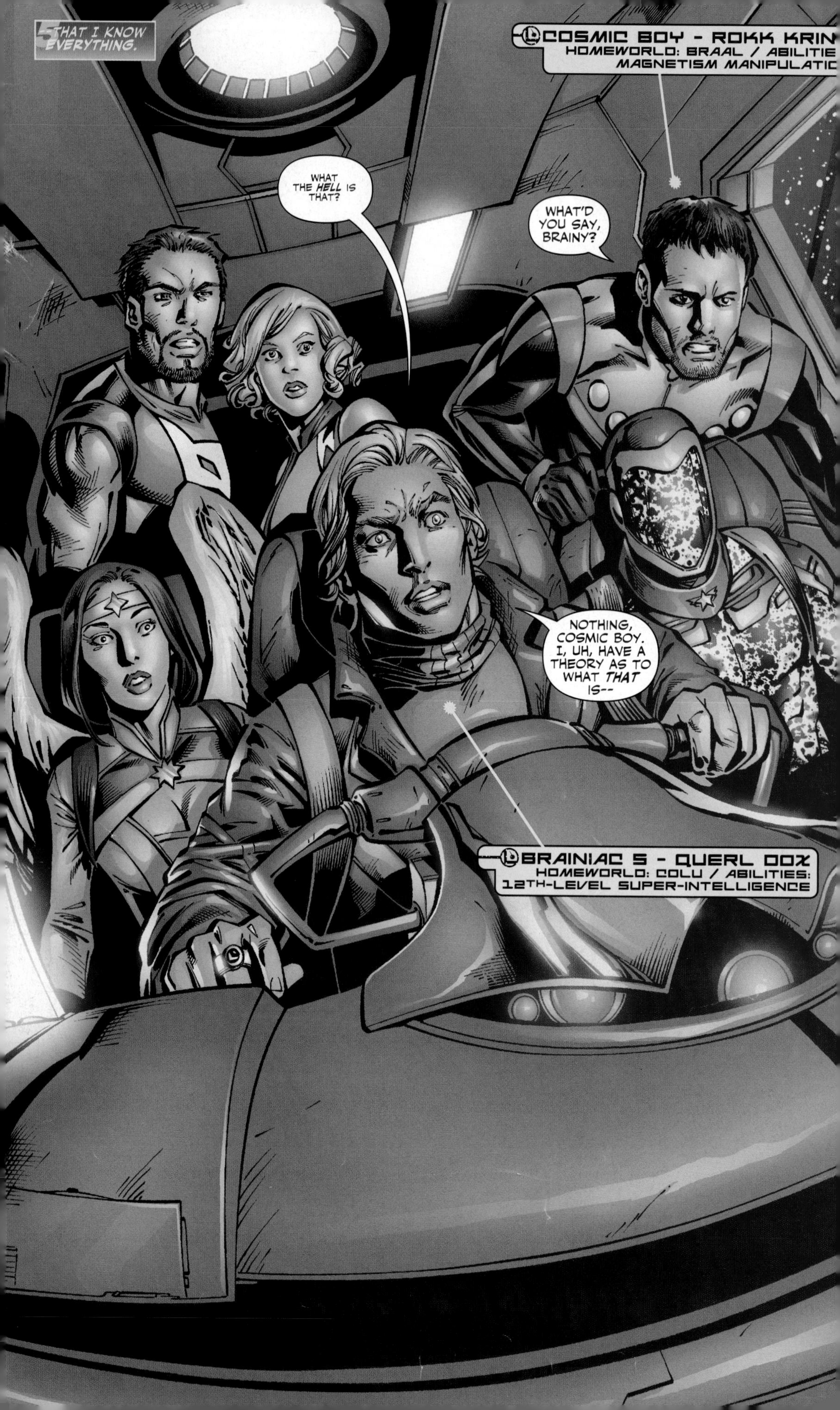

--THAT I KNOW EVERYTHING.
COSMIC BOY - ROKK KRIN
HOMEWORLD: BRAAL / ABILITIE
MAGNETISM MANIPULATIC
WHAT THE HELL IS THAT?
WHAT'D YOU SAY, BRAINY?
NOTHING, COSMIC BOY. I, UH, HAVE A THEORY AS TO WHAT THAT IS--
BRAINIAC 5 - QUERL DOX
HOMEWORLD: COLU / ABILITIES: 12TH-LEVEL SUPER-INTELLIGENCE

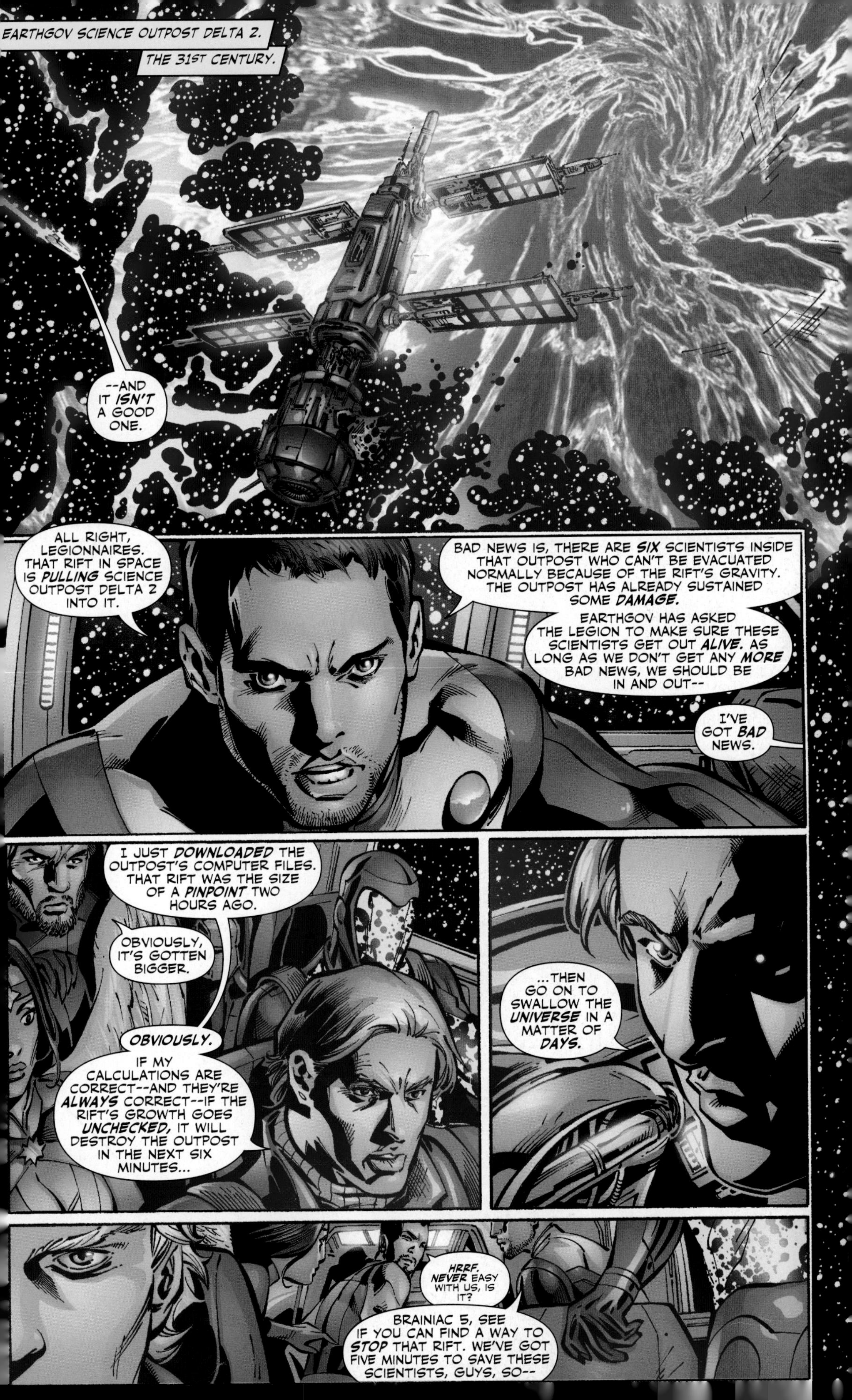
EARTHGOV SCIENCE OUTPOST DELTA 2.
THE 31ST CENTURY.
--AND IT ISN'T A GOOD ONE.
ALL RIGHT, LEGIONNAIRES. THAT RIFT IN SPACE IS PULLING SCIENCE OUTPOST DELTA 2 INTO IT.
BAD NEWS IS, THERE ARE SIX SCIENTISTS INSIDE THAT OUTPOST WHO CAN'T BE EVACUATED NORMALLY BECAUSE OF THE RIFT'S GRAVITY. THE OUTPOST HAS ALREADY SUSTAINED SOME DAMAGE.
EARTHGOV HAS ASKED THE LEGION TO MAKE SURE THESE SCIENTISTS GET OUT ALIVE. AS LONG AS WE DON'T GET ANY MORE BAD NEWS, WE SHOULD BE IN AND OUT--
I'VE GOT BAD NEWS.
I JUST DOWNLOADED THE OUTPOST'S COMPUTER FILES. THAT RIFT WAS THE SIZE OF A PINPOINT TWO HOURS AGO.
OBVIOUSLY, IT'S GOTTEN BIGGER.
OBVIOUSLY.
IF MY CALCULATIONS ARE CORRECT--AND THEY'RE ALWAYS CORRECT--IF THE RIFT'S GROWTH GOES UNCHECKED, IT WILL DESTROY THE OUTPOST IN THE NEXT SIX MINUTES...
...THEN GO ON TO SWALLOW THE UNIVERSE IN A MATTER OF DAYS.
HRRF. NEVER EASY WITH US, IS IT?
BRAINIAC 5, SEE IF YOU CAN FIND A WAY TO STOP THAT RIFT. WE'VE GOT FIVE MINUTES TO SAVE THESE SCIENTISTS, GUYS, SO--

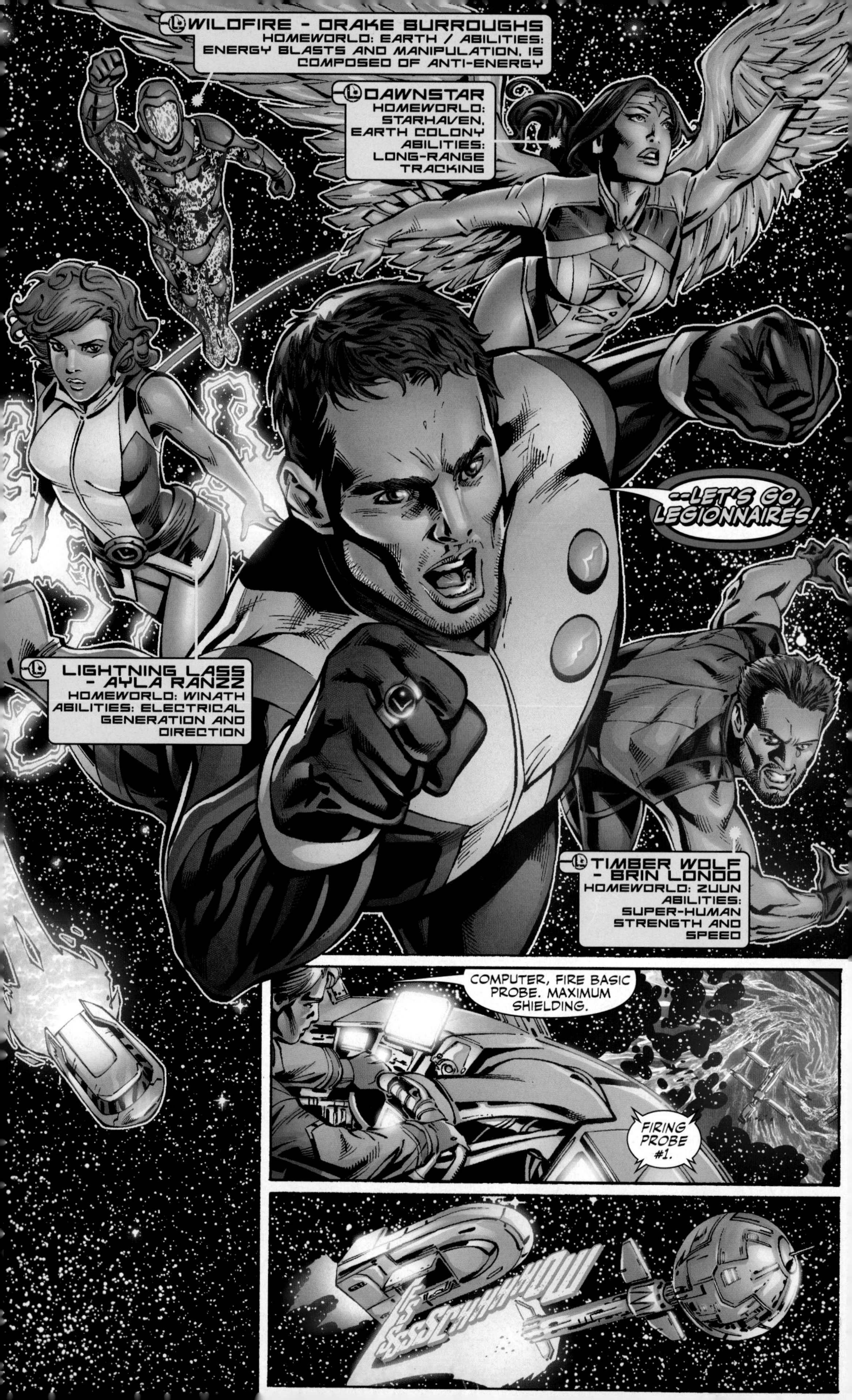
WILDFIRE - DRAKE BURROUGHS
HOMEWORLD: EARTH / ABILITIES: ENERGY BLASTS AND MANIPULATION, IS COMPOSED OF ANTI-ENERGY
DAWNSTAR
HOMEWORLD: STARHAVEN, EARTH COLONY ABILITIES: LONG-RANGE TRACKING
--LET'S GO, LEGIONNAIRES!
LIGHTNING LASS - AYLA RANZZ
HOMEWORLD: WINATH ABILITIES: ELECTRICAL GENERATION AND DIRECTION
TIMBER WOLF - BRIN LONDO
HOMEWORLD: ZUUN ABILITIES: SUPER-HUMAN STRENGTH AND SPEED
COMPUTER, FIRE BASIC PROBE. MAXIMUM SHIELDING.
FIRING PROBE #1.
SSSSSCHHHHHOOM

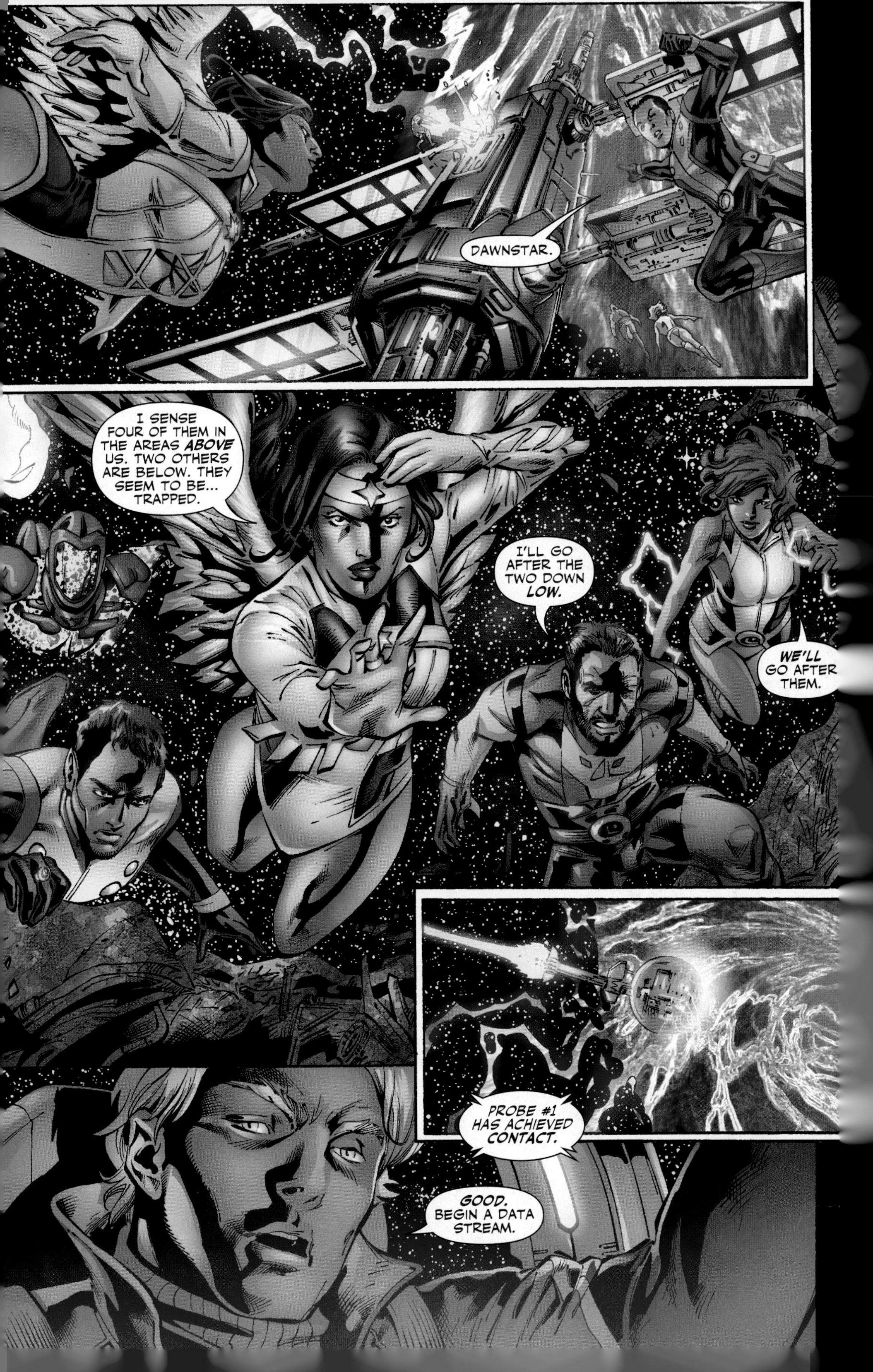
DAWNSTAR.
I SENSE FOUR OF THEM IN THE AREAS ABOVE US. TWO OTHERS ARE BELOW. THEY SEEM TO BE... TRAPPED.
I'LL GO AFTER THE TWO DOWN LOW.
WE'LL GO AFTER THEM.
PROBE #1 HAS ACHIEVED CONTACT.
GOOD. BEGIN A DATA STREAM.

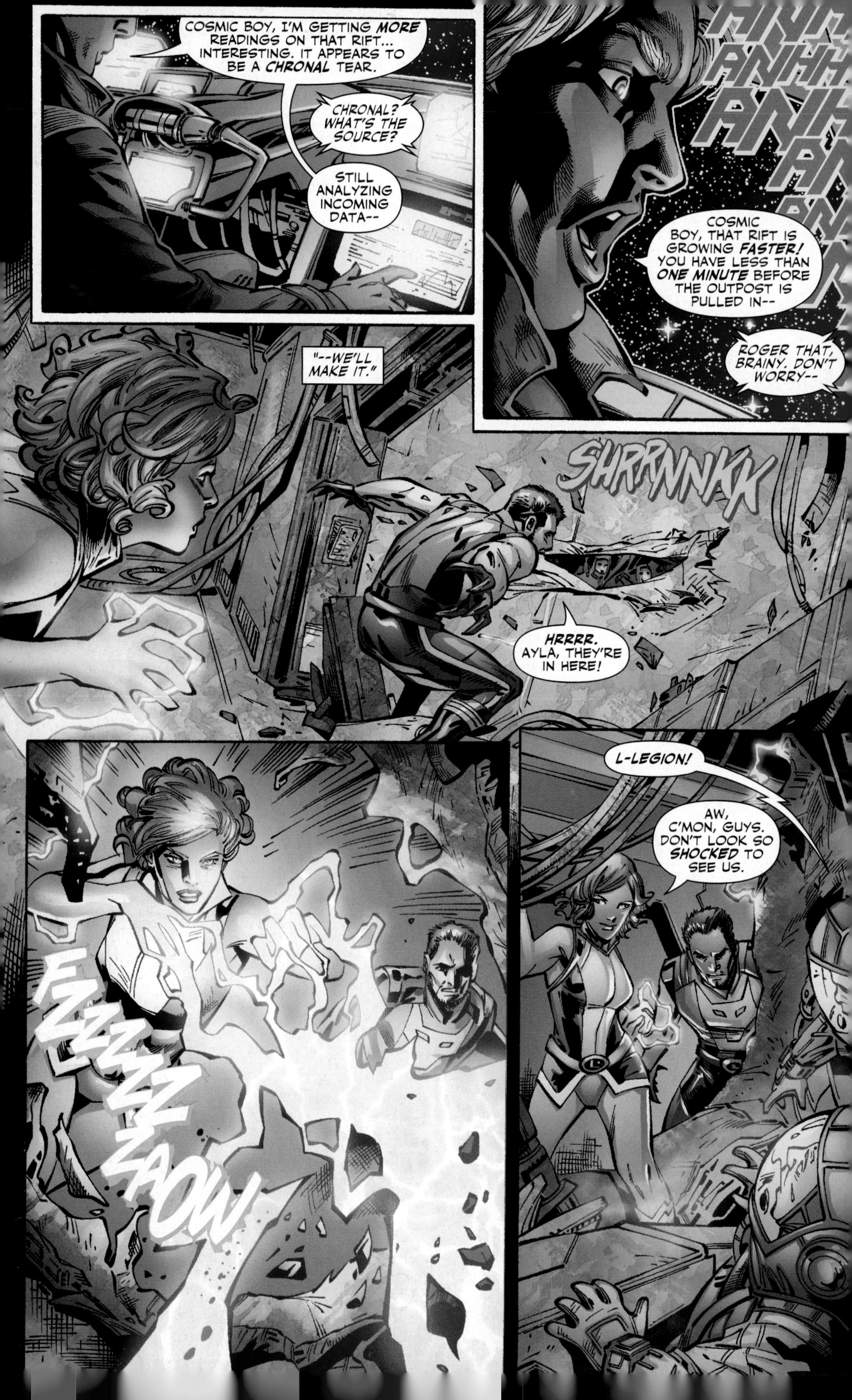
COSMIC BOY, I'M GETTING MORE READINGS ON THAT RIFT... INTERESTING. IT APPEARS TO BE A CHRONAL TEAR.
CHRONAL? WHAT'S THE SOURCE?
STILL ANALYZING INCOMING DATA--
COSMIC BOY, THAT RIFT IS GROWING FASTER! YOU HAVE LESS THAN ONE MINUTE BEFORE THE OUTPOST IS PULLED IN--
ROGER THAT, BRAINY. DON'T WORRY--
"--WE'LL MAKE IT."
SHRRNNKK
HRRRR. AYLA, THEY'RE IN HERE!
L-LEGION!
AW, C'MON, GUYS. DON'T LOOK SO SHOCKED TO SEE US.

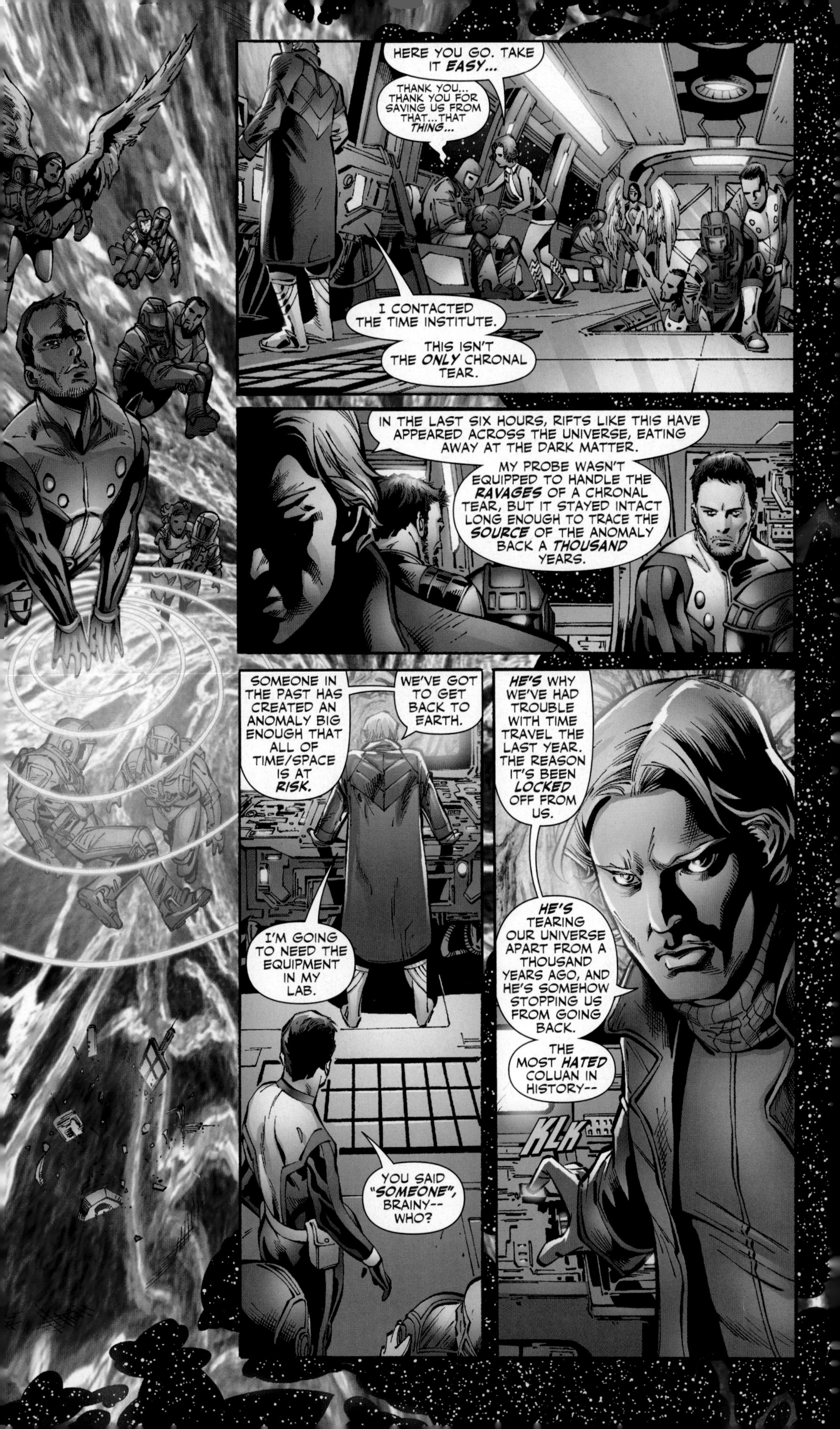

HERE YOU GO. TAKE IT EASY...
THANK YOU... THANK YOU FOR SAVING US FROM THAT...THAT THING...
I CONTACTED THE TIME INSTITUTE.
THIS ISN'T THE ONLY CHRONAL TEAR.
IN THE LAST SIX HOURS, RIFTS LIKE THIS HAVE APPEARED ACROSS THE UNIVERSE, EATING AWAY AT THE DARK MATTER.
MY PROBE WASN'T EQUIPPED TO HANDLE THE RAVAGES OF A CHRONAL TEAR, BUT IT STAYED INTACT LONG ENOUGH TO TRACE THE SOURCE OF THE ANOMALY BACK A THOUSAND YEARS.
SOMEONE IN THE PAST HAS CREATED AN ANOMALY BIG ENOUGH THAT ALL OF TIME/SPACE IS AT RISK.
WE'VE GOT TO GET BACK TO EARTH.
I'M GOING TO NEED THE EQUIPMENT IN MY LAB.
YOU SAID "SOMEONE", BRAINY-- WHO?
HE'S WHY WE'VE HAD TROUBLE WITH TIME TRAVEL THE LAST YEAR. THE REASON IT'S BEEN LOCKED OFF FROM US.
HE'S TEARING OUR UNIVERSE APART FROM A THOUSAND YEARS AGO, AND HE'S SOMEHOW STOPPING US FROM GOING BACK.
THE MOST HATED COLUAN IN HISTORY--
KLK

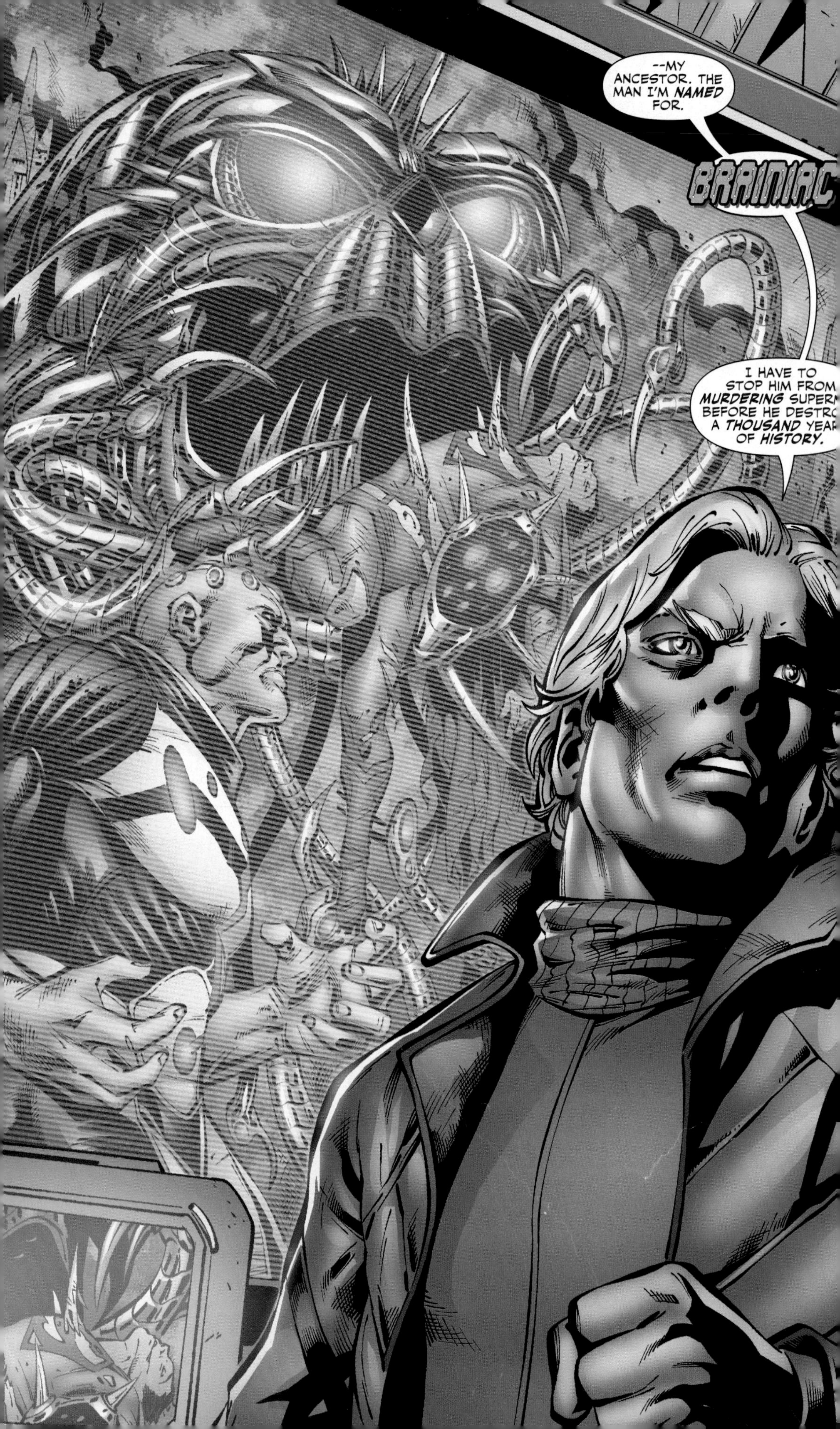
--MY ANCESTOR. THE MAN I'M *NAMED* FOR.
BRAINIAC
I HAVE TO STOP HIM FROM *MURDERING* SUPERM BEFORE HE DESTRO A *THOUSAND* YEAR OF *HISTORY.*

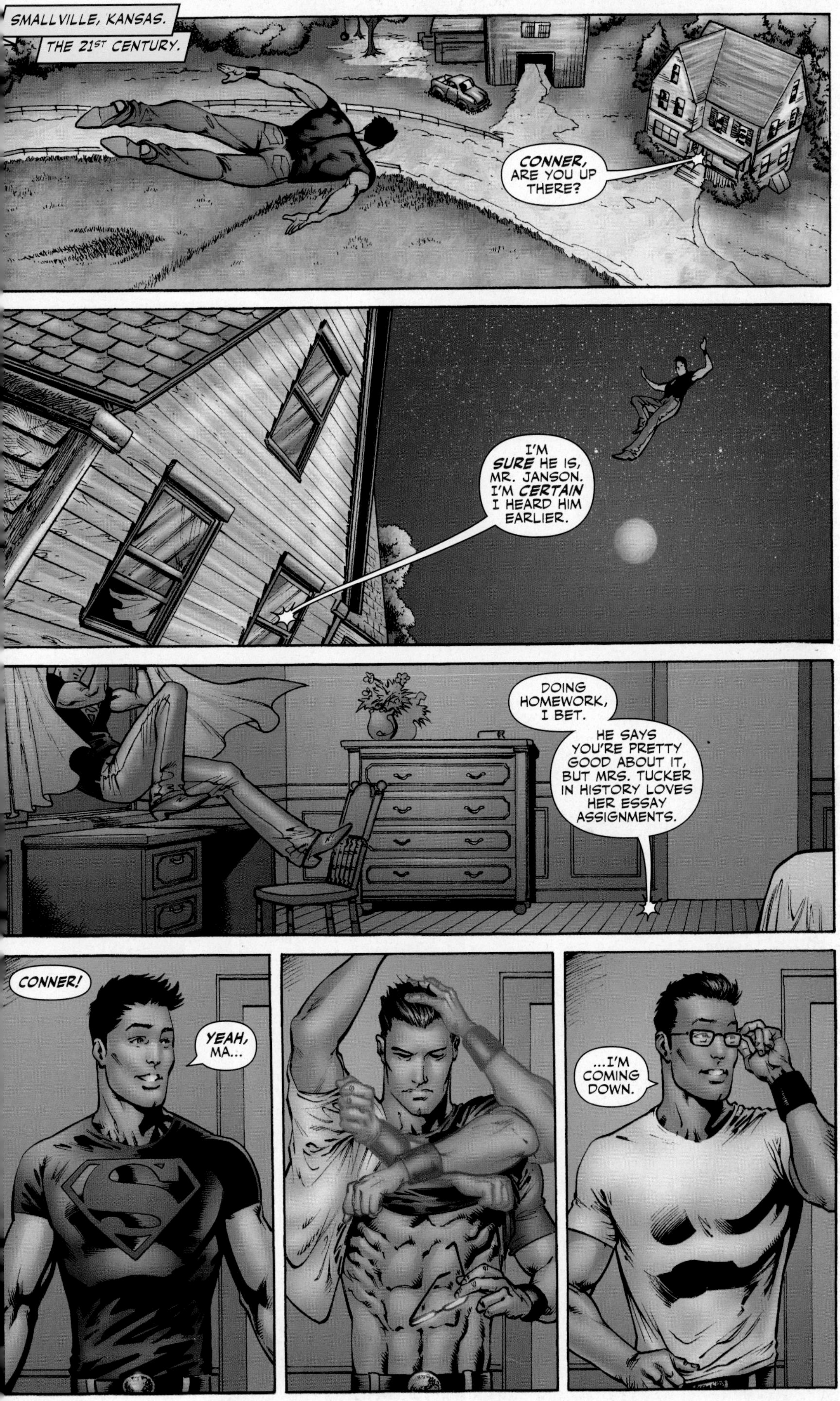
SMALLVILLE, KANSAS.
THE 21ST CENTURY.
CONNER, ARE YOU UP THERE?
I'M SURE HE IS, MR. JANSON. I'M CERTAIN I HEARD HIM EARLIER.
DOING HOMEWORK, I BET.
HE SAYS YOU'RE PRETTY GOOD ABOUT IT, BUT MRS. TUCKER IN HISTORY LOVES HER ESSAY ASSIGNMENTS.
CONNER!
YEAH, MA...
...I'M COMING DOWN.

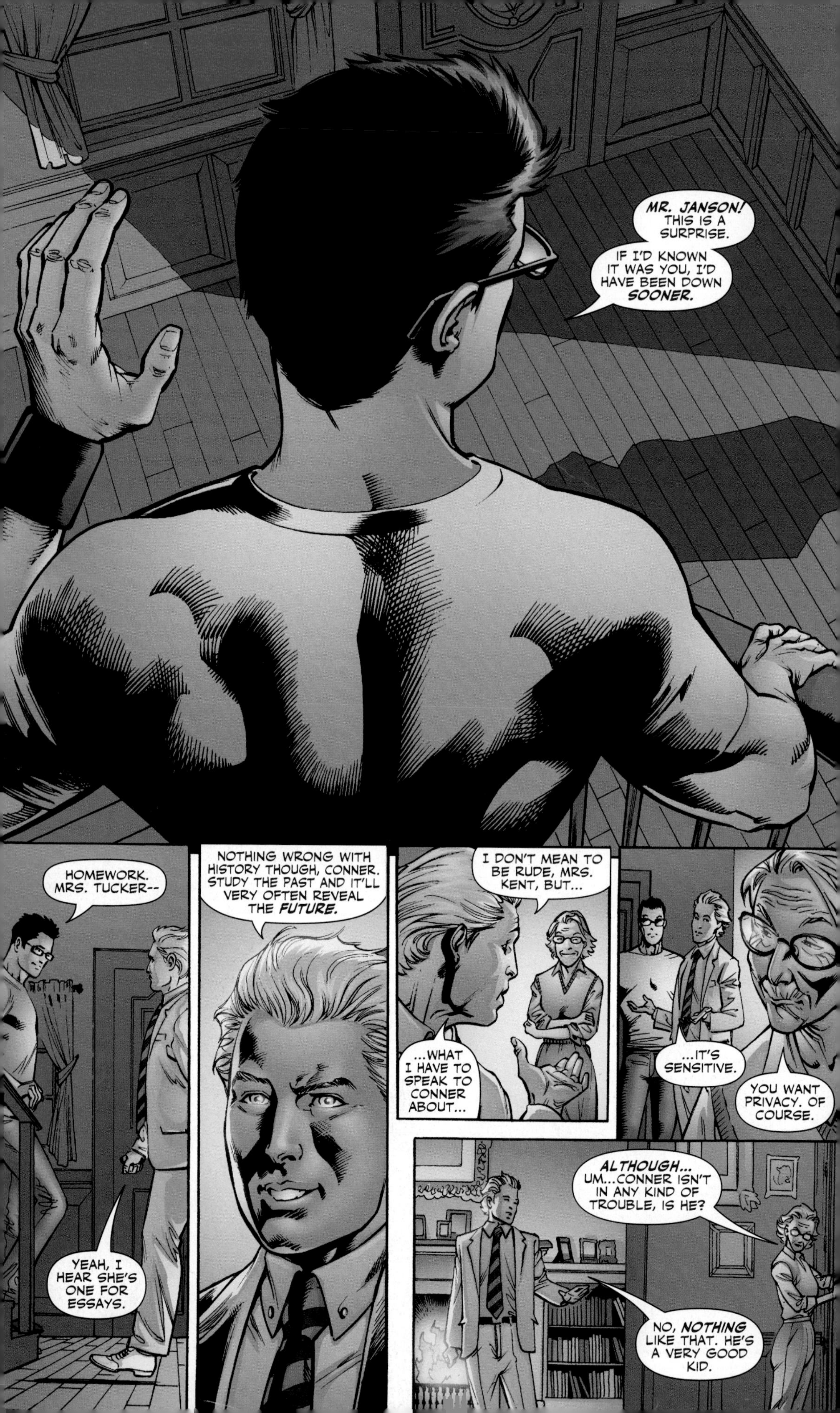
MR. JANSON! THIS IS A SURPRISE.
IF I'D KNOWN IT WAS YOU, I'D HAVE BEEN DOWN SOONER.
HOMEWORK. MRS. TUCKER--
YEAH, I HEAR SHE'S ONE FOR ESSAYS.
NOTHING WRONG WITH HISTORY THOUGH, CONNER. STUDY THE PAST AND IT'LL VERY OFTEN REVEAL THE FUTURE.
I DON'T MEAN TO BE RUDE, MRS. KENT, BUT...
...WHAT I HAVE TO SPEAK TO CONNER ABOUT...
...IT'S SENSITIVE.
YOU WANT PRIVACY. OF COURSE.
ALTHOUGH... UM...CONNER ISN'T IN ANY KIND OF TROUBLE, IS HE?
NO, NOTHING LIKE THAT. HE'S A VERY GOOD KID.

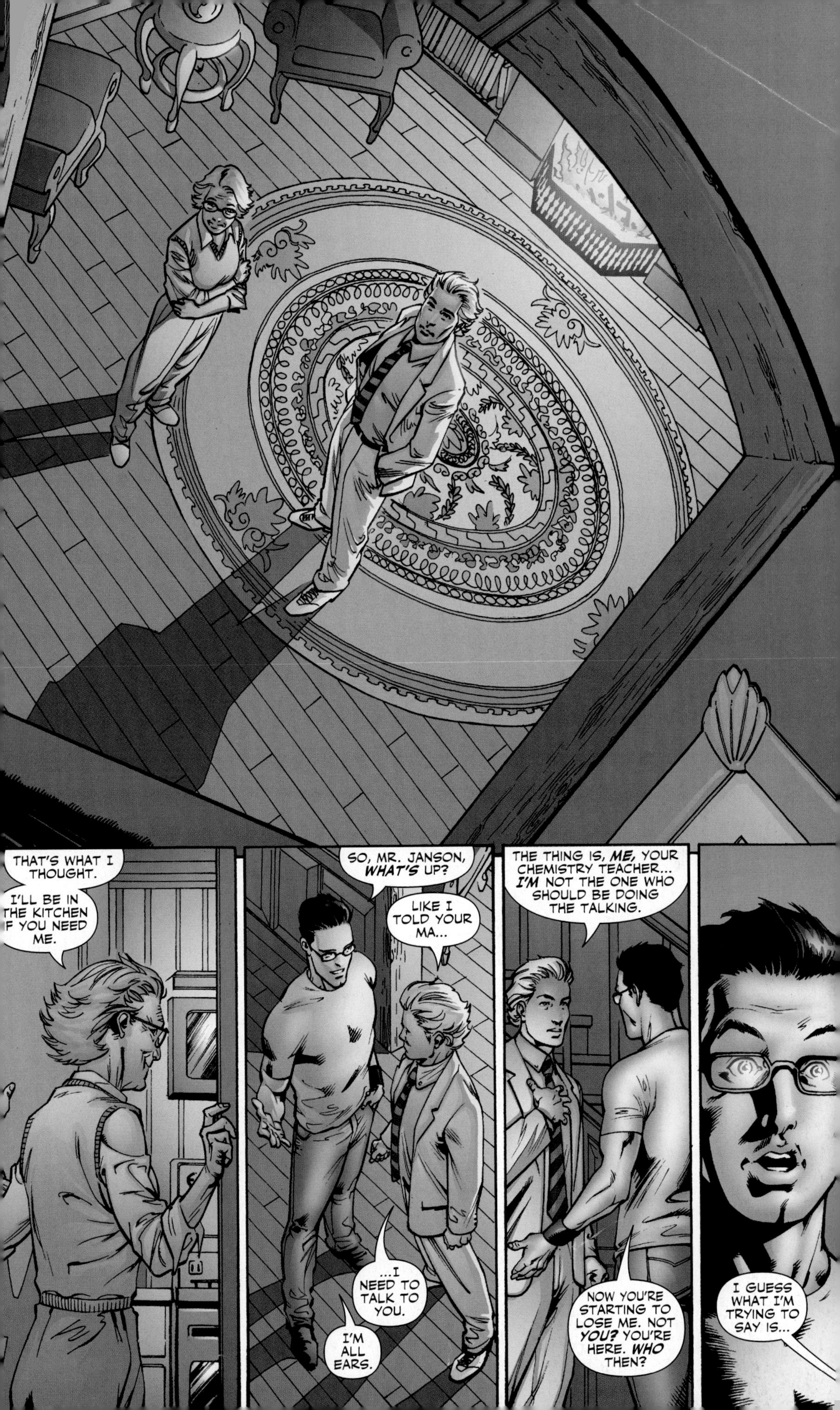
THAT'S WHAT I THOUGHT.
I'LL BE IN THE KITCHEN IF YOU NEED ME.
SO, MR. JANSON, WHAT'S UP?
LIKE I TOLD YOUR MA...
...I NEED TO TALK TO YOU.
I'M ALL EARS.
THE THING IS, ME, YOUR CHEMISTRY TEACHER... I'M NOT THE ONE WHO SHOULD BE DOING THE TALKING.
NOW YOU'RE STARTING TO LOSE ME. NOT YOU? YOU'RE HERE. WHO THEN?
I GUESS WHAT I'M TRYING TO SAY IS...

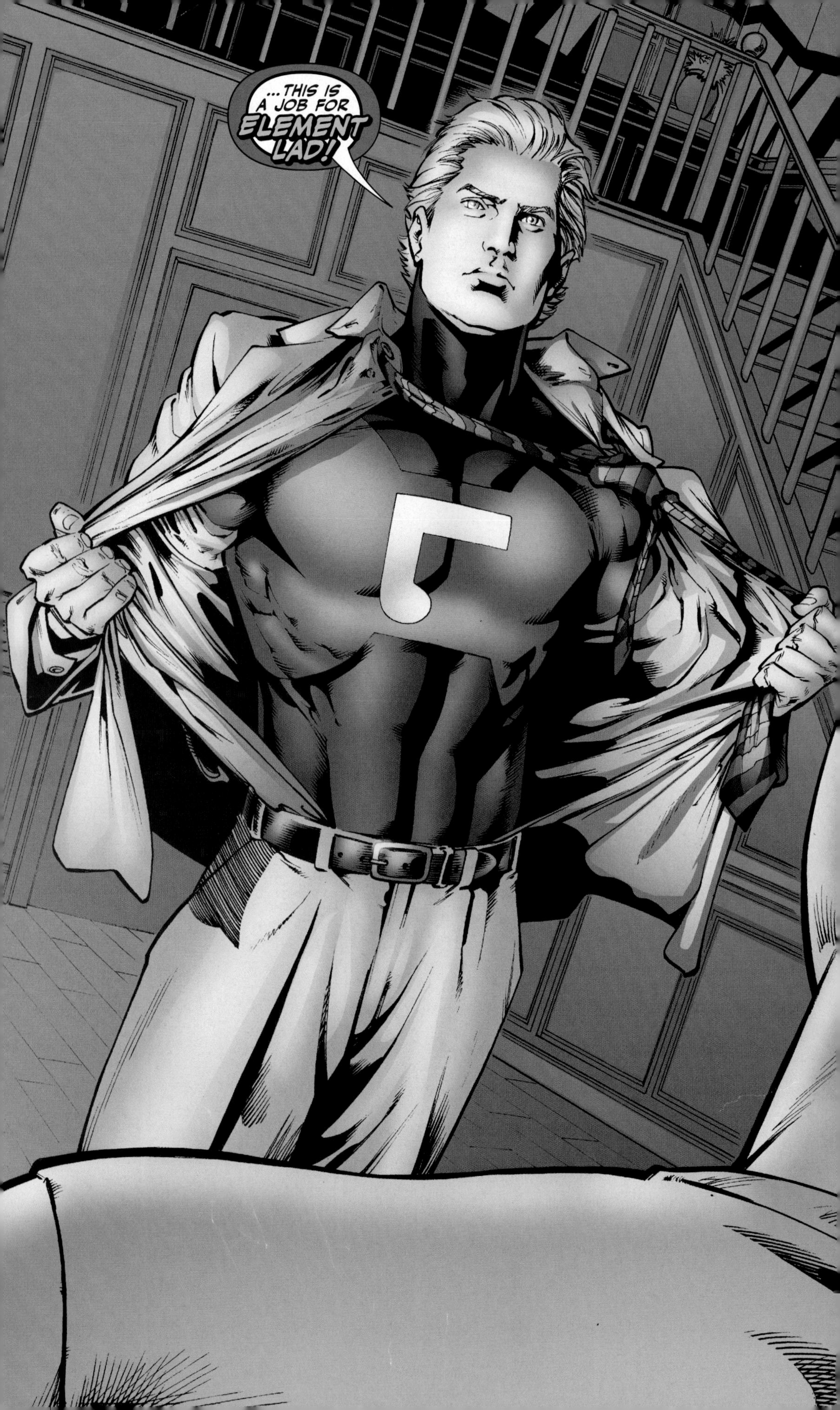
...THIS IS A JOB FOR ELEMENT LAD!

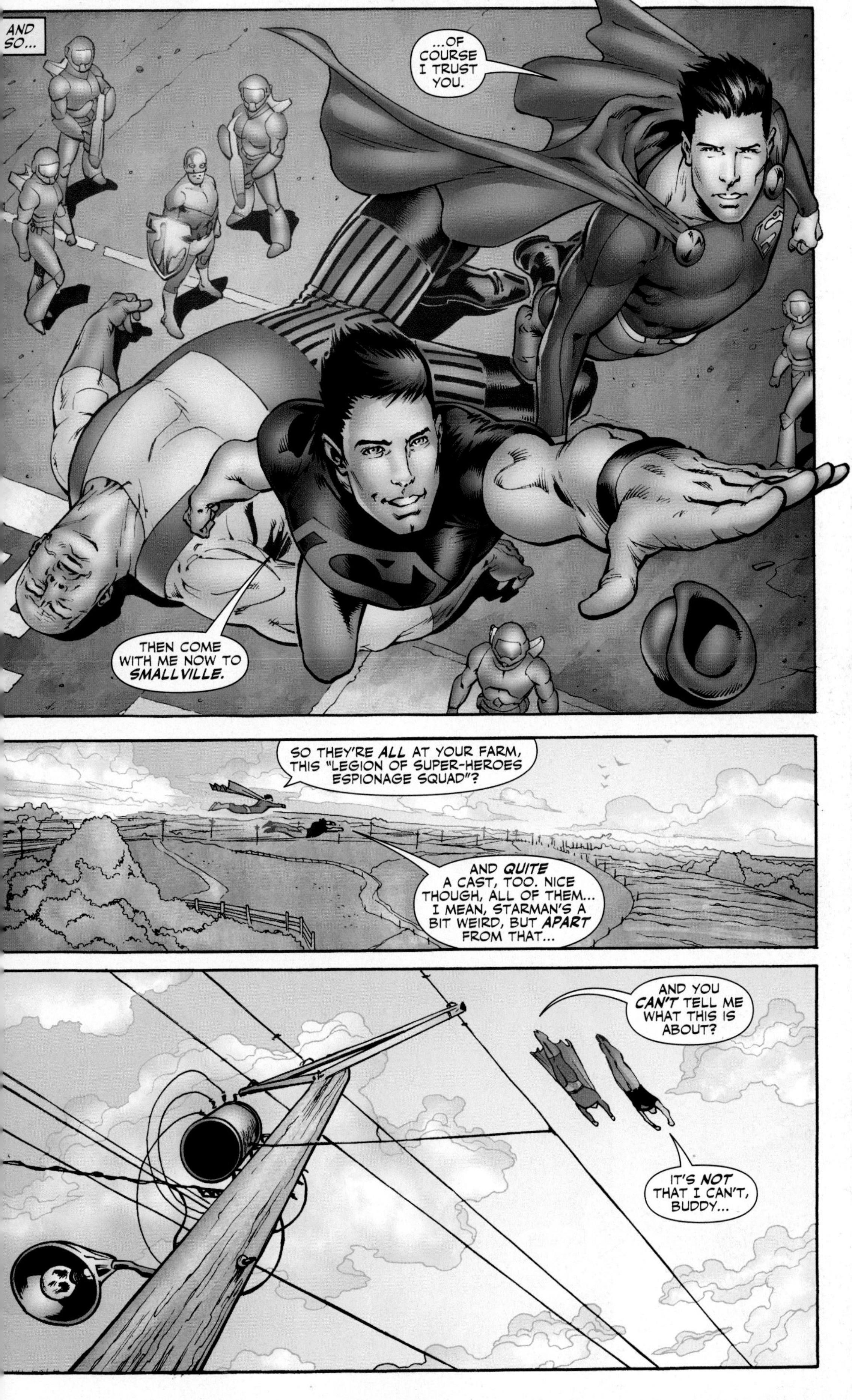
AND SO...
...OF COURSE I TRUST YOU.
THEN COME WITH ME NOW TO SMALLVILLE.
SO THEY'RE ALL AT YOUR FARM, THIS "LEGION OF SUPER-HEROES ESPIONAGE SQUAD"?
AND QUITE A CAST, TOO. NICE THOUGH, ALL OF THEM... I MEAN, STARMAN'S A BIT WEIRD, BUT APART FROM THAT...
AND YOU CAN'T TELL ME WHAT THIS IS ABOUT?
IT'S NOT THAT I CAN'T, BUDDY...

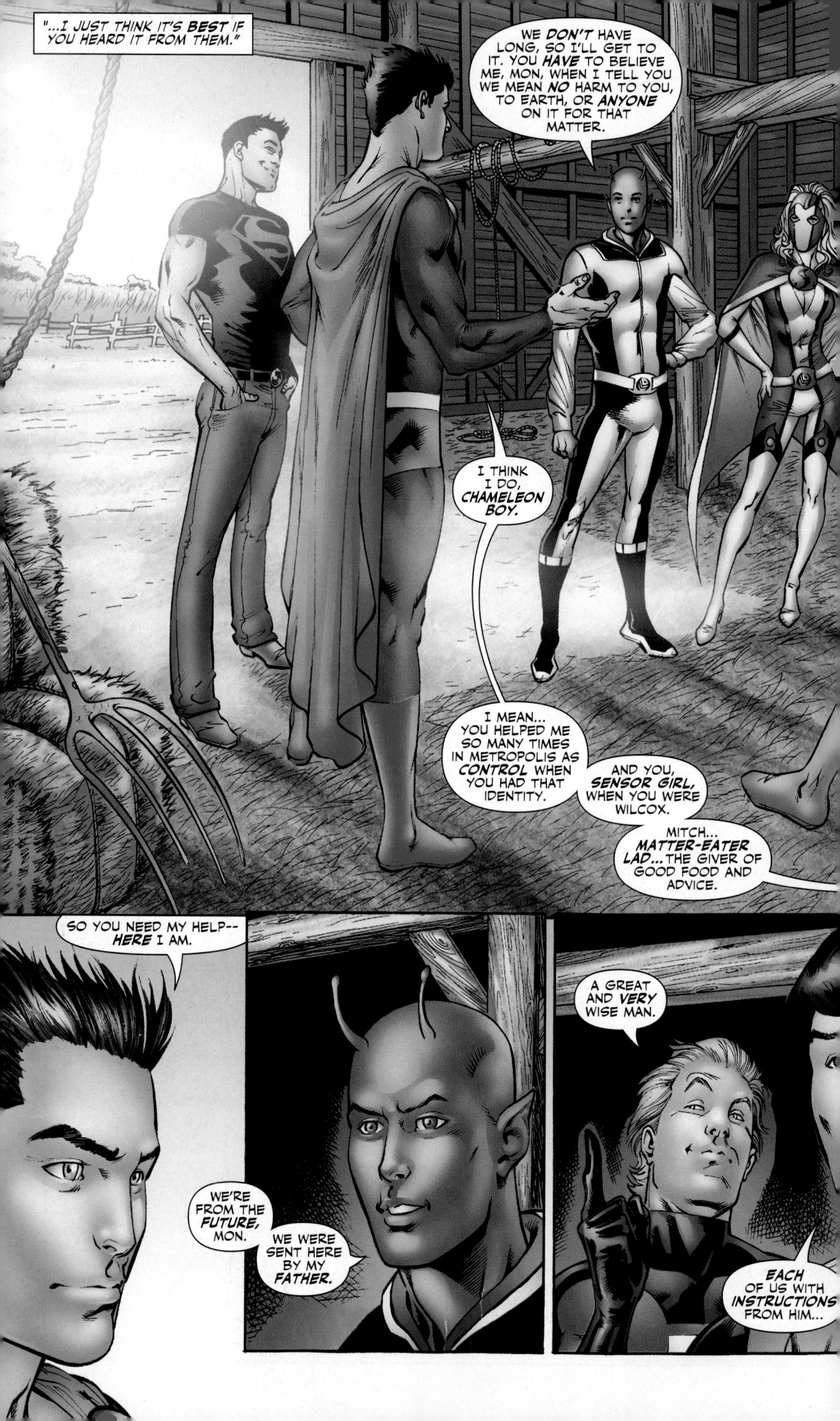
"...I JUST THINK IT'S BEST IF YOU HEARD IT FROM THEM."
WE DON'T HAVE LONG, SO I'LL GET TO IT. YOU HAVE TO BELIEVE ME, MON, WHEN I TELL YOU WE MEAN NO HARM TO YOU, TO EARTH, OR ANYONE ON IT FOR THAT MATTER.
I THINK I DO, CHAMELEON BOY.
I MEAN... YOU HELPED ME SO MANY TIMES IN METROPOLIS AS CONTROL WHEN YOU HAD THAT IDENTITY.
AND YOU, SENSOR GIRL, WHEN YOU WERE WILCOX.
MITCH... MATTER-EATER LAD... THE GIVER OF GOOD FOOD AND ADVICE.
SO YOU NEED MY HELP-- HERE I AM.
WE'RE FROM THE FUTURE, MON.
WE WERE SENT HERE BY MY FATHER.
A GREAT AND VERY WISE MAN.
EACH OF US WITH INSTRUCTIONS FROM HIM...

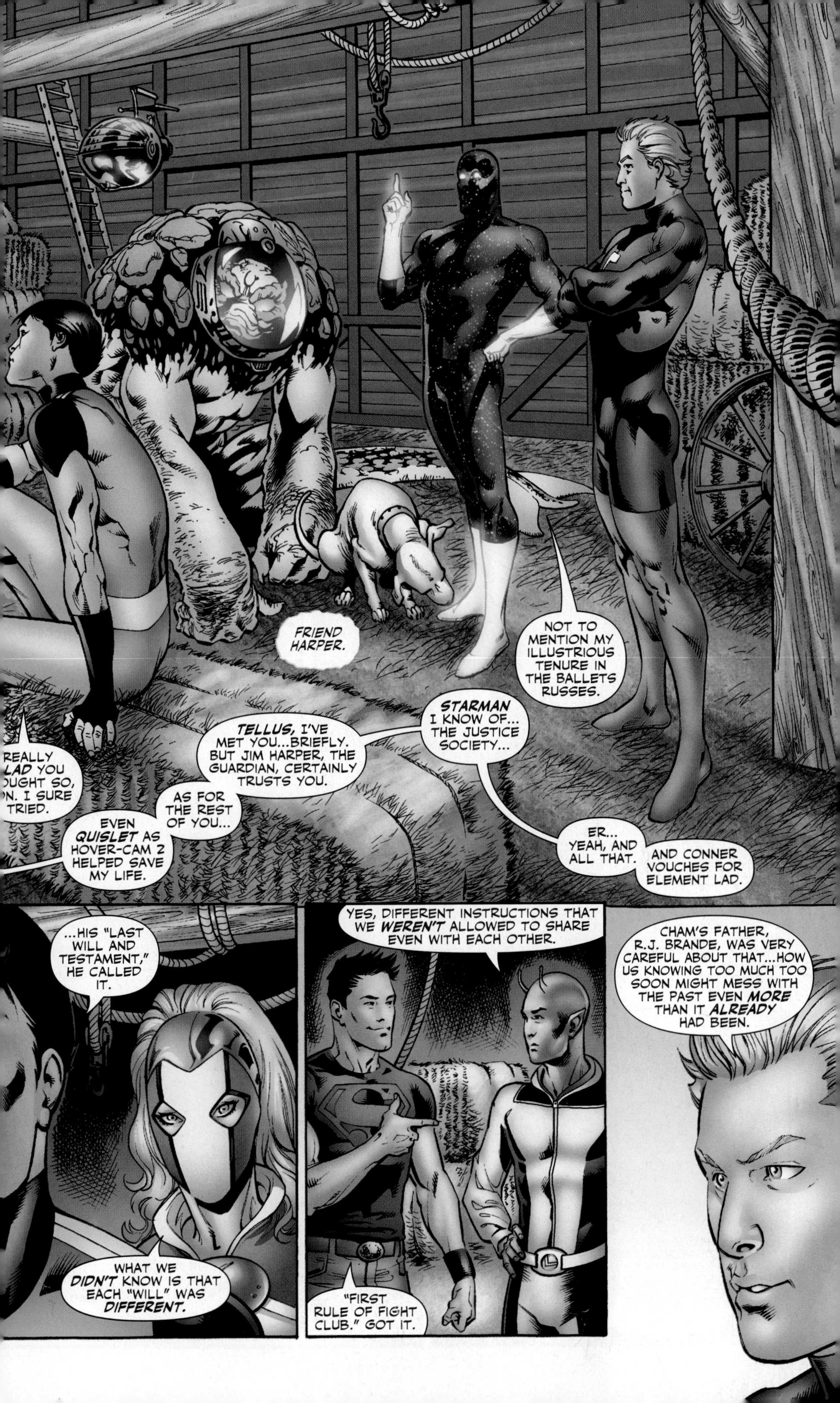

REALLY LAD YOU UGHT SO, N. I SURE TRIED.
EVEN QUISLET AS HOVER-CAM 2 HELPED SAVE MY LIFE.
AS FOR THE REST OF YOU...
TELLUS, I'VE MET YOU...BRIEFLY. BUT JIM HARPER, THE GUARDIAN, CERTAINLY TRUSTS YOU.
FRIEND HARPER.
STARMAN I KNOW OF... THE JUSTICE SOCIETY...
NOT TO MENTION MY ILLUSTRIOUS TENURE IN THE BALLETS RUSSES.
ER... YEAH, AND ALL THAT.
AND CONNER VOUCHES FOR ELEMENT LAD.
...HIS "LAST WILL AND TESTAMENT," HE CALLED IT.
WHAT WE DIDN'T KNOW IS THAT EACH "WILL" WAS DIFFERENT.
YES, DIFFERENT INSTRUCTIONS THAT WE WEREN'T ALLOWED TO SHARE EVEN WITH EACH OTHER.
"FIRST RULE OF FIGHT CLUB." GOT IT.
CHAM'S FATHER, R.J. BRANDE, WAS VERY CAREFUL ABOUT THAT...HOW US KNOWING TOO MUCH TOO SOON MIGHT MESS WITH THE PAST EVEN MORE THAN IT ALREADY HAD BEEN.

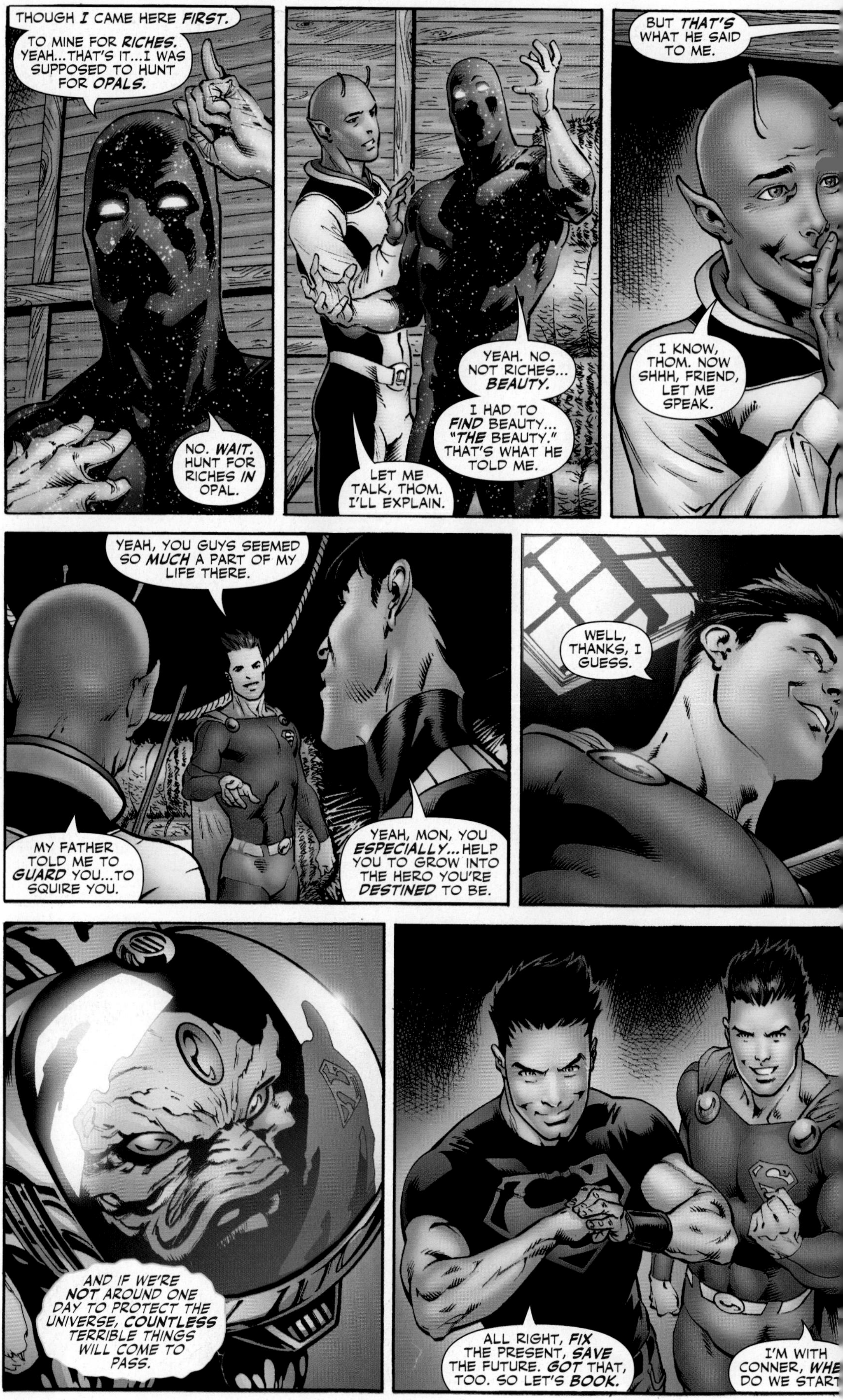
THOUGH I CAME HERE FIRST.
TO MINE FOR RICHES. YEAH...THAT'S IT...I WAS SUPPOSED TO HUNT FOR OPALS.
NO. WAIT. HUNT FOR RICHES IN OPAL.
YEAH. NO. NOT RICHES... BEAUTY.
I HAD TO FIND BEAUTY... "THE BEAUTY." THAT'S WHAT HE TOLD ME.
LET ME TALK, THOM. I'LL EXPLAIN.
BUT THAT'S WHAT HE SAID TO ME.
I KNOW, THOM. NOW SHHH, FRIEND, LET ME SPEAK.
YEAH, YOU GUYS SEEMED SO MUCH A PART OF MY LIFE THERE.
MY FATHER TOLD ME TO GUARD YOU...TO SQUIRE YOU.
YEAH, MON, YOU ESPECIALLY...HELP YOU TO GROW INTO THE HERO YOU'RE DESTINED TO BE.
WELL, THANKS, I GUESS.
AND IF WE'RE NOT AROUND ONE DAY TO PROTECT THE UNIVERSE, COUNTLESS TERRIBLE THINGS WILL COME TO PASS.
ALL RIGHT, FIX THE PRESENT, SAVE THE FUTURE. GOT THAT, TOO. SO LET'S BOOK.
I'M WITH CONNER, WHE
DO WE START

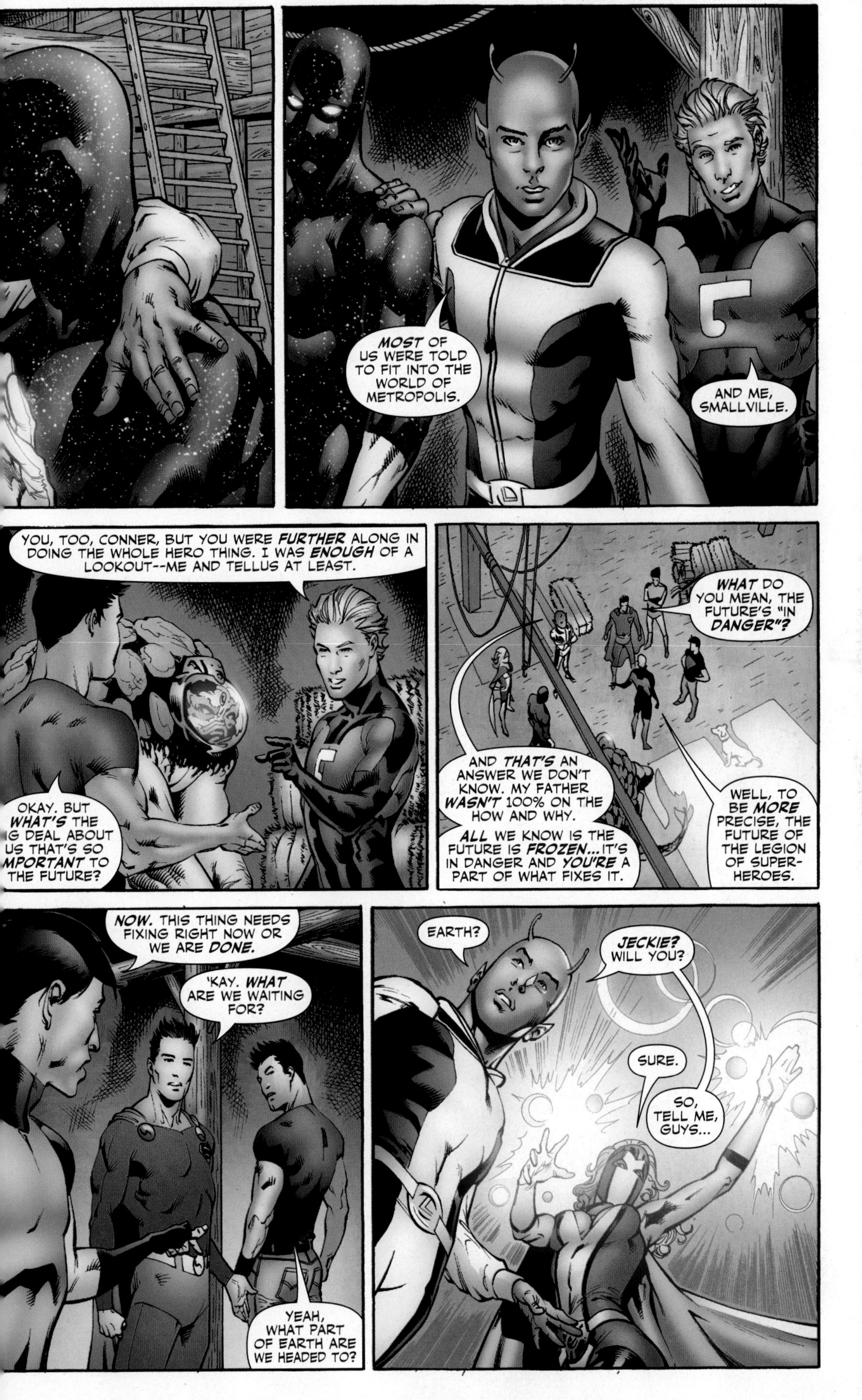

MOST OF US WERE TOLD TO FIT INTO THE WORLD OF METROPOLIS.
AND ME, SMALLVILLE.
YOU, TOO, CONNER, BUT YOU WERE FURTHER ALONG IN DOING THE WHOLE HERO THING. I WAS ENOUGH OF A LOOKOUT--ME AND TELLUS AT LEAST.
OKAY. BUT WHAT'S THE IG DEAL ABOUT US THAT'S SO MPORTANT TO THE FUTURE?
WHAT DO YOU MEAN, THE FUTURE'S "IN DANGER"?
AND THAT'S AN ANSWER WE DON'T KNOW. MY FATHER WASN'T 100% ON THE HOW AND WHY.
ALL WE KNOW IS THE FUTURE IS FROZEN... IT'S IN DANGER AND YOU'RE A PART OF WHAT FIXES IT.
WELL, TO BE MORE PRECISE, THE FUTURE OF THE LEGION OF SUPER-HEROES.
NOW. THIS THING NEEDS FIXING RIGHT NOW OR WE ARE DONE.
'KAY. WHAT ARE WE WAITING FOR?
YEAH, WHAT PART OF EARTH ARE WE HEADED TO?
EARTH?
JECKIE? WILL YOU?
SURE.
SO, TELL ME, GUYS...

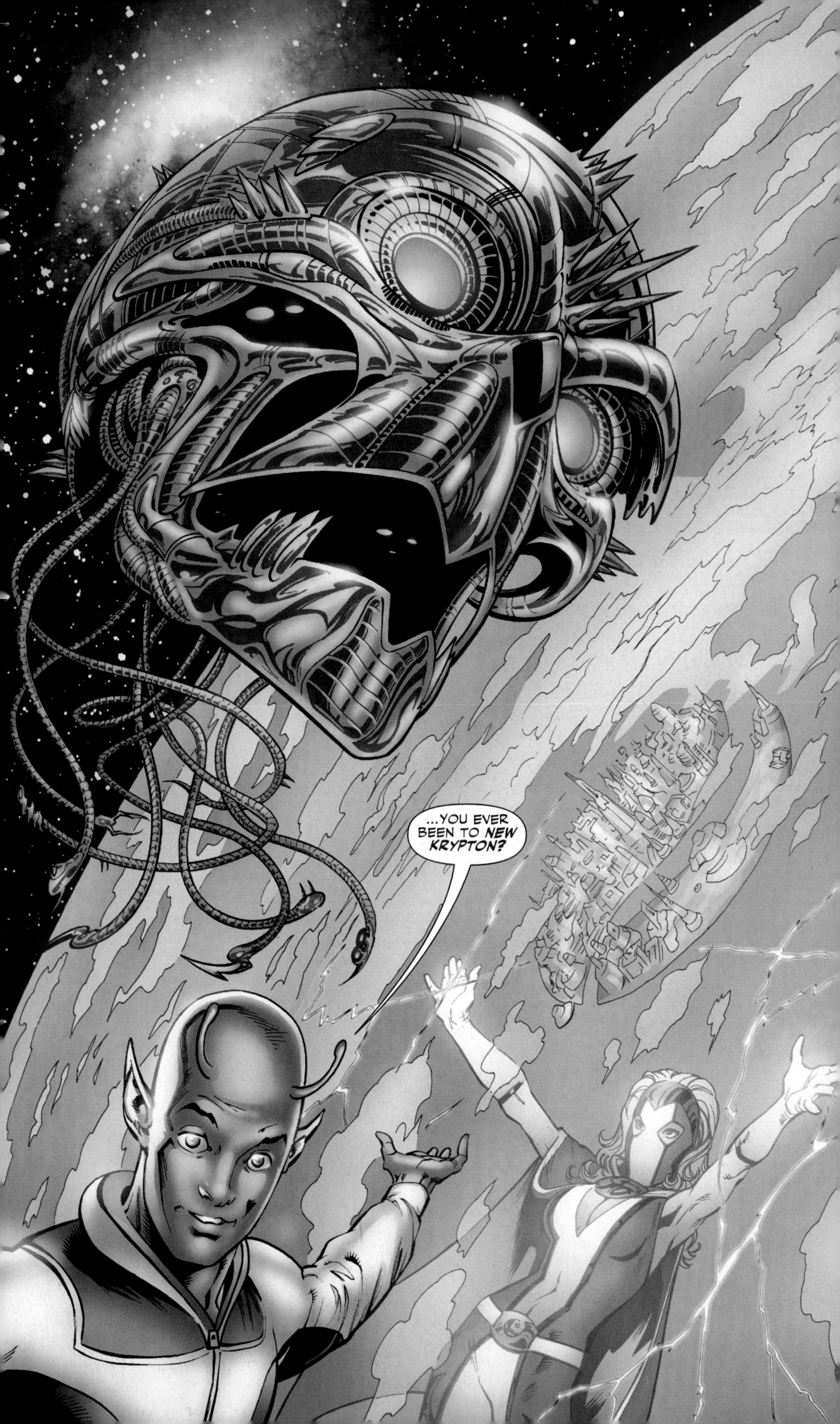
...YOU EVER BEEN TO NEW KRYPTON?

cover by **ANDY KUBERT** & **BRAD ANDERSON**

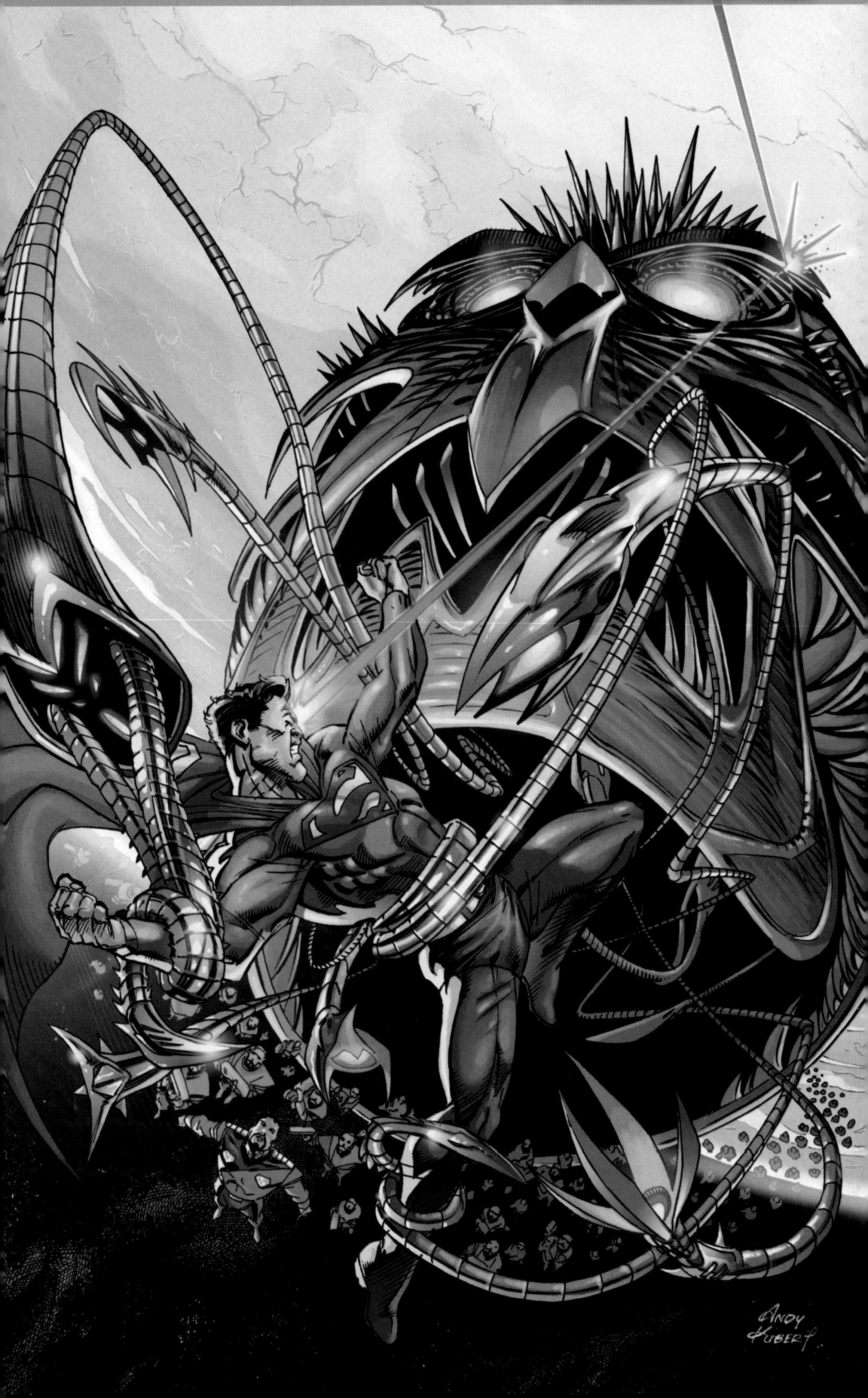
Andy Kubert

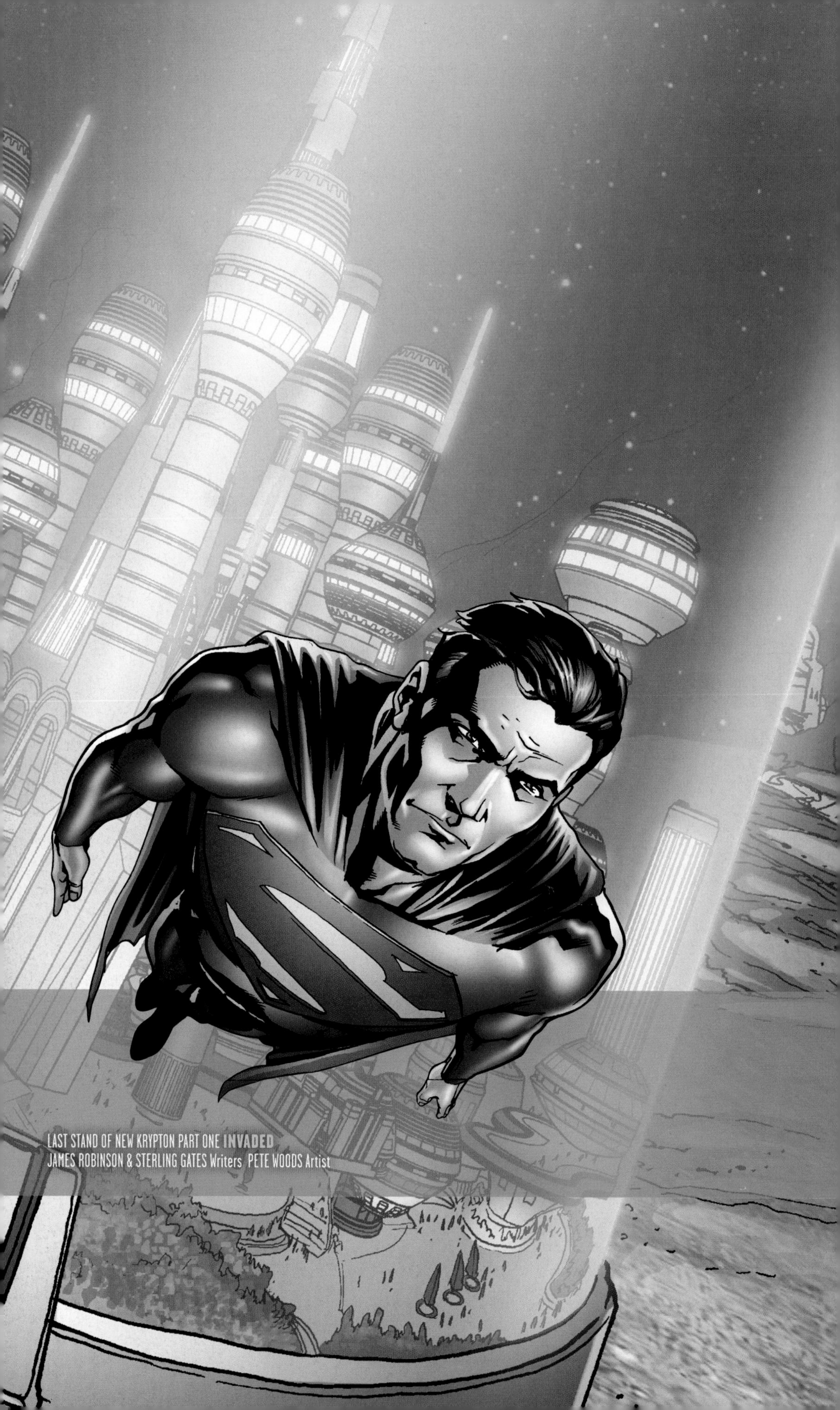

LAST STAND OF NEW KRYPTON PART ONE **INVADED**
JAMES ROBINSON & STERLING GATES Writers PETE WOODS Artist

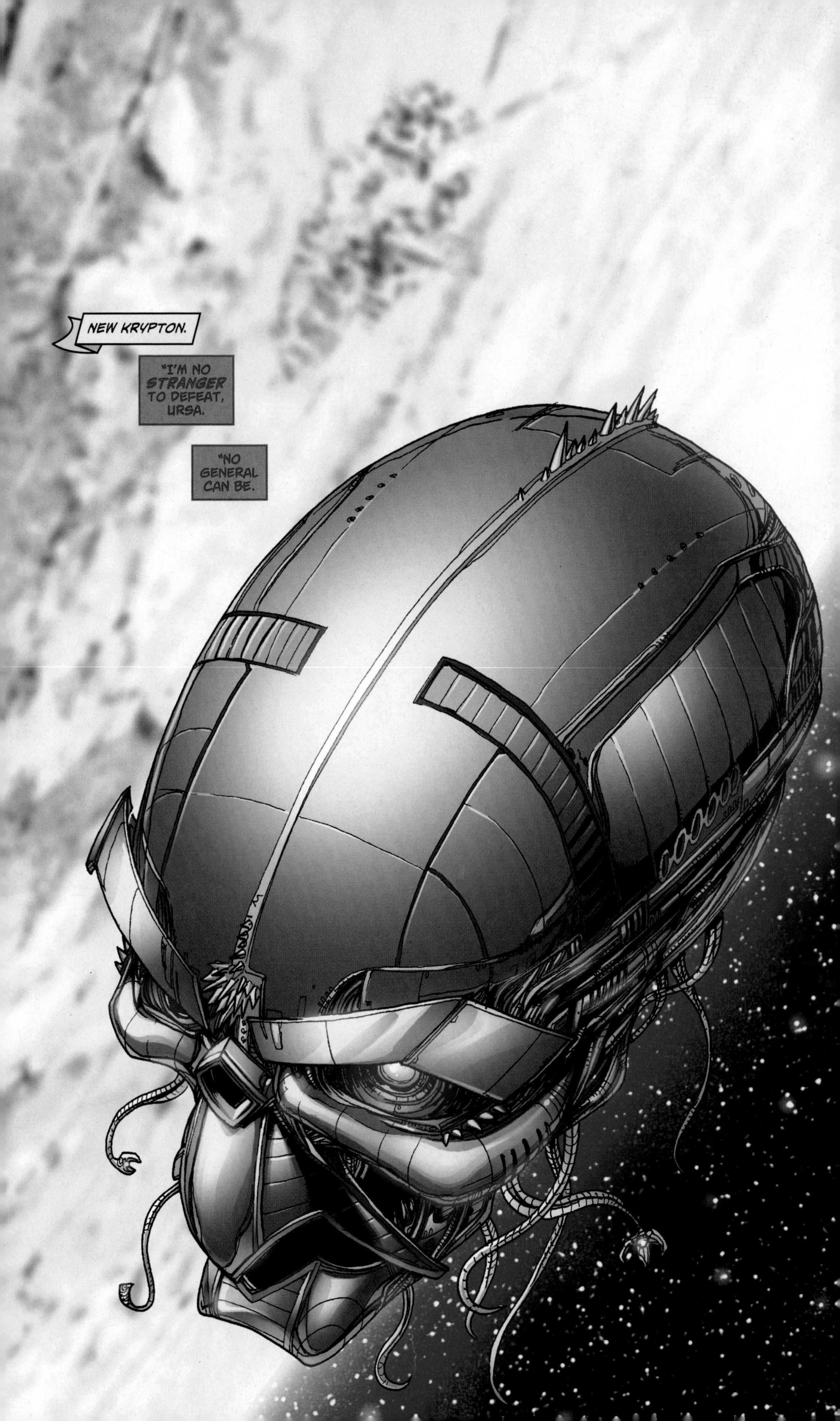
NEW KRYPTON.
"I'M NO STRANGER TO DEFEAT, URSA.
"NO GENERAL CAN BE.

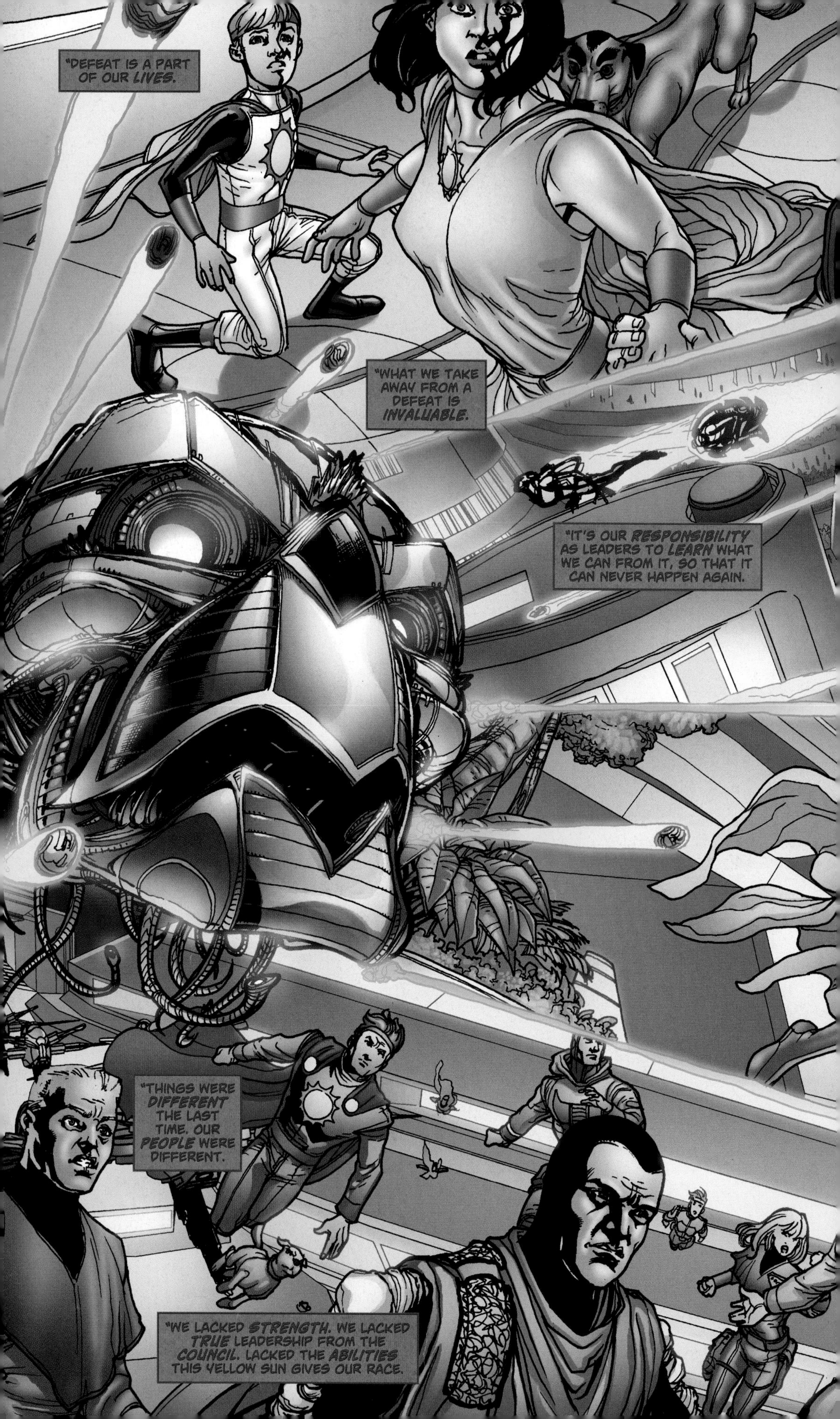
"DEFEAT IS A PART OF OUR LIVES.
"WHAT WE TAKE AWAY FROM A DEFEAT IS INVALUABLE.
"IT'S OUR RESPONSIBILITY AS LEADERS TO LEARN WHAT WE CAN FROM IT, SO THAT IT CAN NEVER HAPPEN AGAIN.
"THINGS WERE DIFFERENT THE LAST TIME. OUR PEOPLE WERE DIFFERENT.
"WE LACKED STRENGTH. WE LACKED TRUE LEADERSHIP FROM THE COUNCIL. LACKED THE ABILITIES THIS YELLOW SUN GIVES OUR RACE.

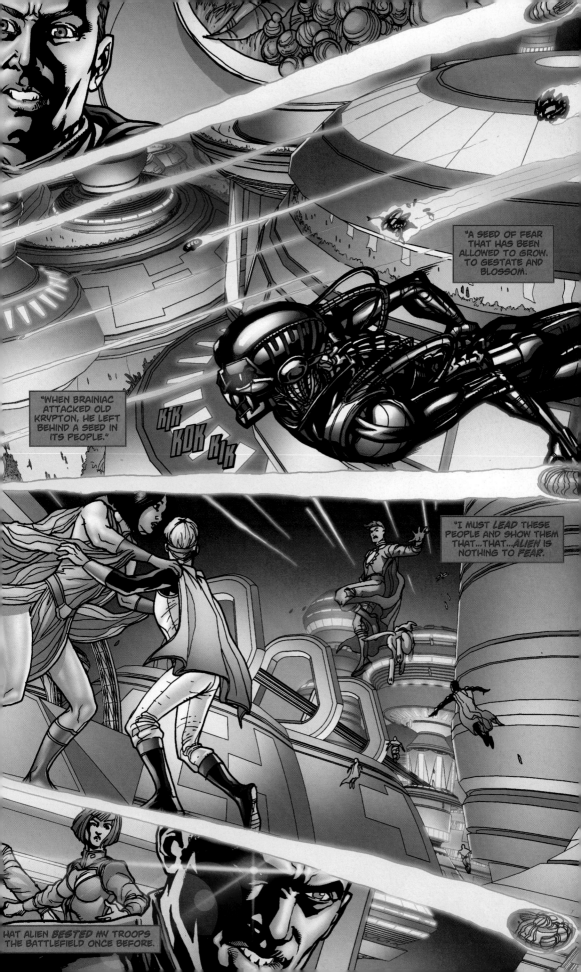

"A SEED OF FEAR THAT HAS BEEN ALLOWED TO GROW. TO GESTATE AND BLOSSOM.

"WHEN BRAINIAC ATTACKED OLD KRYPTON, HE LEFT BEHIND A SEED IN ITS PEOPLE."

KIK KOK KIK

"I MUST *LEAD* THESE PEOPLE AND SHOW THEM THAT...THAT...*ALIEN* IS NOTHING TO *FEAR.*

HAT ALIEN *BESTED* MY TROOPS THE BATTLEFIELD ONCE BEFORE.

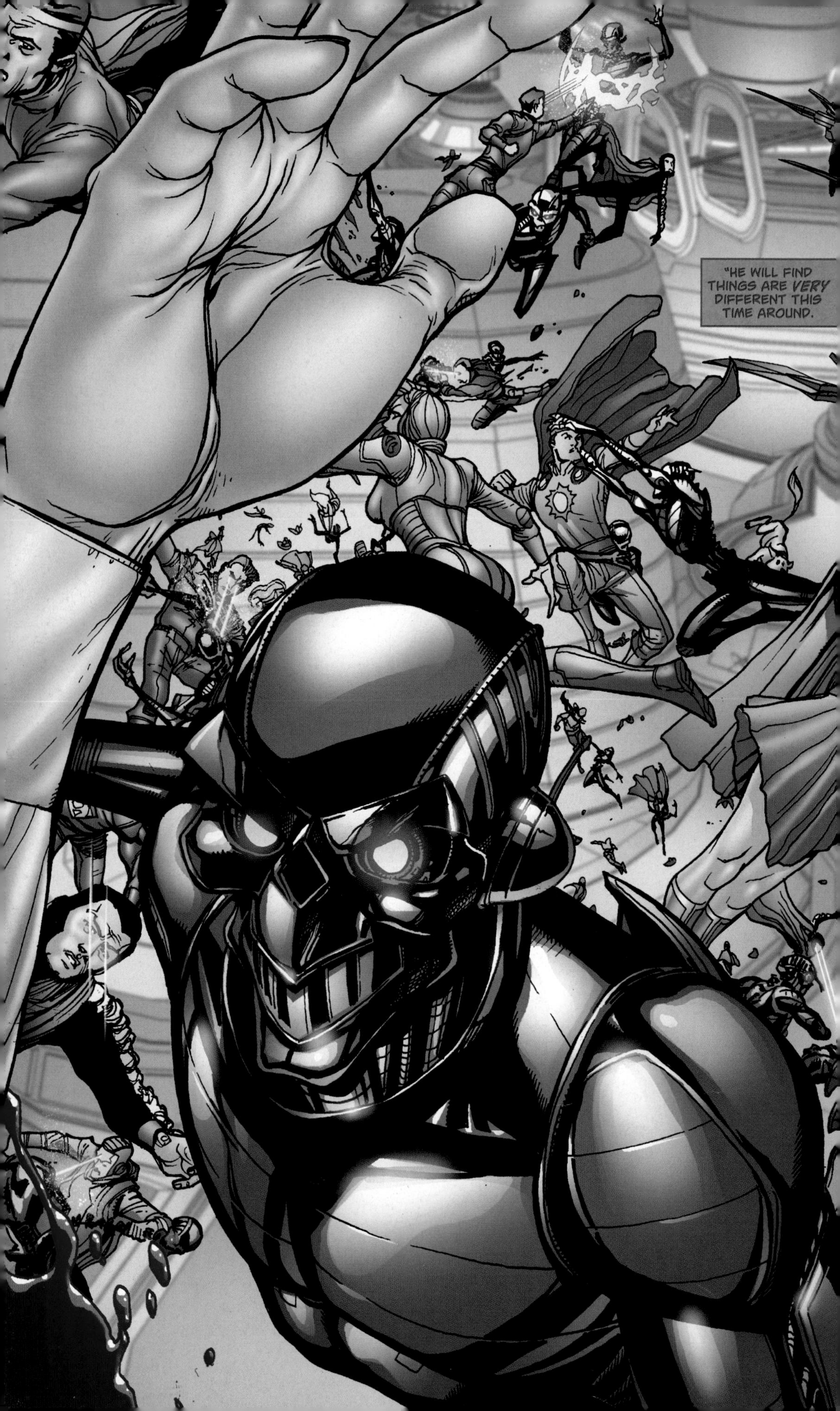
"HE WILL FIND THINGS ARE VERY DIFFERENT THIS TIME AROUND.

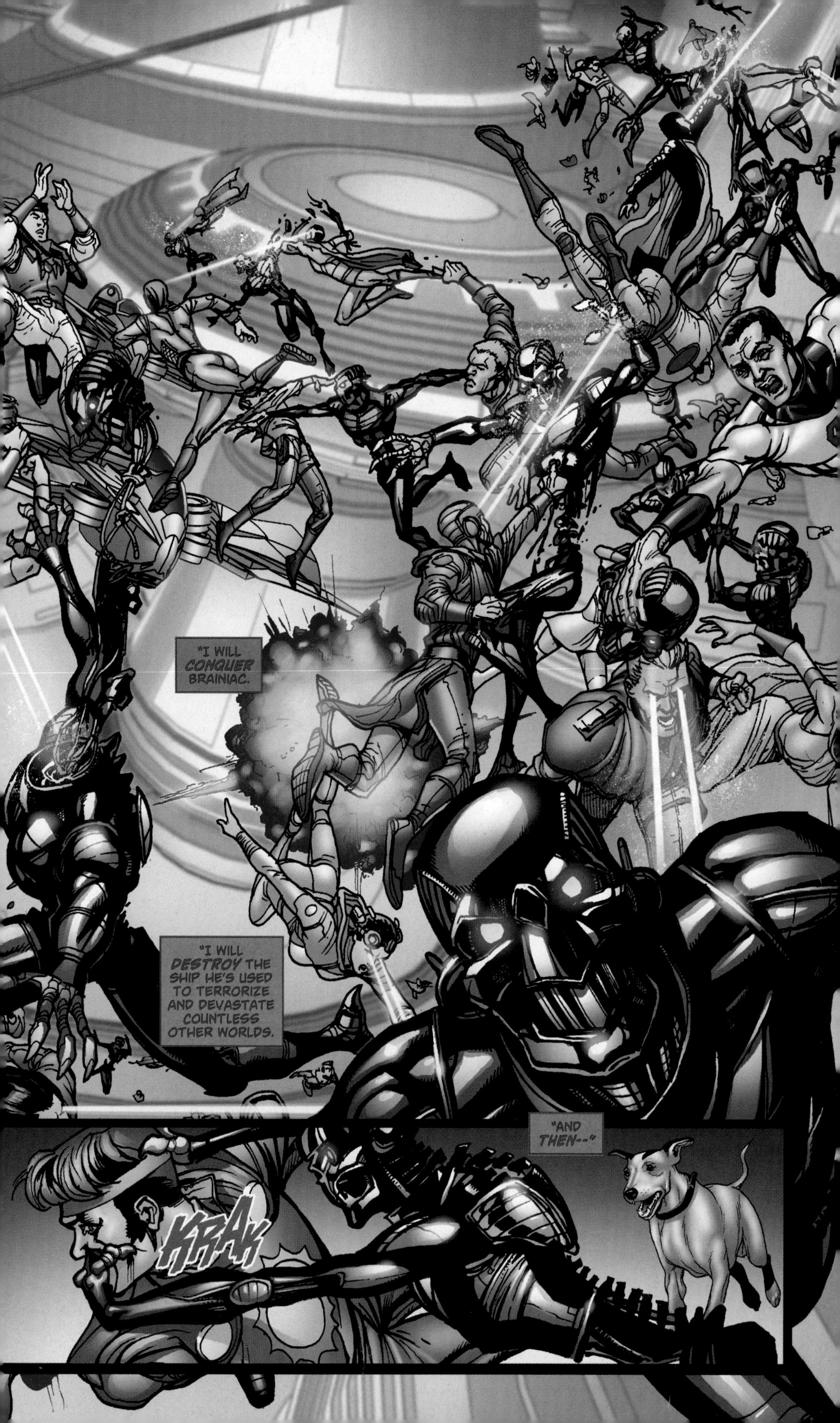
"I WILL CONQUER BRAINIAC.
"I WILL DESTROY THE SHIP HE'S USED TO TERRORIZE AND DEVASTATE COUNTLESS OTHER WORLDS.
"AND THEN--"
KRAK

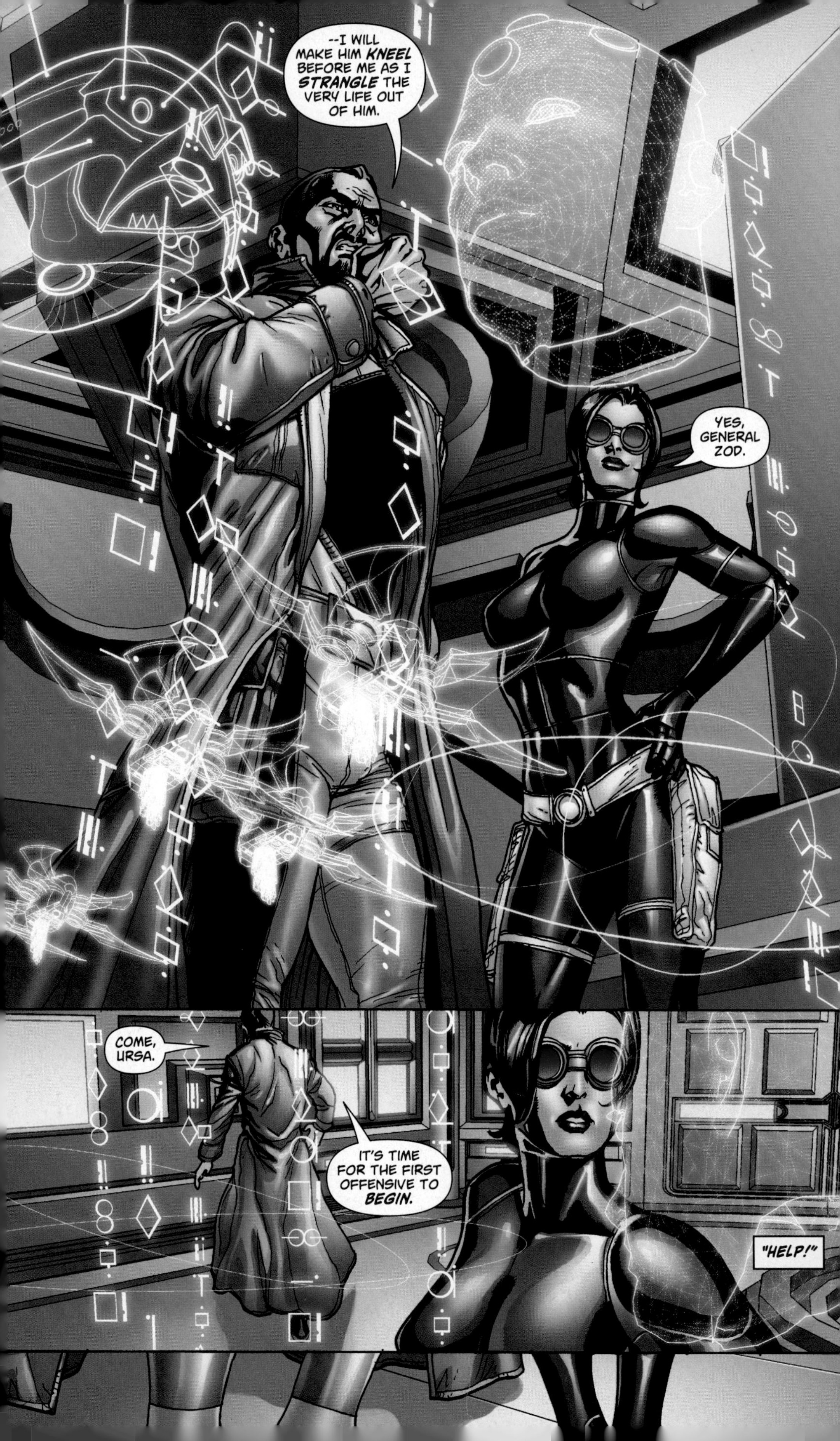
--I WILL MAKE HIM KNEEL BEFORE ME AS I STRANGLE THE VERY LIFE OUT OF HIM.
YES, GENERAL ZOD.
COME, URSA.
IT'S TIME FOR THE FIRST OFFENSIVE TO BEGIN.
"HELP!"

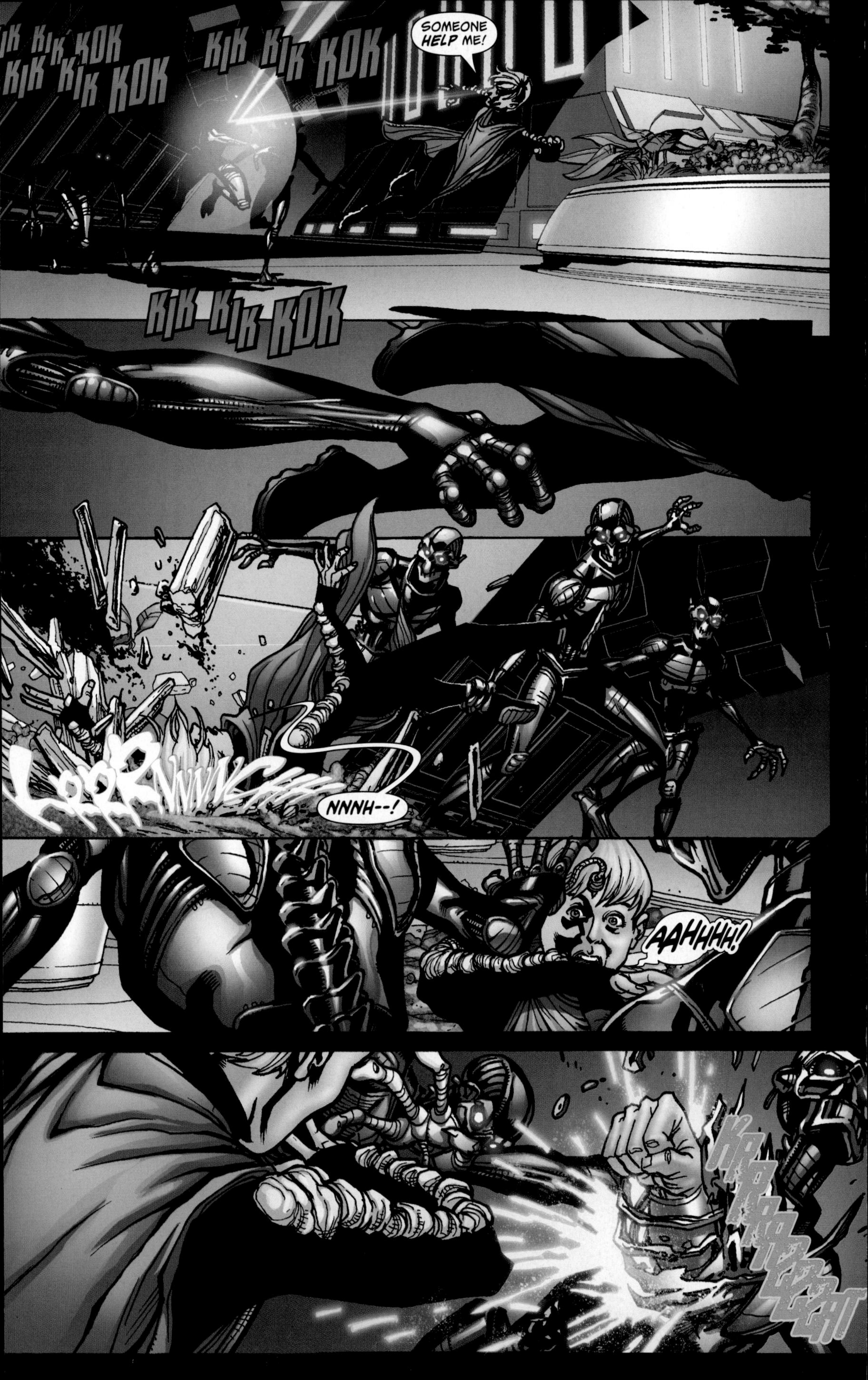
KIK KIK KOK
KIK KIK KOK
KIK KIK KOK
SOMEONE HELP ME!
KIK KIK KOK
NNNH--!
AAHHHH!

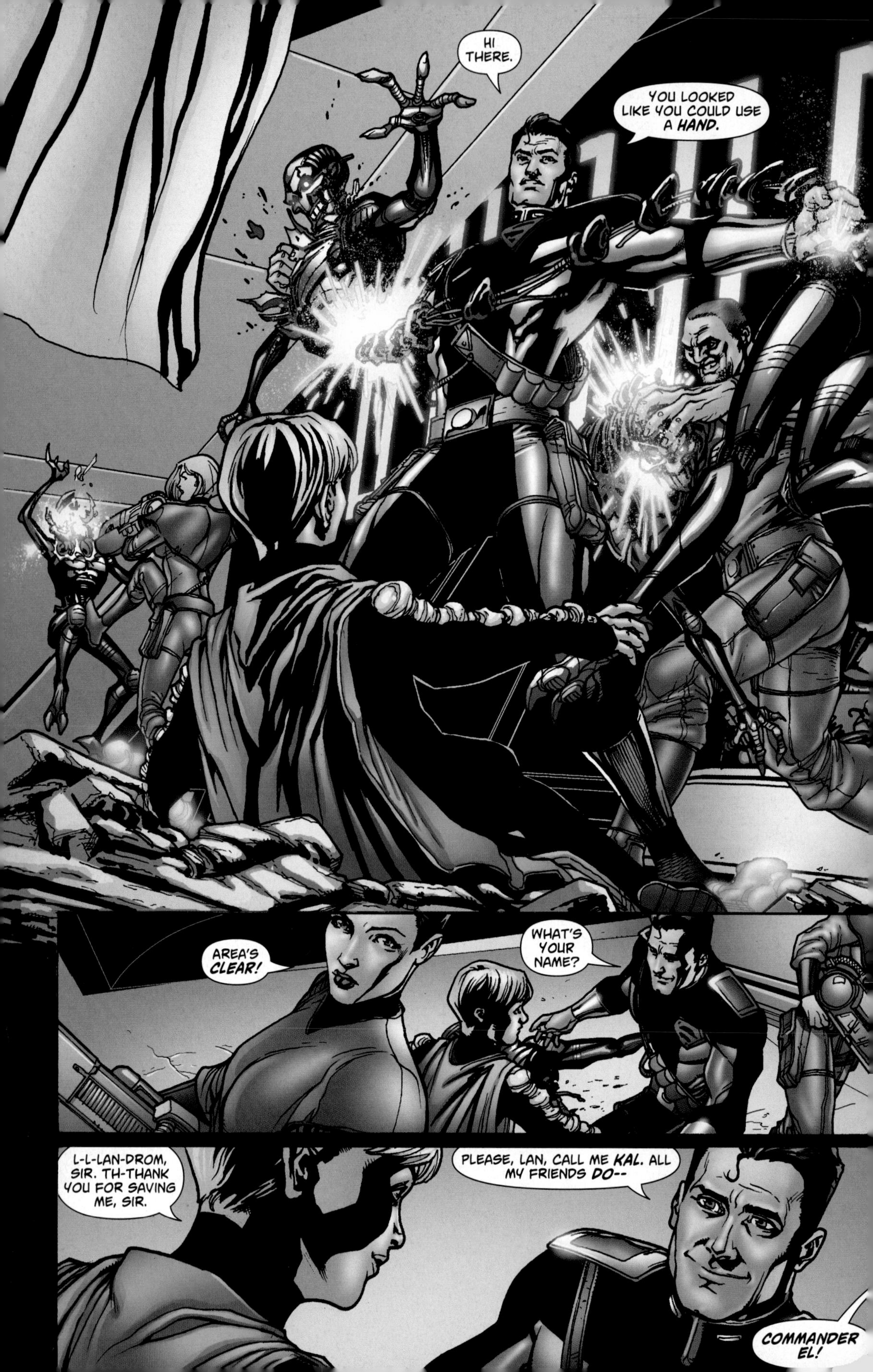
HI THERE.
YOU LOOKED LIKE YOU COULD USE A HAND.
AREA'S CLEAR!
WHAT'S YOUR NAME?
L-L-LAN-DROM, SIR. TH-THANK YOU FOR SAVING ME, SIR.
PLEASE, LAN, CALL ME KAL. ALL MY FRIENDS DO--
COMMANDER EL!

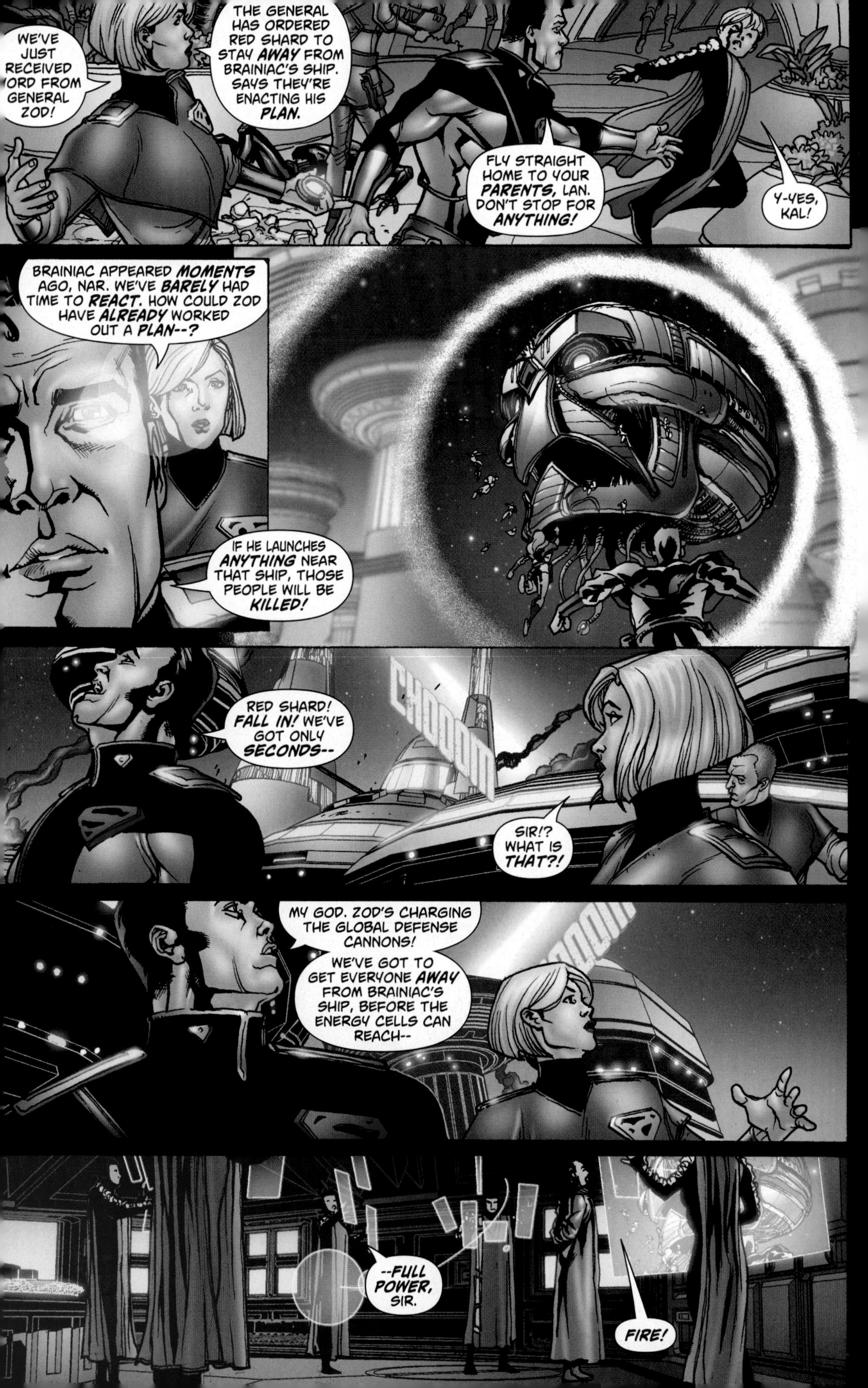
WE'VE JUST RECEIVED WORD FROM GENERAL ZOD!
THE GENERAL HAS ORDERED RED SHARD TO STAY AWAY FROM BRAINIAC'S SHIP. SAYS THEY'RE ENACTING HIS PLAN.
FLY STRAIGHT HOME TO YOUR PARENTS, LAN. DON'T STOP FOR ANYTHING!
Y-YES, KAL!
BRAINIAC APPEARED MOMENTS AGO, NAR. WE'VE BARELY HAD TIME TO REACT. HOW COULD ZOD HAVE ALREADY WORKED OUT A PLAN--?
IF HE LAUNCHES ANYTHING NEAR THAT SHIP, THOSE PEOPLE WILL BE KILLED!
CHOOOM
RED SHARD! FALL IN! WE'VE GOT ONLY SECONDS--
SIR!? WHAT IS THAT?!
MY GOD. ZOD'S CHARGING THE GLOBAL DEFENSE CANNONS!
WE'VE GOT TO GET EVERYONE AWAY FROM BRAINIAC'S SHIP, BEFORE THE ENERGY CELLS CAN REACH--
--FULL POWER, SIR.
FIRE!

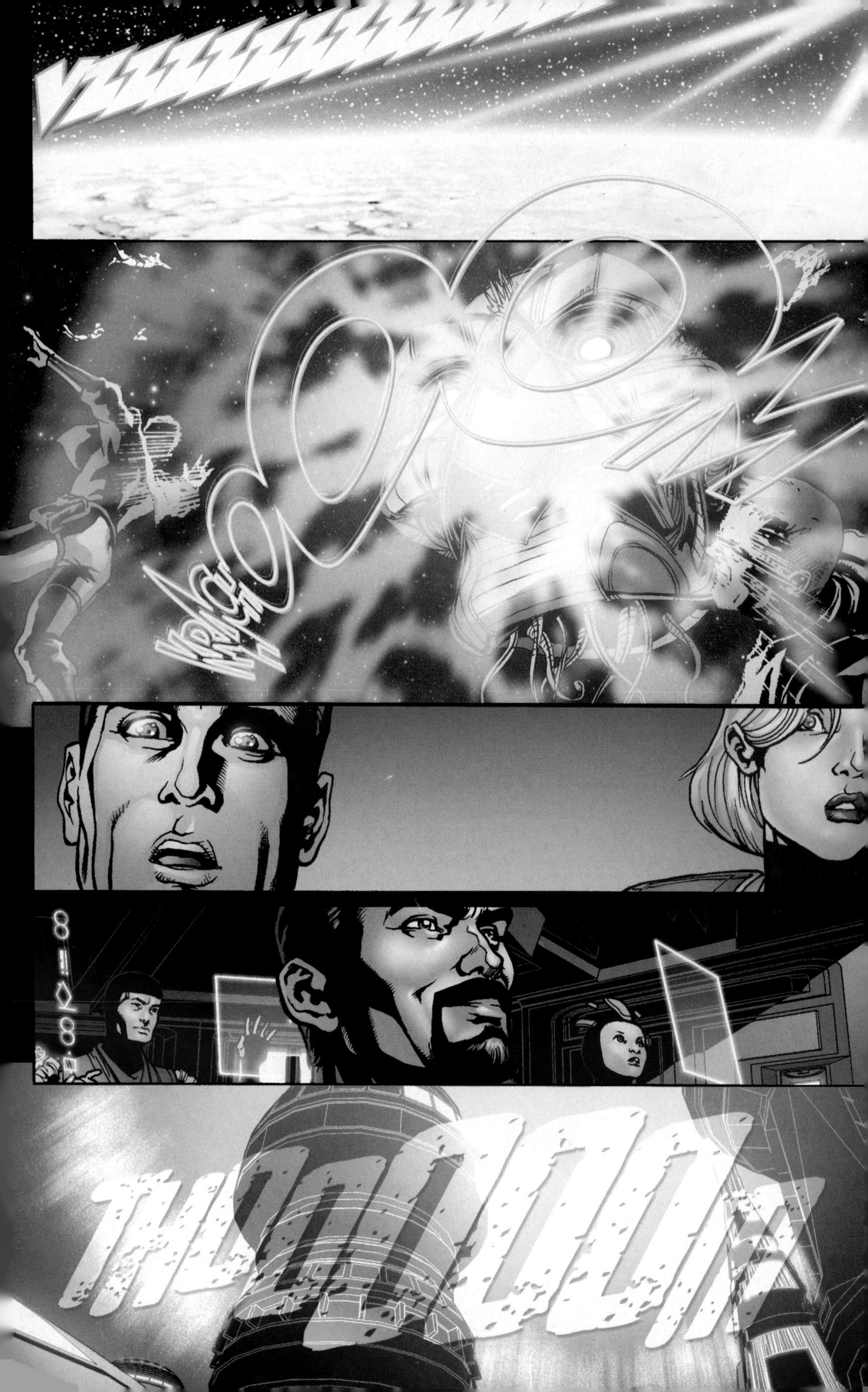
VZZZZZZZZZZZ
KRAKA
BOOM
THOOOOM

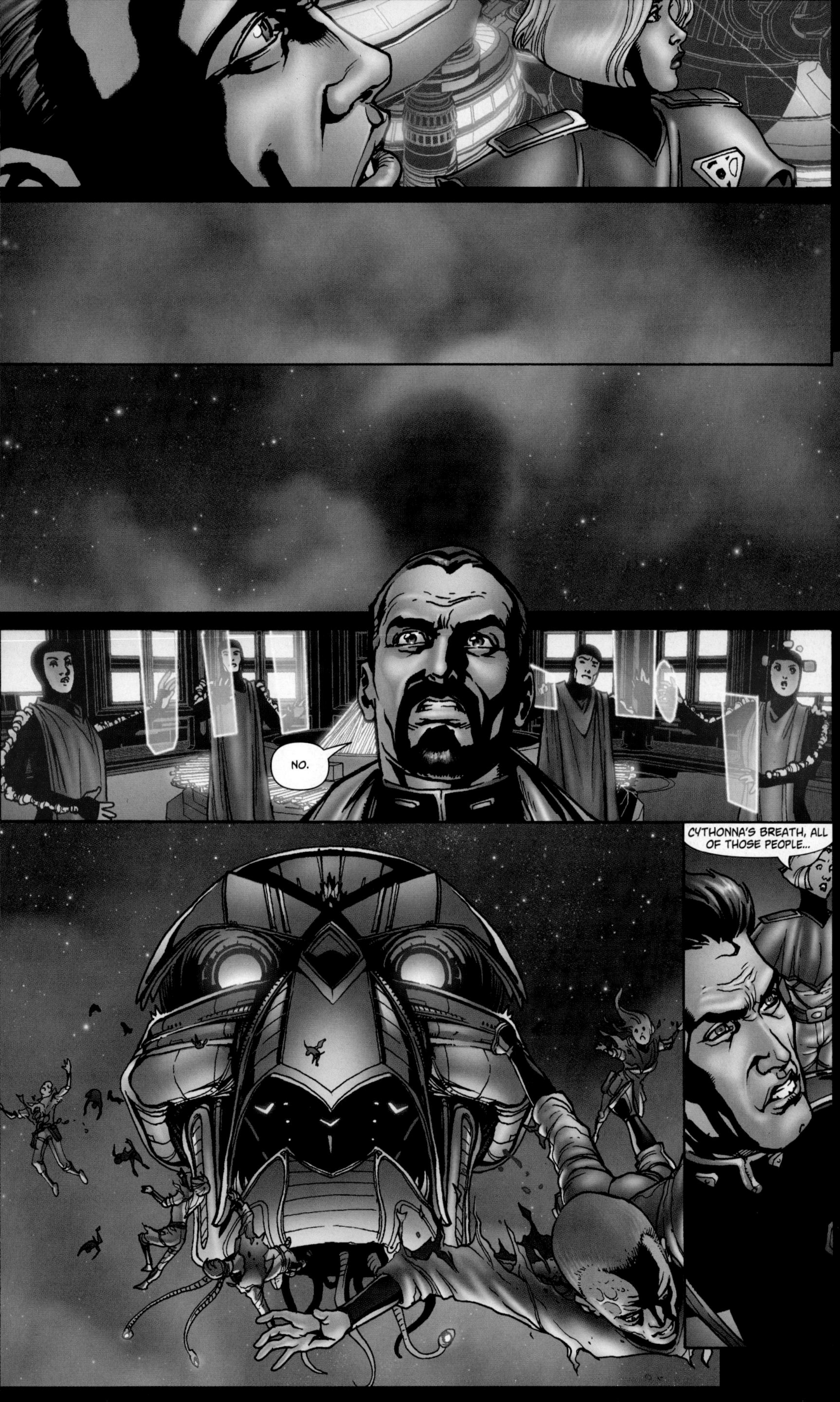
NO.
CYTHONNA'S BREATH, ALL OF THOSE PEOPLE...

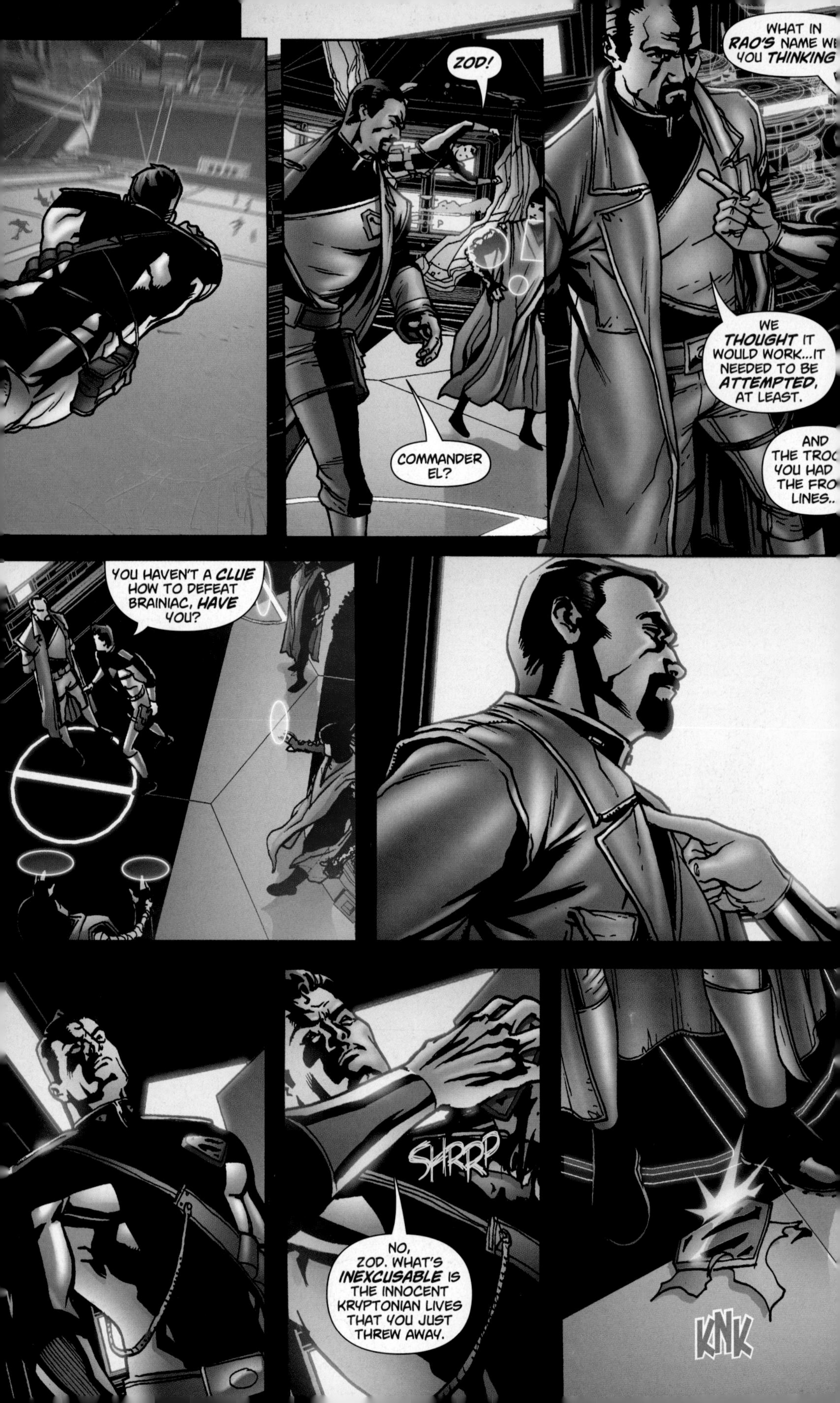
ZOD!
COMMANDER EL?
WHAT IN RAO'S NAME WE YOU THINKING
WE THOUGHT IT WOULD WORK...IT NEEDED TO BE ATTEMPTED, AT LEAST.
AND THE TROC YOU HAD THE FRO LINES..
YOU HAVEN'T A CLUE HOW TO DEFEAT BRAINIAC, HAVE YOU?
SHRRP
NO, ZOD. WHAT'S INEXCUSABLE IS THE INNOCENT KRYPTONIAN LIVES THAT YOU JUST THREW AWAY.
KNK

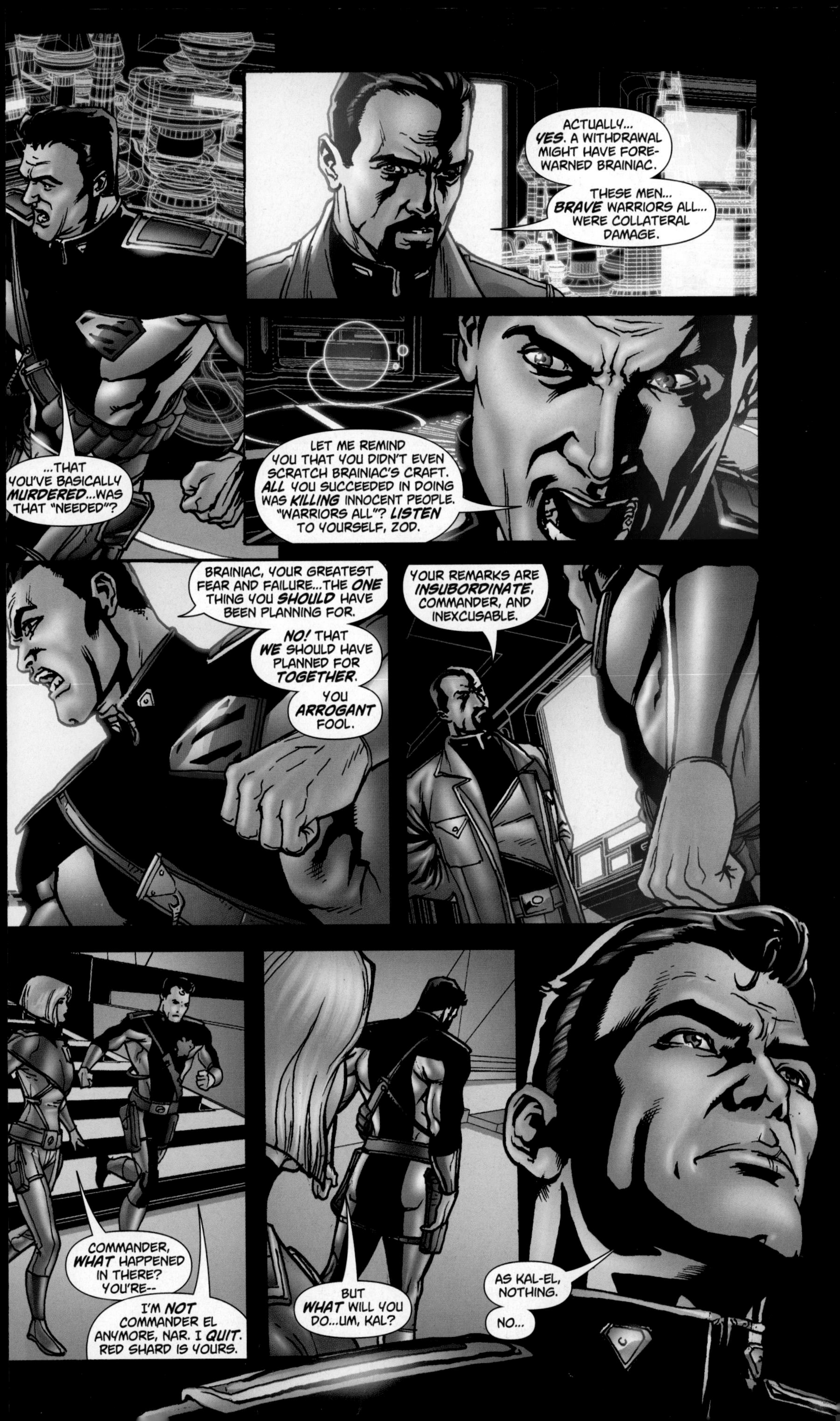
ACTUALLY... YES. A WITHDRAWAL MIGHT HAVE FORE-WARNED BRAINIAC.
THESE MEN... BRAVE WARRIORS ALL... WERE COLLATERAL DAMAGE.
...THAT YOU'VE BASICALLY MURDERED...WAS THAT "NEEDED"?
LET ME REMIND YOU THAT YOU DIDN'T EVEN SCRATCH BRAINIAC'S CRAFT. ALL YOU SUCCEEDED IN DOING WAS KILLING INNOCENT PEOPLE. "WARRIORS ALL"? LISTEN TO YOURSELF, ZOD.
BRAINIAC, YOUR GREATEST FEAR AND FAILURE...THE ONE THING YOU SHOULD HAVE BEEN PLANNING FOR.
NO! THAT WE SHOULD HAVE PLANNED FOR TOGETHER.
YOU ARROGANT FOOL.
YOUR REMARKS ARE INSUBORDINATE, COMMANDER, AND INEXCUSABLE.
COMMANDER, WHAT HAPPENED IN THERE? YOU'RE--
I'M NOT COMMANDER EL ANYMORE, NAR. I QUIT. RED SHARD IS YOURS.
BUT WHAT WILL YOU DO...UM, KAL?
AS KAL-EL, NOTHING.
NO...

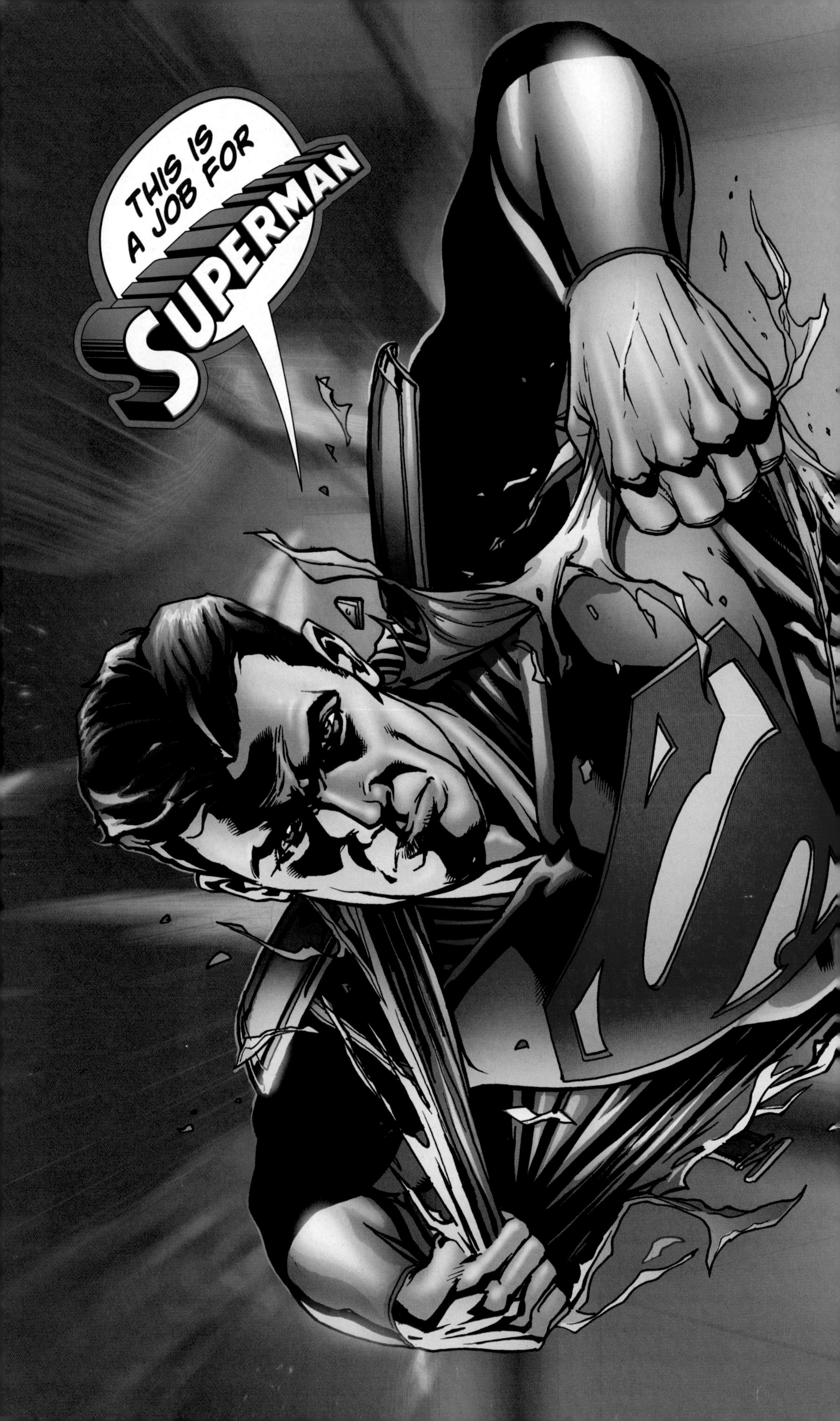
THIS IS A JOB FOR SUPERMAN

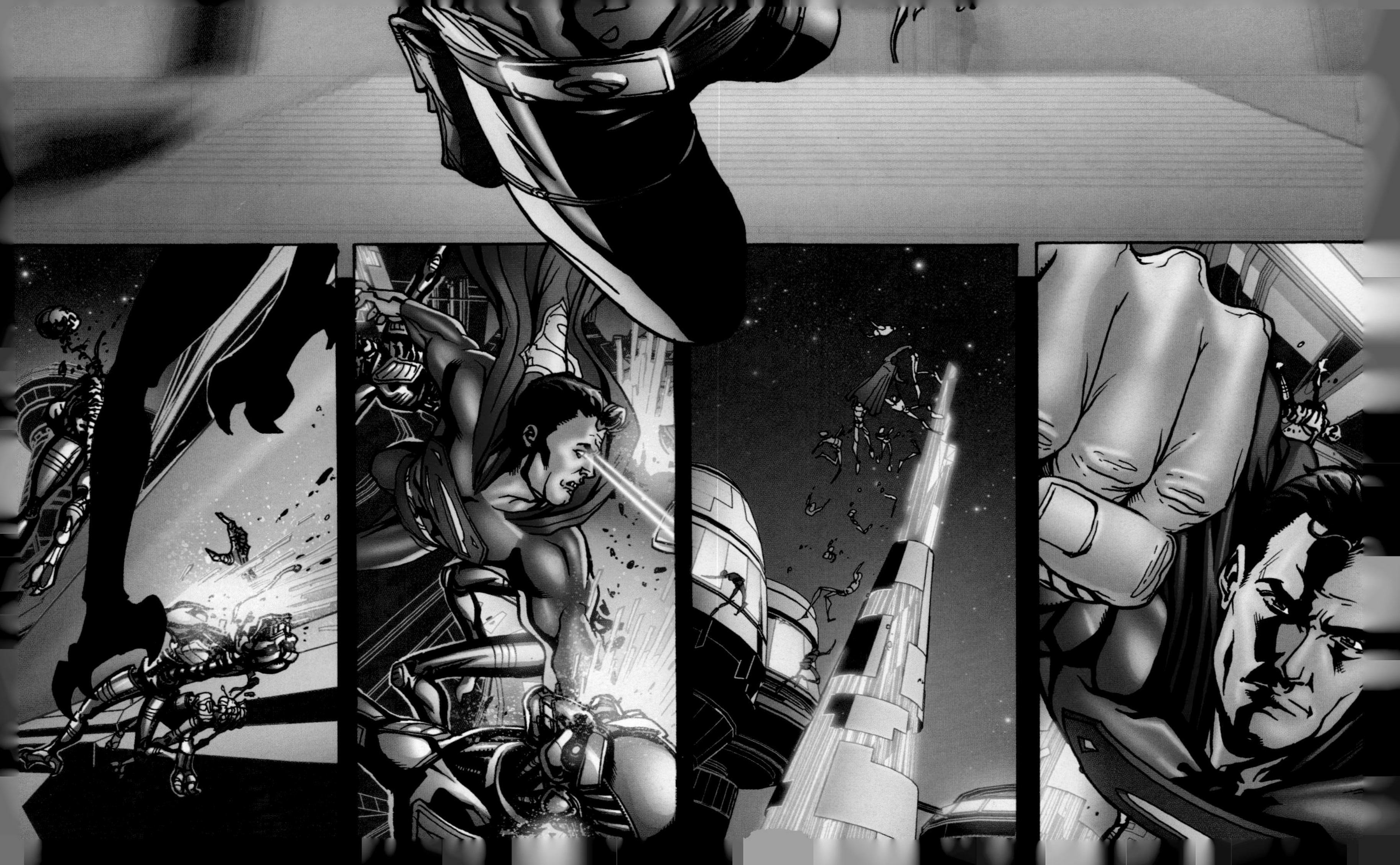

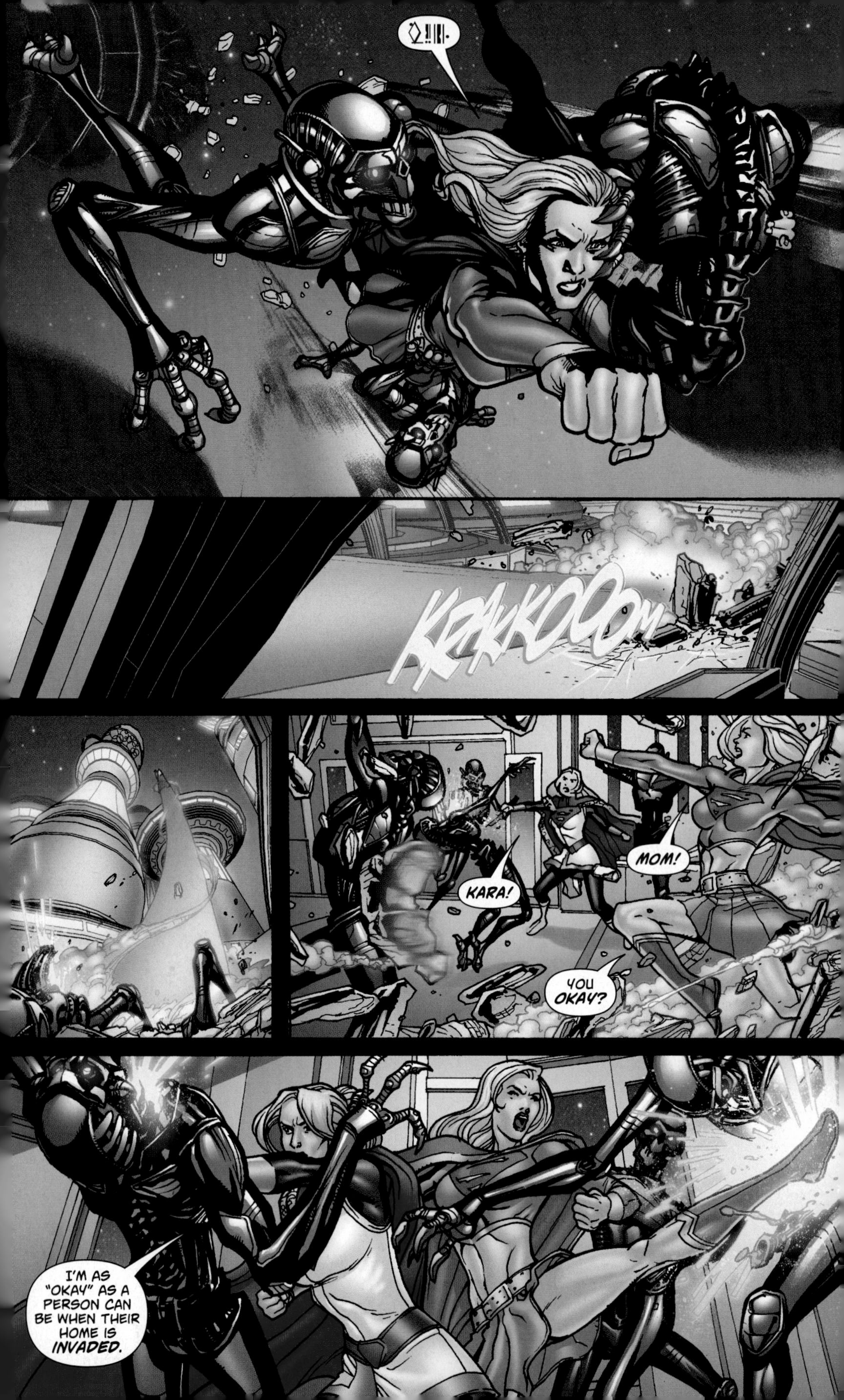
KRAKKOOOOM
KARA!
MOM!
YOU OKAY?
I'M AS "OKAY" AS A PERSON CAN BE WHEN THEIR HOME IS INVADED.

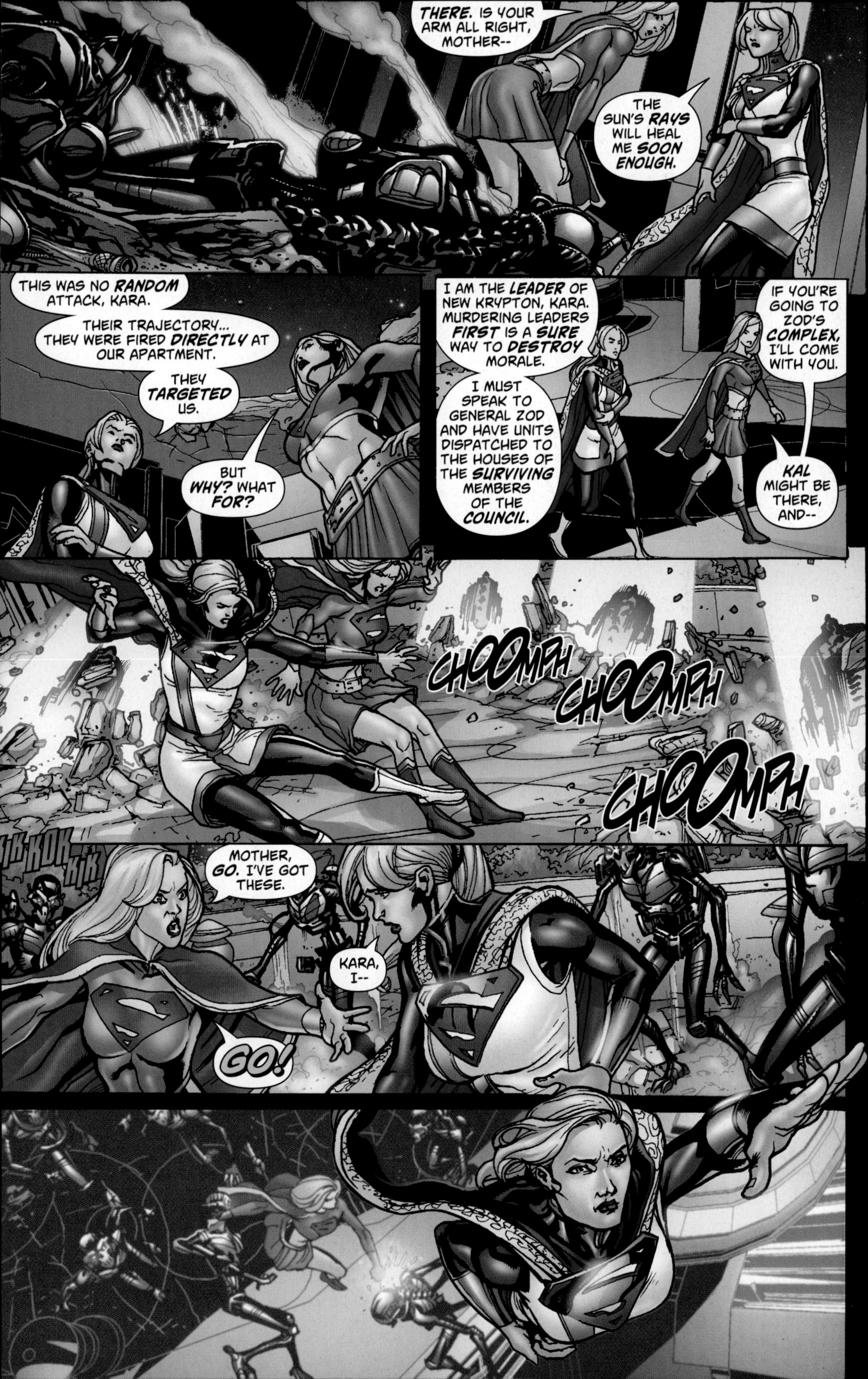
THERE. IS YOUR ARM ALL RIGHT, MOTHER--
THE SUN'S RAYS WILL HEAL ME SOON ENOUGH.
THIS WAS NO RANDOM ATTACK, KARA.
THEIR TRAJECTORY... THEY WERE FIRED DIRECTLY AT OUR APARTMENT.
THEY TARGETED US.
BUT WHY? WHAT FOR?
I AM THE LEADER OF NEW KRYPTON, KARA. MURDERING LEADERS FIRST IS A SURE WAY TO DESTROY MORALE.
I MUST SPEAK TO GENERAL ZOD AND HAVE UNITS DISPATCHED TO THE HOUSES OF THE SURVIVING MEMBERS OF THE COUNCIL.
IF YOU'RE GOING TO ZOD'S COMPLEX, I'LL COME WITH YOU.
KAL MIGHT BE THERE, AND--
CHOOOMPH
CHOOOMPH
CHOOOMPH
KIK KOK KIK
MOTHER, GO. I'VE GOT THESE.
KARA, I--
GO!

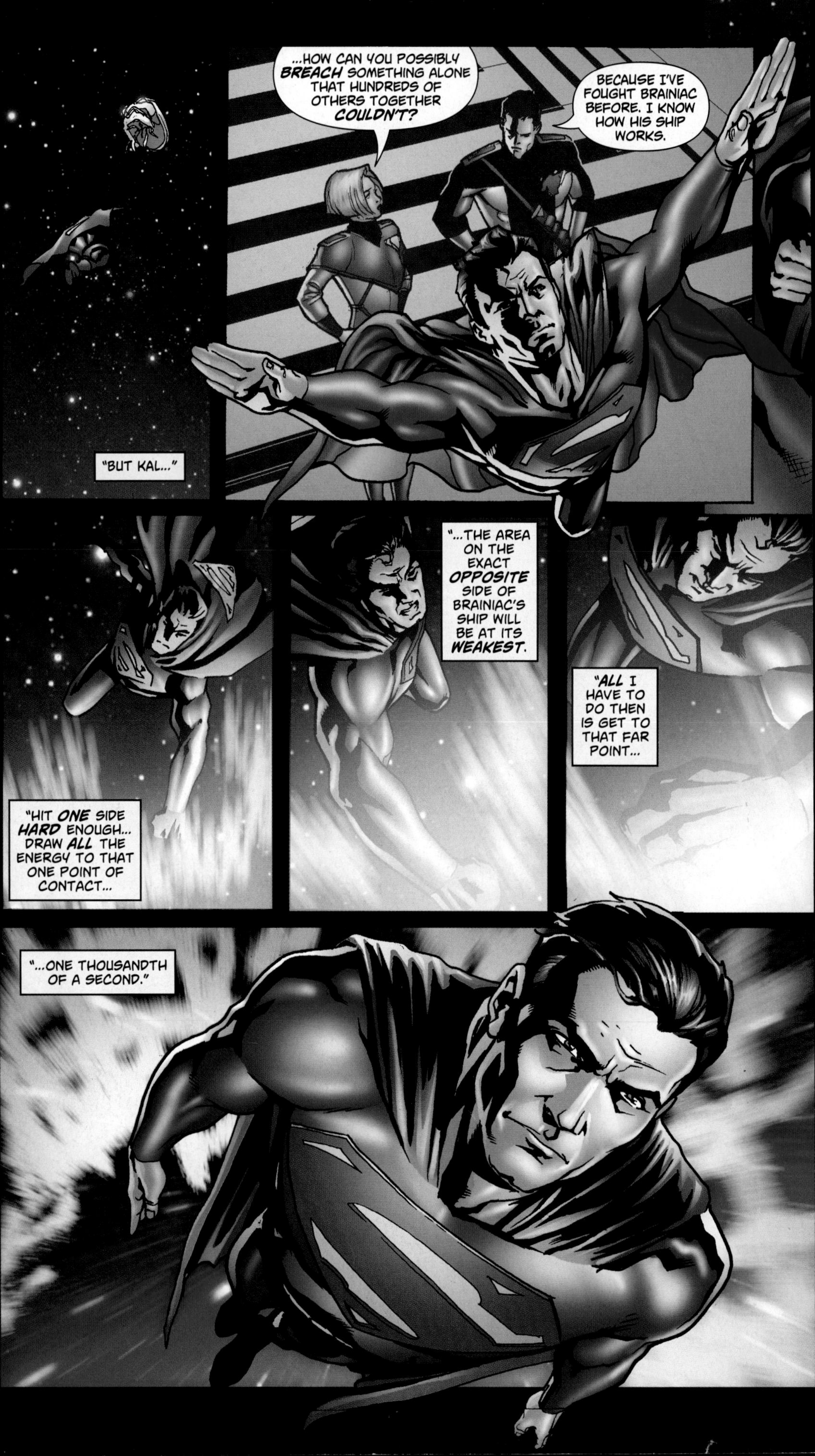
"BUT KAL..."
...HOW CAN YOU POSSIBLY BREACH SOMETHING ALONE THAT HUNDREDS OF OTHERS TOGETHER COULDN'T?
BECAUSE I'VE FOUGHT BRAINIAC BEFORE. I KNOW HOW HIS SHIP WORKS.
"HIT ONE SIDE HARD ENOUGH... DRAW ALL THE ENERGY TO THAT ONE POINT OF CONTACT...
"...THE AREA ON THE EXACT OPPOSITE SIDE OF BRAINIAC'S SHIP WILL BE AT ITS WEAKEST.
"ALL I HAVE TO DO THEN IS GET TO THAT FAR POINT...
"...ONE THOUSANDTH OF A SECOND."

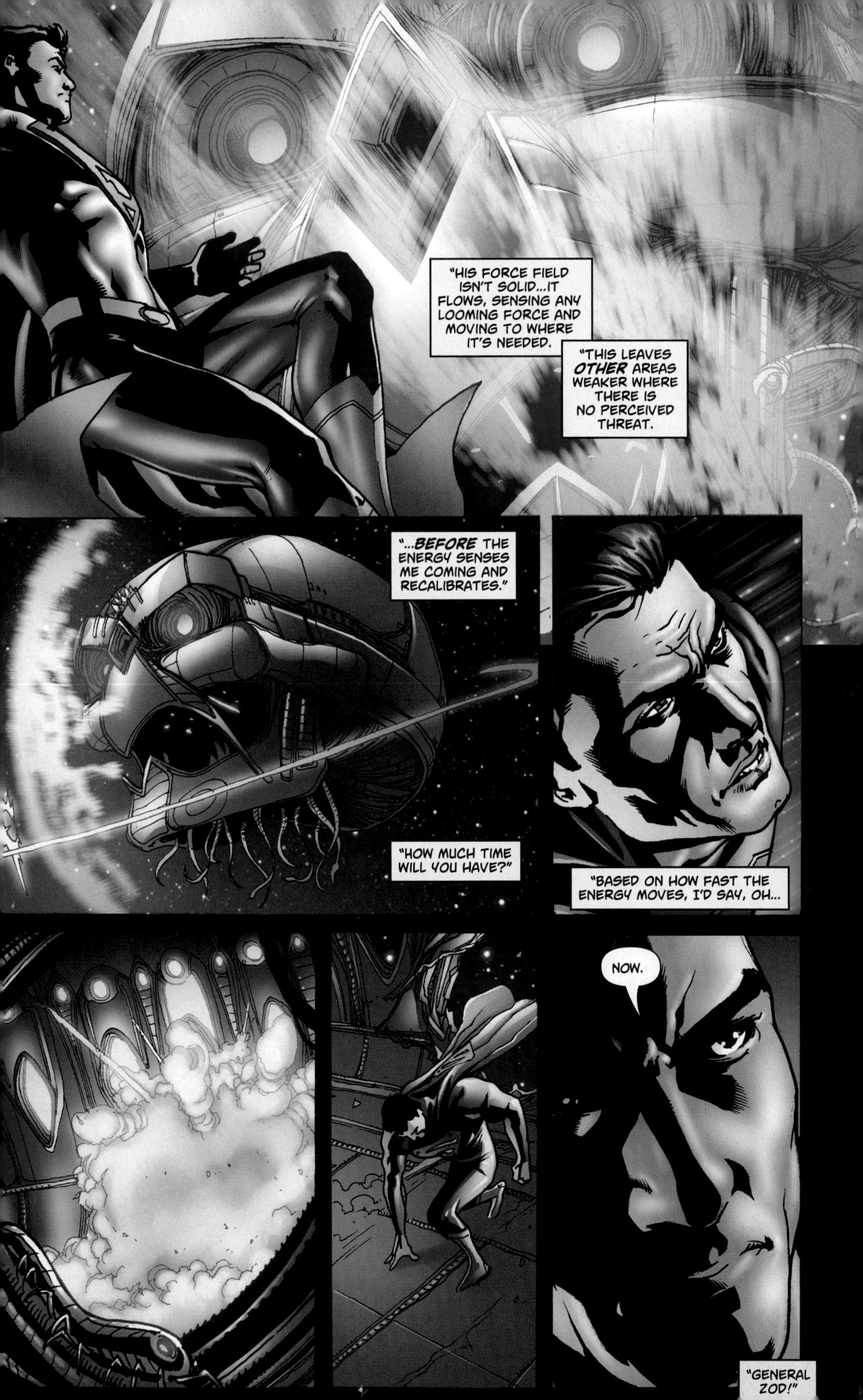
"HIS FORCE FIELD ISN'T SOLID...IT FLOWS, SENSING ANY LOOMING FORCE AND MOVING TO WHERE IT'S NEEDED.
"THIS LEAVES OTHER AREAS WEAKER WHERE THERE IS NO PERCEIVED THREAT.
"...BEFORE THE ENERGY SENSES ME COMING AND RECALIBRATES."
"HOW MUCH TIME WILL YOU HAVE?"
"BASED ON HOW FAST THE ENERGY MOVES, I'D SAY, OH...
NOW.
"GENERAL ZOD!"

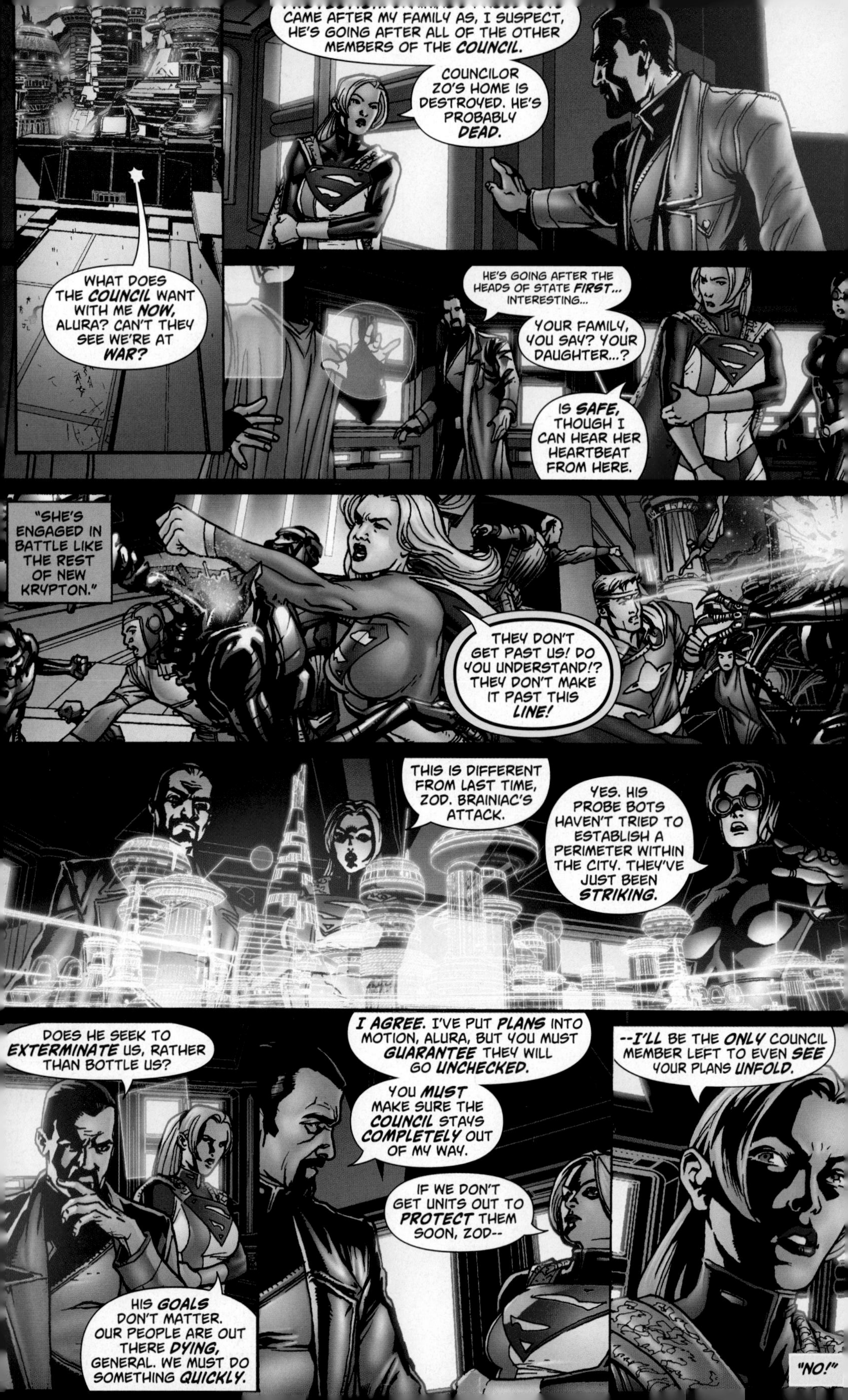
CAME AFTER MY FAMILY AS, I SUSPECT, HE'S GOING AFTER ALL OF THE OTHER MEMBERS OF THE COUNCIL.
COUNCILOR ZO'S HOME IS DESTROYED. HE'S PROBABLY DEAD.
WHAT DOES THE COUNCIL WANT WITH ME NOW, ALURA? CAN'T THEY SEE WE'RE AT WAR?
HE'S GOING AFTER THE HEADS OF STATE FIRST... INTERESTING...
YOUR FAMILY, YOU SAY? YOUR DAUGHTER...?
IS SAFE, THOUGH I CAN HEAR HER HEARTBEAT FROM HERE.
"SHE'S ENGAGED IN BATTLE LIKE THE REST OF NEW KRYPTON."
THEY DON'T GET PAST US! DO YOU UNDERSTAND!? THEY DON'T MAKE IT PAST THIS LINE!
THIS IS DIFFERENT FROM LAST TIME, ZOD. BRAINIAC'S ATTACK.
YES. HIS PROBE BOTS HAVEN'T TRIED TO ESTABLISH A PERIMETER WITHIN THE CITY. THEY'VE JUST BEEN STRIKING.
DOES HE SEEK TO EXTERMINATE US, RATHER THAN BOTTLE US?
HIS GOALS DON'T MATTER. OUR PEOPLE ARE OUT THERE DYING, GENERAL. WE MUST DO SOMETHING QUICKLY.
I AGREE. I'VE PUT PLANS INTO MOTION, ALURA, BUT YOU MUST GUARANTEE THEY WILL GO UNCHECKED.
YOU MUST MAKE SURE THE COUNCIL STAYS COMPLETELY OUT OF MY WAY.
IF WE DON'T GET UNITS OUT TO PROTECT THEM SOON, ZOD--
--I'LL BE THE ONLY COUNCIL MEMBER LEFT TO EVEN SEE YOUR PLANS UNFOLD.
"NO!"

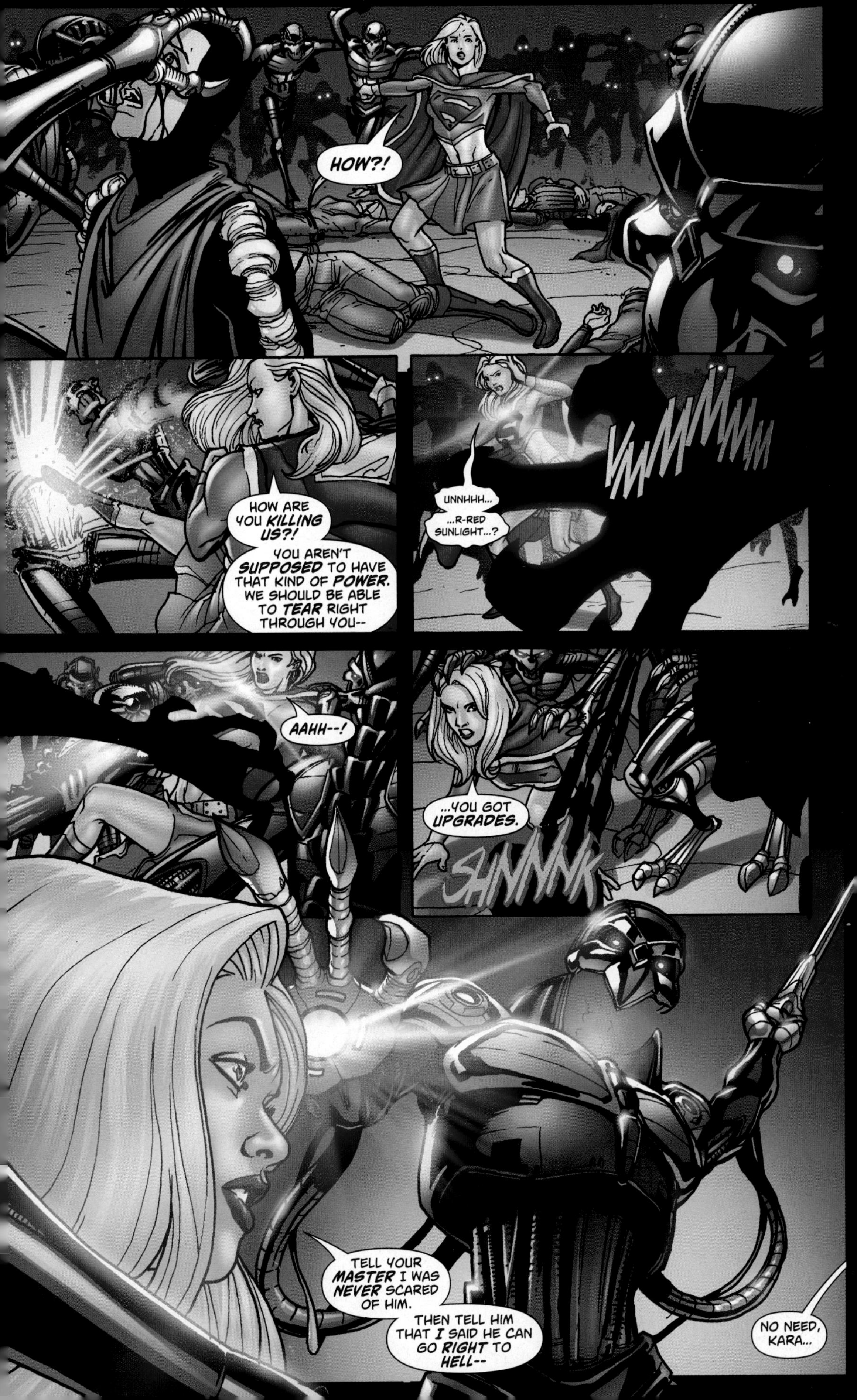

HOW?!
HOW ARE YOU KILLING US?!
YOU AREN'T SUPPOSED TO HAVE THAT KIND OF POWER. WE SHOULD BE ABLE TO TEAR RIGHT THROUGH YOU--
UNNHHH...
...R-RED SUNLIGHT...?
VMMMMMM
AAHH--!
...YOU GOT UPGRADES.
SHNNNK
TELL YOUR MASTER I WAS NEVER SCARED OF HIM.
THEN TELL HIM THAT I SAID HE CAN GO RIGHT TO HELL--
NO NEED, KARA...

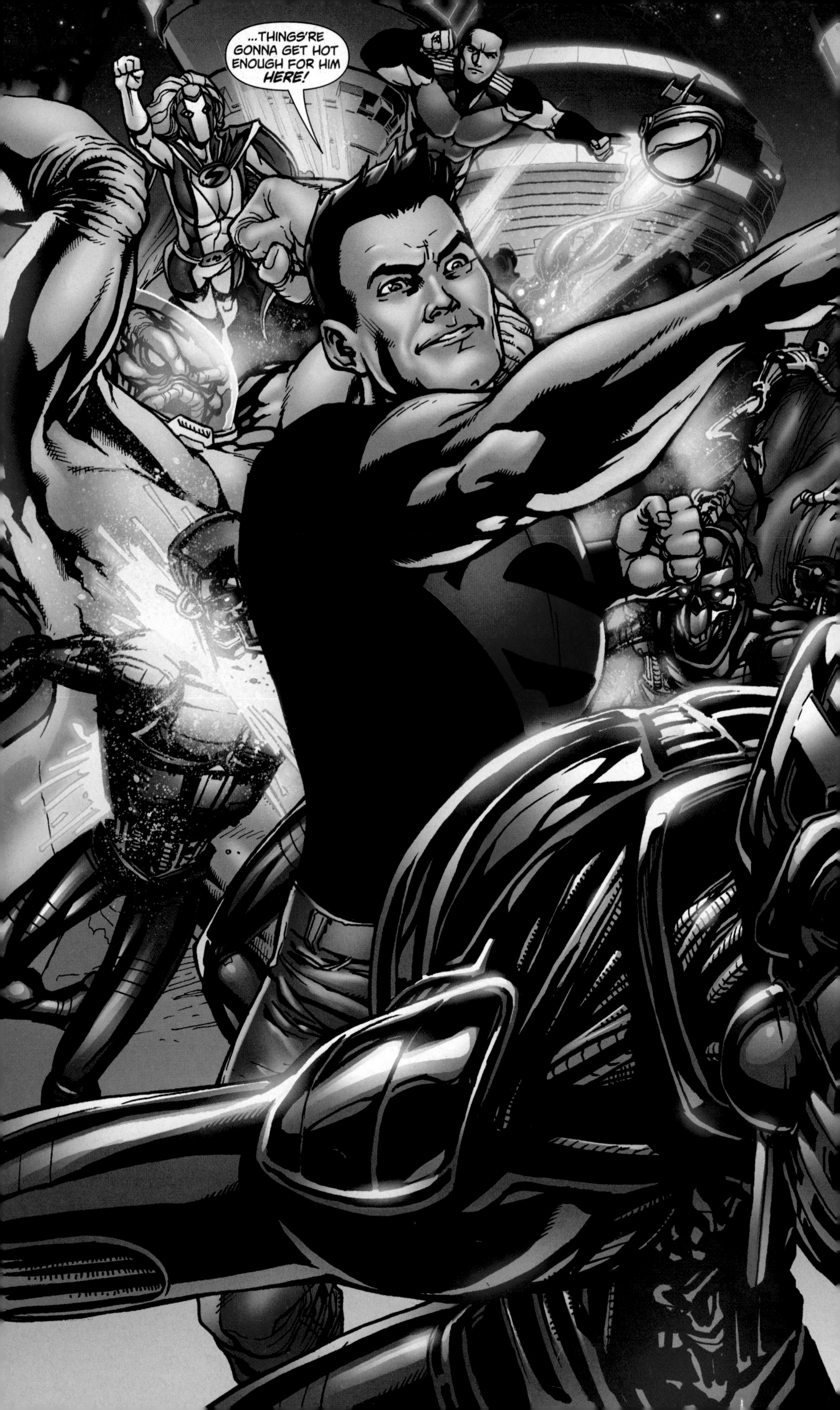
...THINGS'RE GONNA GET HOT ENOUGH FOR HIM HERE!

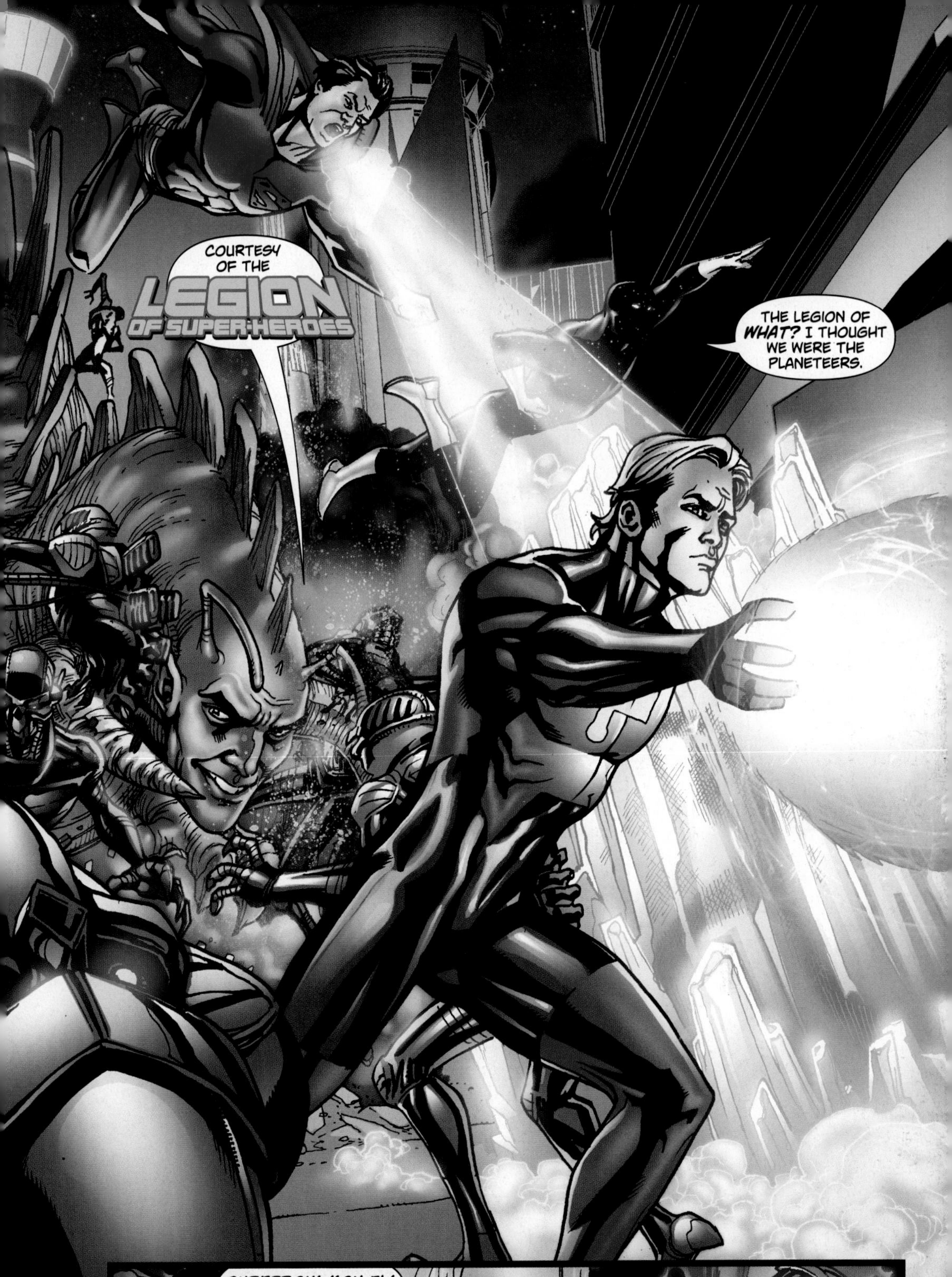
COURTESY OF THE
LEGION OF SUPER-HEROES
THE LEGION OF WHAT? I THOUGHT WE WERE THE PLANETEERS.

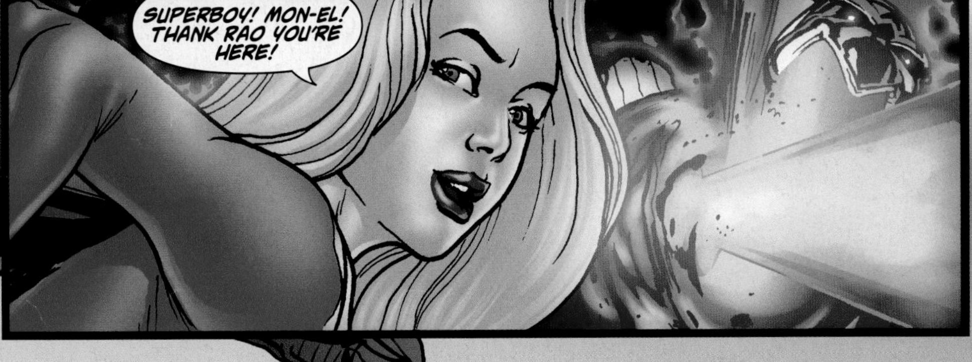
SUPERBOY! MON-EL! THANK RAO YOU'RE HERE!

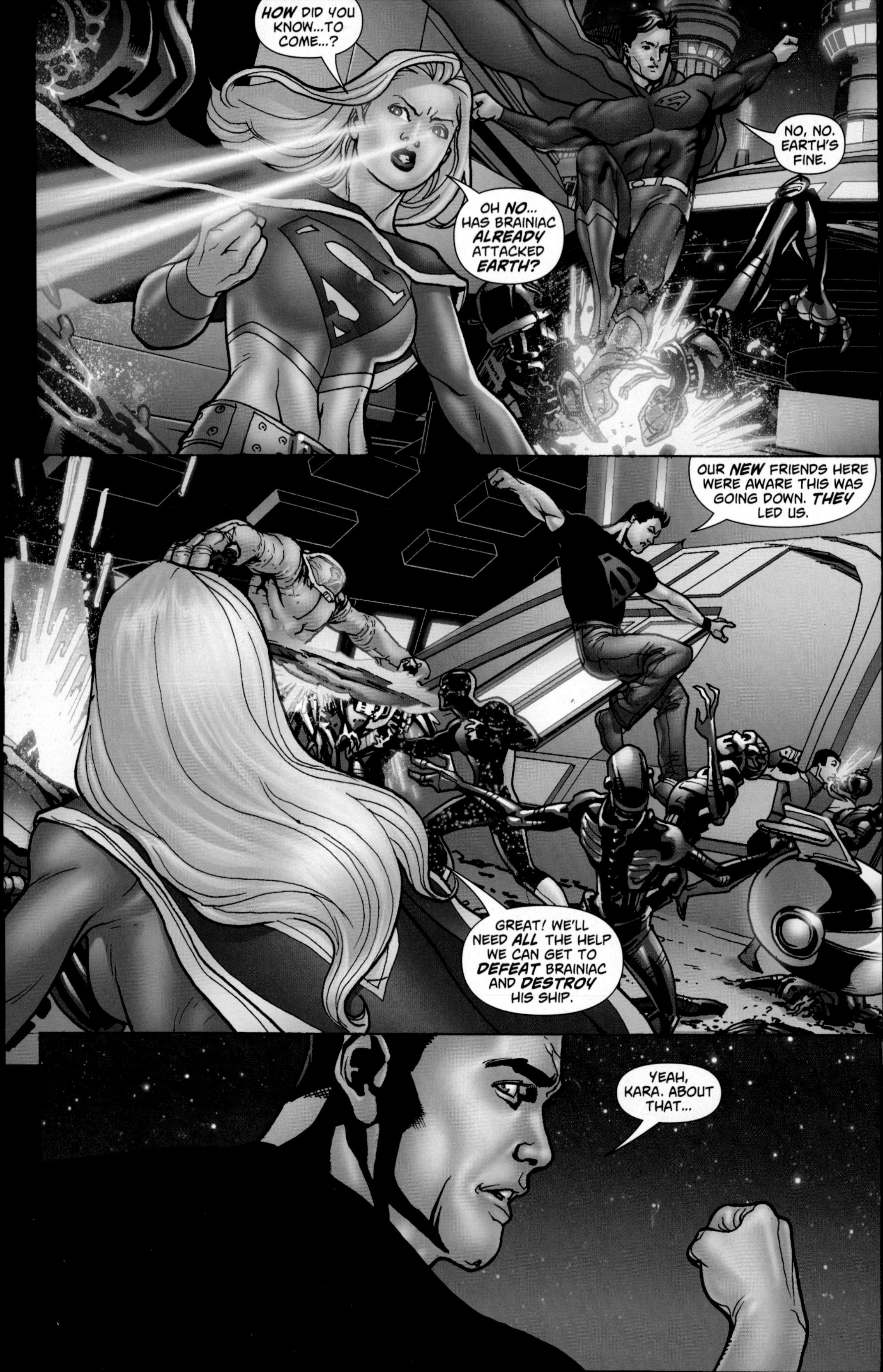
HOW DID YOU KNOW...TO COME...?
OH NO... HAS BRAINIAC ALREADY ATTACKED EARTH?
NO, NO. EARTH'S FINE.
OUR NEW FRIENDS HERE WERE AWARE THIS WAS GOING DOWN. THEY LED US.
GREAT! WE'LL NEED ALL THE HELP WE CAN GET TO DEFEAT BRAINIAC AND DESTROY HIS SHIP.
YEAH, KARA. ABOUT THAT...

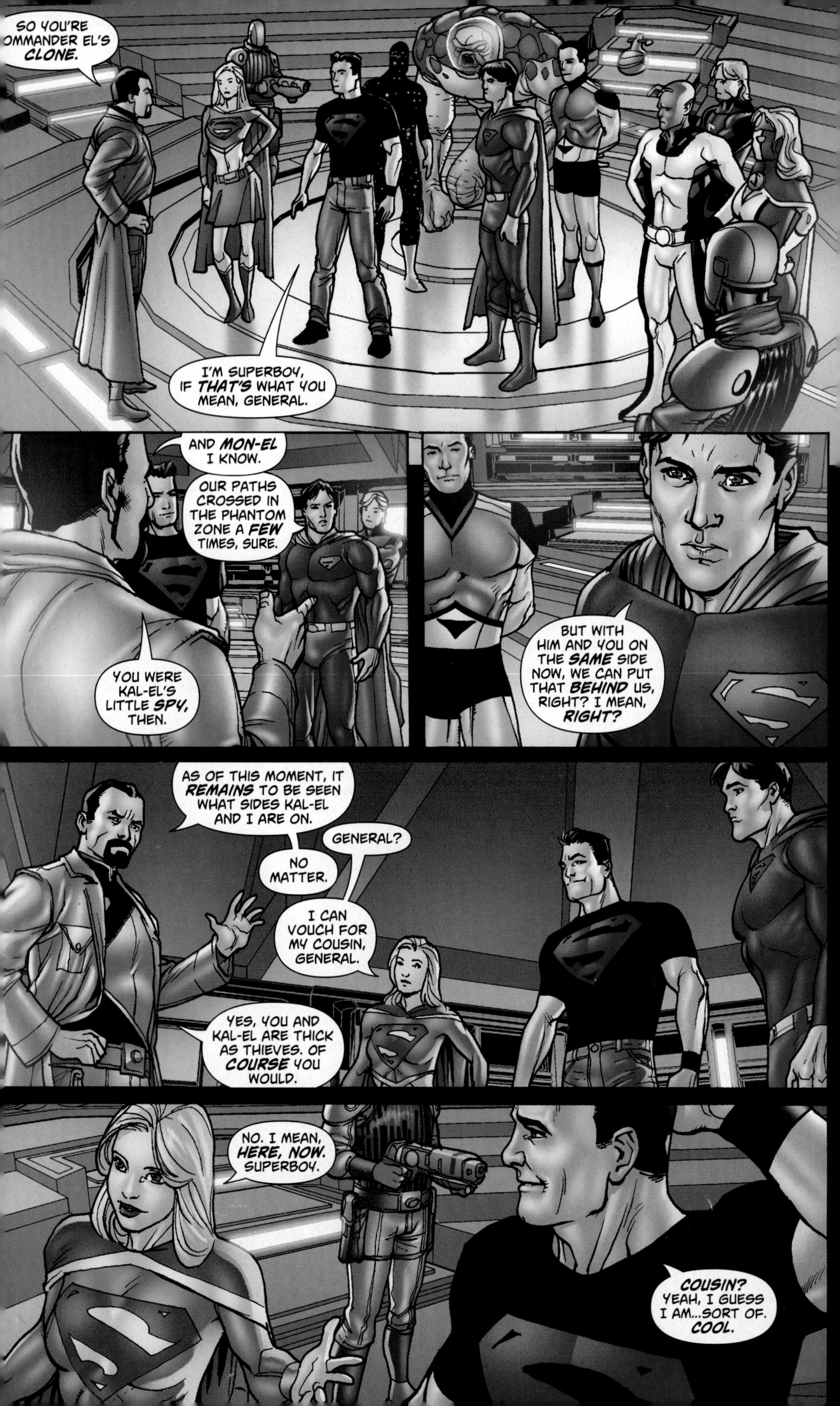
SO YOU'RE
OMMANDER EL'S
CLONE.
I'M SUPERBOY, IF THAT'S WHAT YOU MEAN, GENERAL.
AND MON-EL I KNOW.
OUR PATHS CROSSED IN THE PHANTOM ZONE A FEW TIMES, SURE.
YOU WERE KAL-EL'S LITTLE SPY, THEN.
BUT WITH HIM AND YOU ON THE SAME SIDE NOW, WE CAN PUT THAT BEHIND US, RIGHT? I MEAN, RIGHT?
AS OF THIS MOMENT, IT REMAINS TO BE SEEN WHAT SIDES KAL-EL AND I ARE ON.
GENERAL?
NO MATTER.
I CAN VOUCH FOR MY COUSIN, GENERAL.
YES, YOU AND KAL-EL ARE THICK AS THIEVES. OF COURSE YOU WOULD.
NO. I MEAN, HERE, NOW. SUPERBOY.
COUSIN? YEAH, I GUESS I AM...SORT OF. COOL.

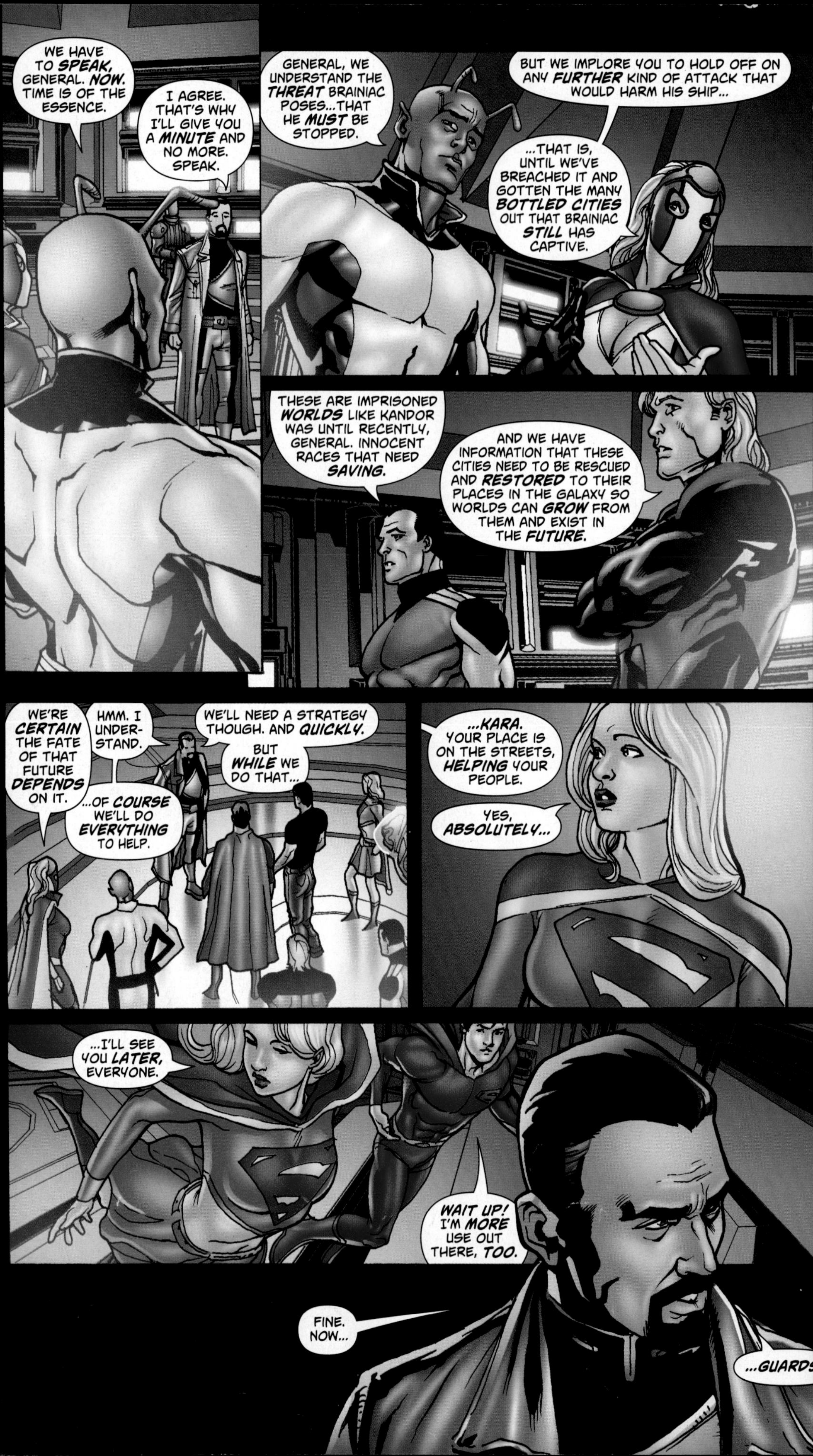
WE HAVE TO SPEAK, GENERAL. NOW. TIME IS OF THE ESSENCE.
I AGREE. THAT'S WHY I'LL GIVE YOU A MINUTE AND NO MORE. SPEAK.
GENERAL, WE UNDERSTAND THE THREAT BRAINIAC POSES...THAT HE MUST BE STOPPED.
BUT WE IMPLORE YOU TO HOLD OFF ON ANY FURTHER KIND OF ATTACK THAT WOULD HARM HIS SHIP...
...THAT IS, UNTIL WE'VE BREACHED IT AND GOTTEN THE MANY BOTTLED CITIES OUT THAT BRAINIAC STILL HAS CAPTIVE.
THESE ARE IMPRISONED WORLDS LIKE KANDOR WAS UNTIL RECENTLY, GENERAL. INNOCENT RACES THAT NEED SAVING.
AND WE HAVE INFORMATION THAT THESE CITIES NEED TO BE RESCUED AND RESTORED TO THEIR PLACES IN THE GALAXY SO WORLDS CAN GROW FROM THEM AND EXIST IN THE FUTURE.
WE'RE CERTAIN THE FATE OF THAT FUTURE DEPENDS ON IT.
HMM. I UNDER-STAND.
...OF COURSE WE'LL DO EVERYTHING TO HELP.
WE'LL NEED A STRATEGY THOUGH. AND QUICKLY.
BUT WHILE WE DO THAT...
...KARA. YOUR PLACE IS ON THE STREETS, HELPING YOUR PEOPLE.
YES, ABSOLUTELY...
...I'LL SEE YOU LATER, EVERYONE.
WAIT UP! I'M MORE USE OUT THERE, TOO.
FINE. NOW...
...GUARDS

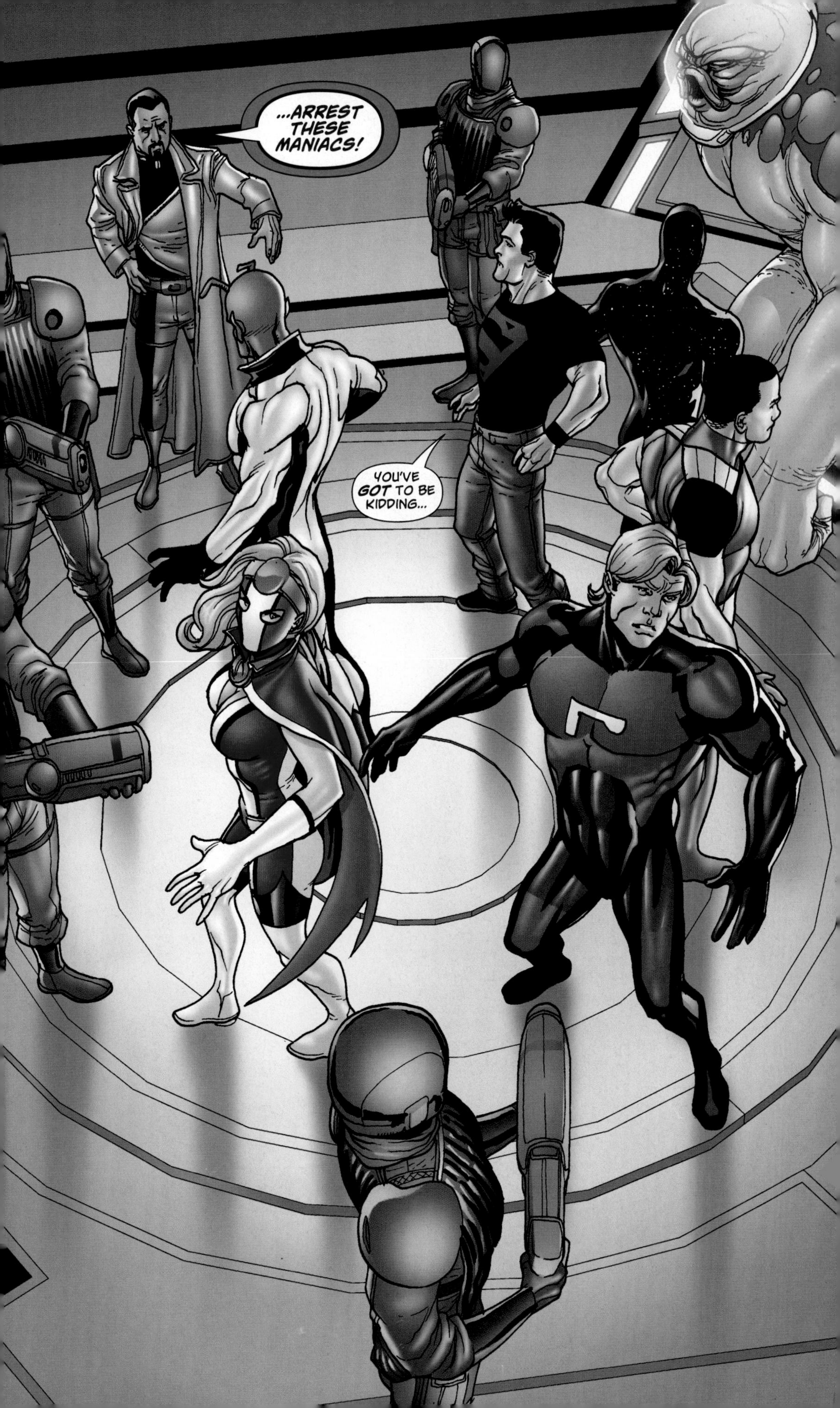
...ARREST THESE MANIACS!
YOU'VE GOT TO BE KIDDING...

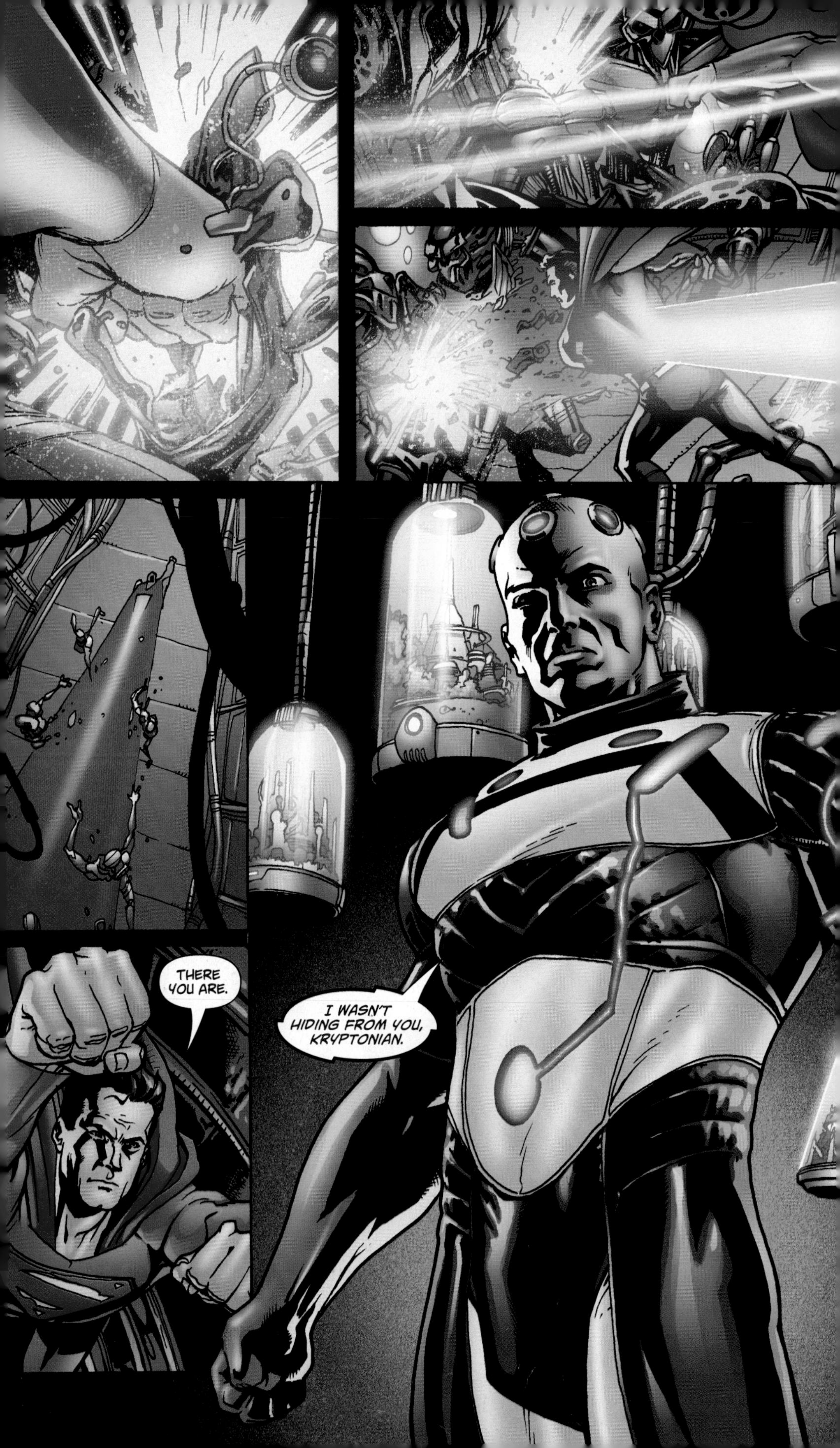
THERE YOU ARE.
I WASN'T HIDING FROM YOU, KRYPTONIAN.

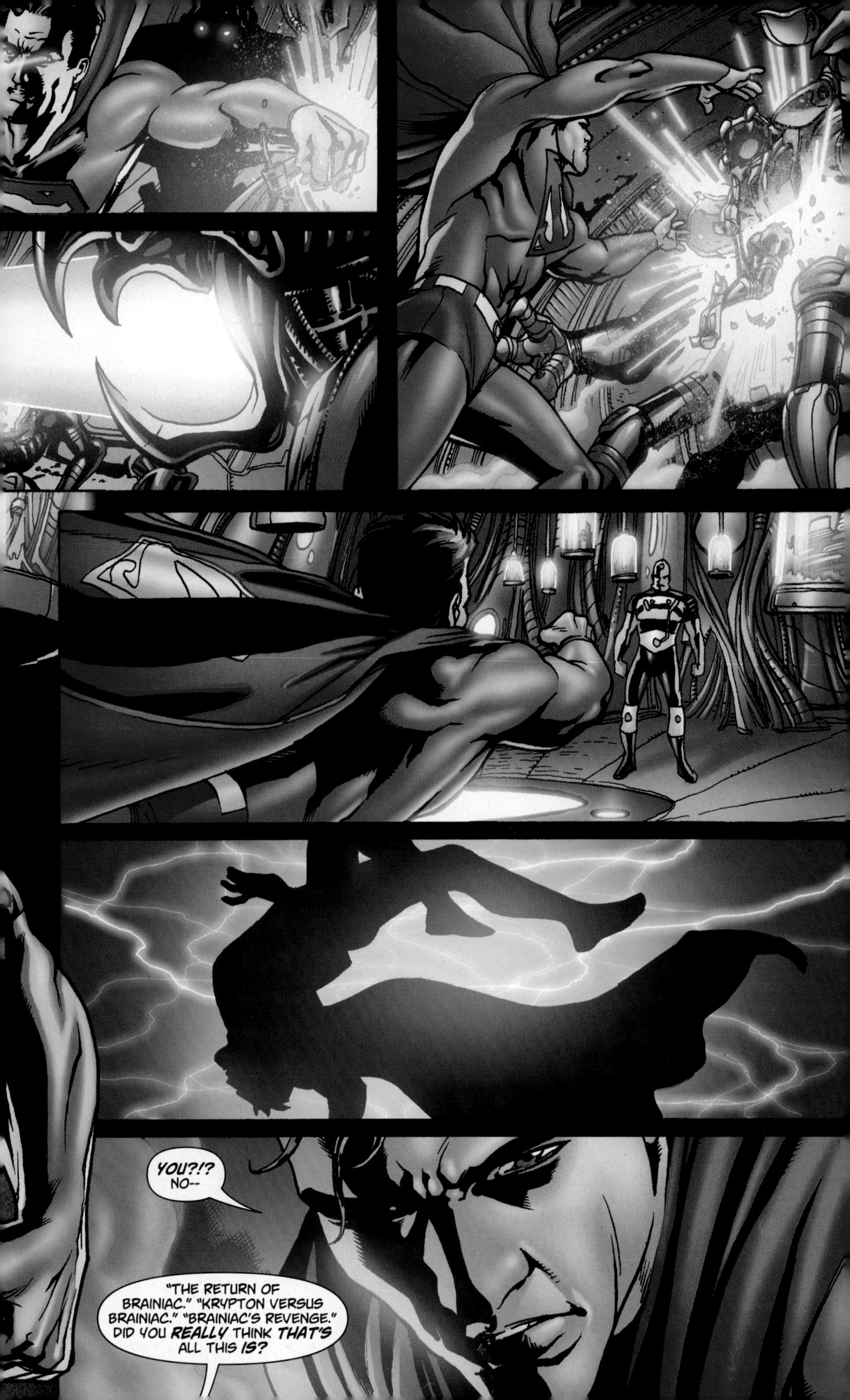
YOU?!? NO--
"THE RETURN OF BRAINIAC." "KRYPTON VERSUS BRAINIAC." "BRAINIAC'S REVENGE." DID YOU **REALLY** THINK **THAT'S** ALL THIS **IS**?

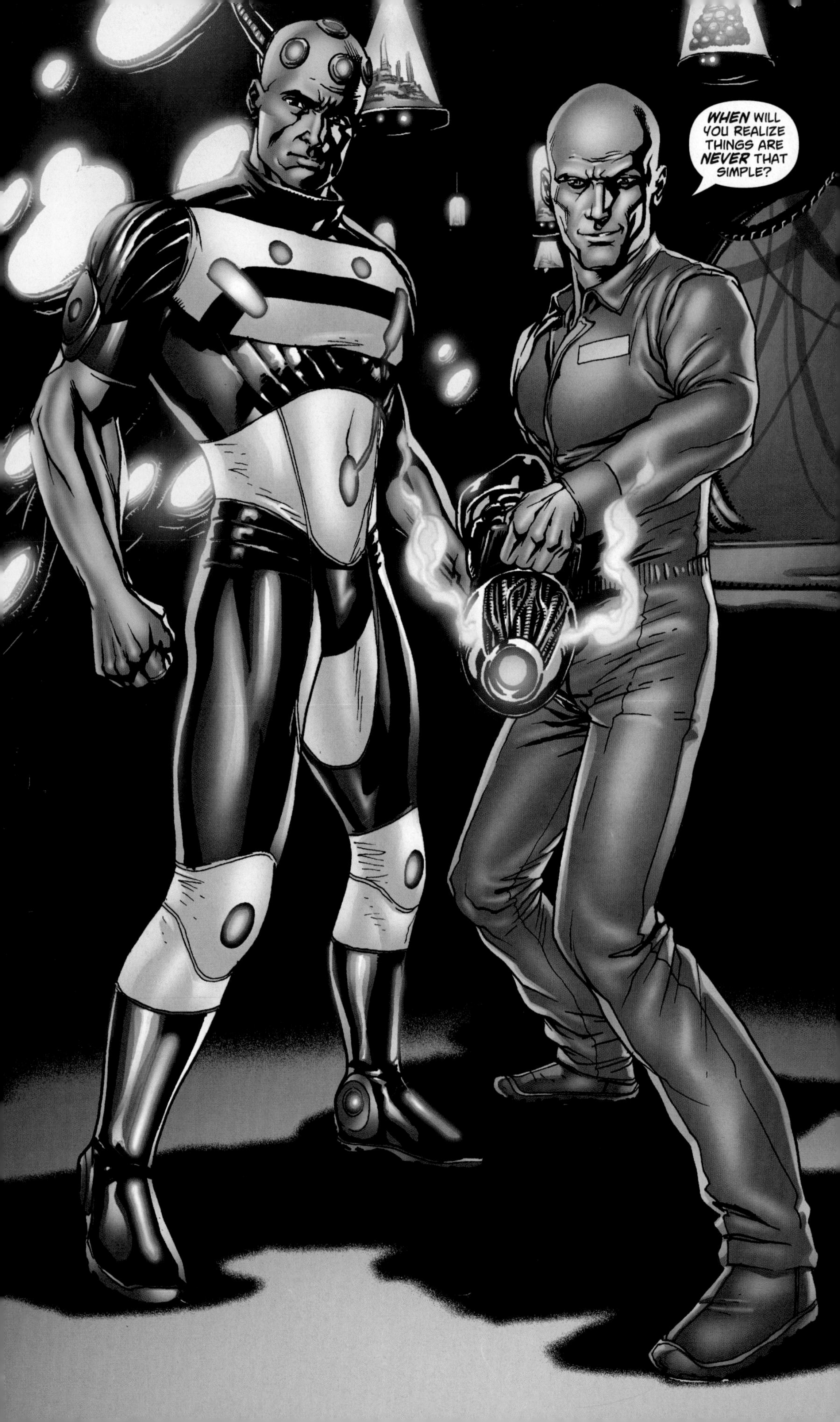
WHEN WILL YOU REALIZE THINGS ARE **NEVER** THAT SIMPLE?

cover by JOSHUA MIDDLETON

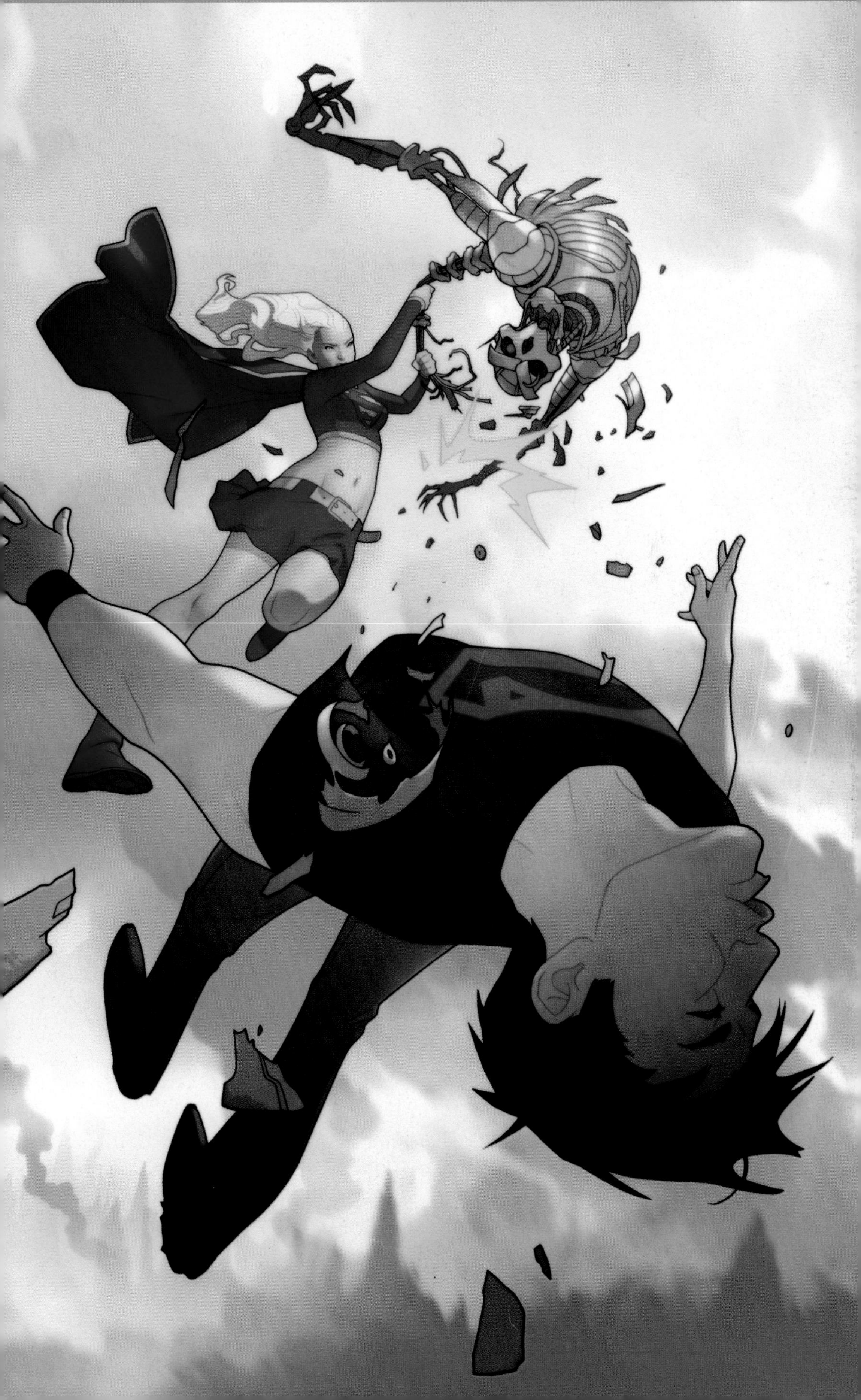

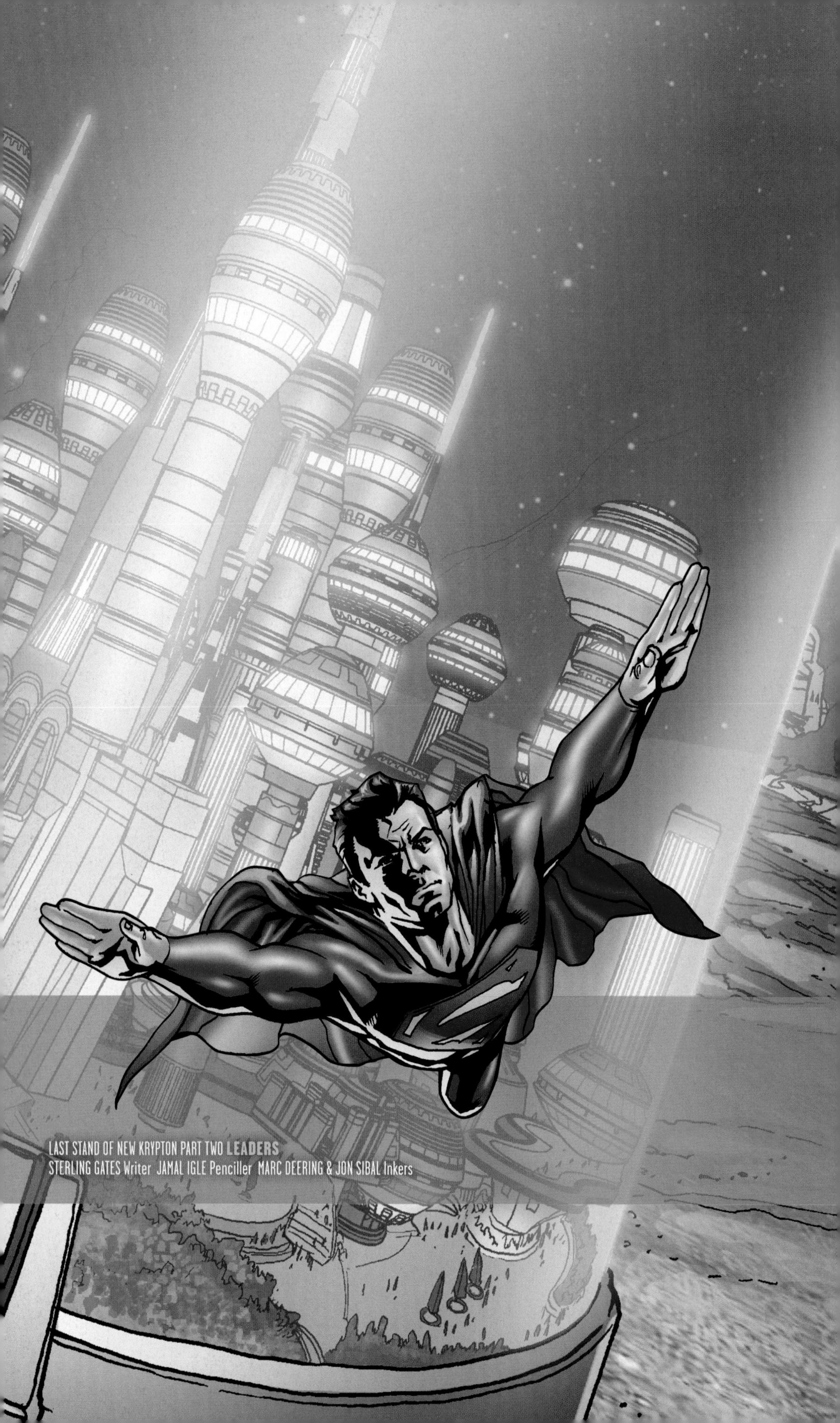
LAST STAND OF NEW KRYPTON PART TWO LEADERS
STERLING GATES Writer JAMAL IGLE Penciller MARC DEERING & JON SIBAL Inkers

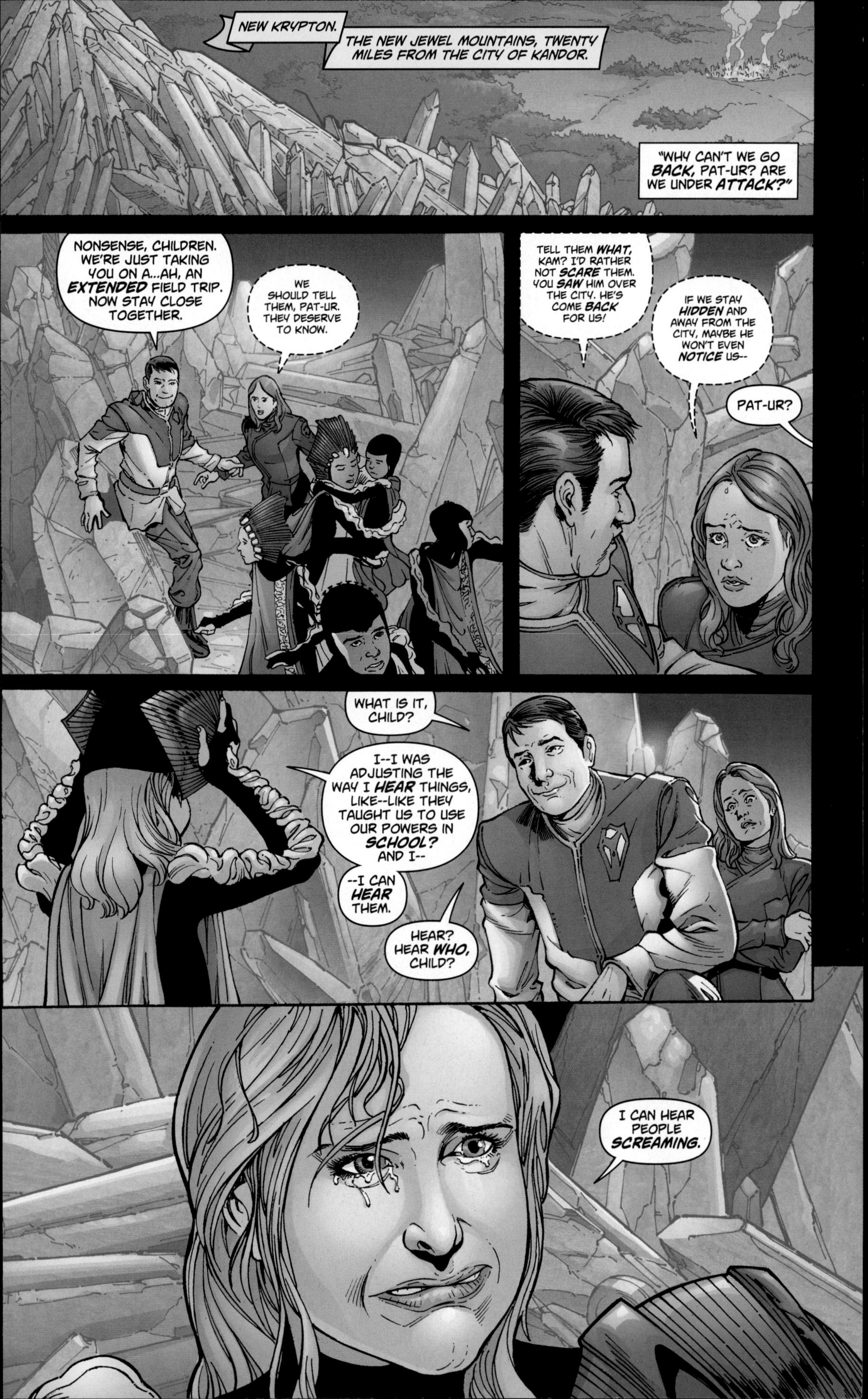
NEW KRYPTON.
THE NEW JEWEL MOUNTAINS, TWENTY MILES FROM THE CITY OF KANDOR.
"WHY CAN'T WE GO BACK, PAT-UR? ARE WE UNDER ATTACK?"
NONSENSE, CHILDREN. WE'RE JUST TAKING YOU ON A...AH, AN EXTENDED FIELD TRIP. NOW STAY CLOSE TOGETHER.
WE SHOULD TELL THEM, PAT-UR. THEY DESERVE TO KNOW.
TELL THEM WHAT, KAM? I'D RATHER NOT SCARE THEM. YOU SAW HIM OVER THE CITY. HE'S COME BACK FOR US!
IF WE STAY HIDDEN AND AWAY FROM THE CITY, MAYBE HE WON'T EVEN NOTICE US--
PAT-UR?
WHAT IS IT, CHILD?
I--I WAS ADJUSTING THE WAY I HEAR THINGS, LIKE--LIKE THEY TAUGHT US TO USE OUR POWERS IN SCHOOL? AND I--
--I CAN HEAR THEM.
HEAR? HEAR WHO, CHILD?
I CAN HEAR PEOPLE SCREAMING.

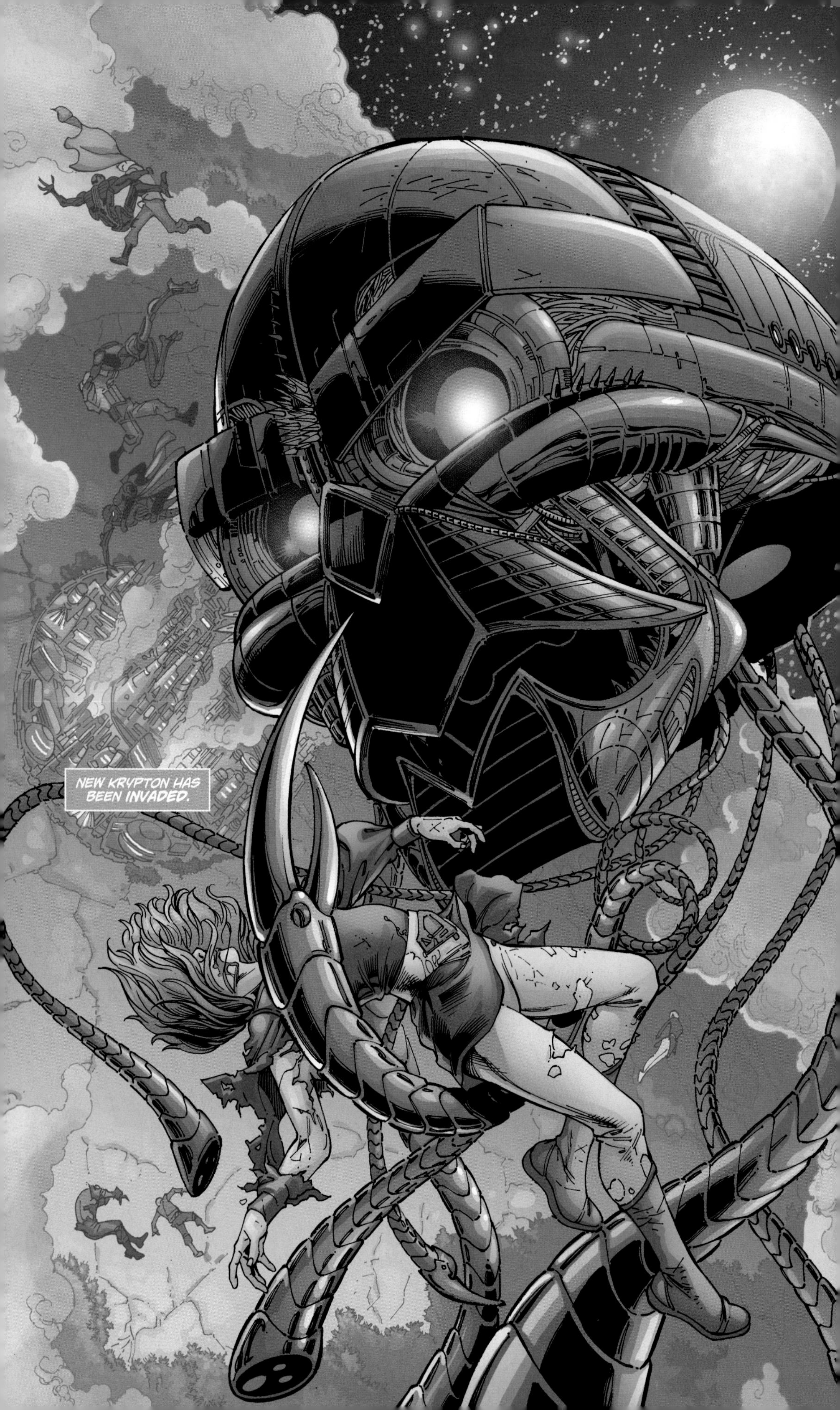
NEW KRYPTON HAS BEEN INVADED.

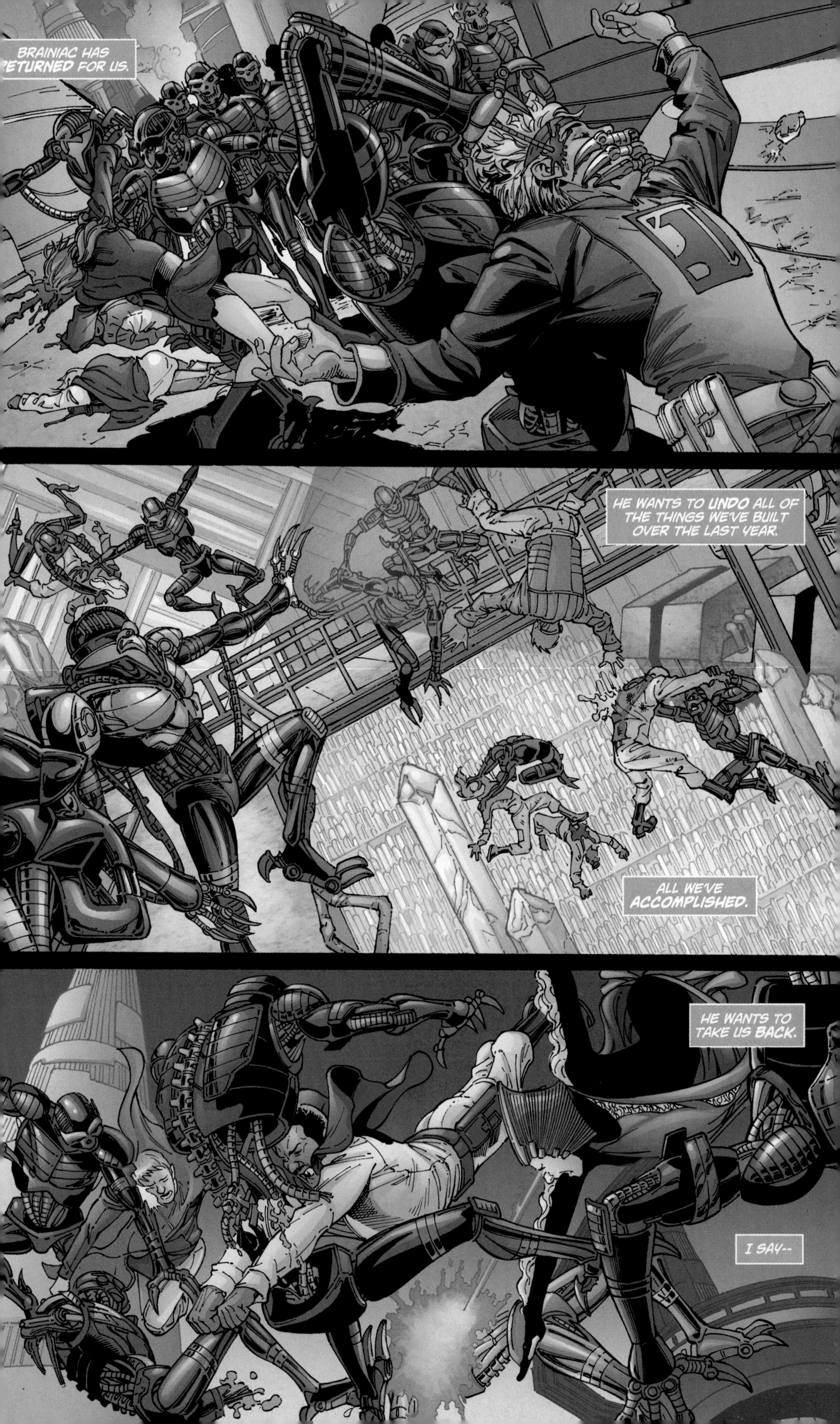
BRAINIAC HAS RETURNED FOR US.
HE WANTS TO UNDO ALL OF THE THINGS WE'VE BUILT OVER THE LAST YEAR.
ALL WE'VE ACCOMPLISHED.
HE WANTS TO TAKE US BACK.
I SAY--

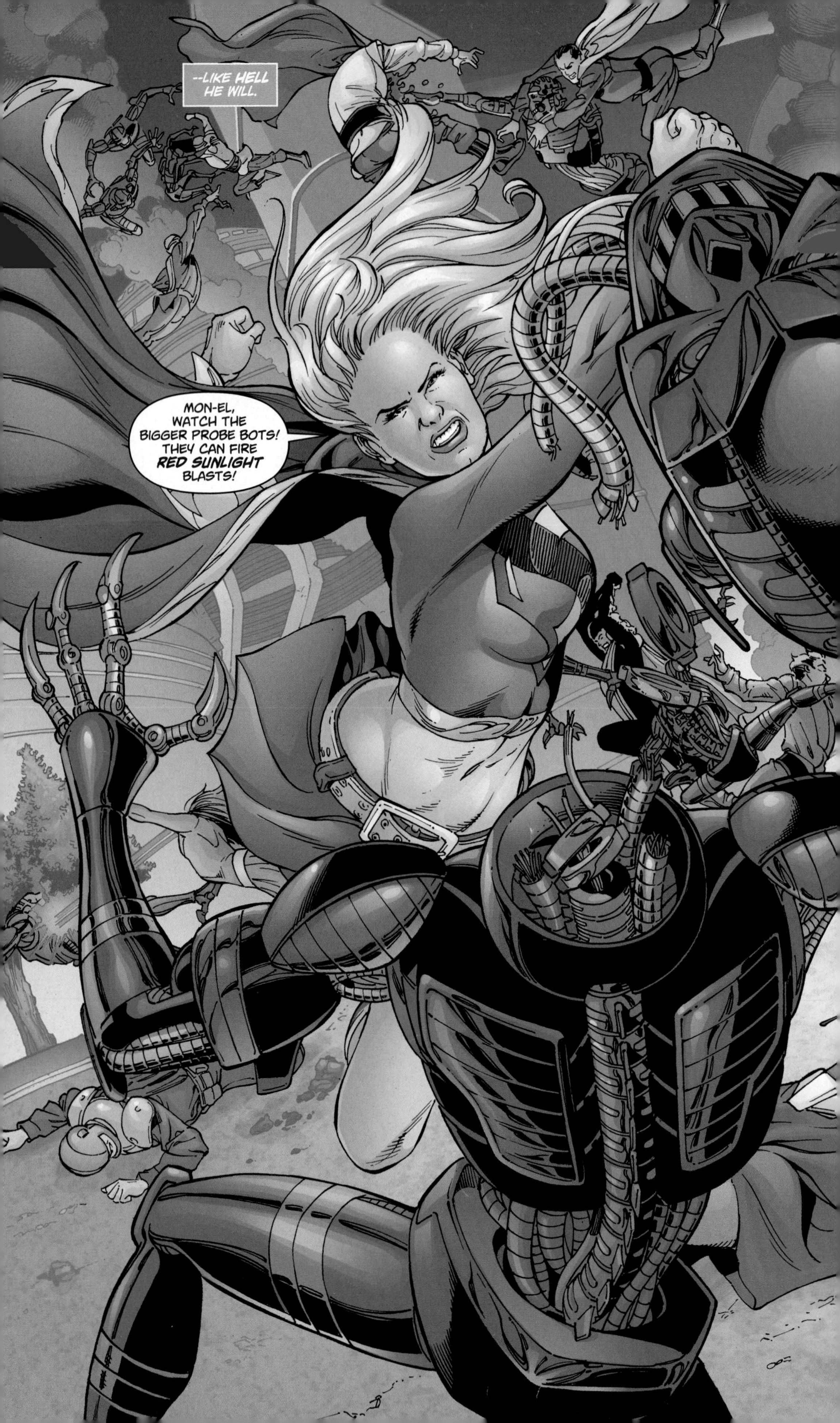
--LIKE HELL HE WILL.
MON-EL, WATCH THE BIGGER PROBE BOTS! THEY CAN FIRE RED SUNLIGHT BLASTS!

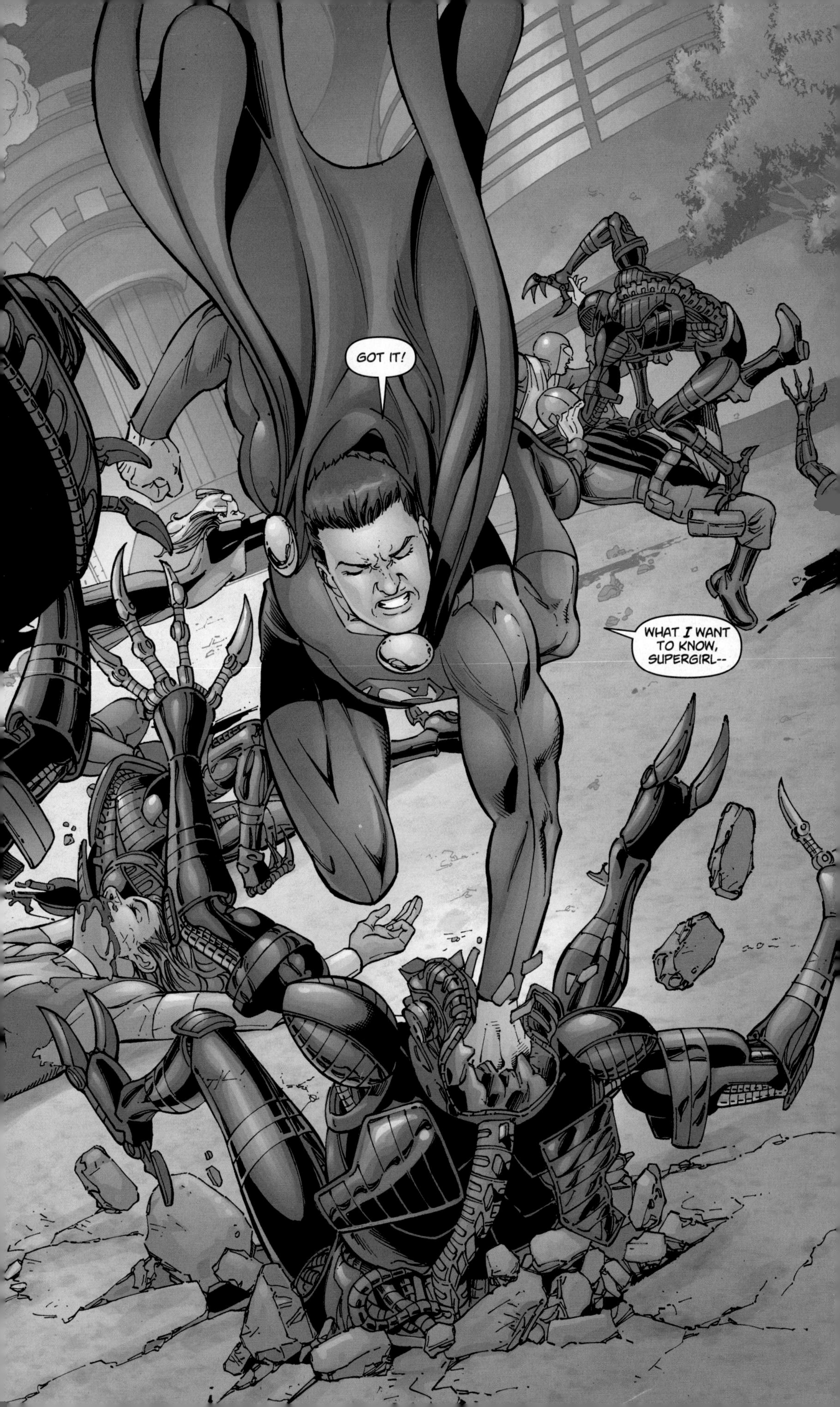
GOT IT!
WHAT I WANT TO KNOW, SUPERGIRL--

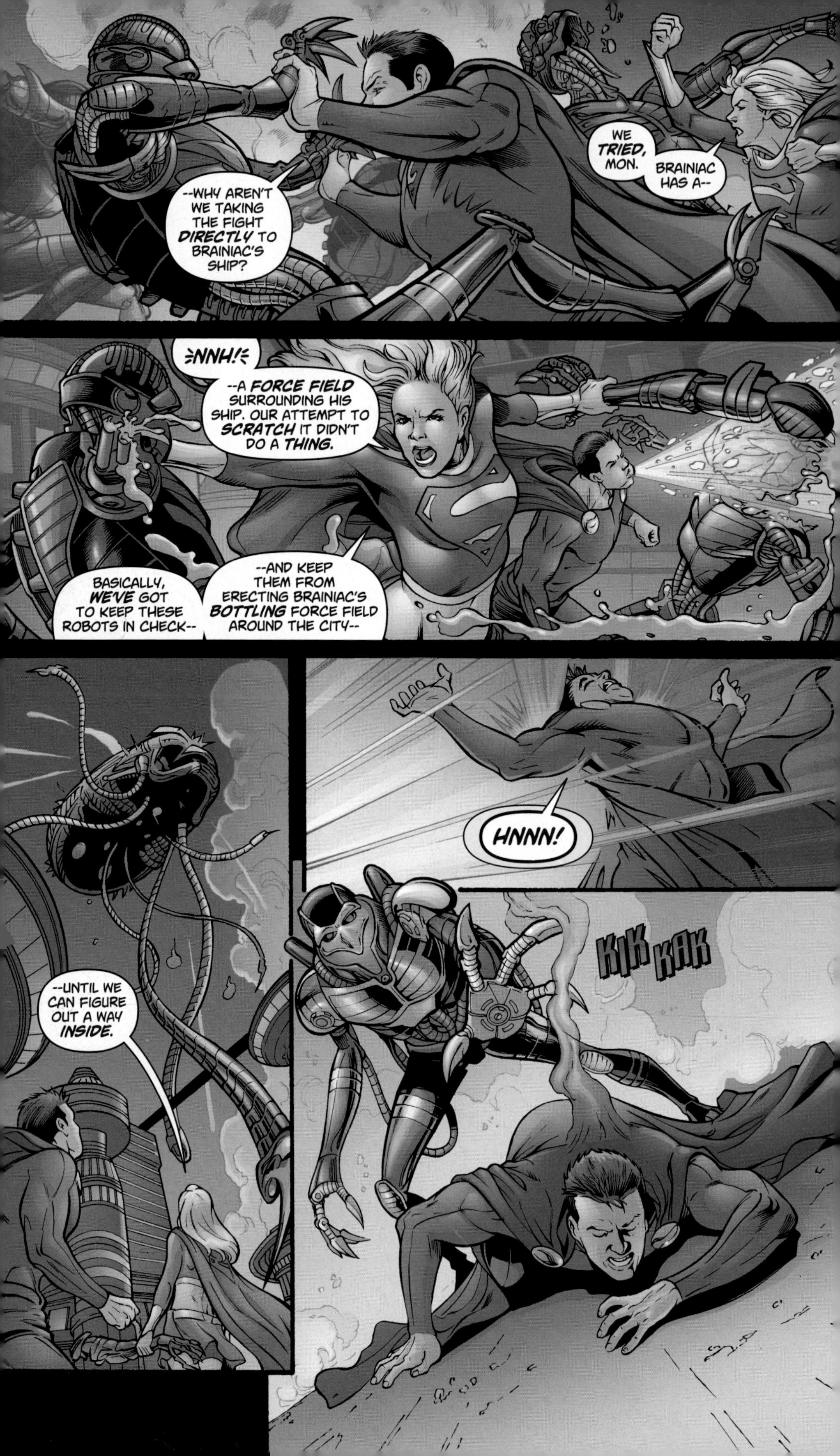
--WHY AREN'T WE TAKING THE FIGHT DIRECTLY TO BRAINIAC'S SHIP?
WE TRIED, MON.
BRAINIAC HAS A--
NNH!
--A FORCE FIELD SURROUNDING HIS SHIP. OUR ATTEMPT TO SCRATCH IT DIDN'T DO A THING.
BASICALLY, WE'VE GOT TO KEEP THESE ROBOTS IN CHECK--
--AND KEEP THEM FROM ERECTING BRAINIAC'S BOTTLING FORCE FIELD AROUND THE CITY--
--UNTIL WE CAN FIGURE OUT A WAY INSIDE.
HNNN!
KIK KAK

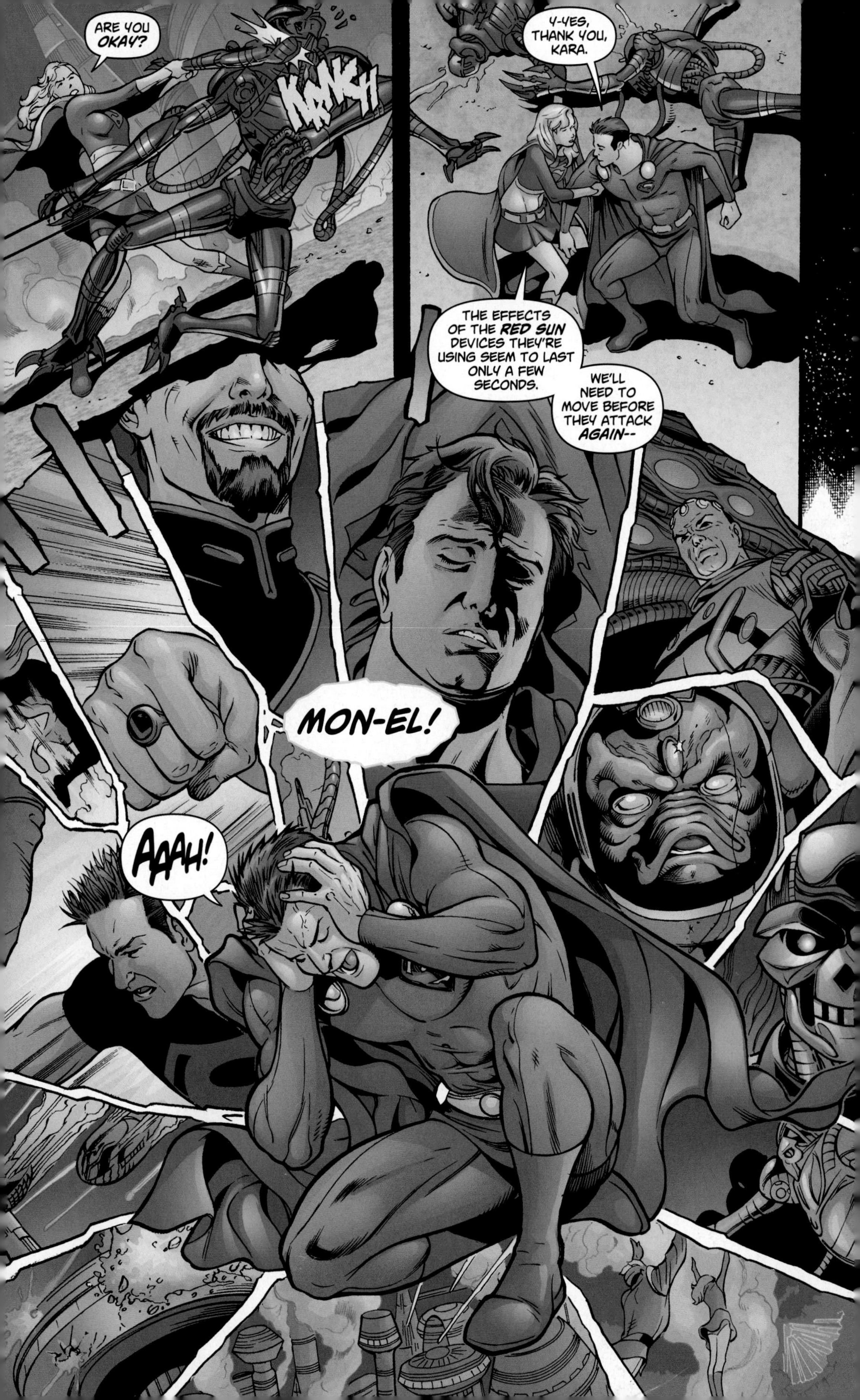
ARE YOU OKAY?
KRAKK
Y-YES, THANK YOU, KARA.
THE EFFECTS OF THE RED SUN DEVICES THEY'RE USING SEEM TO LAST ONLY A FEW SECONDS.
WE'LL NEED TO MOVE BEFORE THEY ATTACK AGAIN--
MON-EL!
AAAH!

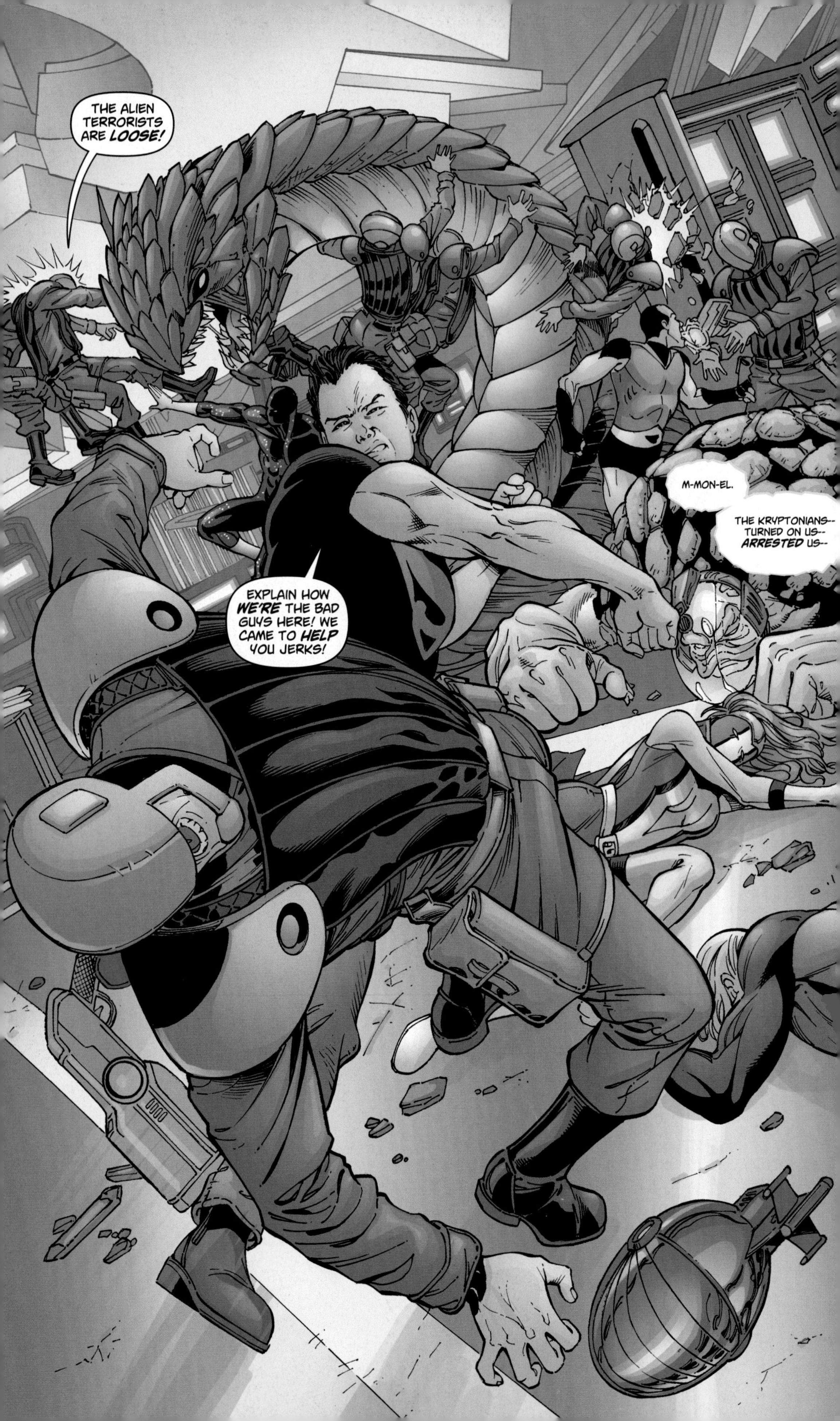
THE ALIEN TERRORISTS ARE LOOSE!
M-MON-EL.
THE KRYPTONIANS-- TURNED ON US-- ARRESTED US--
EXPLAIN HOW WE'RE THE BAD GUYS HERE! WE CAME TO HELP YOU JERKS!

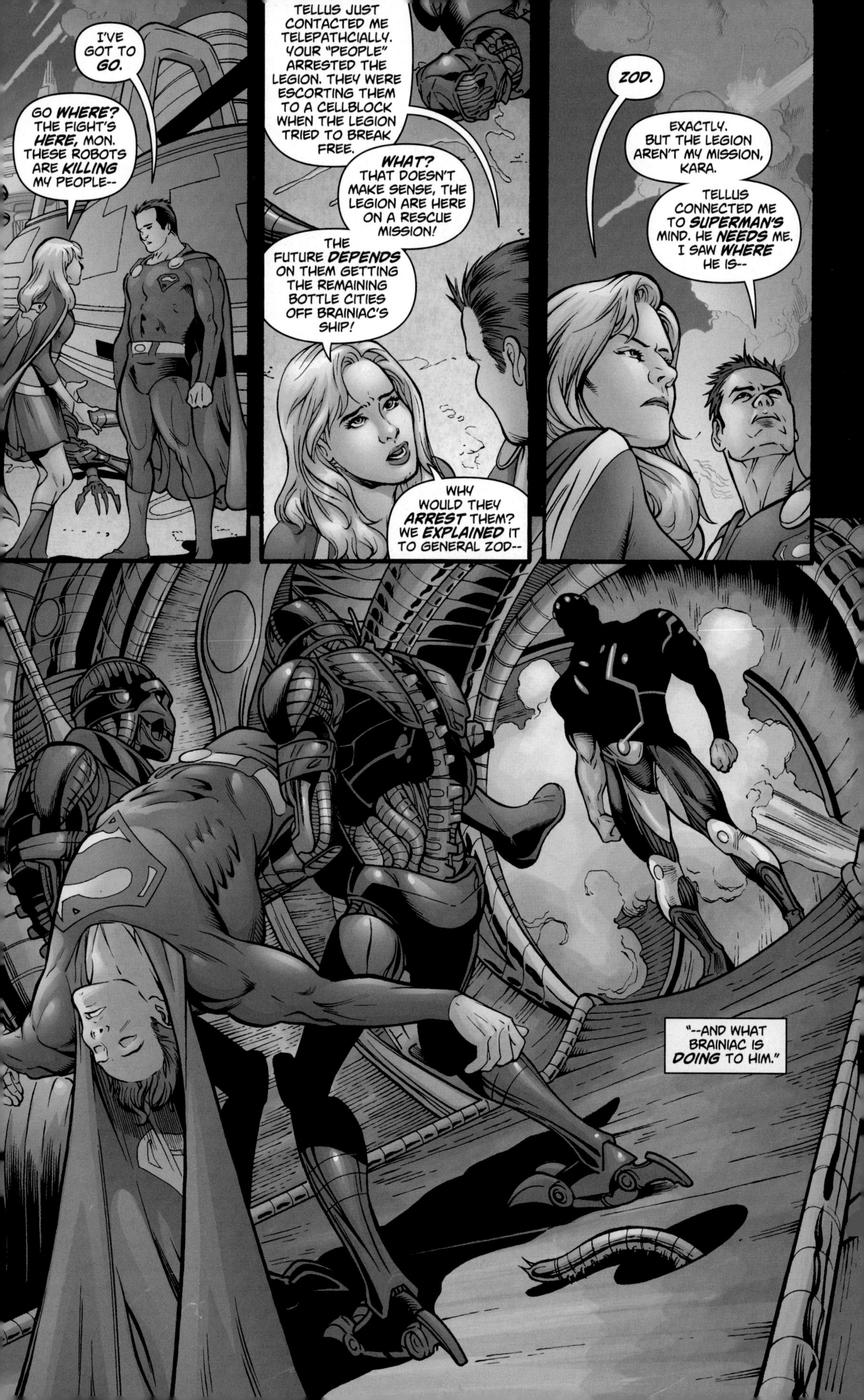
I'VE GOT TO GO.
GO WHERE? THE FIGHT'S HERE, MON. THESE ROBOTS ARE KILLING MY PEOPLE--
TELLUS JUST CONTACTED ME TELEPATHCIALLY. YOUR "PEOPLE" ARRESTED THE LEGION. THEY WERE ESCORTING THEM TO A CELLBLOCK WHEN THE LEGION TRIED TO BREAK FREE.
WHAT? THAT DOESN'T MAKE SENSE, THE LEGION ARE HERE ON A RESCUE MISSION!
THE FUTURE DEPENDS ON THEM GETTING THE REMAINING BOTTLE CITIES OFF BRAINIAC'S SHIP!
WHY WOULD THEY ARREST THEM? WE EXPLAINED IT TO GENERAL ZOD--
ZOD.
EXACTLY. BUT THE LEGION AREN'T MY MISSION, KARA.
TELLUS CONNECTED ME TO SUPERMAN'S MIND. HE NEEDS ME. I SAW WHERE HE IS--
"--AND WHAT BRAINIAC IS DOING TO HIM."

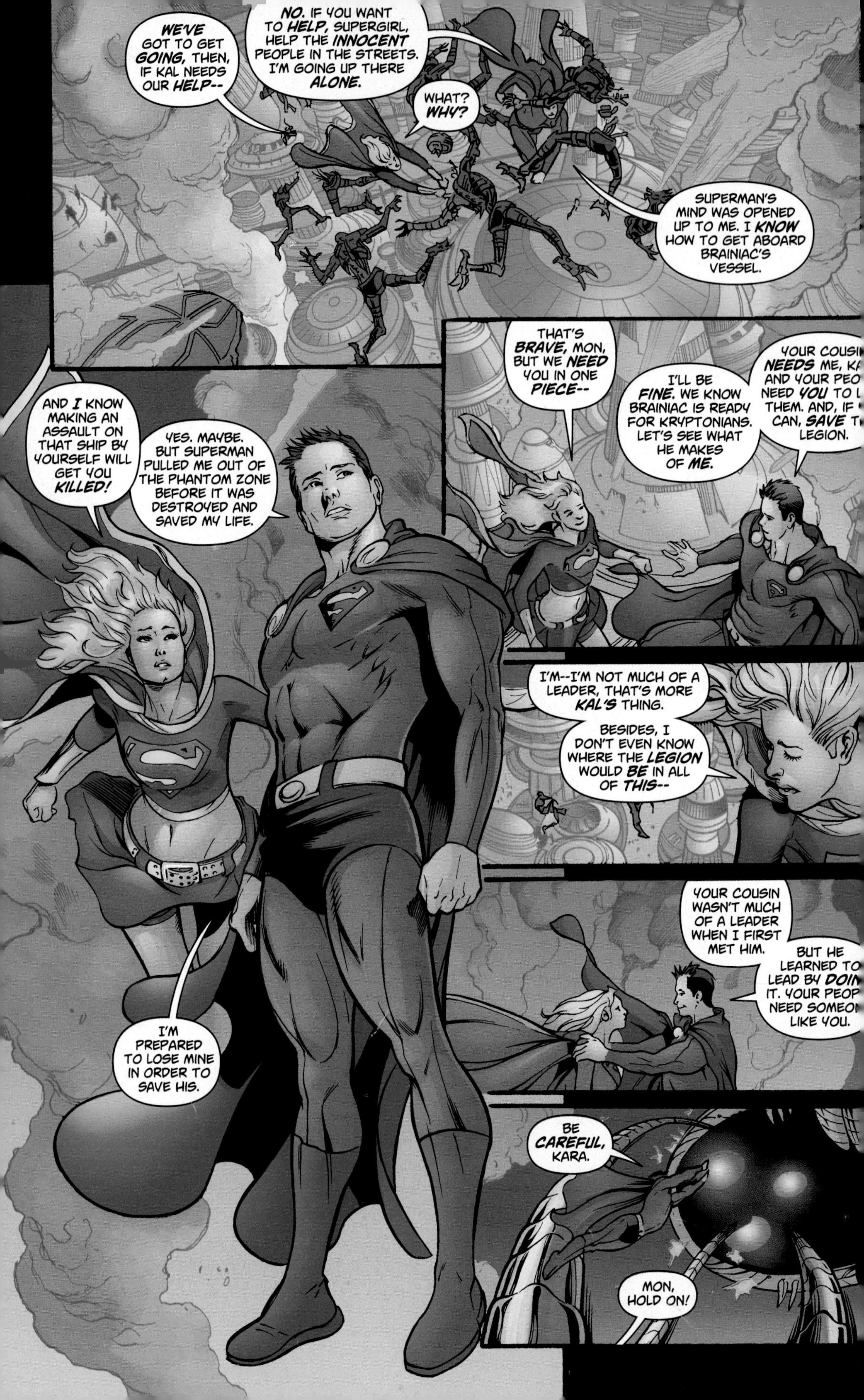
WE'VE GOT TO GET GOING, THEN, IF KAL NEEDS OUR HELP--
NO. IF YOU WANT TO HELP, SUPERGIRL, HELP THE INNOCENT PEOPLE IN THE STREETS. I'M GOING UP THERE ALONE.
WHAT? WHY?
SUPERMAN'S MIND WAS OPENED UP TO ME. I KNOW HOW TO GET ABOARD BRAINIAC'S VESSEL.
AND I KNOW MAKING AN ASSAULT ON THAT SHIP BY YOURSELF WILL GET YOU KILLED!
YES. MAYBE. BUT SUPERMAN PULLED ME OUT OF THE PHANTOM ZONE BEFORE IT WAS DESTROYED AND SAVED MY LIFE.
I'M PREPARED TO LOSE MINE IN ORDER TO SAVE HIS.
THAT'S BRAVE, MON, BUT WE NEED YOU IN ONE PIECE--
I'LL BE FINE. WE KNOW BRAINIAC IS READY FOR KRYPTONIANS. LET'S SEE WHAT HE MAKES OF ME.
YOUR COUSI NEEDS ME, KA AND YOUR PEO NEED YOU TO THEM. AND, IF CAN, SAVE T LEGION.
I'M--I'M NOT MUCH OF A LEADER, THAT'S MORE KAL'S THING.
BESIDES, I DON'T EVEN KNOW WHERE THE LEGION WOULD BE IN ALL OF THIS--
YOUR COUSIN WASN'T MUCH OF A LEADER WHEN I FIRST MET HIM.
BUT HE LEARNED TO LEAD BY DOI IT. YOUR PEOP NEED SOMEO LIKE YOU.
BE CAREFUL, KARA.
MON, HOLD ON!

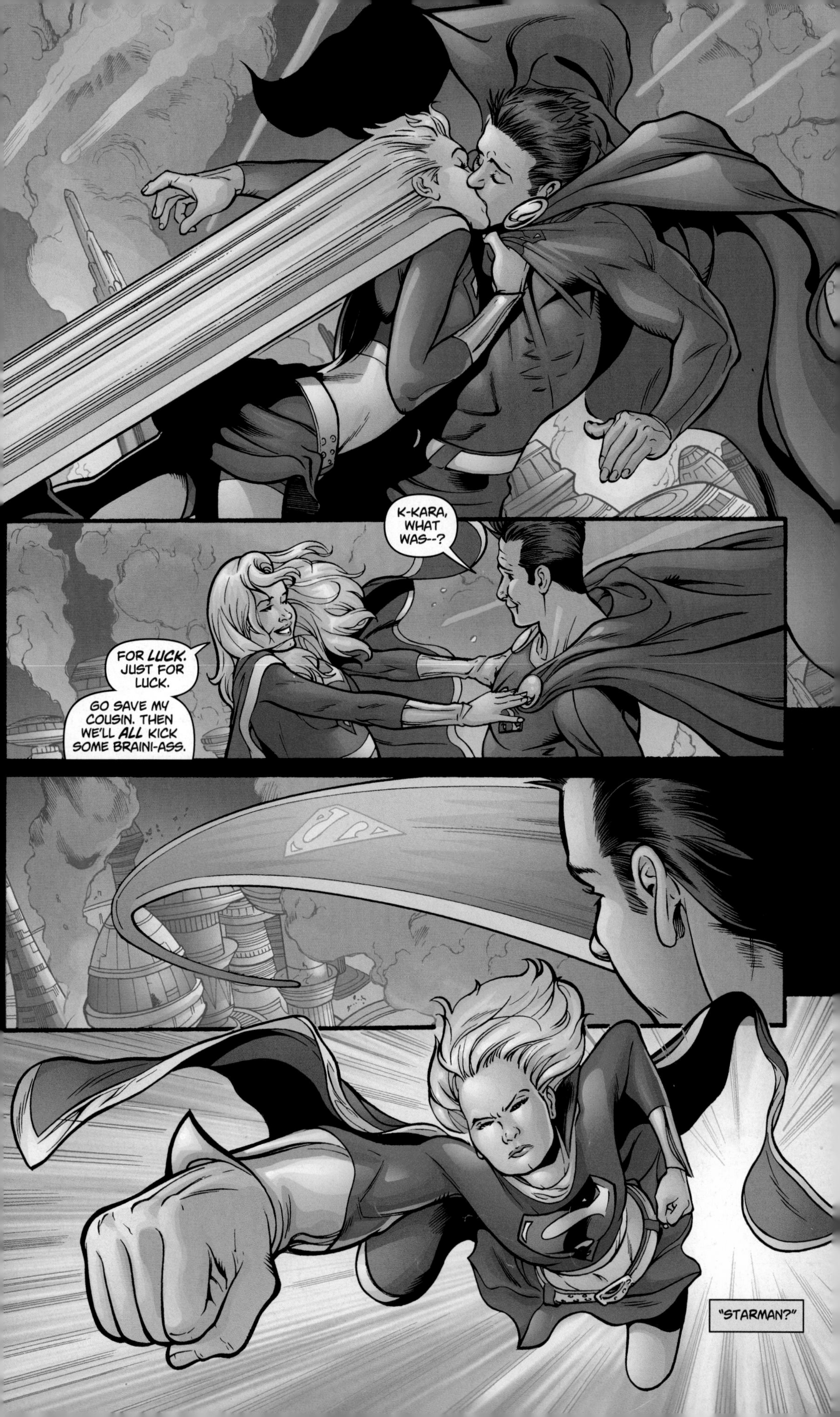
K-KARA, WHAT WAS--?
FOR LUCK. JUST FOR LUCK.
GO SAVE MY COUSIN. THEN WE'LL ALL KICK SOME BRAINI-ASS.
"STARMAN?"

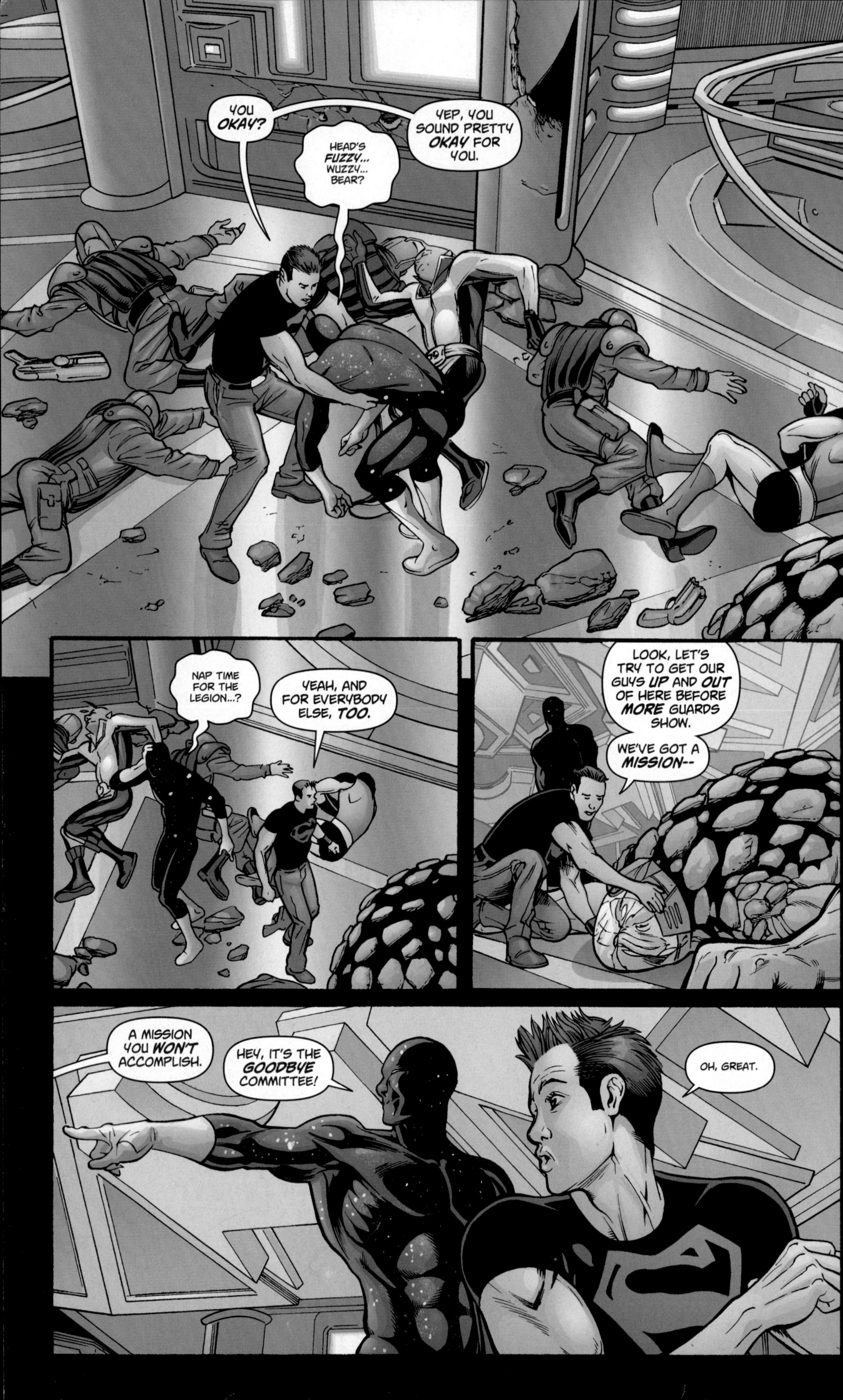
YOU OKAY?
HEAD'S FUZZY... WUZZY... BEAR?
YEP, YOU SOUND PRETTY OKAY FOR YOU.
NAP TIME FOR THE LEGION...?
YEAH, AND FOR EVERYBODY ELSE, TOO.
LOOK, LET'S TRY TO GET OUR GUYS UP AND OUT OF HERE BEFORE MORE GUARDS SHOW.
WE'VE GOT A MISSION--
A MISSION YOU WON'T ACCOMPLISH.
HEY, IT'S THE GOODBYE COMMITTEE!
OH, GREAT.

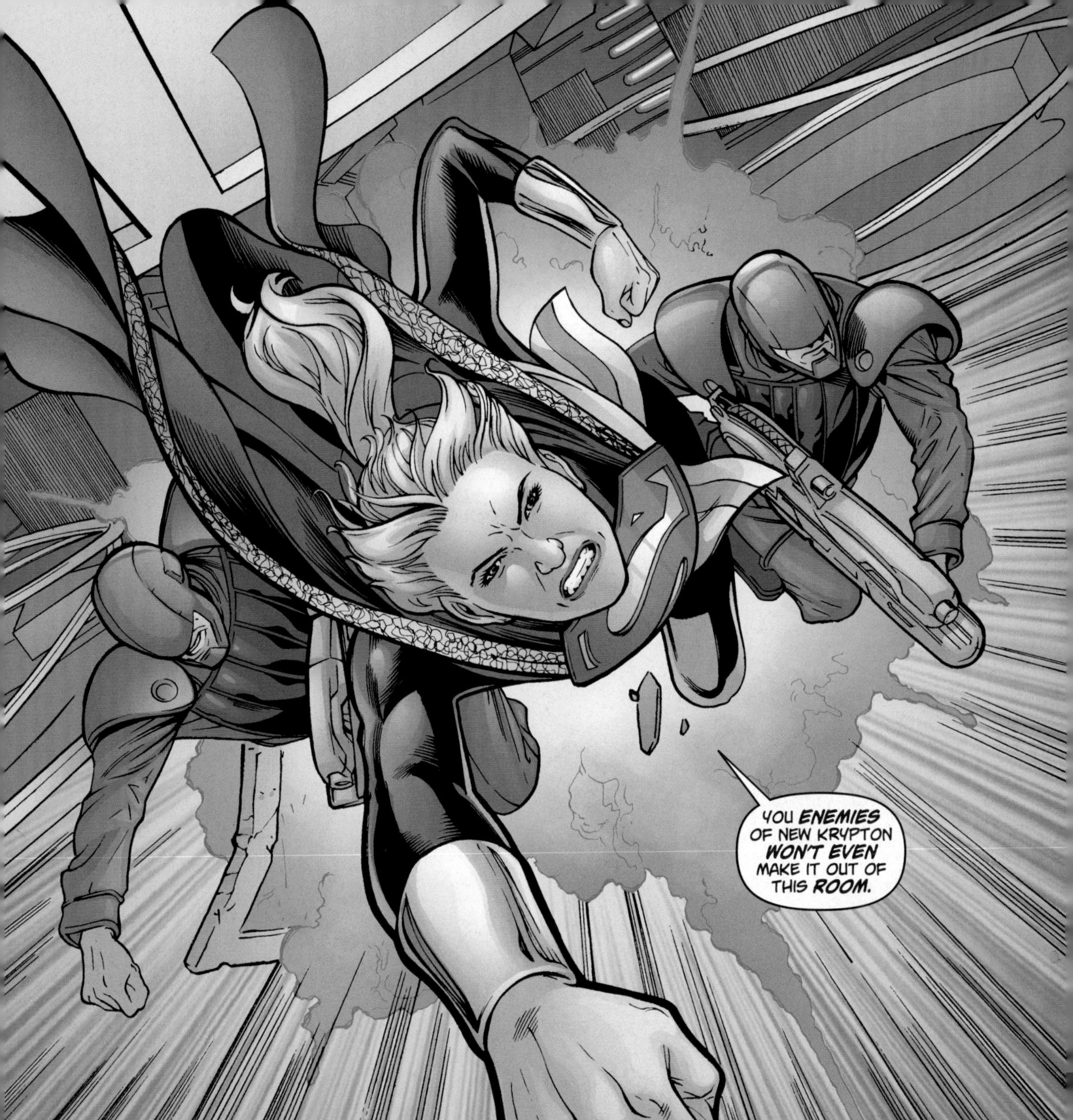
YOU ENEMIES OF NEW KRYPTON WON'T EVEN MAKE IT OUT OF THIS ROOM.

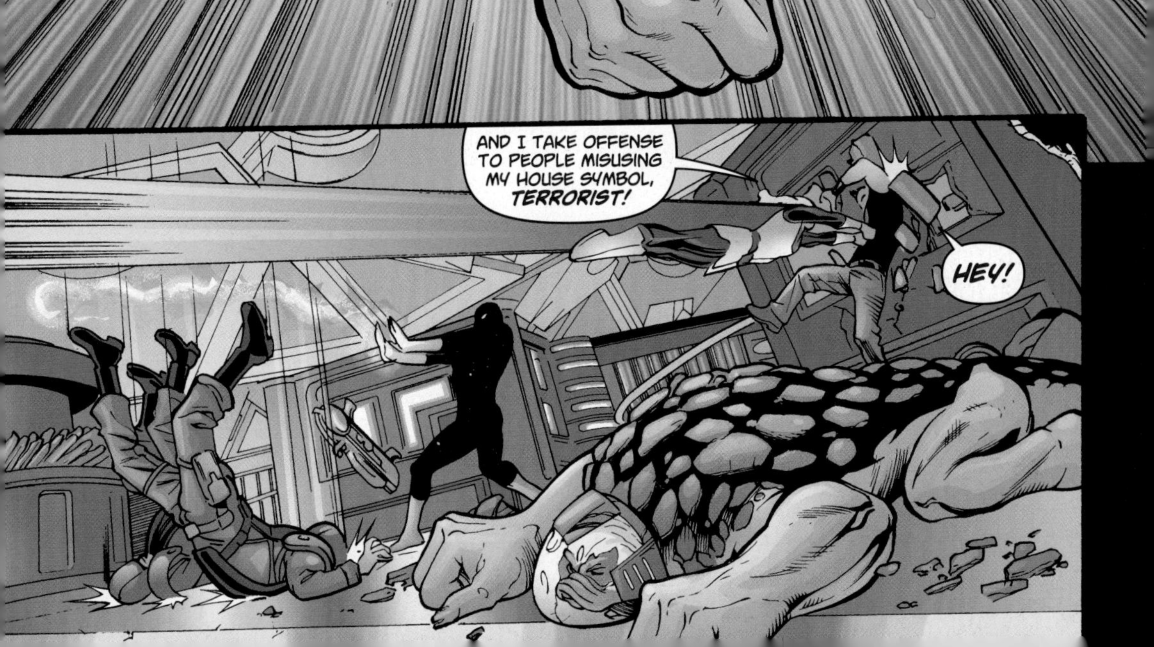
AND I TAKE OFFENSE TO PEOPLE MISUSING MY HOUSE SYMBOL, TERRORIST!
HEY!

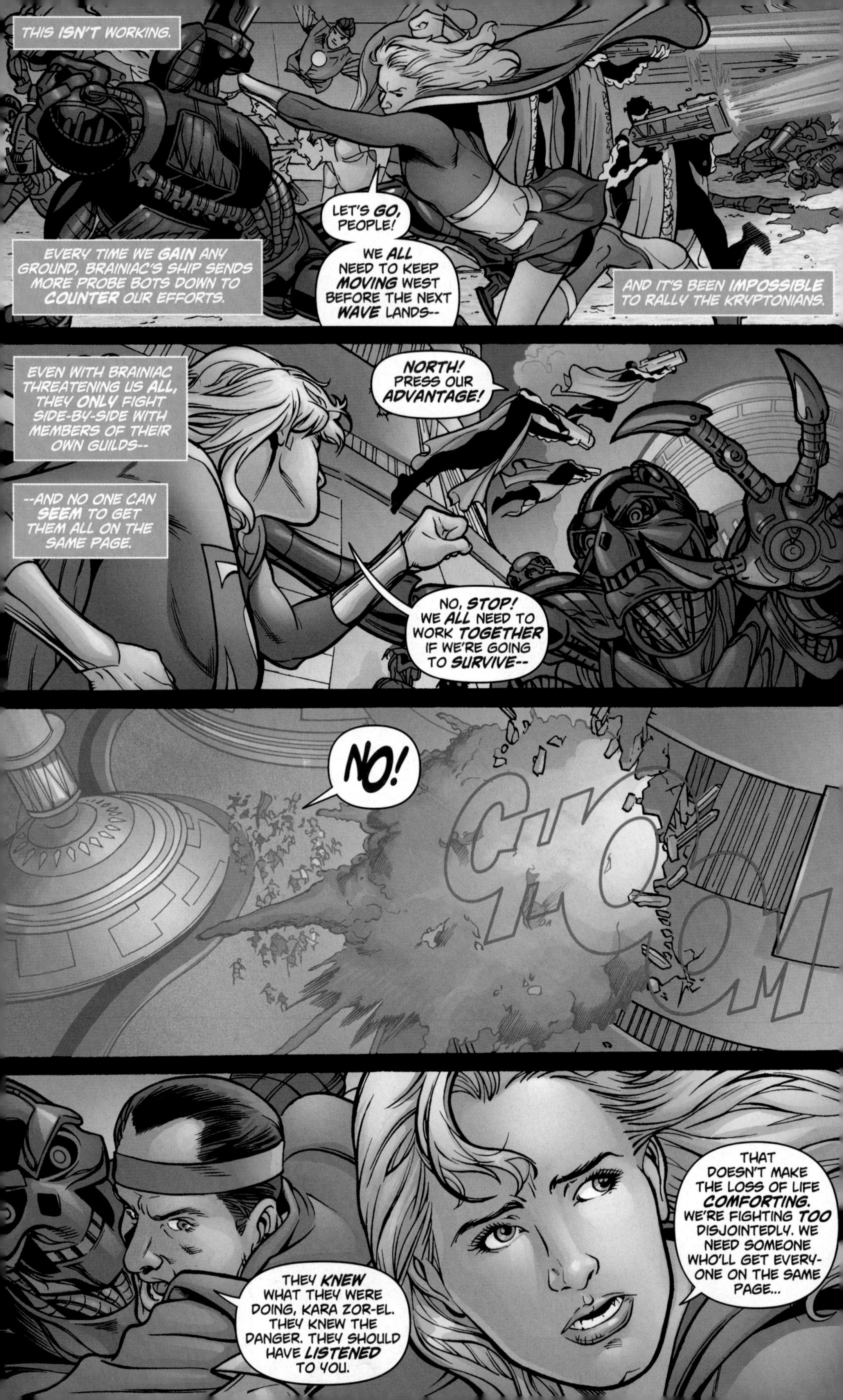

THIS ISN'T WORKING.
LET'S GO, PEOPLE!
EVERY TIME WE GAIN ANY GROUND, BRAINIAC'S SHIP SENDS MORE PROBE BOTS DOWN TO COUNTER OUR EFFORTS.
WE ALL NEED TO KEEP MOVING WEST BEFORE THE NEXT WAVE LANDS--
AND IT'S BEEN IMPOSSIBLE TO RALLY THE KRYPTONIANS.
EVEN WITH BRAINIAC THREATENING US ALL, THEY ONLY FIGHT SIDE-BY-SIDE WITH MEMBERS OF THEIR OWN GUILDS--
NORTH! PRESS OUR ADVANTAGE!
--AND NO ONE CAN SEEM TO GET THEM ALL ON THE SAME PAGE.
NO, STOP! WE ALL NEED TO WORK TOGETHER IF WE'RE GOING TO SURVIVE--
NO!
CHOOM
THAT DOESN'T MAKE THE LOSS OF LIFE COMFORTING. WE'RE FIGHTING TOO DISJOINTEDLY. WE NEED SOMEONE WHO'LL GET EVERY-ONE ON THE SAME PAGE...
THEY KNEW WHAT THEY WERE DOING, KARA ZOR-EL. THEY KNEW THE DANGER. THEY SHOULD HAVE LISTENED TO YOU.

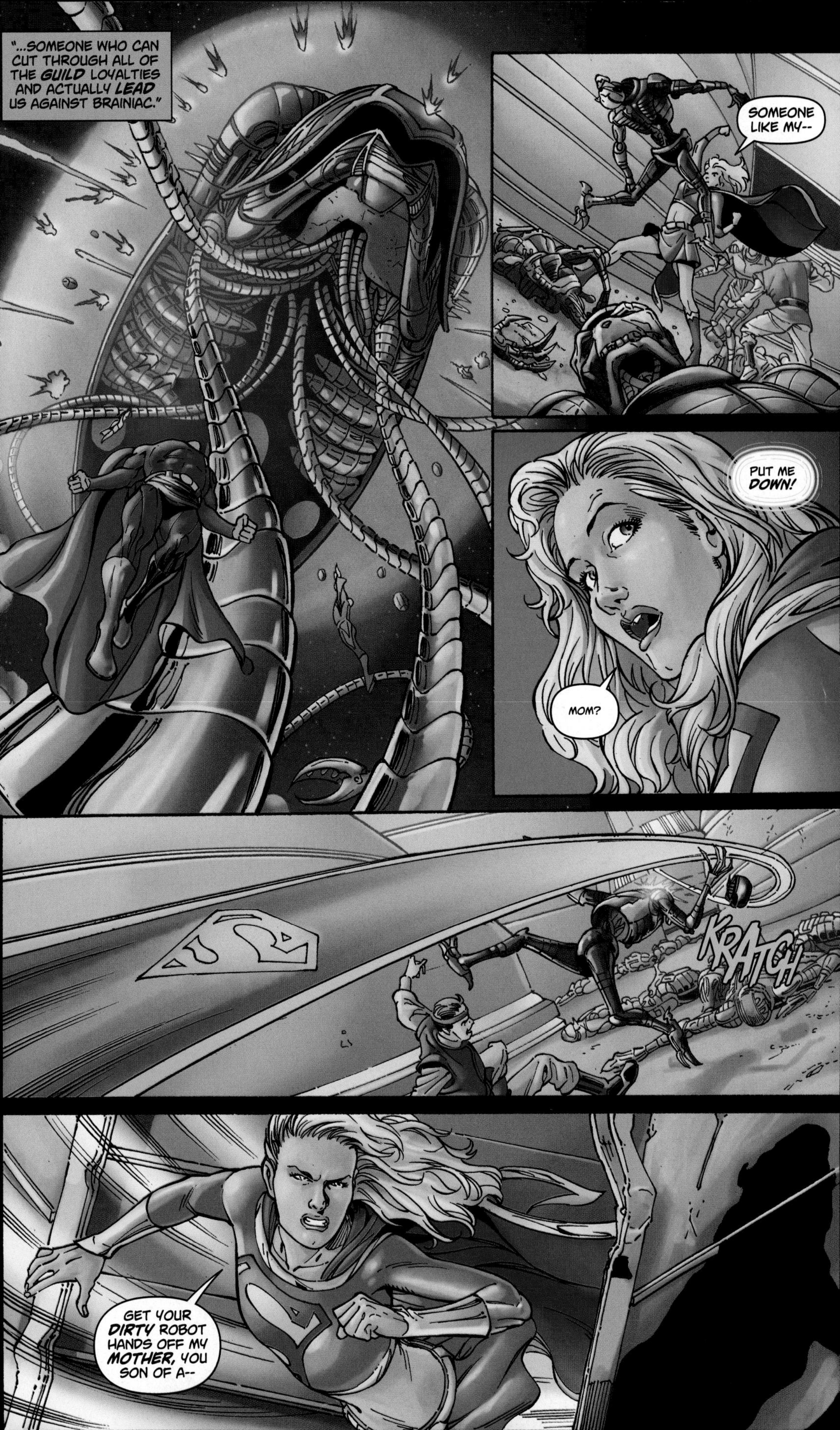
"...SOMEONE WHO CAN CUT THROUGH ALL OF THE GUILD LOYALTIES AND ACTUALLY LEAD US AGAINST BRAINIAC."
SOMEONE LIKE MY--
PUT ME DOWN!
MOM?
KRATCH
GET YOUR DIRTY ROBOT HANDS OFF MY MOTHER, YOU SON OF A--

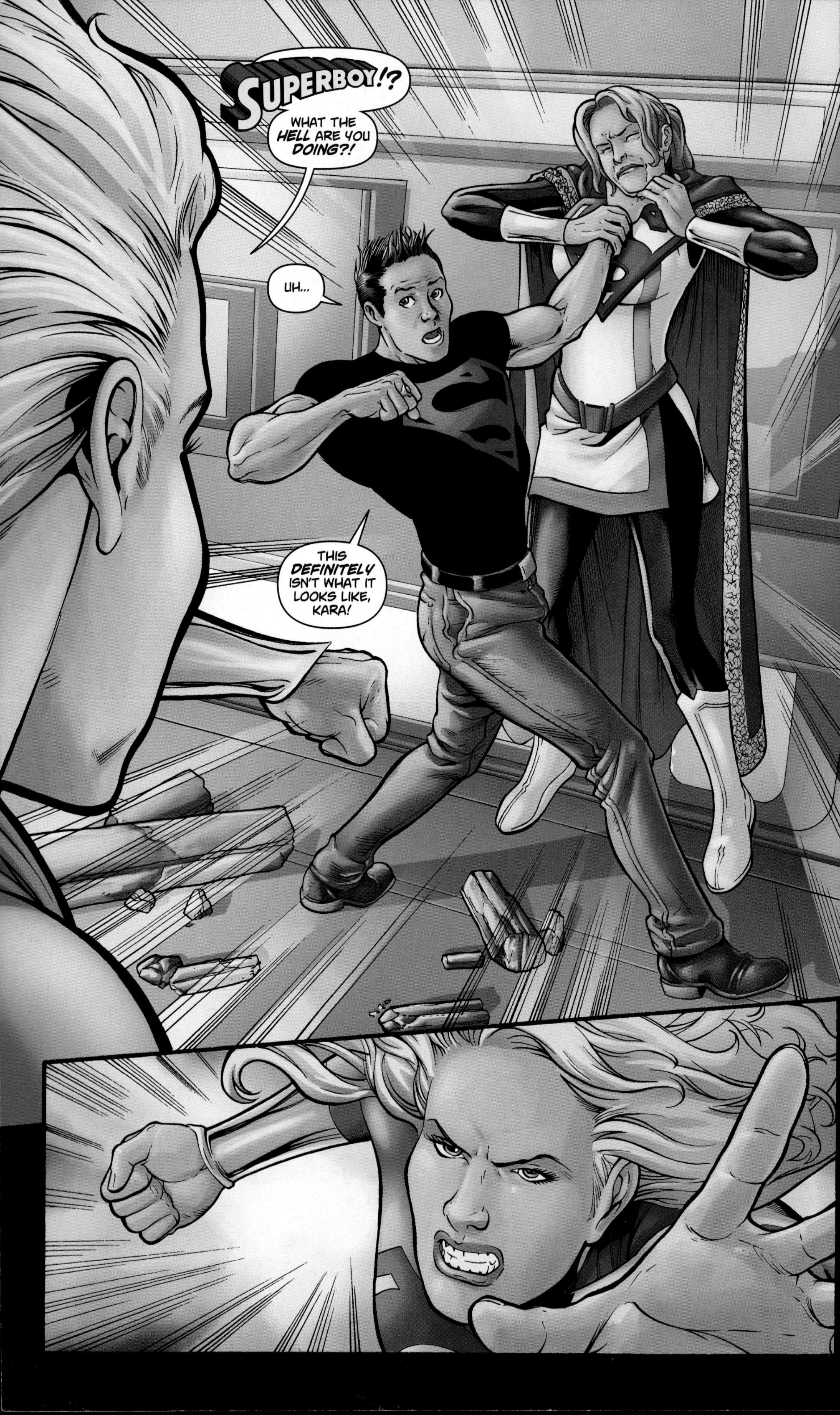
SUPERBOY!?
WHAT THE HELL ARE YOU DOING?!
UH...
THIS DEFINITELY ISN'T WHAT IT LOOKS LIKE, KARA!

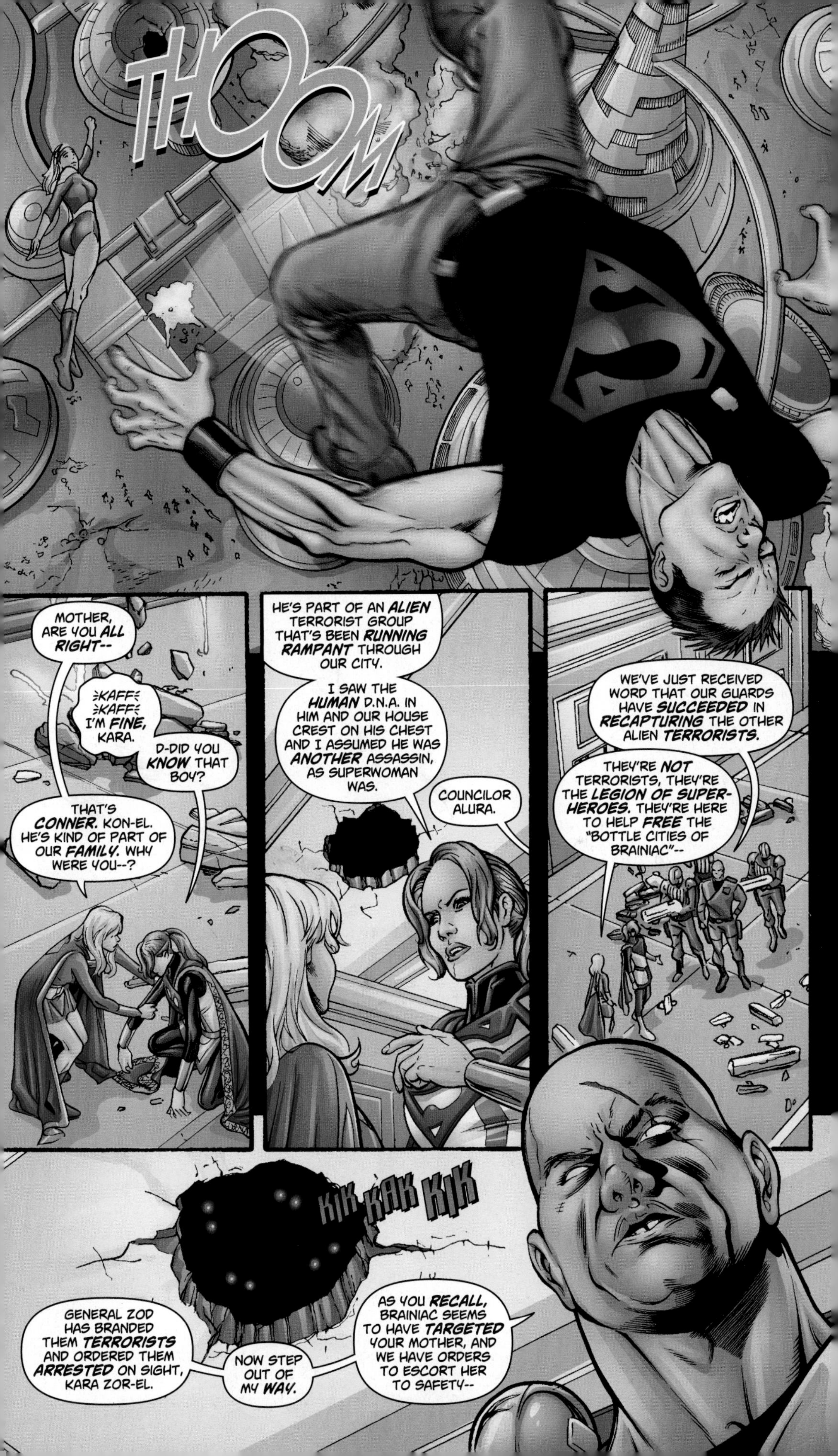
THOOM
MOTHER, ARE YOU ALL RIGHT--
KAFF KAFF I'M FINE, KARA.
D-DID YOU KNOW THAT BOY?
THAT'S CONNER. KON-EL. HE'S KIND OF PART OF OUR FAMILY. WHY WERE YOU--?
HE'S PART OF AN ALIEN TERRORIST GROUP THAT'S BEEN RUNNING RAMPANT THROUGH OUR CITY.
I SAW THE HUMAN D.N.A. IN HIM AND OUR HOUSE CREST ON HIS CHEST AND I ASSUMED HE WAS ANOTHER ASSASSIN, AS SUPERWOMAN WAS.
COUNCILOR ALURA.
WE'VE JUST RECEIVED WORD THAT OUR GUARDS HAVE SUCCEEDED IN RECAPTURING THE OTHER ALIEN TERRORISTS.
THEY'RE NOT TERRORISTS, THEY'RE THE LEGION OF SUPER-HEROES. THEY'RE HERE TO HELP FREE THE "BOTTLE CITIES OF BRAINIAC"--
KIK KAK KIK
GENERAL ZOD HAS BRANDED THEM TERRORISTS AND ORDERED THEM ARRESTED ON SIGHT, KARA ZOR-EL.
NOW STEP OUT OF MY WAY.
AS YOU RECALL, BRAINIAC SEEMS TO HAVE TARGETED YOUR MOTHER, AND WE HAVE ORDERS TO ESCORT HER TO SAFETY--

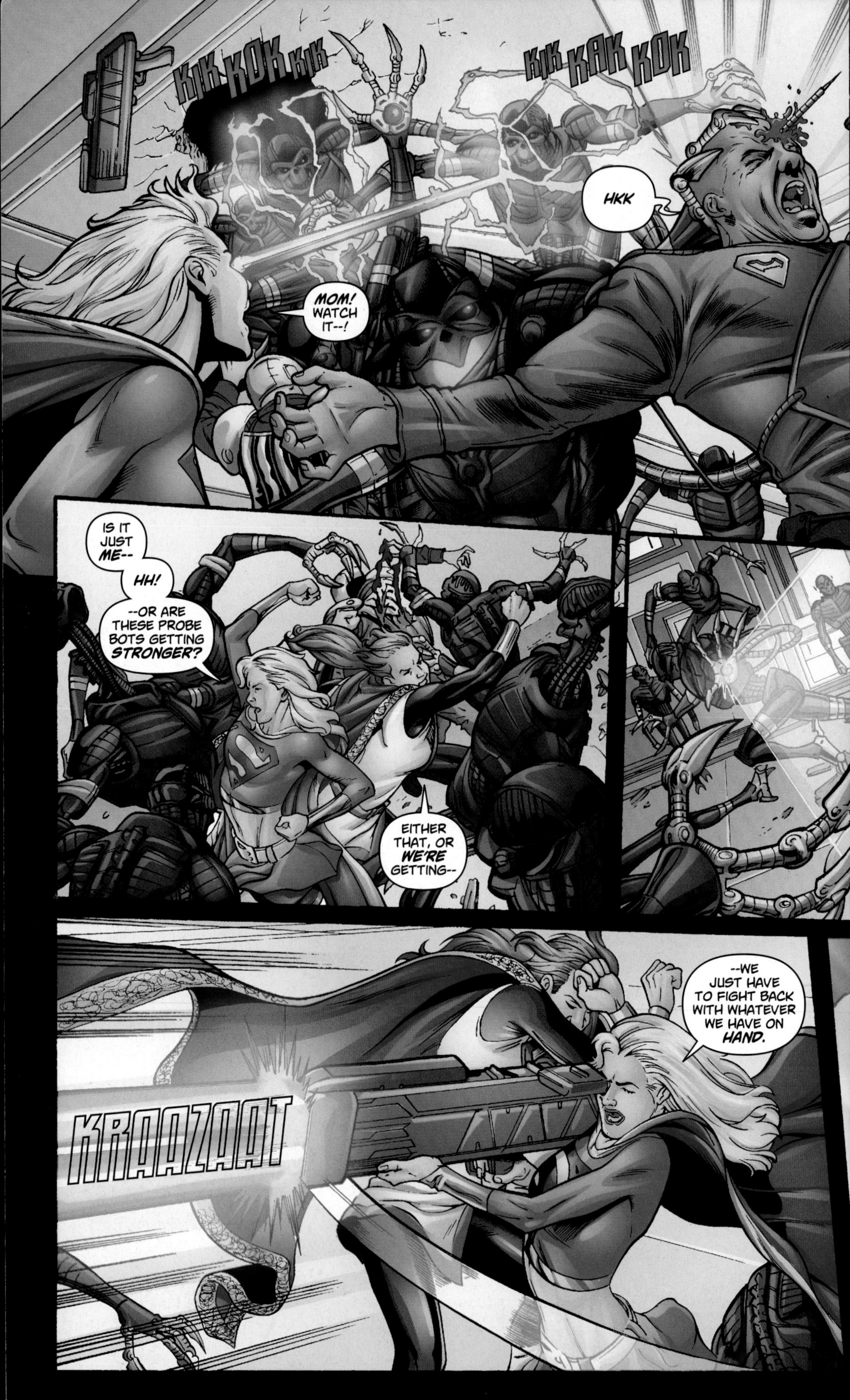
KIK KOK KIK
KIK KAK KOK
HKK
MOM! WATCH IT--!
IS IT JUST ME--
HH!
--OR ARE THESE PROBE BOTS GETTING STRONGER?
EITHER THAT, OR WE'RE GETTING--
--WE JUST HAVE TO FIGHT BACK WITH WHATEVER WE HAVE ON HAND.
KRAAZAAT

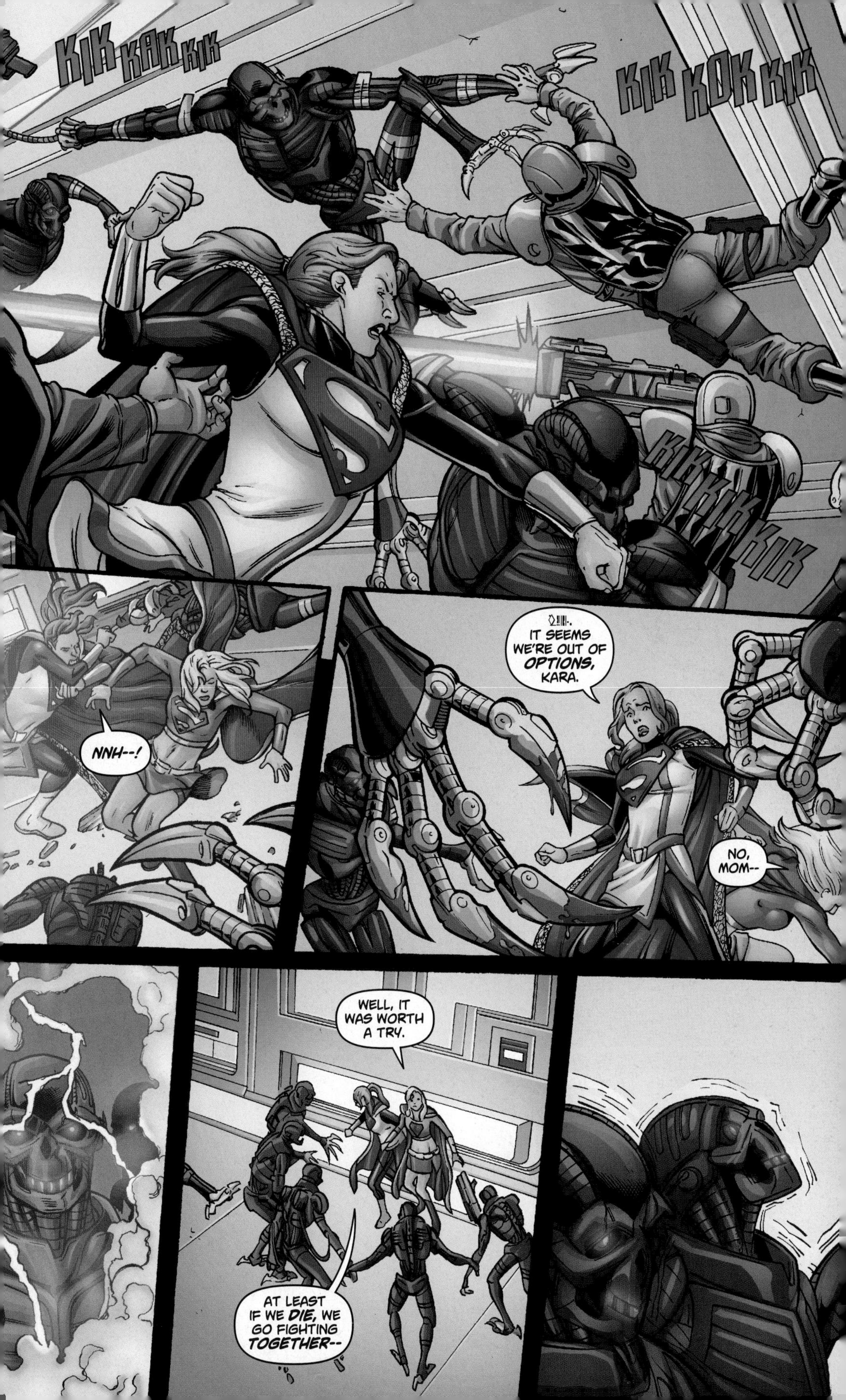
KIK KAK KIK
KIK KOK KIK
KIK KIK KIK
NNH--!
IT SEEMS WE'RE OUT OF OPTIONS, KARA.
NO, MOM--
WELL, IT WAS WORTH A TRY.
AT LEAST IF WE DIE, WE GO FIGHTING TOGETHER--

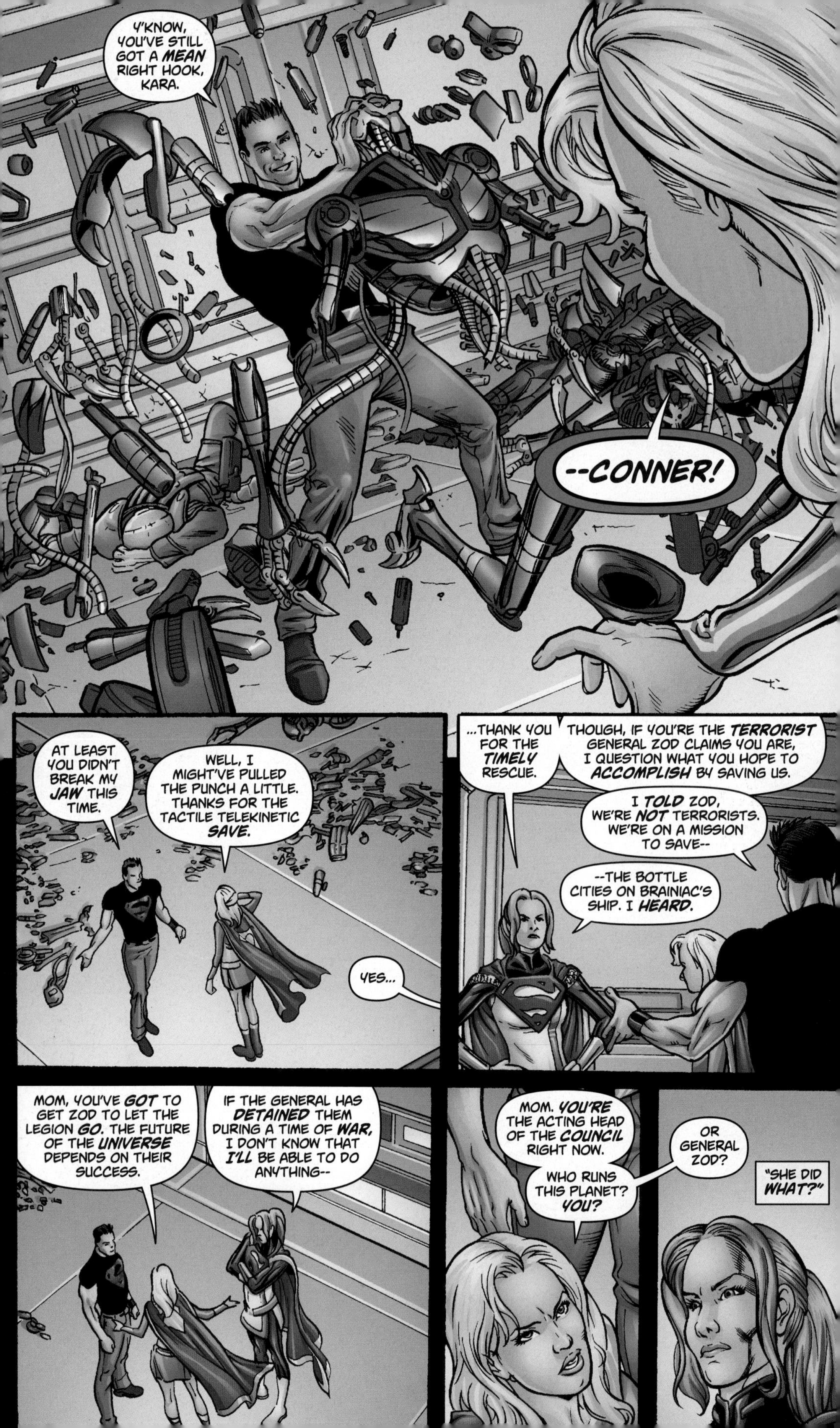
Y'KNOW, YOU'VE STILL GOT A MEAN RIGHT HOOK, KARA.
--CONNER!
AT LEAST YOU DIDN'T BREAK MY JAW THIS TIME.
WELL, I MIGHT'VE PULLED THE PUNCH A LITTLE. THANKS FOR THE TACTILE TELEKINETIC SAVE.
YES...
...THANK YOU FOR THE TIMELY RESCUE.
THOUGH, IF YOU'RE THE TERRORIST GENERAL ZOD CLAIMS YOU ARE, I QUESTION WHAT YOU HOPE TO ACCOMPLISH BY SAVING US.
I TOLD ZOD, WE'RE NOT TERRORISTS. WE'RE ON A MISSION TO SAVE--
--THE BOTTLE CITIES ON BRAINIAC'S SHIP. I HEARD.
MOM, YOU'VE GOT TO GET ZOD TO LET THE LEGION GO. THE FUTURE OF THE UNIVERSE DEPENDS ON THEIR SUCCESS.
IF THE GENERAL HAS DETAINED THEM DURING A TIME OF WAR, I DON'T KNOW THAT I'LL BE ABLE TO DO ANYTHING--
MOM. YOU'RE THE ACTING HEAD OF THE COUNCIL RIGHT NOW.
WHO RUNS THIS PLANET? YOU?
OR GENERAL ZOD?
"SHE DID WHAT?"

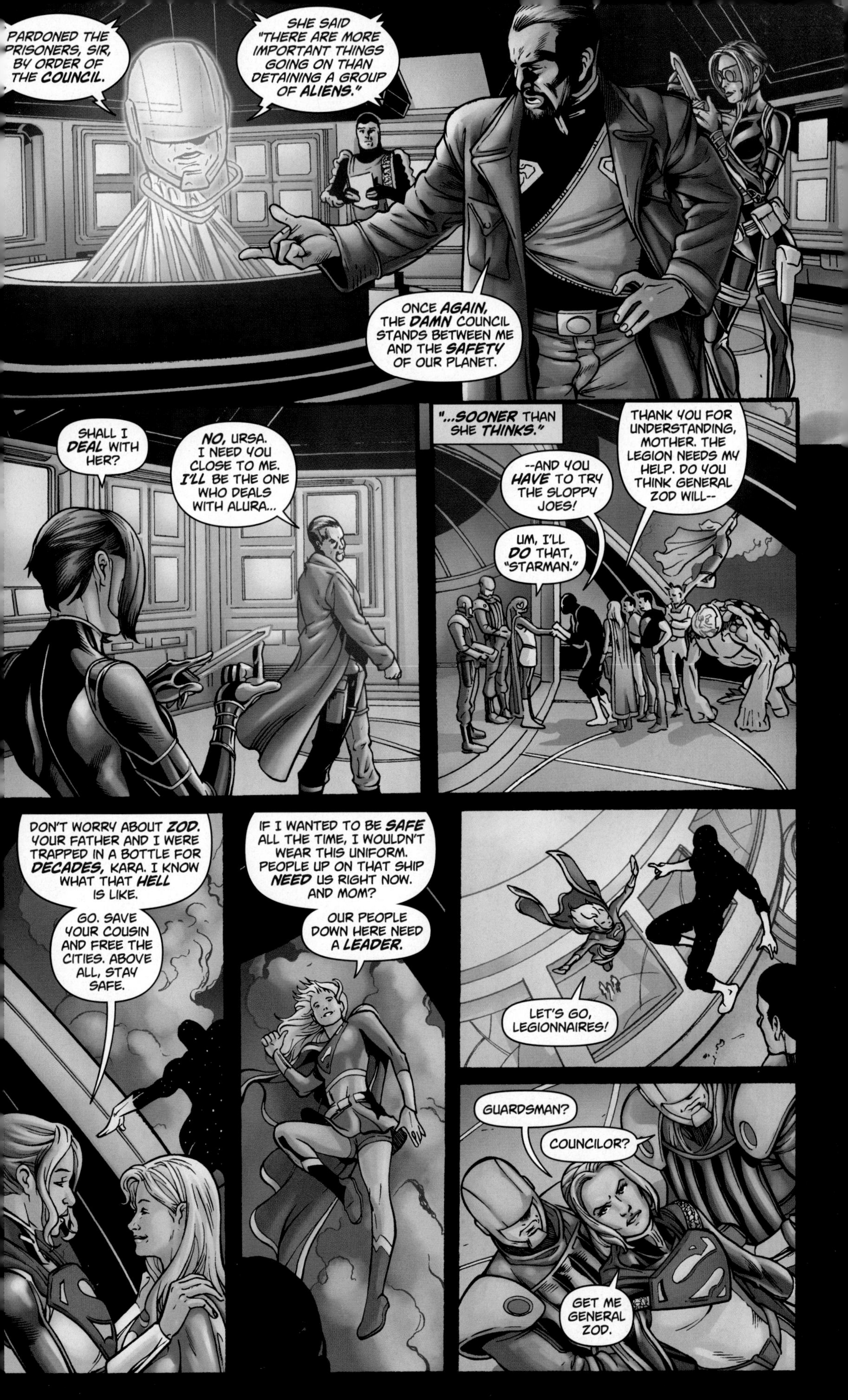
PARDONED THE PRISONERS, SIR, BY ORDER OF THE COUNCIL.
SHE SAID "THERE ARE MORE IMPORTANT THINGS GOING ON THAN DETAINING A GROUP OF ALIENS."
ONCE AGAIN, THE DAMN COUNCIL STANDS BETWEEN ME AND THE SAFETY OF OUR PLANET.
SHALL I DEAL WITH HER?
NO, URSA. I NEED YOU CLOSE TO ME. I'LL BE THE ONE WHO DEALS WITH ALURA...
"...SOONER THAN SHE THINKS."
--AND YOU HAVE TO TRY THE SLOPPY JOES!
UM, I'LL DO THAT, "STARMAN."
THANK YOU FOR UNDERSTANDING, MOTHER. THE LEGION NEEDS MY HELP. DO YOU THINK GENERAL ZOD WILL--
DON'T WORRY ABOUT ZOD. YOUR FATHER AND I WERE TRAPPED IN A BOTTLE FOR DECADES, KARA. I KNOW WHAT THAT HELL IS LIKE.
GO. SAVE YOUR COUSIN AND FREE THE CITIES. ABOVE ALL, STAY SAFE.
IF I WANTED TO BE SAFE ALL THE TIME, I WOULDN'T WEAR THIS UNIFORM. PEOPLE UP ON THAT SHIP NEED US RIGHT NOW. AND MOM?
OUR PEOPLE DOWN HERE NEED A LEADER.
LET'S GO, LEGIONNAIRES!
GUARDSMAN?
COUNCILOR?
GET ME GENERAL ZOD.

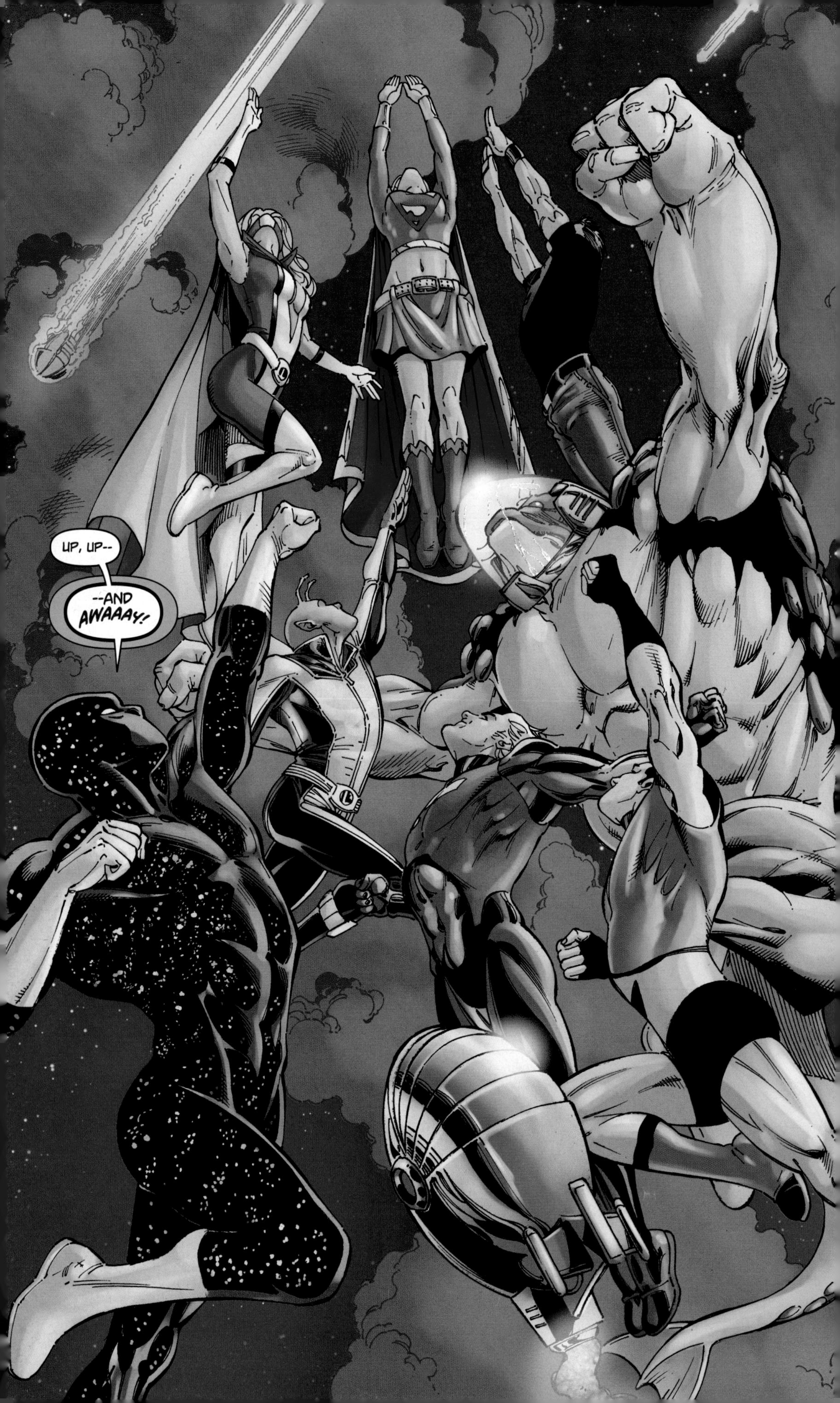
UP, UP--
--AND AWAAAY!

cover by **JULIAN LÓPEZ, BIT & SANTIAGO ARCAS**

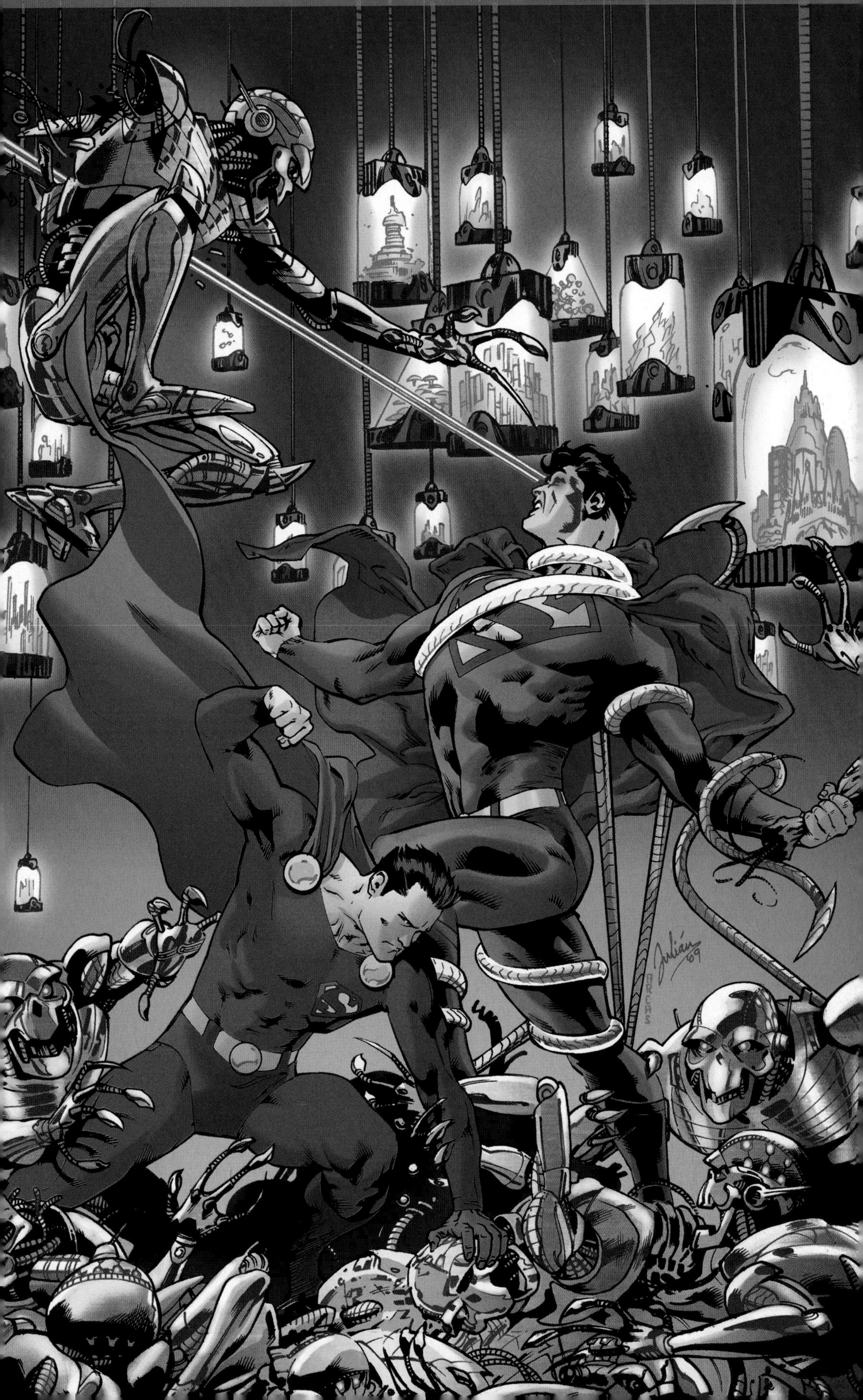
Julián '09
ARCAS

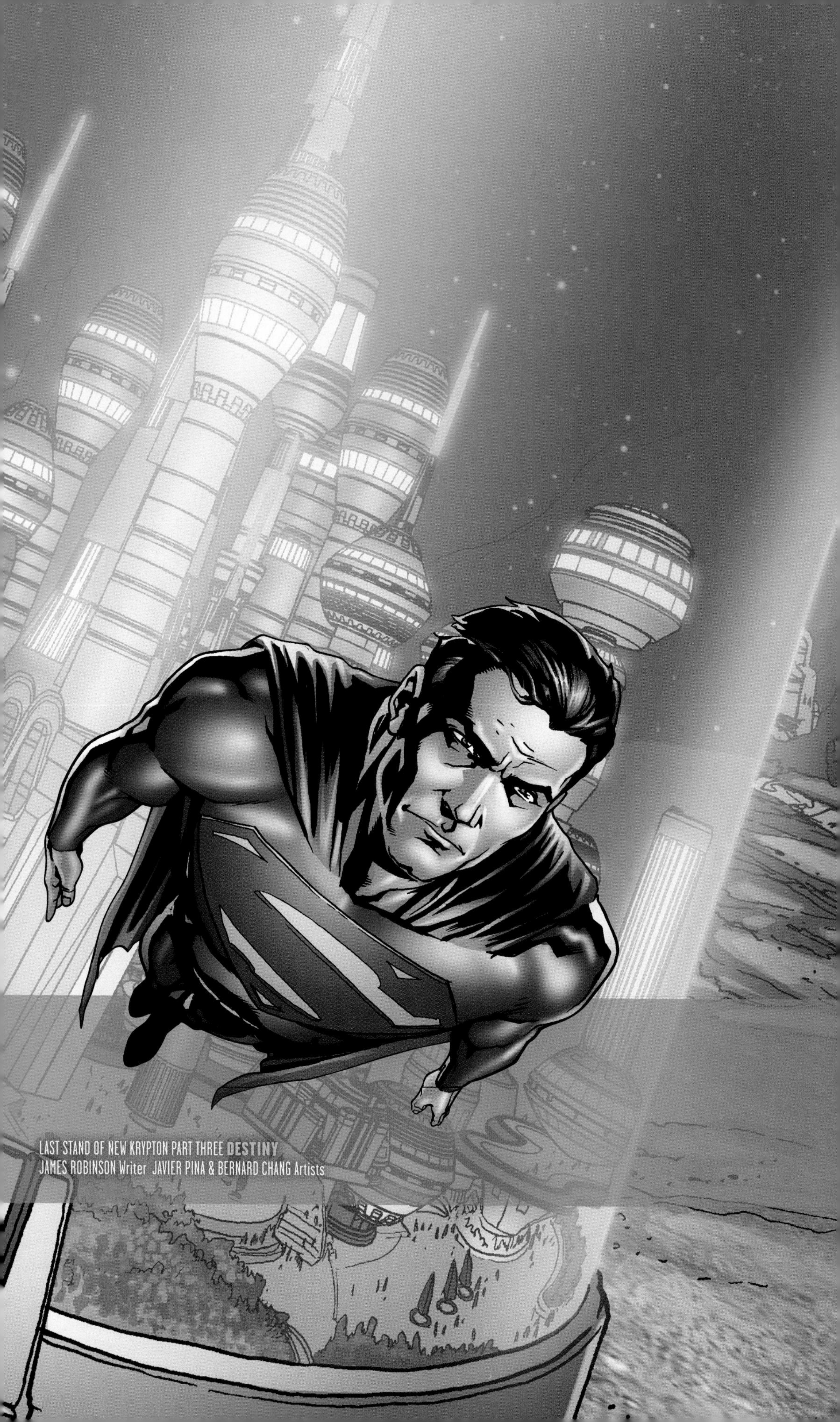

LAST STAND OF NEW KRYPTON PART THREE **DESTINY**

JAMES ROBINSON Writer JAVIER PINA & BERNARD CHANG Artists

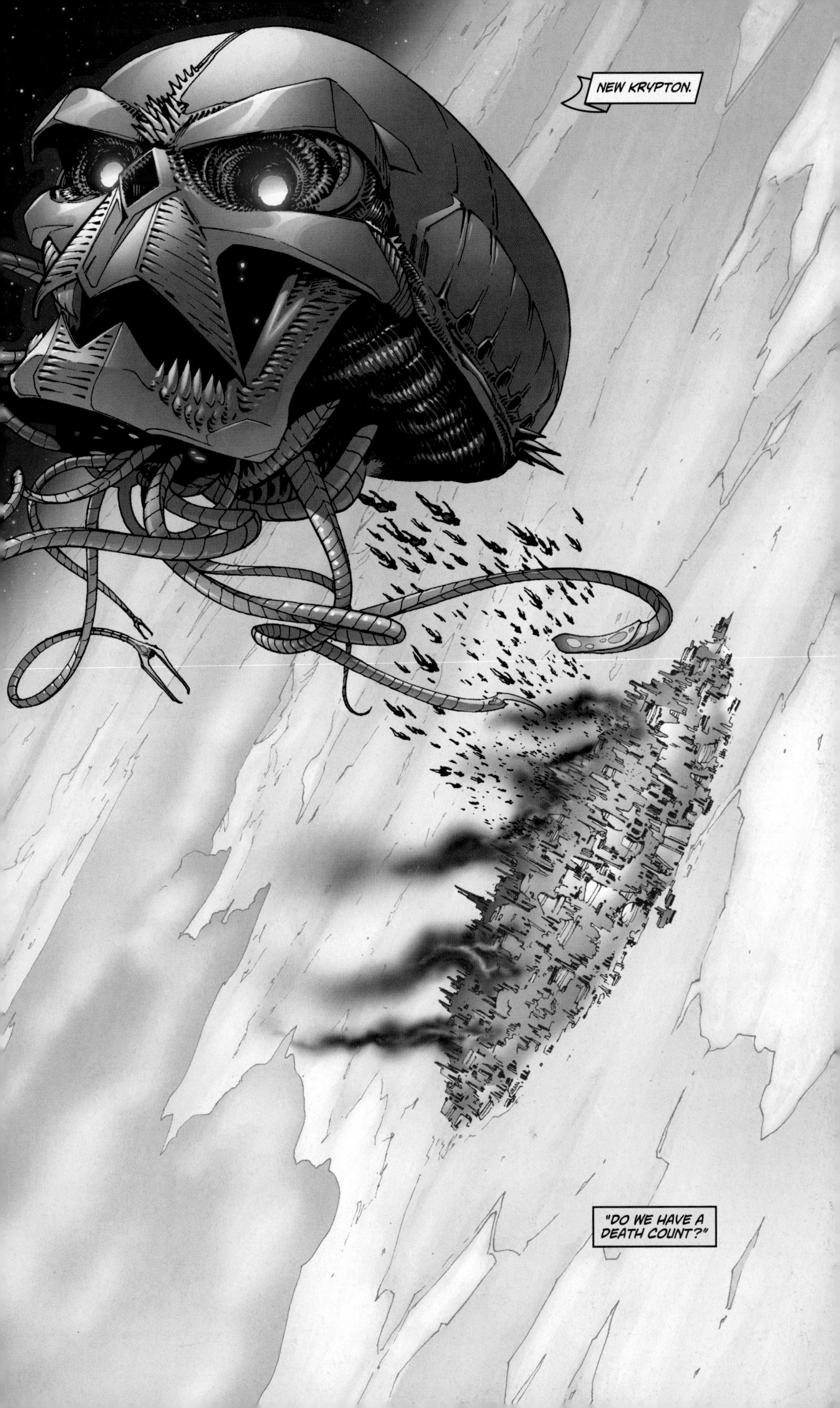
NEW KRYPTON.
"DO WE HAVE A DEATH COUNT?"

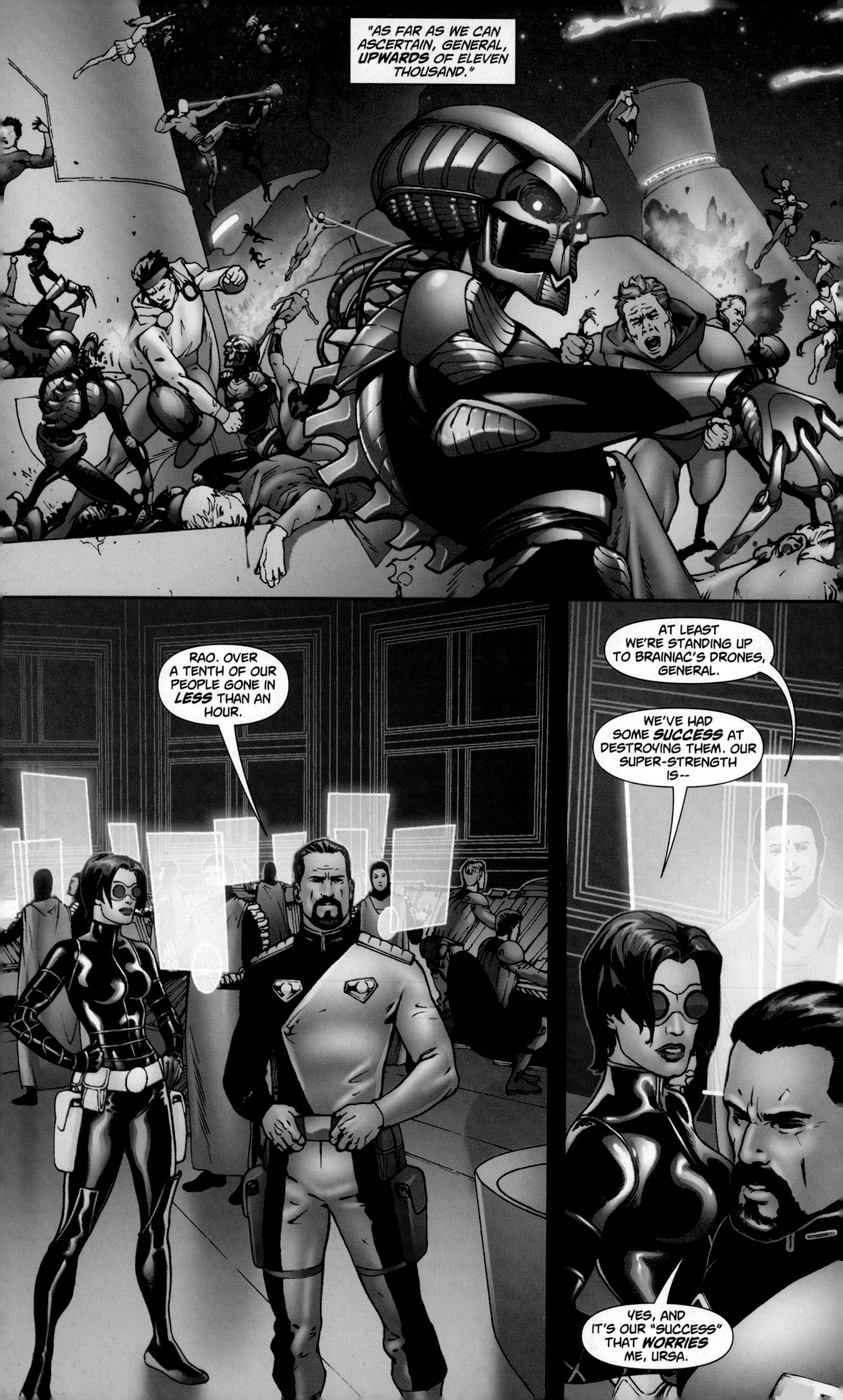
"AS FAR AS WE CAN ASCERTAIN, GENERAL, UPWARDS OF ELEVEN THOUSAND."
RAO. OVER A TENTH OF OUR PEOPLE GONE IN LESS THAN AN HOUR.
AT LEAST WE'RE STANDING UP TO BRAINIAC'S DRONES, GENERAL.
WE'VE HAD SOME SUCCESS AT DESTROYING THEM. OUR SUPER-STRENGTH IS--
YES, AND IT'S OUR "SUCCESS" THAT WORRIES ME, URSA.

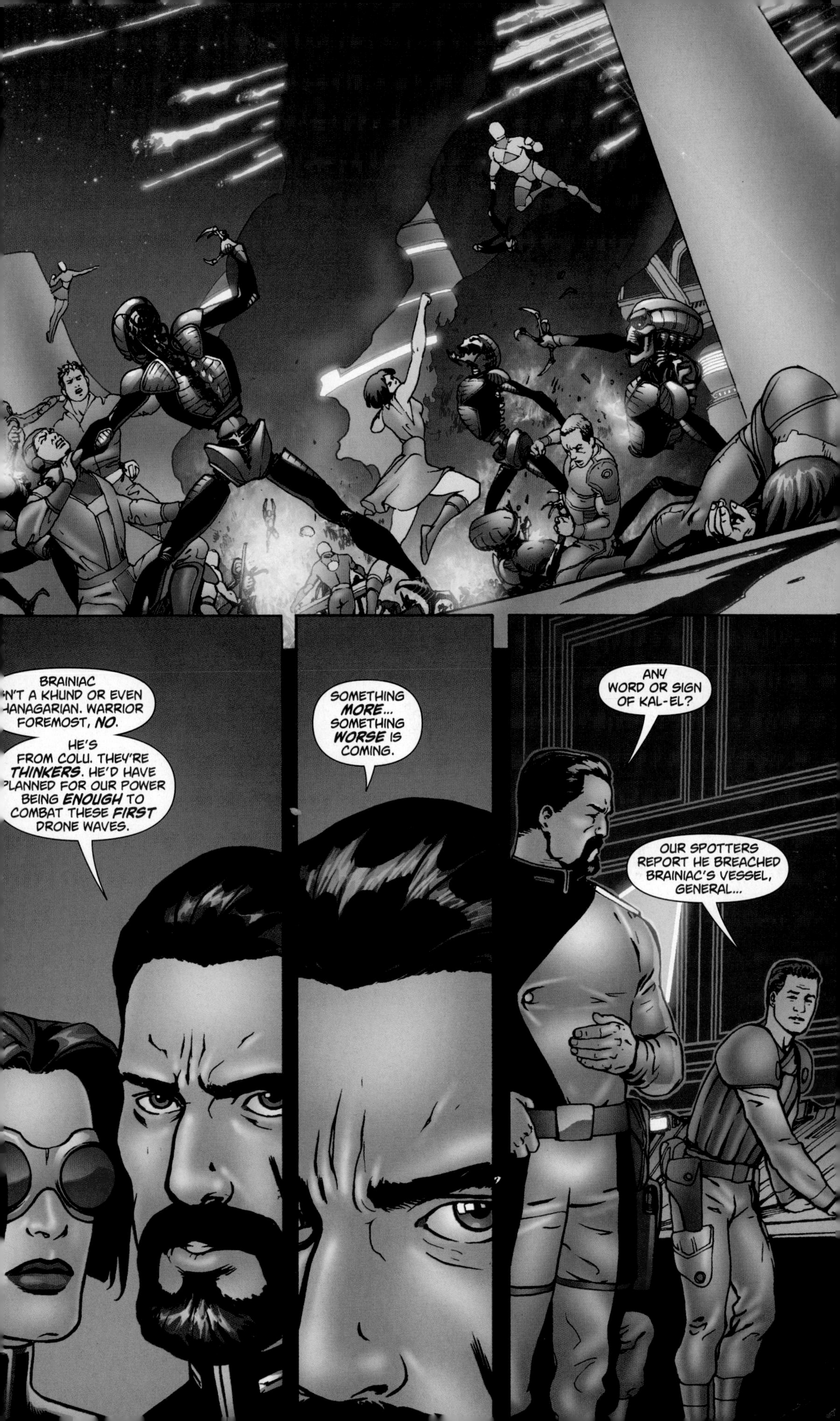
BRAINIAC 'N'T A KHUND OR EVEN HANAGARIAN. WARRIOR FOREMOST, NO.
HE'S FROM COLU. THEY'RE THINKERS. HE'D HAVE PLANNED FOR OUR POWER BEING ENOUGH TO COMBAT THESE FIRST DRONE WAVES.
SOMETHING MORE... SOMETHING WORSE IS COMING.
ANY WORD OR SIGN OF KAL-EL?
OUR SPOTTERS REPORT HE BREACHED BRAINIAC'S VESSEL, GENERAL...

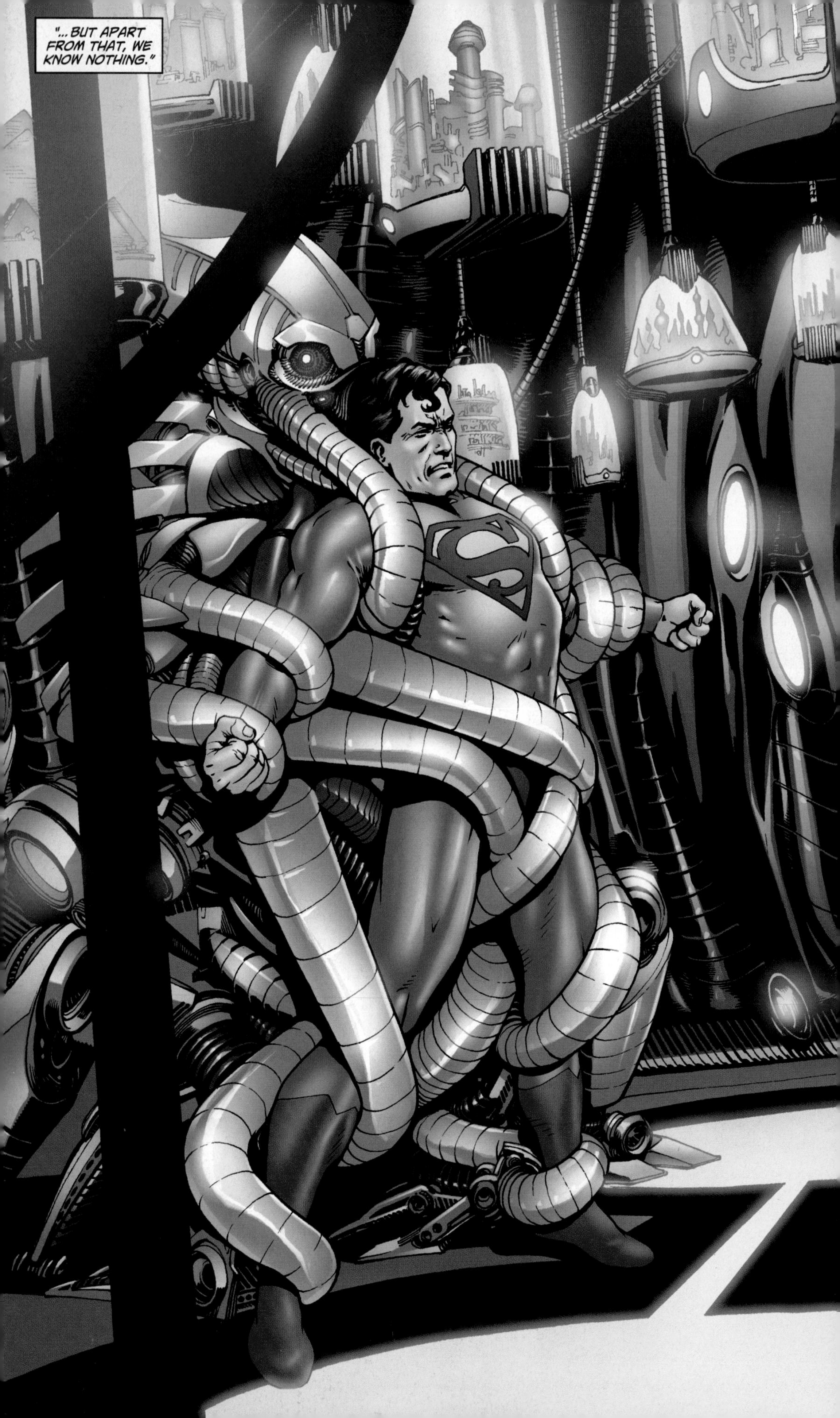
"... BUT APART FROM THAT, WE KNOW NOTHING."

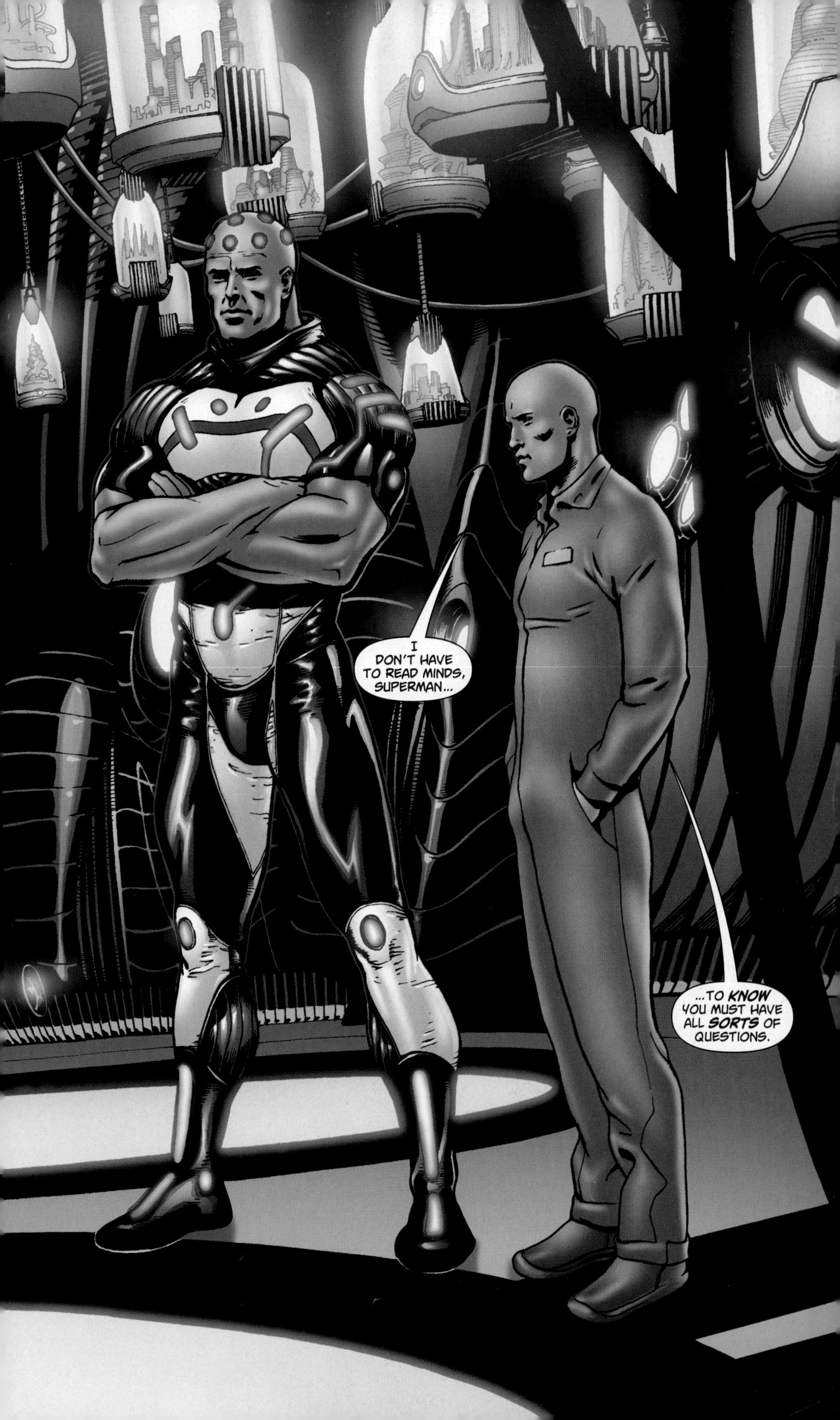
I DON'T HAVE TO READ MINDS, SUPERMAN...
...TO KNOW YOU MUST HAVE ALL SORTS OF QUESTIONS.

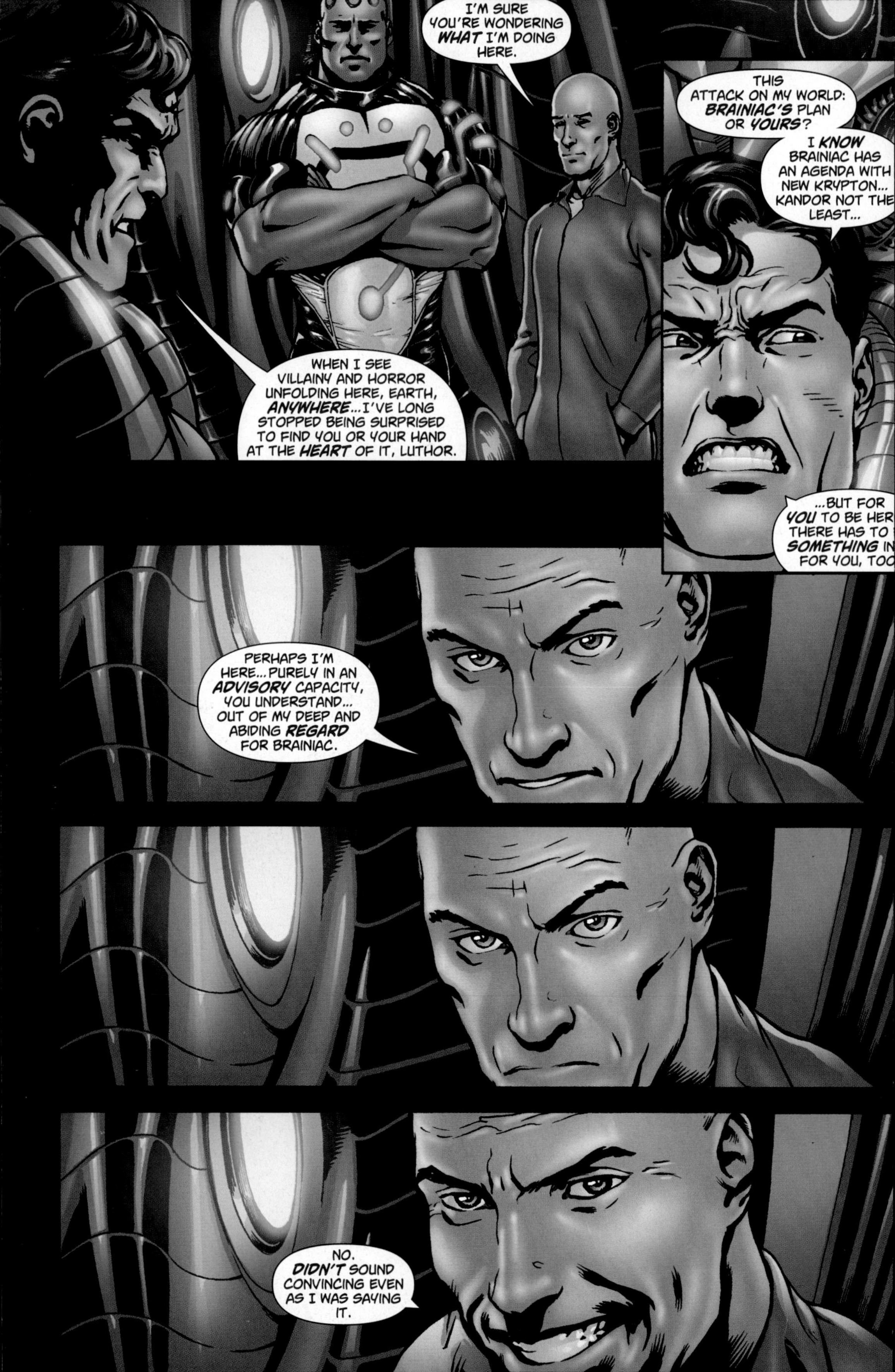
I'M SURE YOU'RE WONDERING WHAT I'M DOING HERE.
WHEN I SEE VILLAINY AND HORROR UNFOLDING HERE, EARTH, ANYWHERE...I'VE LONG STOPPED BEING SURPRISED TO FIND YOU OR YOUR HAND AT THE HEART OF IT, LUTHOR.
THIS ATTACK ON MY WORLD: BRAINIAC'S PLAN OR YOURS?
I KNOW BRAINIAC HAS AN AGENDA WITH NEW KRYPTON... KANDOR NOT THE LEAST...
...BUT FOR YOU TO BE HER THERE HAS TO SOMETHING IN FOR YOU, TOO
PERHAPS I'M HERE...PURELY IN AN ADVISORY CAPACITY, YOU UNDERSTAND... OUT OF MY DEEP AND ABIDING REGARD FOR BRAINIAC.
NO. DIDN'T SOUND CONVINCING EVEN AS I WAS SAYING IT.

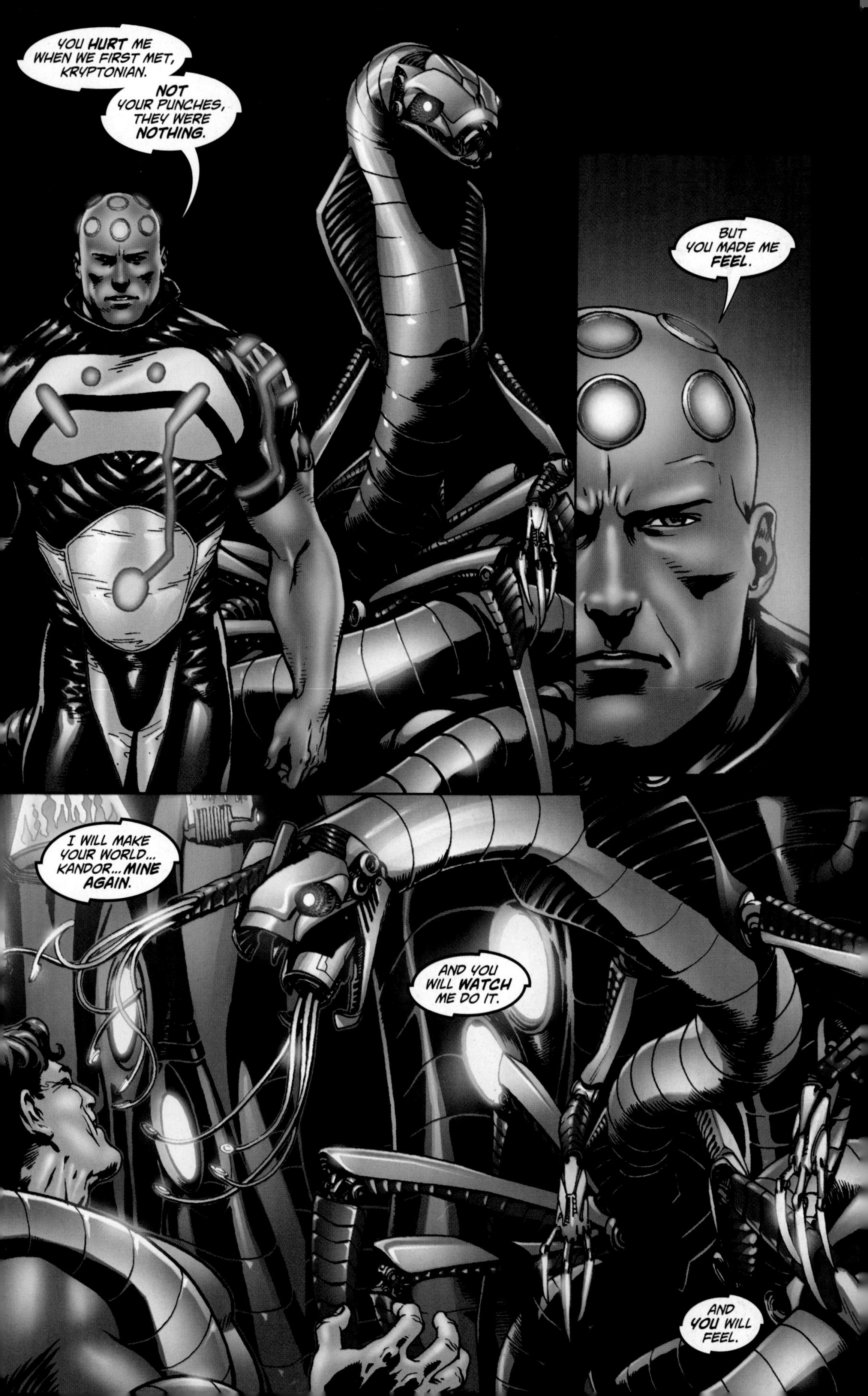
YOU HURT ME WHEN WE FIRST MET, KRYPTONIAN.
NOT YOUR PUNCHES, THEY WERE NOTHING.
BUT YOU MADE ME FEEL.
I WILL MAKE YOUR WORLD... KANDOR... MINE AGAIN.
AND YOU WILL WATCH ME DO IT.
AND YOU WILL FEEL.

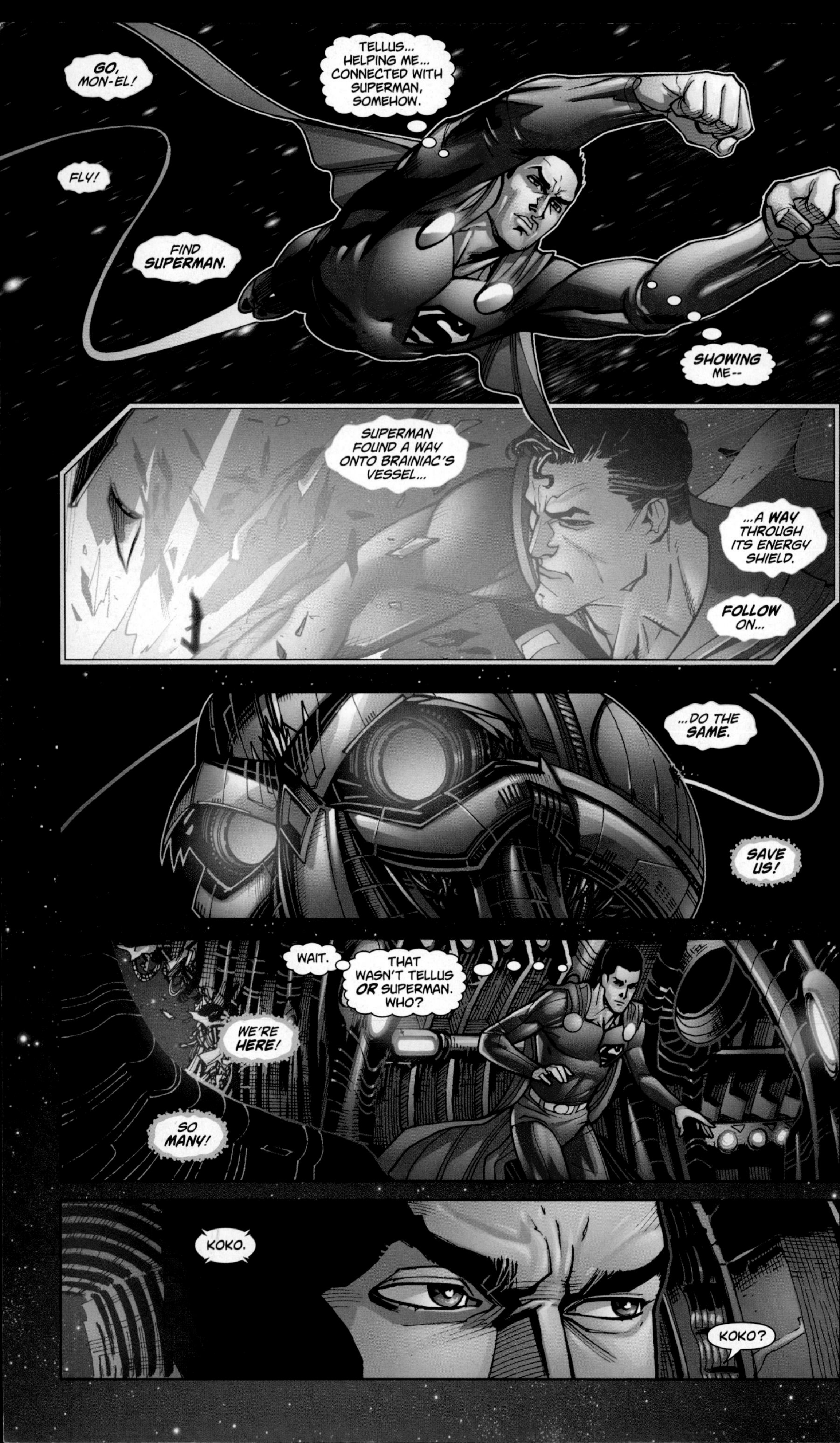
GO, MON-EL!
TELLUS... HELPING ME... CONNECTED WITH SUPERMAN, SOMEHOW.
FLY!
FIND SUPERMAN.
SHOWING ME--
SUPERMAN FOUND A WAY ONTO BRAINIAC'S VESSEL...
...A WAY THROUGH ITS ENERGY SHIELD.
FOLLOW ON...
...DO THE SAME.
SAVE US!
WAIT.
THAT WASN'T TELLUS OR SUPERMAN. WHO?
WE'RE HERE!
SO MANY!
KOKO.
KOKO?

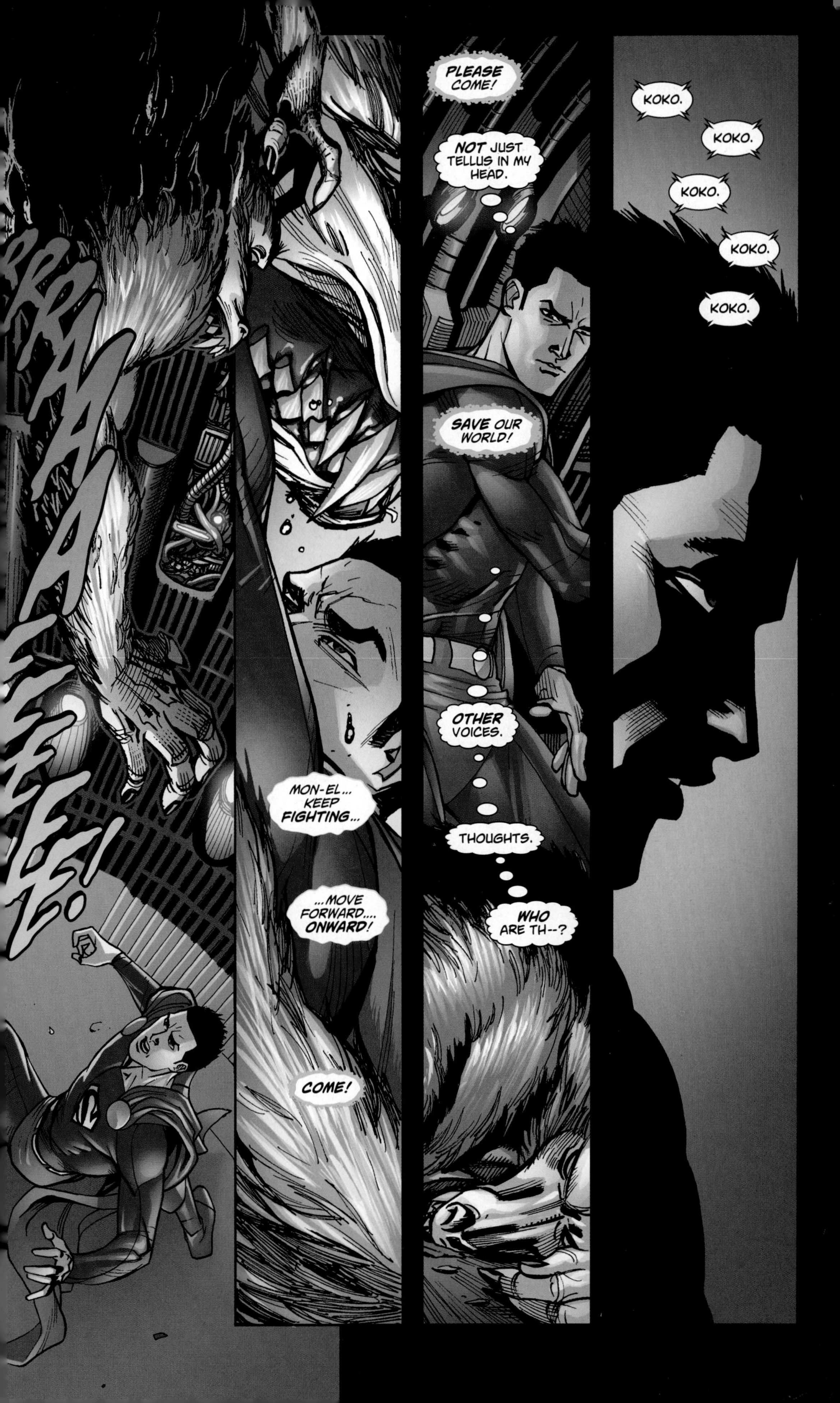
MON-EL... KEEP FIGHTING...
...MOVE FORWARD.... ONWARD!
COME!
PLEASE COME!
NOT JUST TELLUS IN MY HEAD.
SAVE OUR WORLD!
OTHER VOICES.
THOUGHTS.
WHO ARE TH--?
KOKO.
KOKO.
KOKO.
KOKO.
KOKO.

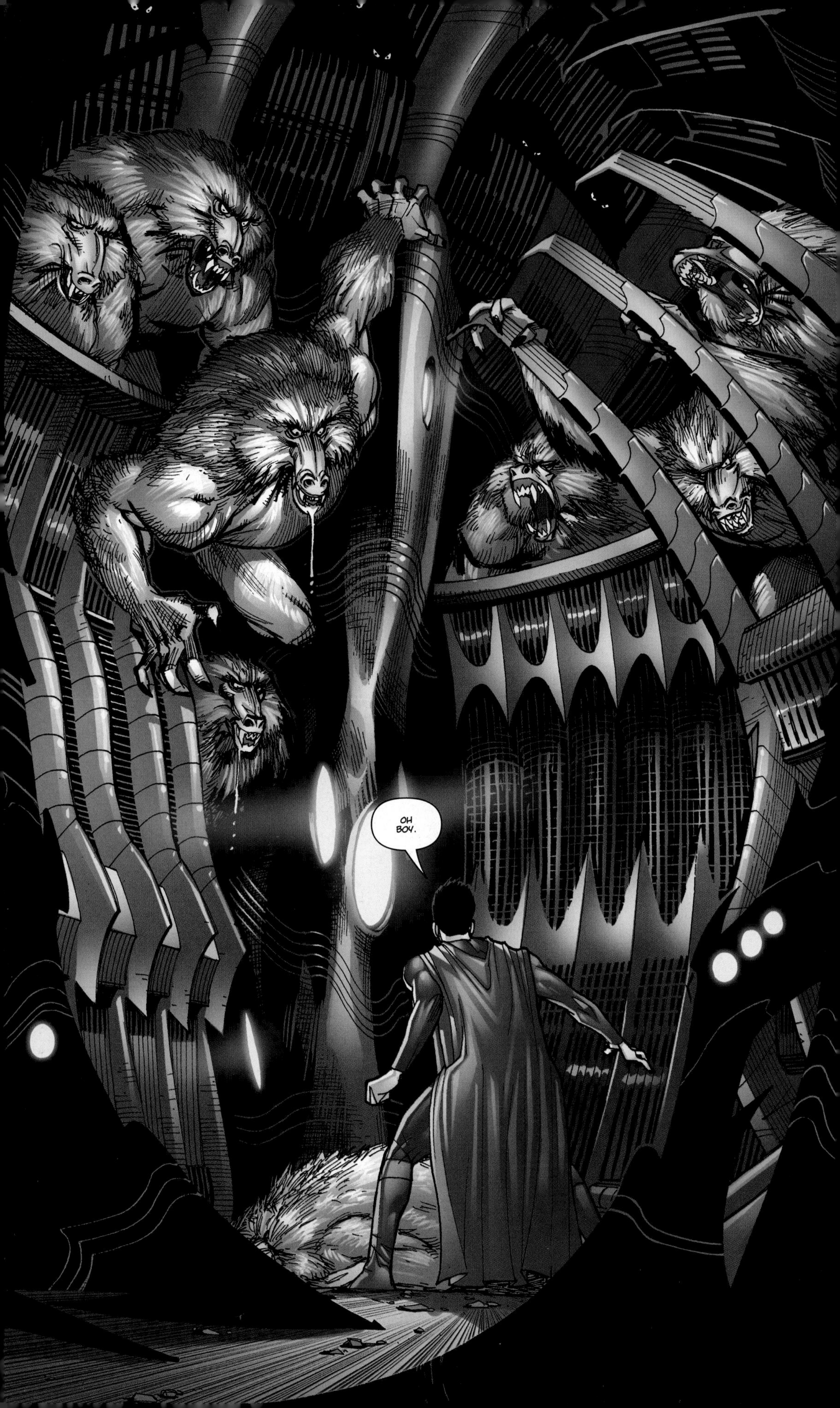
OH BOY.

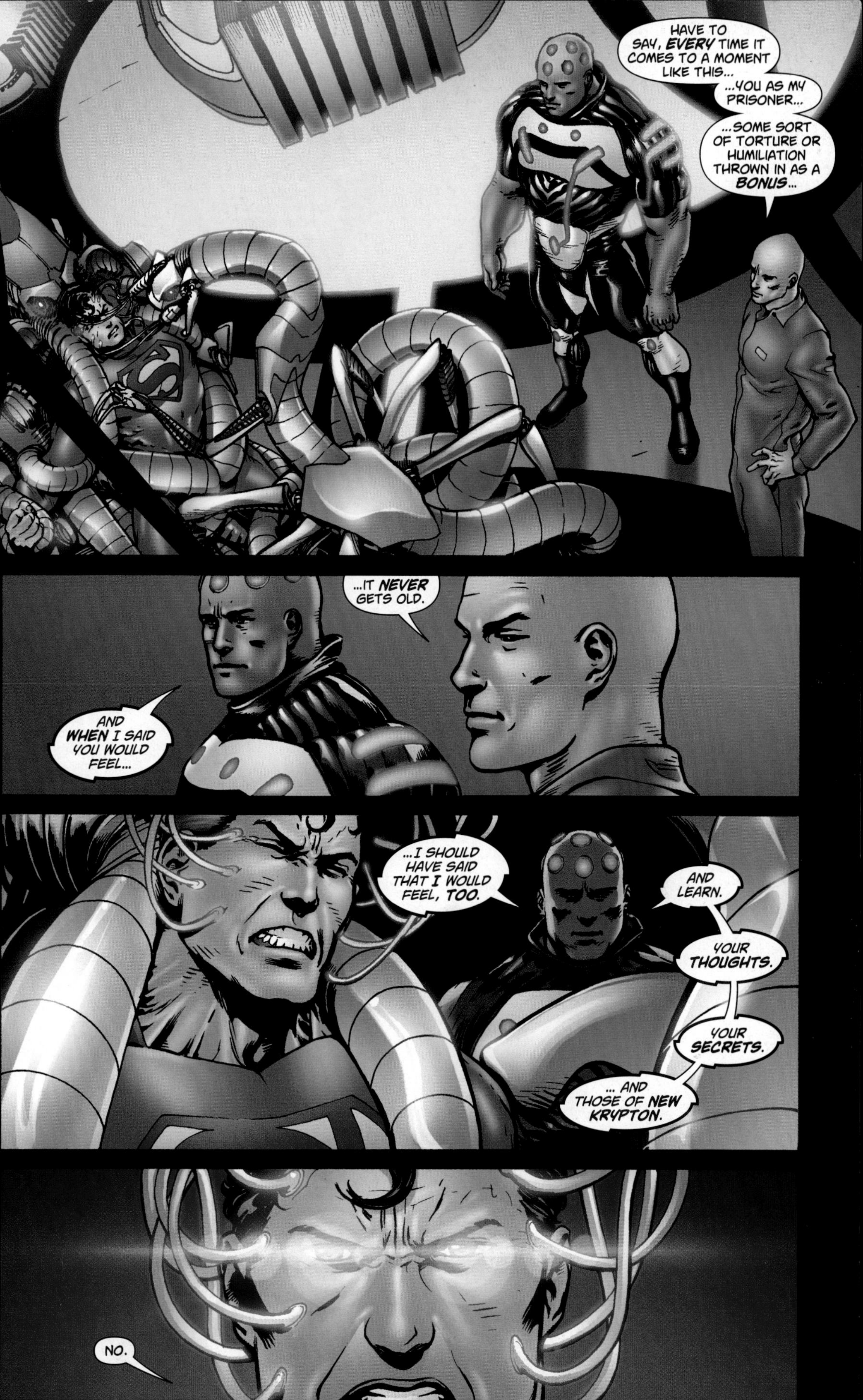
HAVE TO SAY, EVERY TIME IT COMES TO A MOMENT LIKE THIS...
...YOU AS MY PRISONER...
...SOME SORT OF TORTURE OR HUMILIATION THROWN IN AS A BONUS...
...IT NEVER GETS OLD.
AND WHEN I SAID YOU WOULD FEEL...
...I SHOULD HAVE SAID THAT I WOULD FEEL, TOO.
AND LEARN.
YOUR THOUGHTS.
YOUR SECRETS.
... AND THOSE OF NEW KRYPTON.
NO.

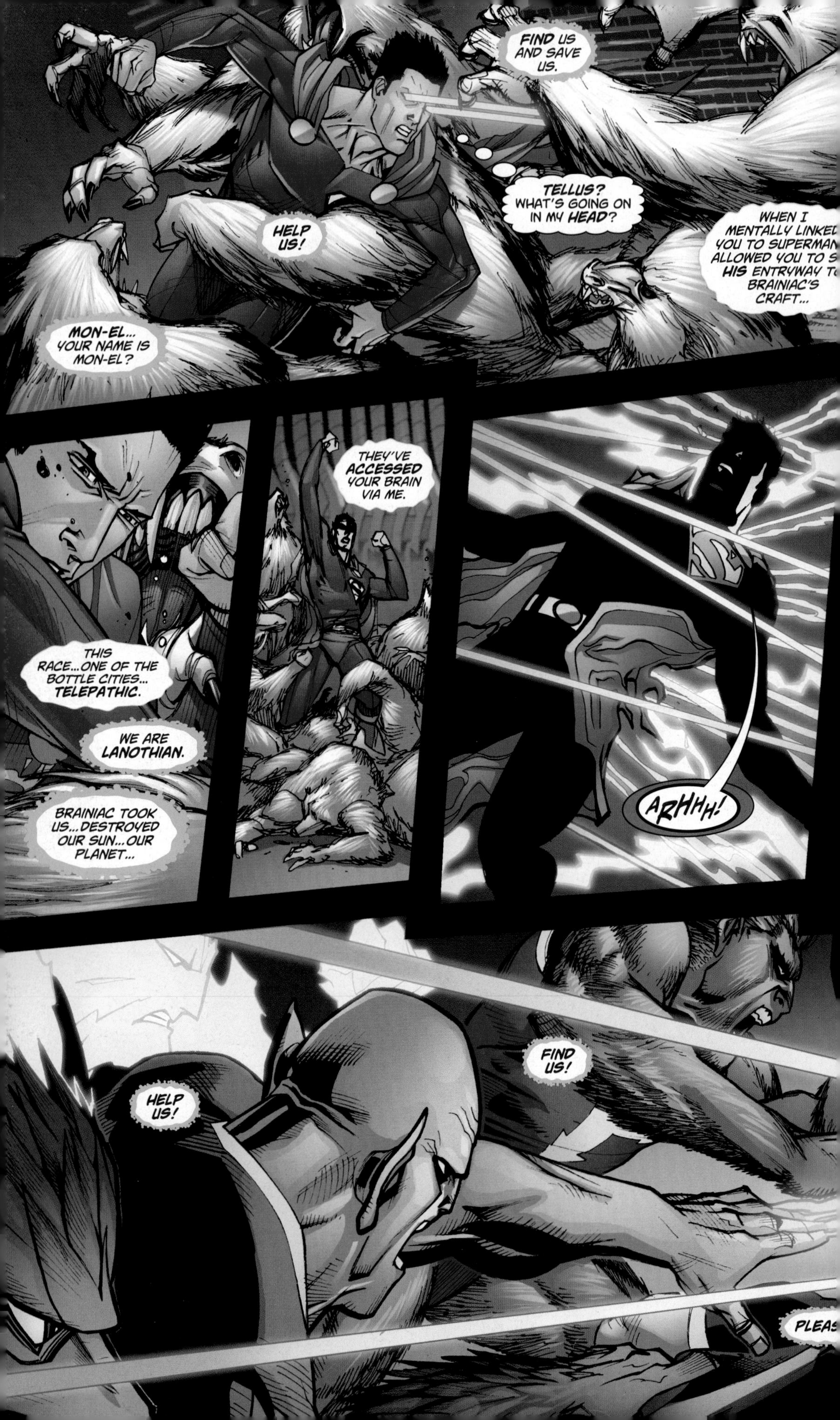
FIND US AND SAVE US.
HELP US!
TELLUS? WHAT'S GOING ON IN MY HEAD?
WHEN I MENTALLY LINKED YOU TO SUPERMAN ALLOWED YOU TO S HIS ENTRYWAY TO BRAINIAC'S CRAFT...
MON-EL... YOUR NAME IS MON-EL?
THIS RACE...ONE OF THE BOTTLE CITIES... TELEPATHIC.
WE ARE LANOTHIAN.
BRAINIAC TOOK US...DESTROYED OUR SUN...OUR PLANET...
THEY'VE ACCESSED YOUR BRAIN VIA ME.
ARHHH!
FIND US!
HELP US!
PLEAS

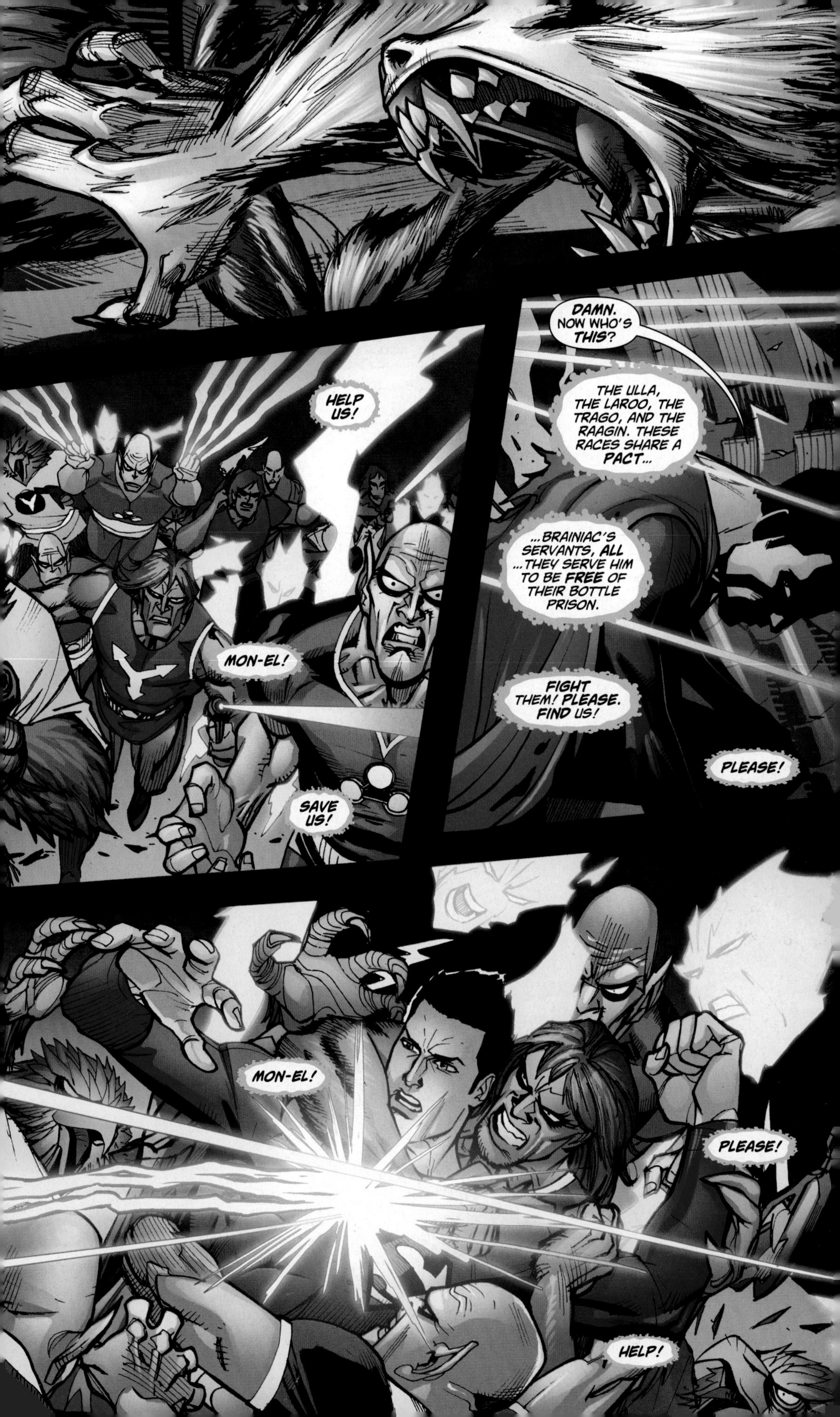
HELP US!
MON-EL!
SAVE US!
DAMN. NOW WHO'S THIS?
THE ULLA, THE LAROO, THE TRAGO, AND THE RAAGIN. THESE RACES SHARE A PACT...
...BRAINIAC'S SERVANTS, ALL ...THEY SERVE HIM TO BE FREE OF THEIR BOTTLE PRISON.
FIGHT THEM! PLEASE. FIND US!
PLEASE!
MON-EL!
PLEASE!
HELP!

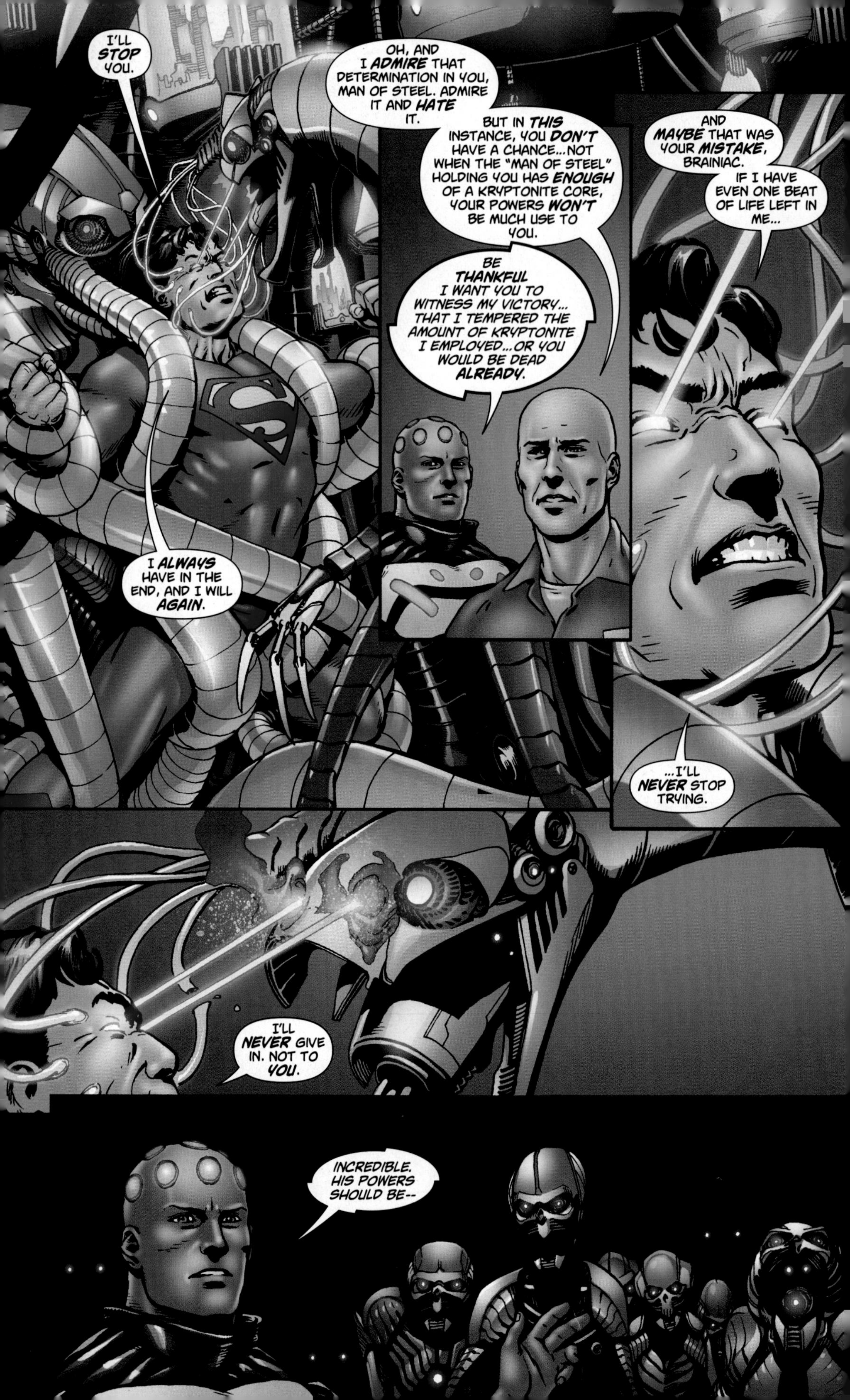

I'LL STOP YOU.
OH, AND I ADMIRE THAT DETERMINATION IN YOU, MAN OF STEEL. ADMIRE IT AND HATE IT.
I ALWAYS HAVE IN THE END, AND I WILL AGAIN.
BUT IN THIS INSTANCE, YOU DON'T HAVE A CHANCE...NOT WHEN THE "MAN OF STEEL" HOLDING YOU HAS ENOUGH OF A KRYPTONITE CORE, YOUR POWERS WON'T BE MUCH USE TO YOU.
BE THANKFUL I WANT YOU TO WITNESS MY VICTORY... THAT I TEMPERED THE AMOUNT OF KRYPTONITE I EMPLOYED...OR YOU WOULD BE DEAD ALREADY.
AND MAYBE THAT WAS YOUR MISTAKE, BRAINIAC.
IF I HAVE EVEN ONE BEAT OF LIFE LEFT IN ME...
...I'LL NEVER STOP TRYING.
I'LL NEVER GIVE IN. NOT TO YOU.
INCREDIBLE. HIS POWERS SHOULD BE--

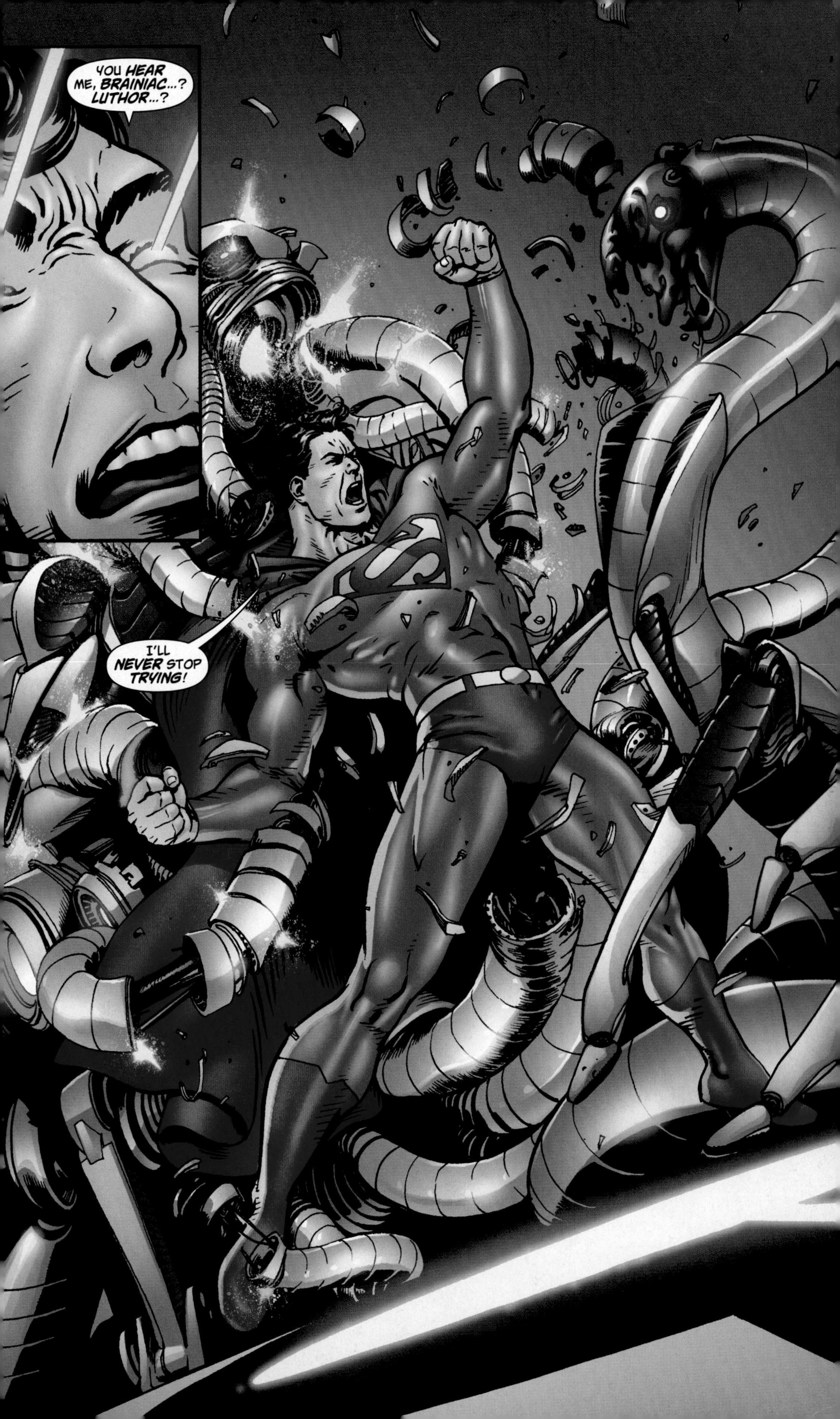
YOU HEAR ME, BRAINIAC...? LUTHOR...?
I'LL NEVER STOP TRYING!

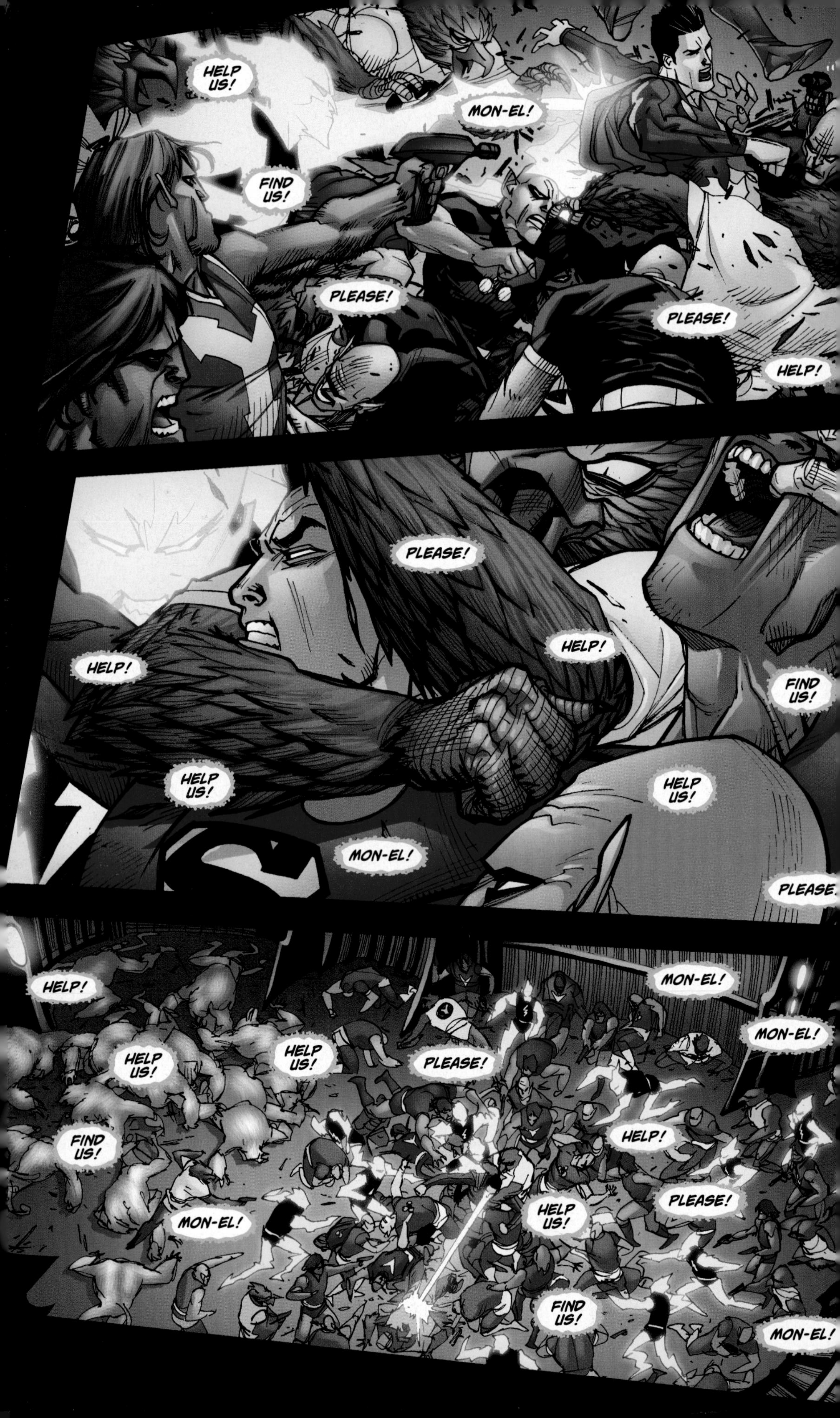
HELP US!
MON-EL!
FIND US!
PLEASE!
PLEASE!
HELP!
PLEASE!
HELP!
HELP!
FIND US!
HELP US!
HELP US!
MON-EL!
PLEASE.
HELP!
MON-EL!
MON-EL!
HELP US!
HELP US!
PLEASE!
FIND US!
HELP!
PLEASE!
MON-EL!
HELP US!
FIND US!
MON-EL!

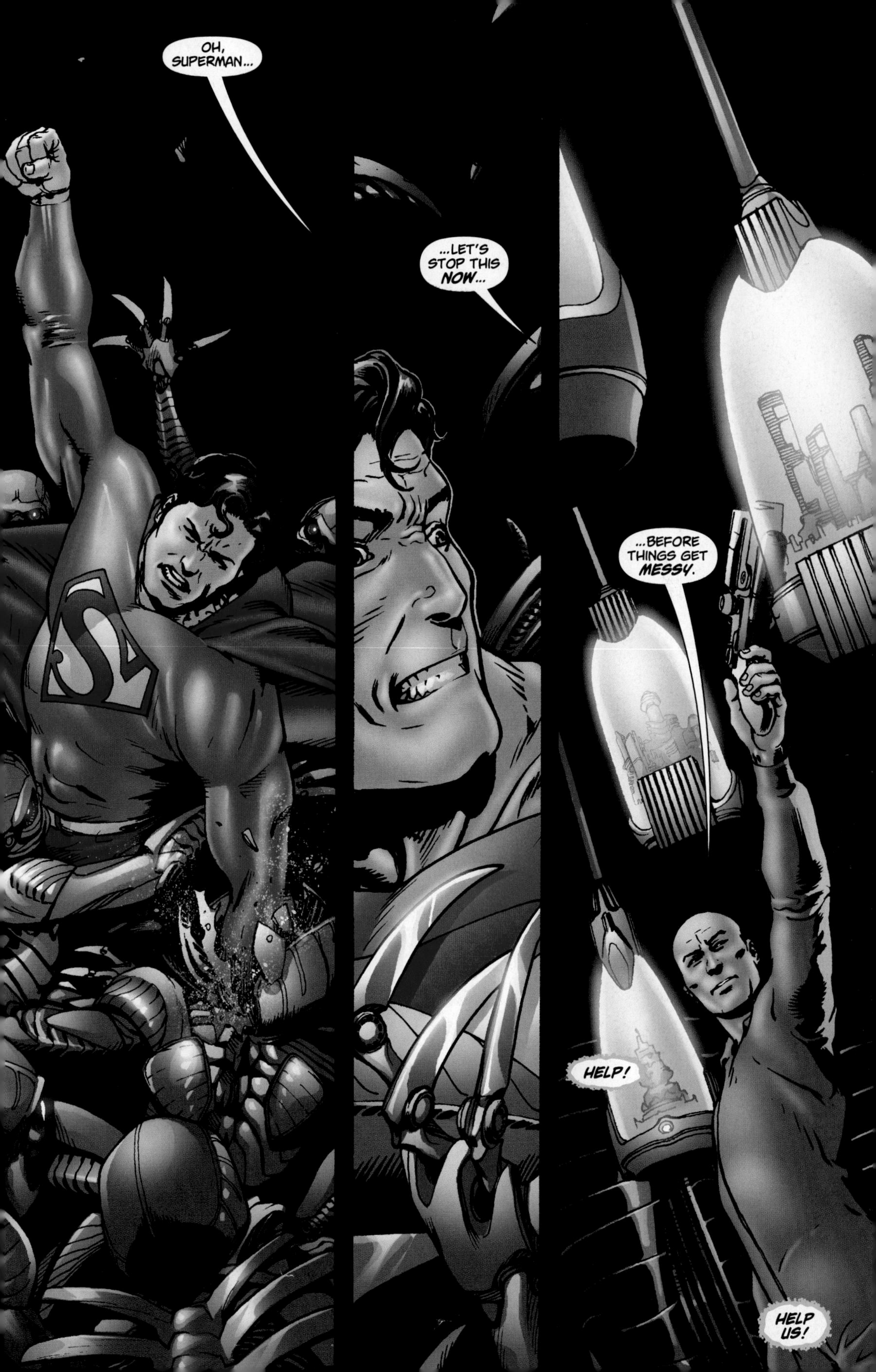
OH, SUPERMAN...
...LET'S STOP THIS NOW...
...BEFORE THINGS GET MESSY.
HELP!
HELP US!

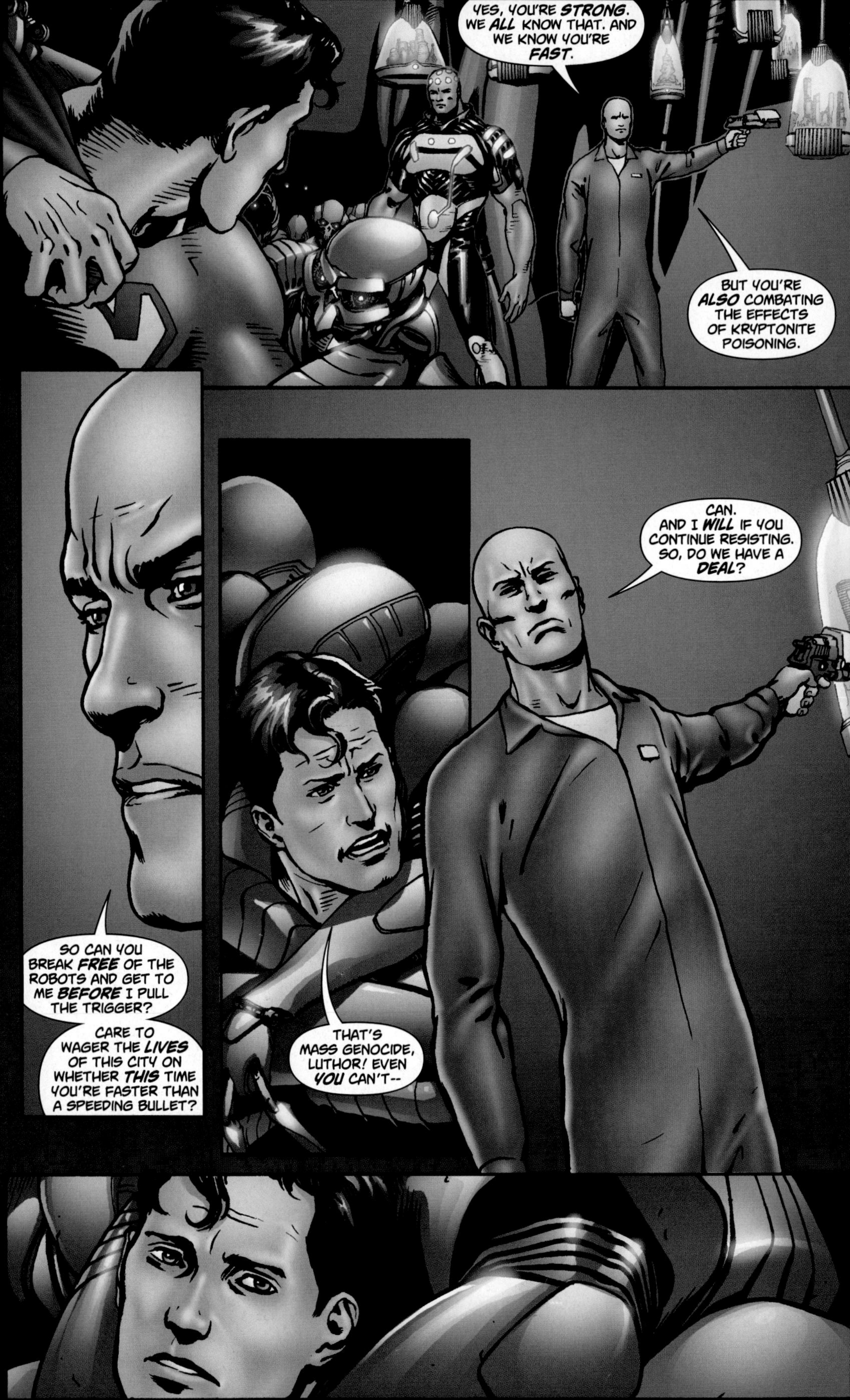
YES, YOU'RE STRONG. WE ALL KNOW THAT. AND WE KNOW YOU'RE FAST.
BUT YOU'RE ALSO COMBATING THE EFFECTS OF KRYPTONITE POISONING.
SO CAN YOU BREAK FREE OF THE ROBOTS AND GET TO ME BEFORE I PULL THE TRIGGER?
CARE TO WAGER THE LIVES OF THIS CITY ON WHETHER THIS TIME YOU'RE FASTER THAN A SPEEDING BULLET?
THAT'S MASS GENOCIDE, LUTHOR! EVEN YOU CAN'T--
CAN. AND I WILL IF YOU CONTINUE RESISTING. SO, DO WE HAVE A DEAL?

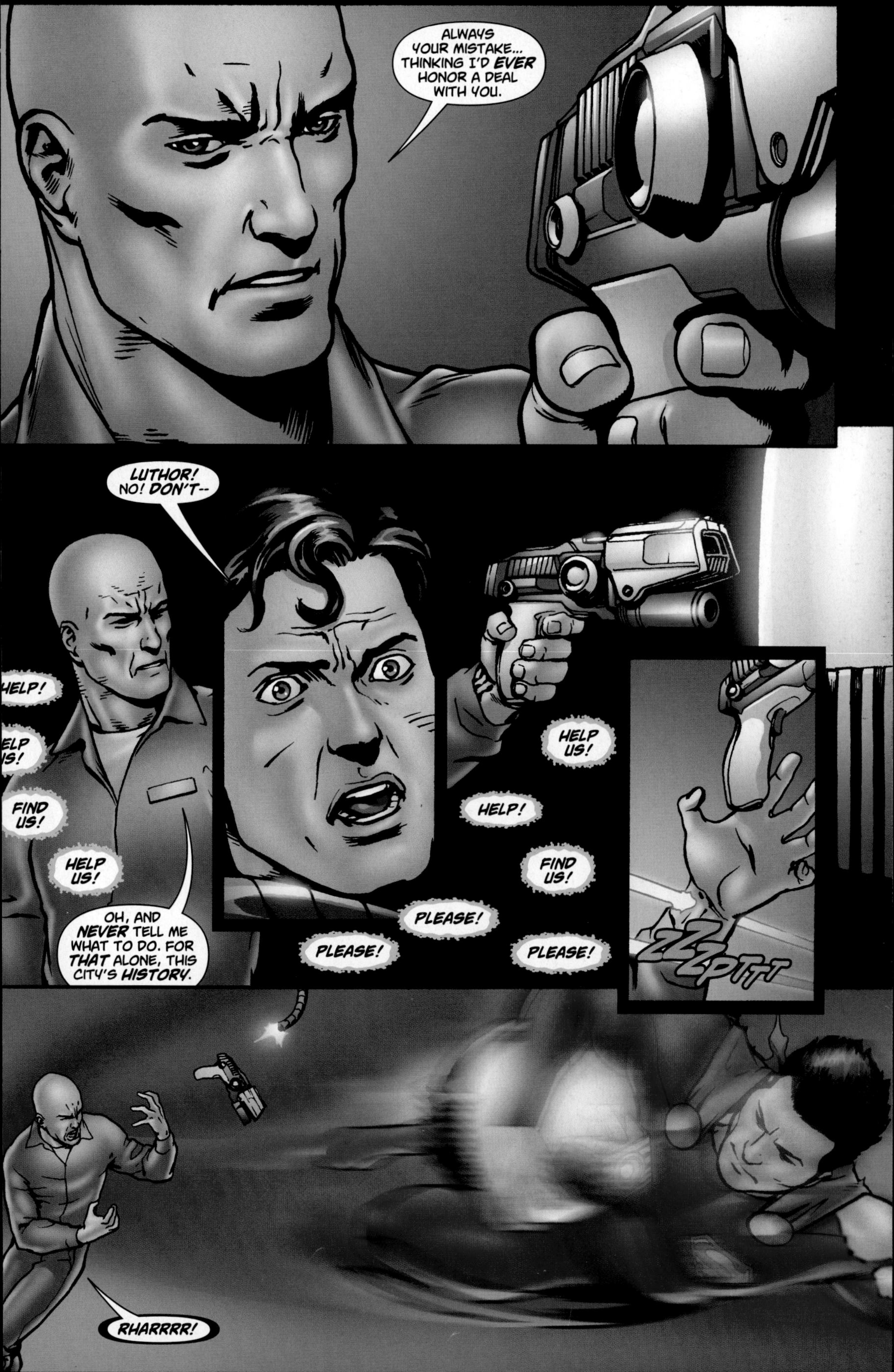
ALWAYS YOUR MISTAKE... THINKING I'D EVER HONOR A DEAL WITH YOU.
LUTHOR! NO! DON'T--
HELP!
HELP US!
FIND US!
HELP US!
OH, AND NEVER TELL ME WHAT TO DO. FOR THAT ALONE, THIS CITY'S HISTORY.
HELP US!
HELP!
FIND US!
PLEASE!
PLEASE!
PLEASE!
ZZZPTTT
RHARRRR!

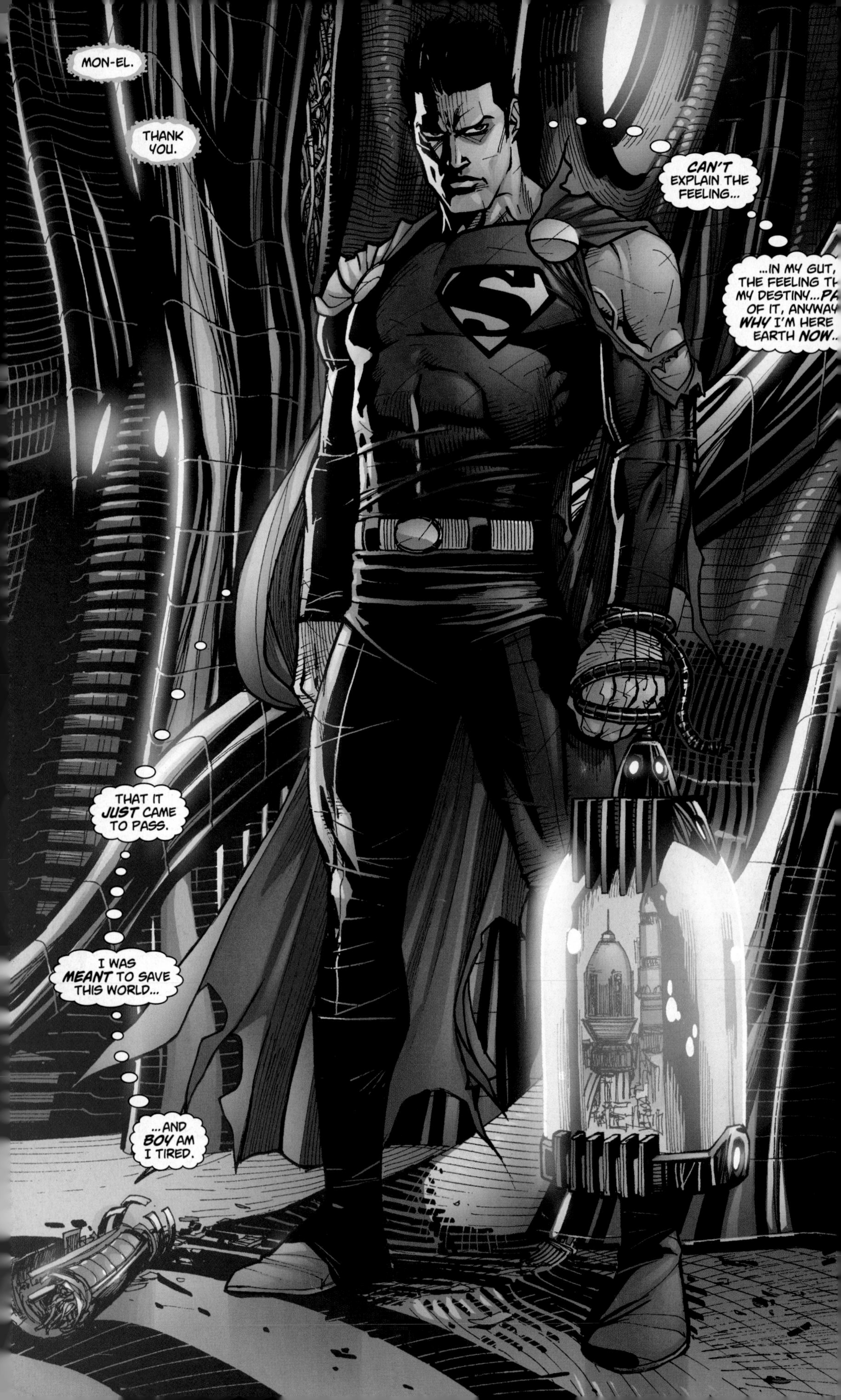

MON-EL.
THANK YOU.
CAN'T EXPLAIN THE FEELING...
...IN MY GUT, THE FEELING TH MY DESTINY...PA OF IT, ANYWAY WHY I'M HERE EARTH NOW...
THAT IT JUST CAME TO PASS.
I WAS MEANT TO SAVE THIS WORLD...
...AND BOY AM I TIRED.

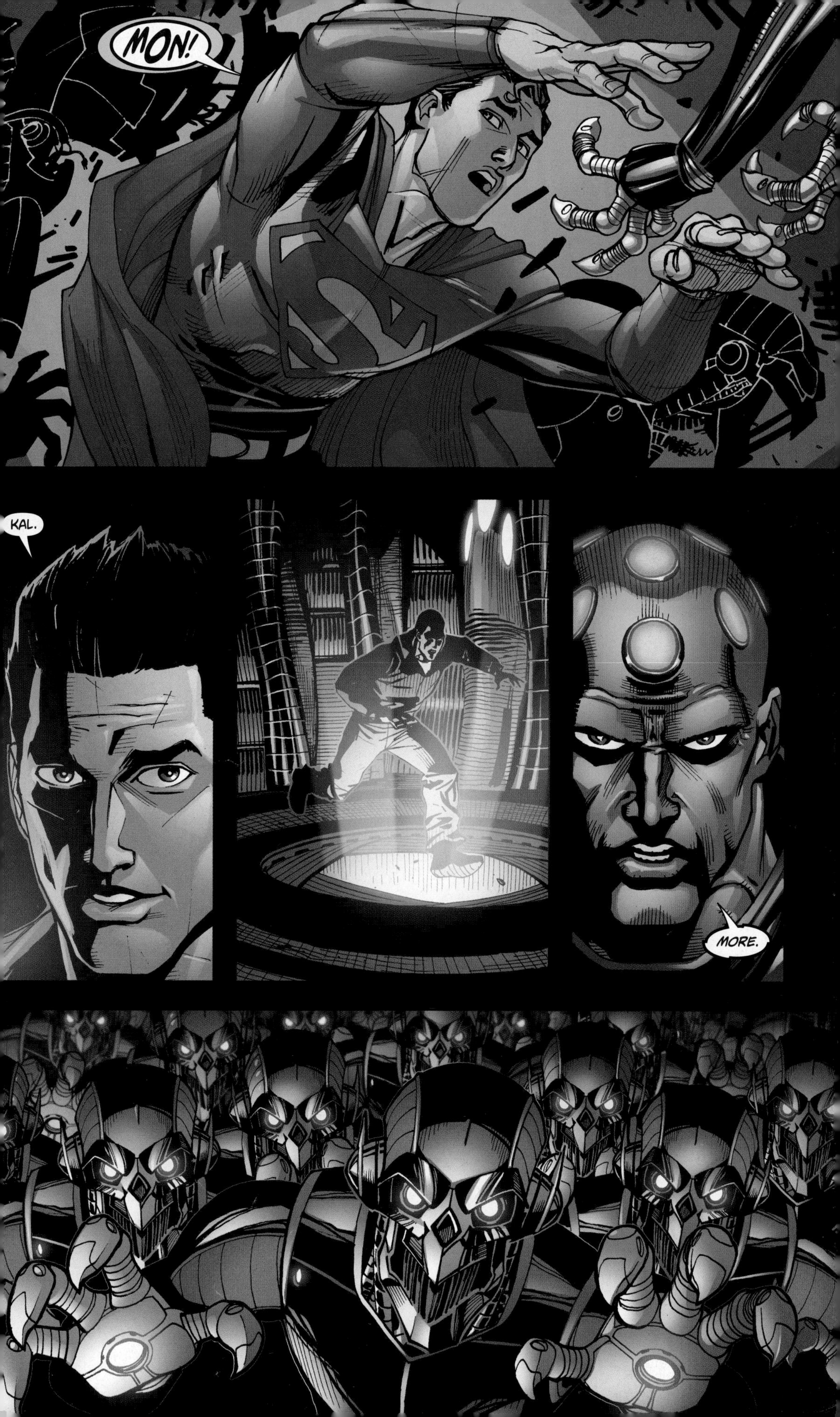
MON!
KAL.
MORE.

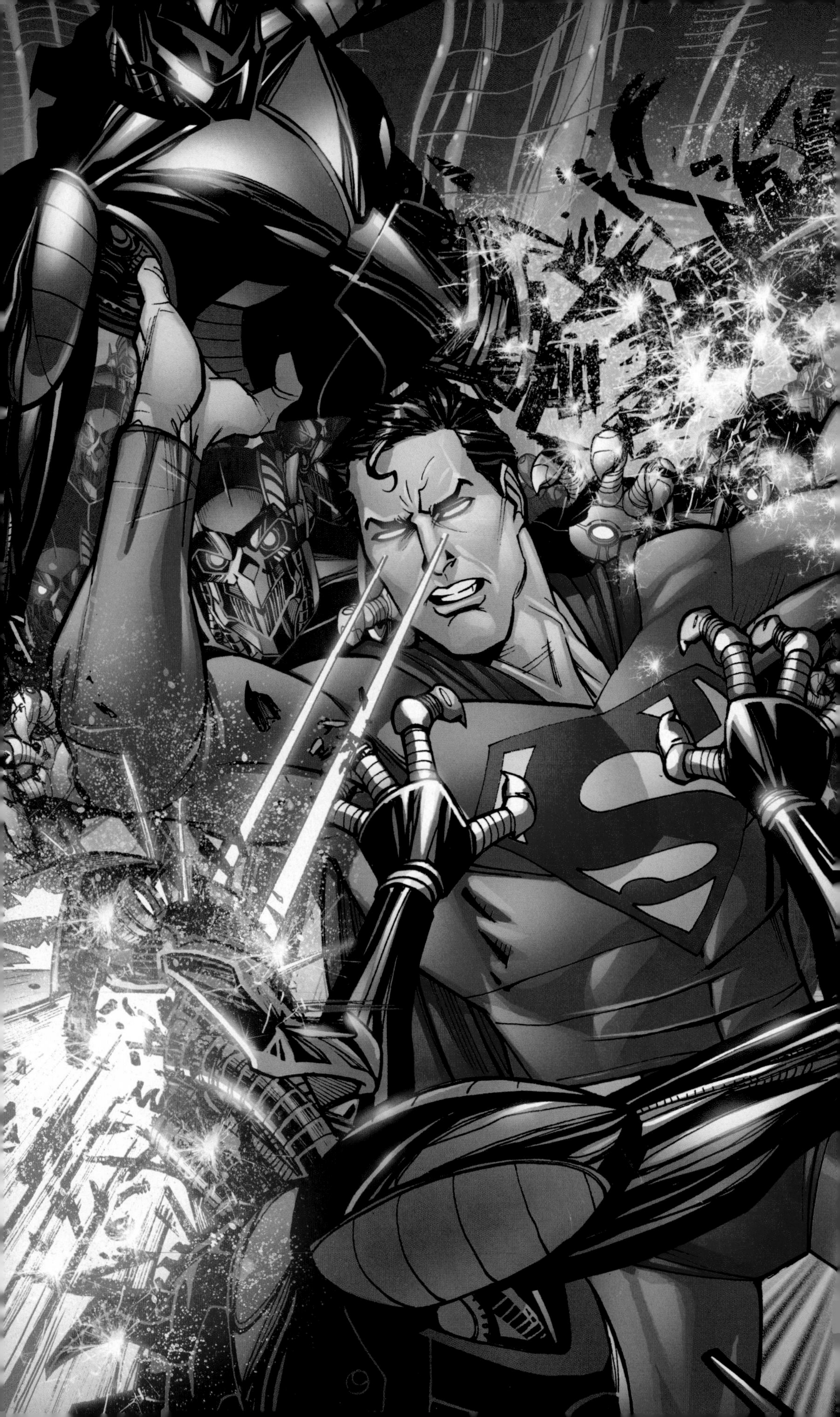

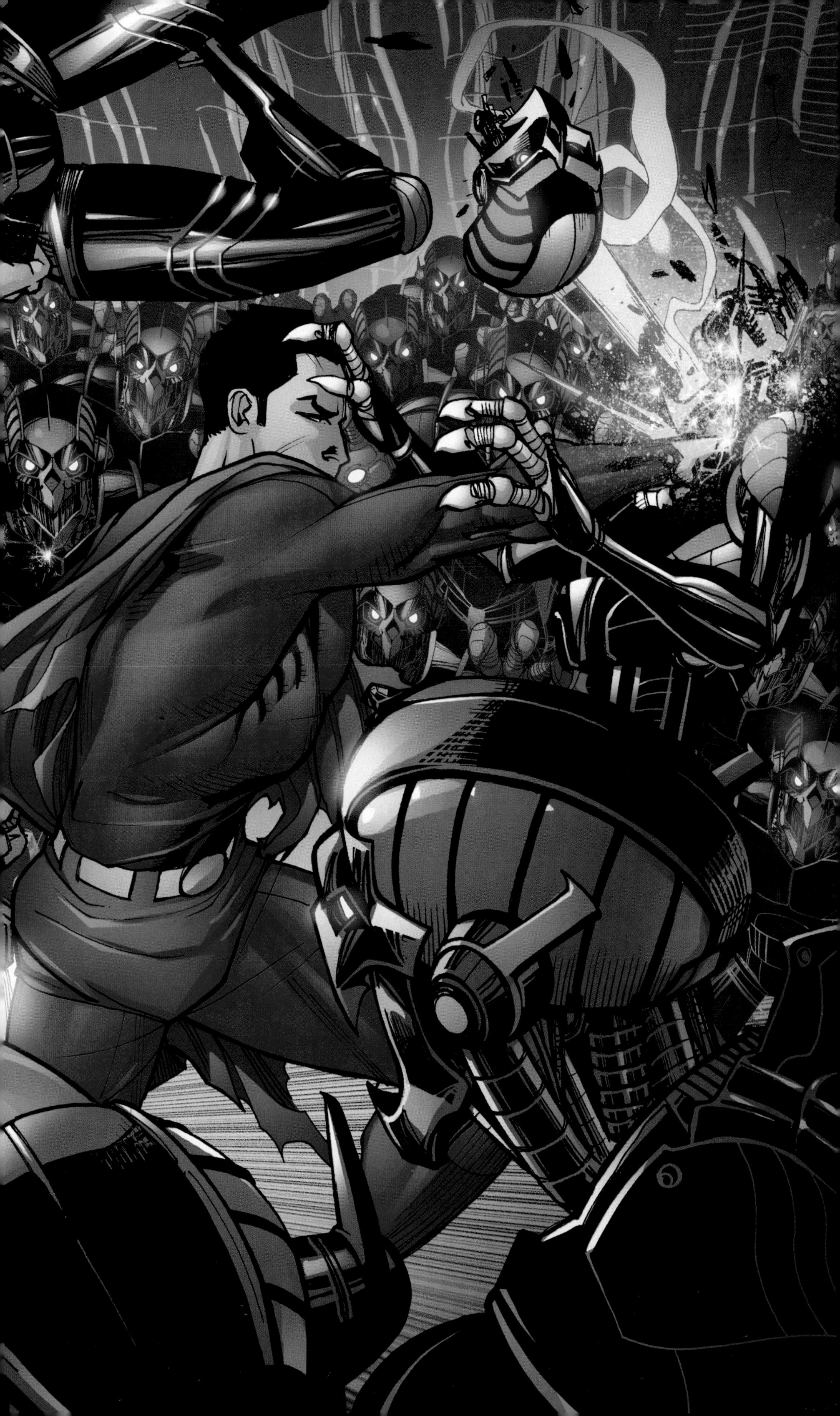

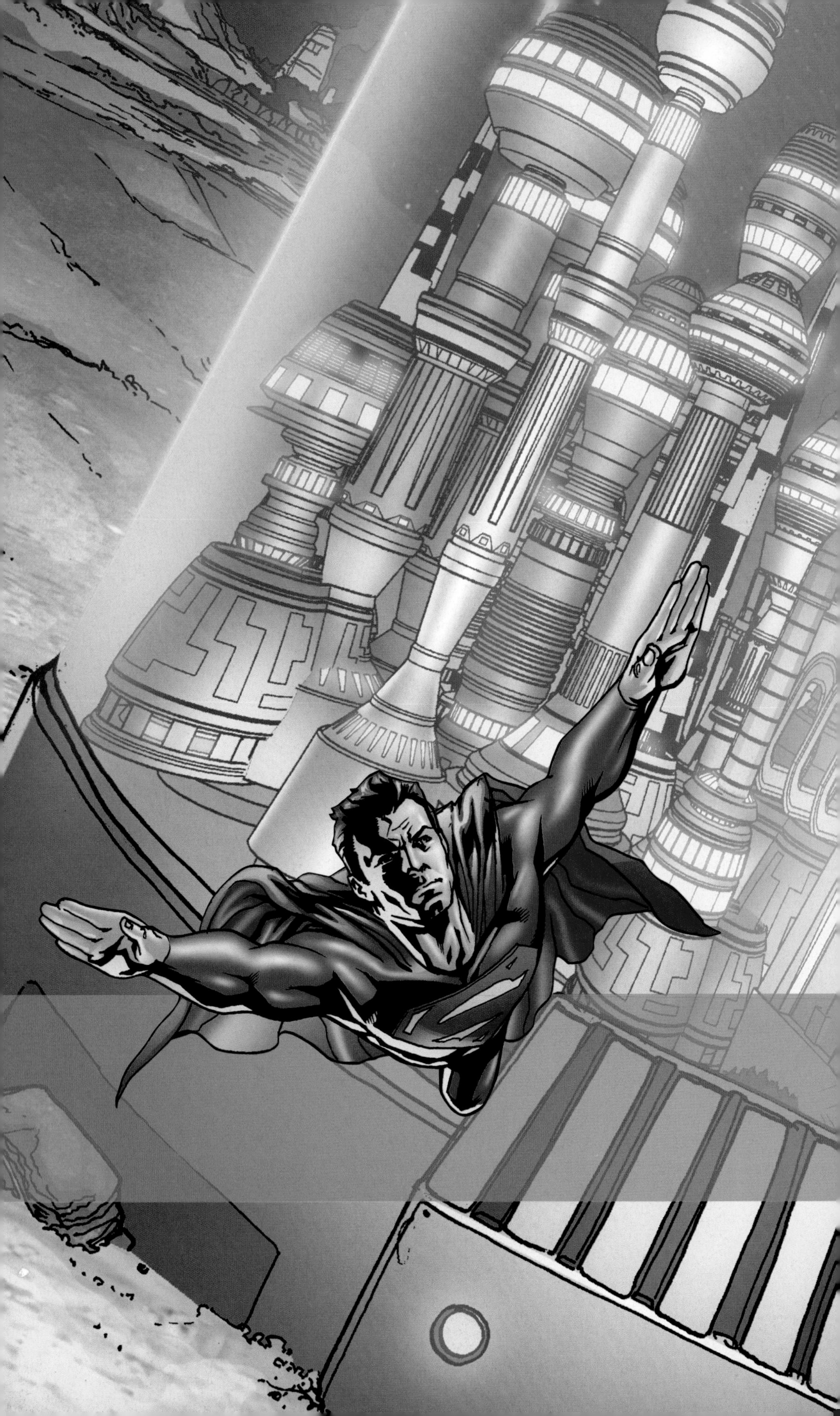

cover by JOE QUINONES

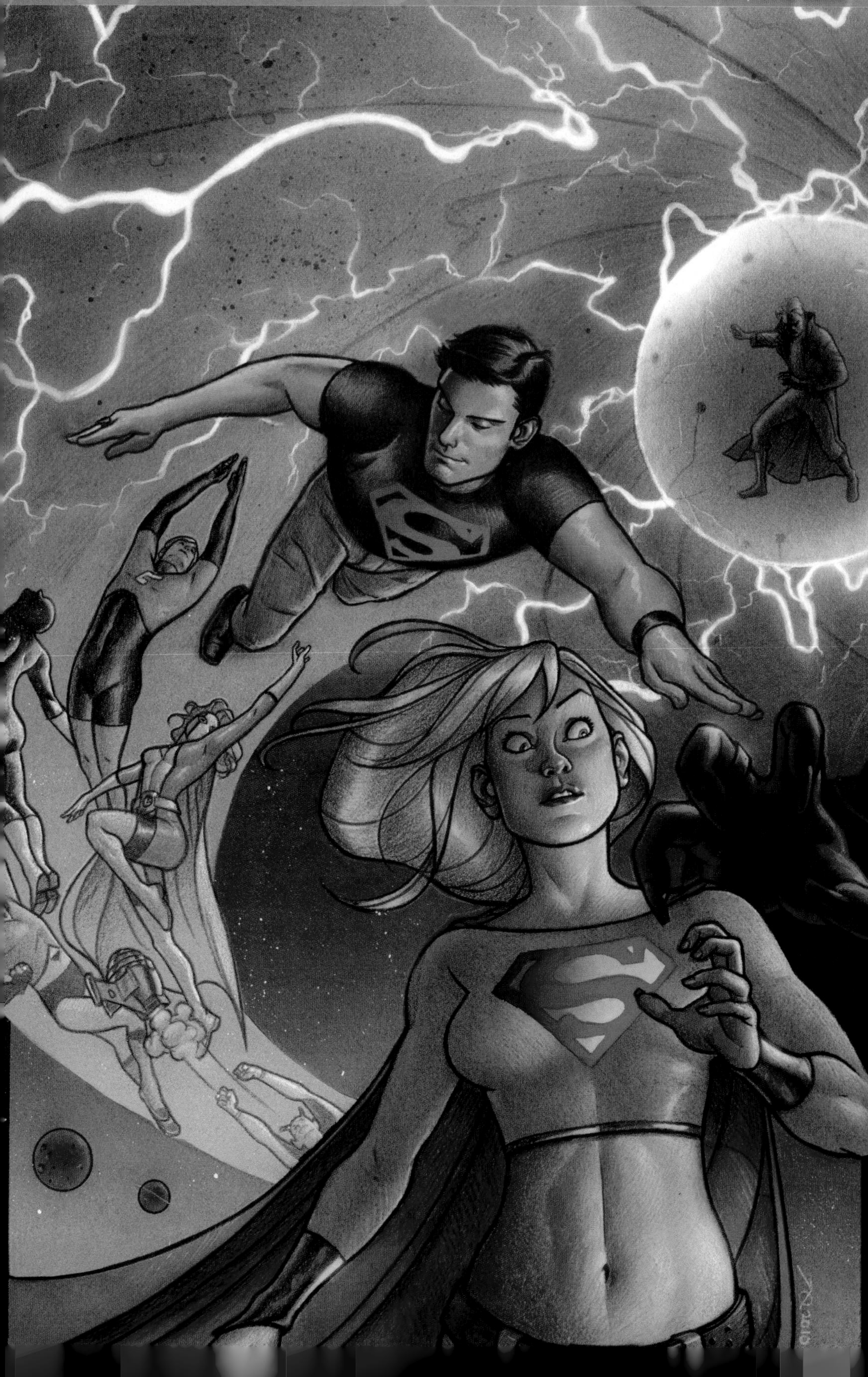

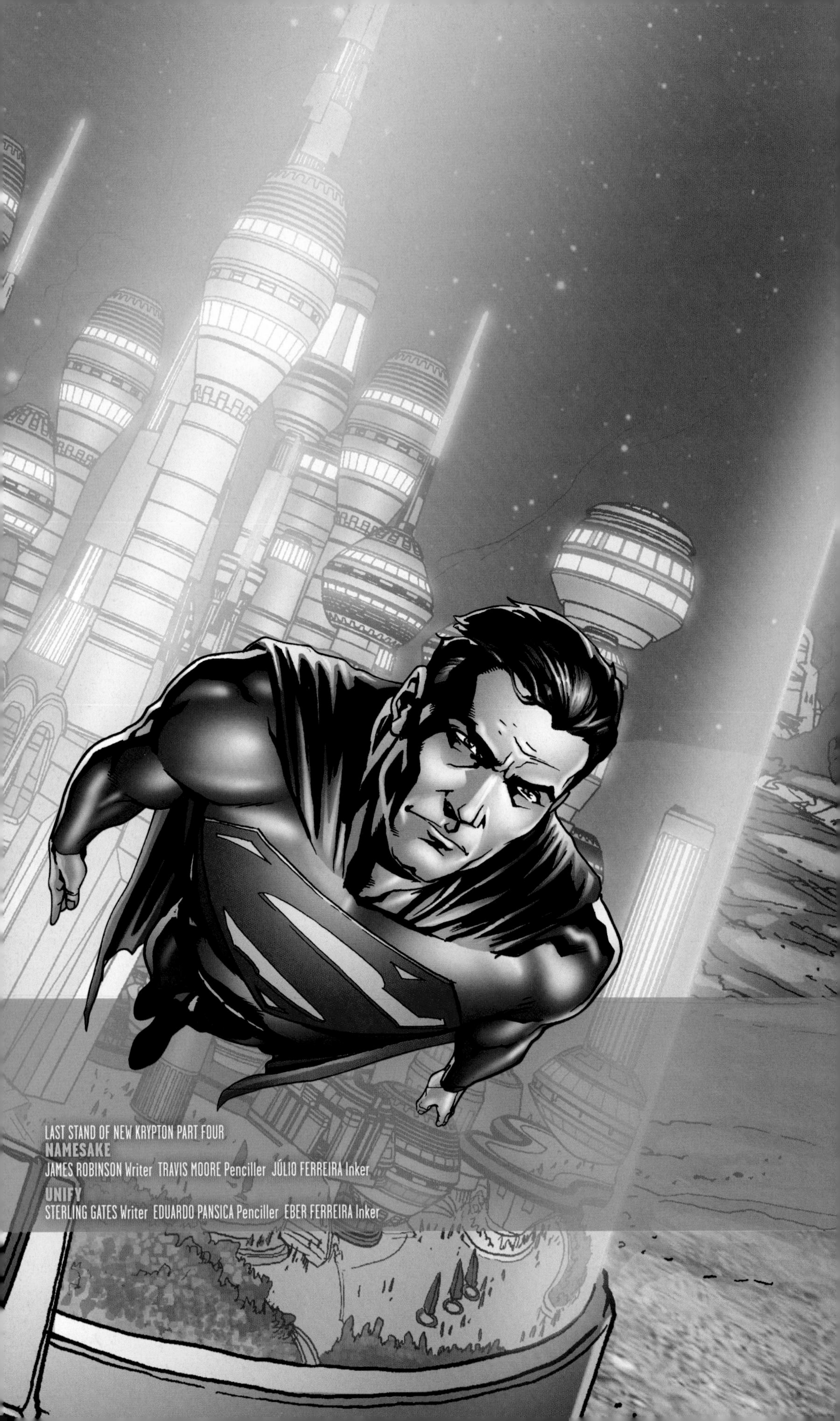

LAST STAND OF NEW KRYPTON PART FOUR
NAMESAKE
JAMES ROBINSON Writer TRAVIS MOORE Penciller JÚLIO FERREIRA Inker
UNIFY
STERLING GATES Writer EDUARDO PANSICA Penciller EBER FERREIRA Inker

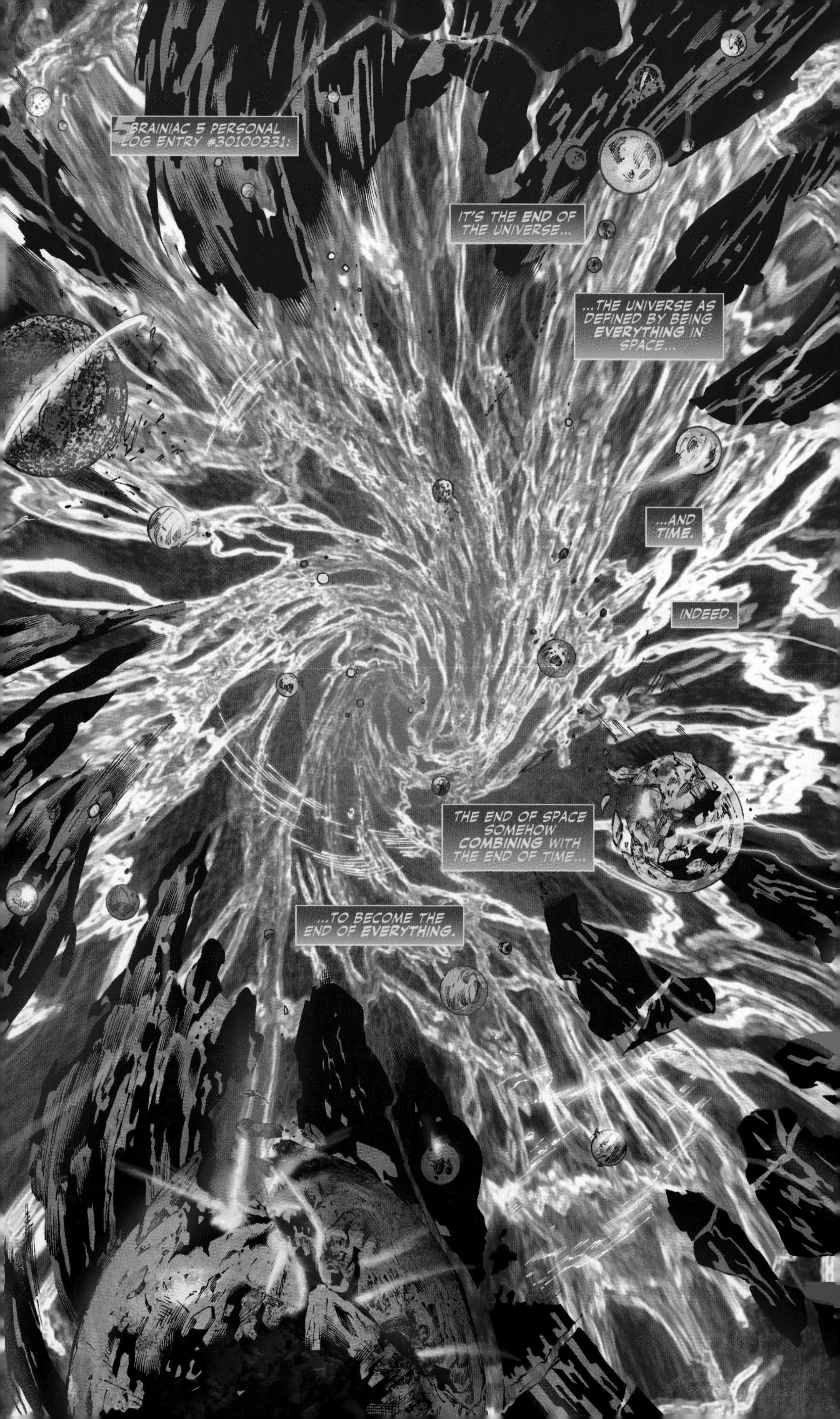
BRAINIAC 5 PERSONAL LOG ENTRY #30100331:
IT'S THE END OF THE UNIVERSE...
...THE UNIVERSE AS DEFINED BY BEING EVERYTHING IN SPACE...
...AND TIME.
INDEED.
THE END OF SPACE SOMEHOW COMBINING WITH THE END OF TIME...
...TO BECOME THE END OF EVERYTHING.

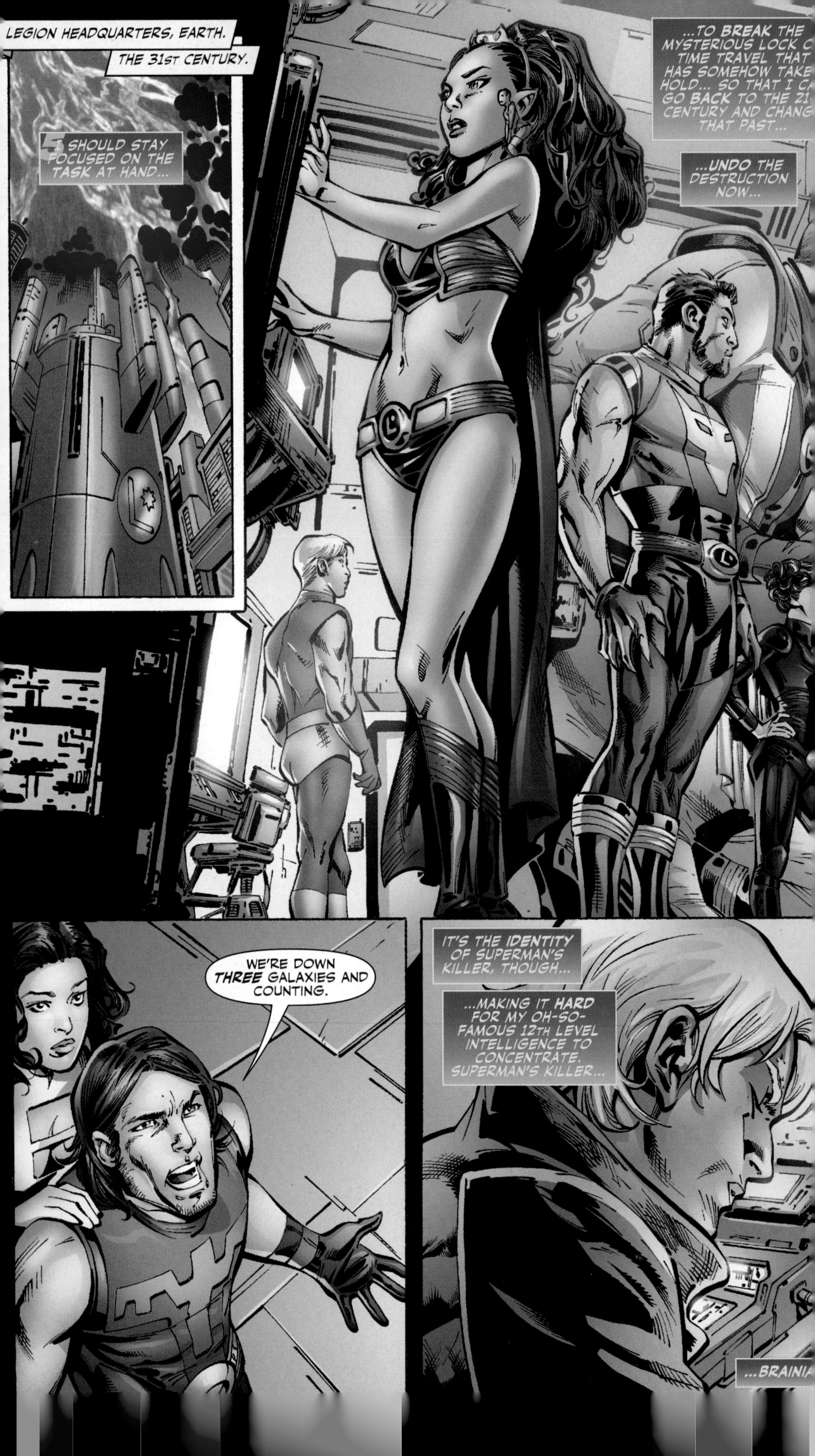
LEGION HEADQUARTERS, EARTH.
THE 31ST CENTURY.
I SHOULD STAY FOCUSED ON THE TASK AT HAND...
...TO BREAK THE MYSTERIOUS LOCK
TIME TRAVEL THAT HAS SOMEHOW TAKE
HOLD... SO THAT I C
GO BACK TO THE 21
CENTURY AND CHANG
THAT PAST...
...UNDO THE DESTRUCTION NOW...
WE'RE DOWN THREE GALAXIES AND COUNTING.
IT'S THE IDENTITY OF SUPERMAN'S KILLER, THOUGH...
...MAKING IT HARD FOR MY OH-SO-FAMOUS 12TH LEVEL INTELLIGENCE TO CONCENTRATE. SUPERMAN'S KILLER...
...BRAINIA

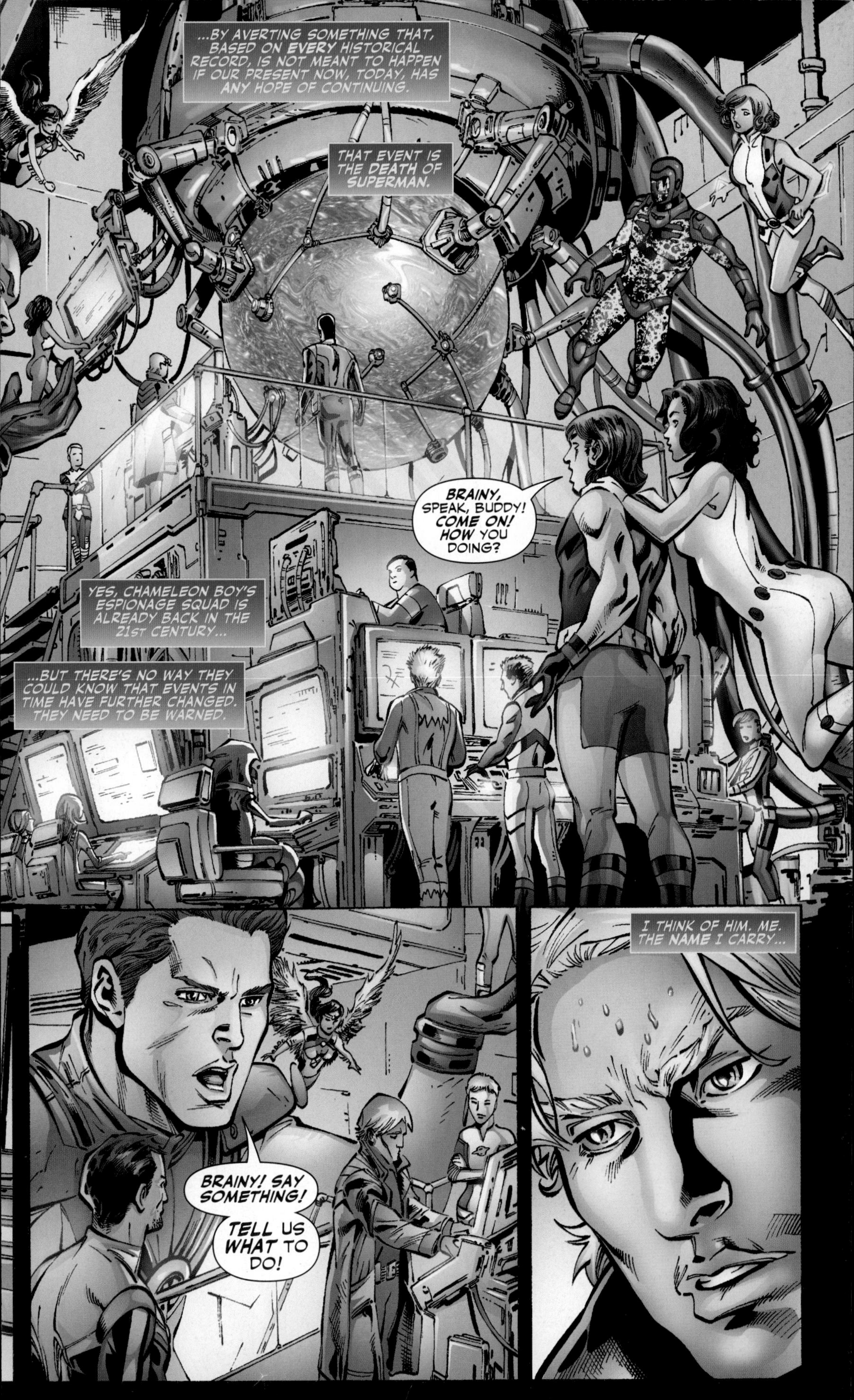
...BY AVERTING SOMETHING THAT, BASED ON EVERY HISTORICAL RECORD, IS NOT MEANT TO HAPPEN IF OUR PRESENT NOW, TODAY, HAS ANY HOPE OF CONTINUING.
THAT EVENT IS THE DEATH OF SUPERMAN.
BRAINY, SPEAK, BUDDY! COME ON! HOW YOU DOING?
YES, CHAMELEON BOY'S ESPIONAGE SQUAD IS ALREADY BACK IN THE 21ST CENTURY...
...BUT THERE'S NO WAY THEY COULD KNOW THAT EVENTS IN TIME HAVE FURTHER CHANGED. THEY NEED TO BE WARNED.
BRAINY! SAY SOMETHING!
TELL US WHAT TO DO!
I THINK OF HIM. ME. THE NAME I CARRY...

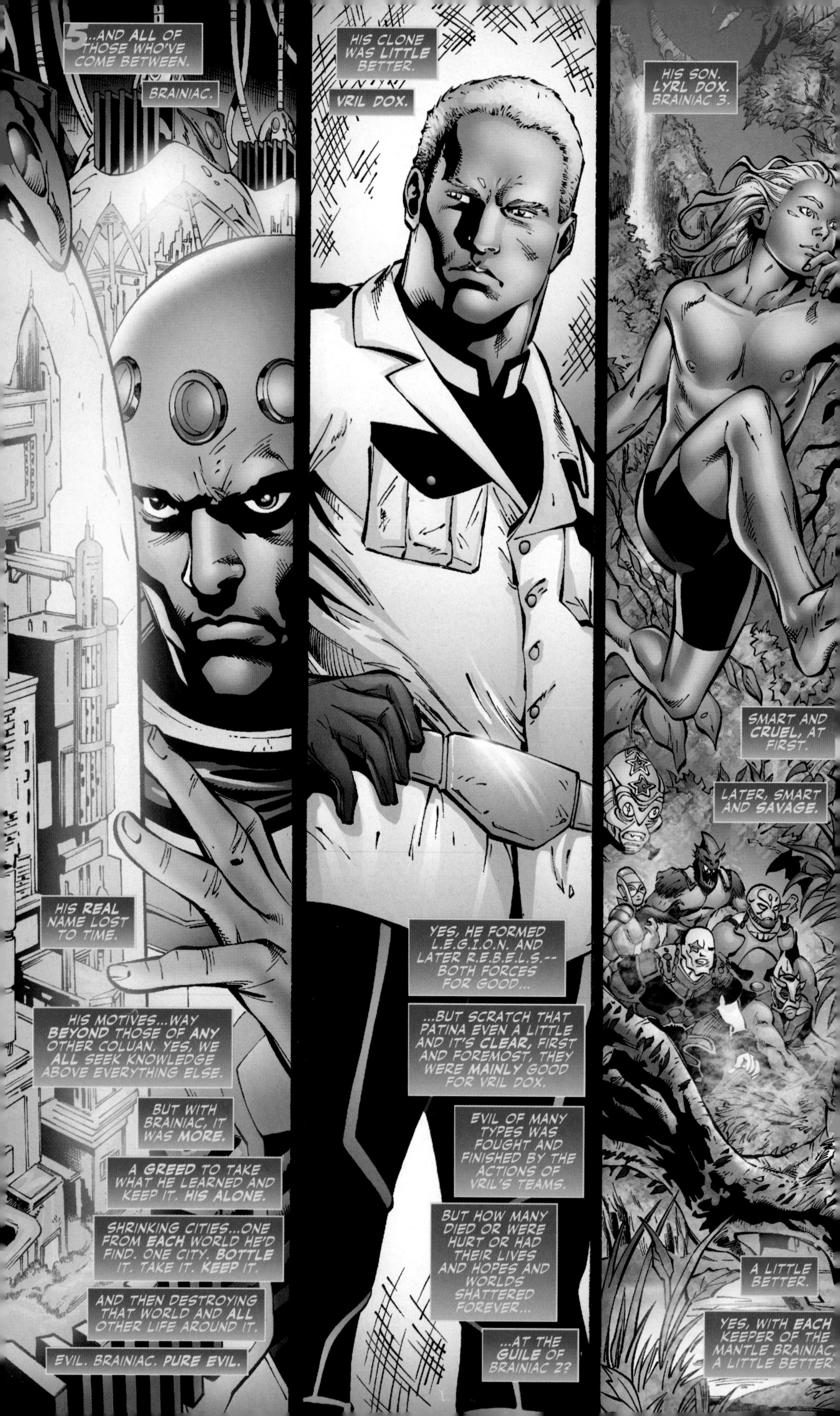
5
...AND ALL OF THOSE WHO'VE COME BETWEEN.
BRAINIAC.
HIS REAL NAME LOST TO TIME.
HIS MOTIVES...WAY BEYOND THOSE OF ANY OTHER COLUAN. YES, WE ALL SEEK KNOWLEDGE ABOVE EVERYTHING ELSE.
BUT WITH BRAINIAC, IT WAS MORE.
A GREED TO TAKE WHAT HE LEARNED AND KEEP IT. HIS ALONE.
SHRINKING CITIES...ONE FROM EACH WORLD HE'D FIND. ONE CITY. BOTTLE IT. TAKE IT. KEEP IT.
AND THEN DESTROYING THAT WORLD AND ALL OTHER LIFE AROUND IT.
EVIL. BRAINIAC. PURE EVIL.
HIS CLONE WAS LITTLE BETTER.
VRIL DOX.
YES, HE FORMED L.E.G.I.O.N. AND LATER R.E.B.E.L.S.--BOTH FORCES FOR GOOD...
...BUT SCRATCH THAT PATINA EVEN A LITTLE AND IT'S CLEAR, FIRST AND FOREMOST, THEY WERE MAINLY GOOD FOR VRIL DOX.
EVIL OF MANY TYPES WAS FOUGHT AND FINISHED BY THE ACTIONS OF VRIL'S TEAMS.
BUT HOW MANY DIED OR WERE HURT OR HAD THEIR LIVES AND HOPES AND WORLDS SHATTERED FOREVER...
...AT THE GUILE OF BRAINIAC 2?
HIS SON. LYRL DOX. BRAINIAC 3.
SMART AND CRUEL, AT FIRST.
LATER, SMART AND SAVAGE.
A LITTLE BETTER.
YES, WITH EACH KEEPER OF THE MANTLE BRAINIAC A LITTLE BETTER

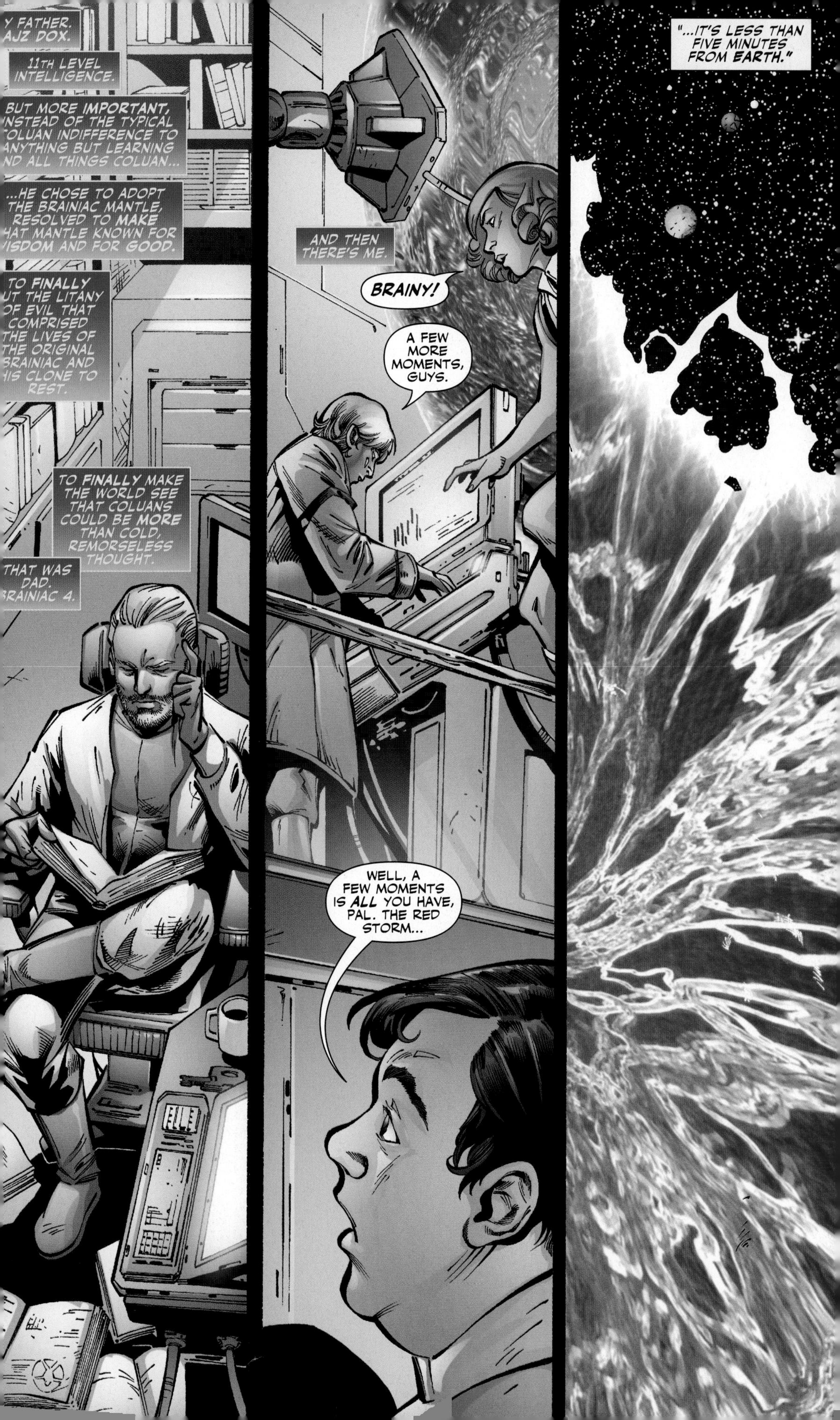
Y FATHER. AJZ DOX.
11TH LEVEL INTELLIGENCE.
BUT MORE IMPORTANT, NSTEAD OF THE TYPICAL OLUAN INDIFFERENCE TO ANYTHING BUT LEARNING ND ALL THINGS COLUAN...
...HE CHOSE TO ADOPT THE BRAINIAC MANTLE, RESOLVED TO MAKE THAT MANTLE KNOWN FOR WISDOM AND FOR GOOD.
TO FINALLY UT THE LITANY OF EVIL THAT COMPRISED THE LIVES OF THE ORIGINAL BRAINIAC AND HIS CLONE TO REST.
TO FINALLY MAKE THE WORLD SEE THAT COLUANS COULD BE MORE THAN COLD, REMORSELESS THOUGHT.
THAT WAS DAD. BRAINIAC 4.
AND THEN THERE'S ME.
BRAINY!
A FEW MORE MOMENTS, GUYS.
WELL, A FEW MOMENTS IS ALL YOU HAVE, PAL. THE RED STORM...
"...IT'S LESS THAN FIVE MINUTES FROM EARTH."

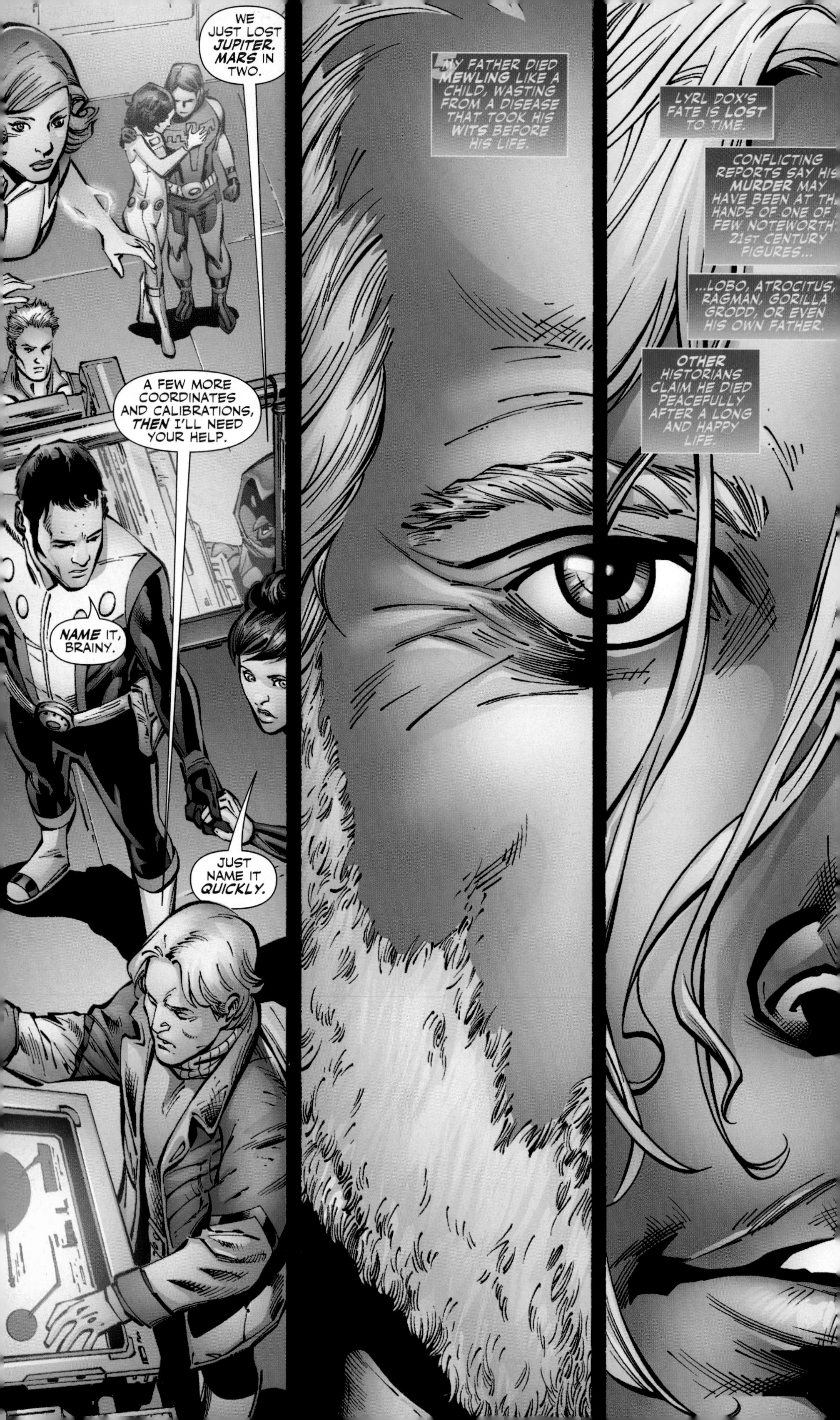

WE JUST LOST JUPITER. MARS IN TWO.
A FEW MORE COORDINATES AND CALIBRATIONS, THEN I'LL NEED YOUR HELP.
NAME IT, BRAINY.
JUST NAME IT QUICKLY.
MY FATHER DIED MEWLING LIKE A CHILD, WASTING FROM A DISEASE THAT TOOK HIS WITS BEFORE HIS LIFE.
LYRL DOX'S FATE IS LOST TO TIME.
CONFLICTING REPORTS SAY HIS MURDER MAY HAVE BEEN AT THE HANDS OF ONE OF FEW NOTEWORTHY 21ST CENTURY FIGURES...
...LOBO, ATROCITUS, RAGMAN, GORILLA GRODD, OR EVEN HIS OWN FATHER.
OTHER HISTORIANS CLAIM HE DIED PEACEFULLY AFTER A LONG AND HAPPY LIFE.

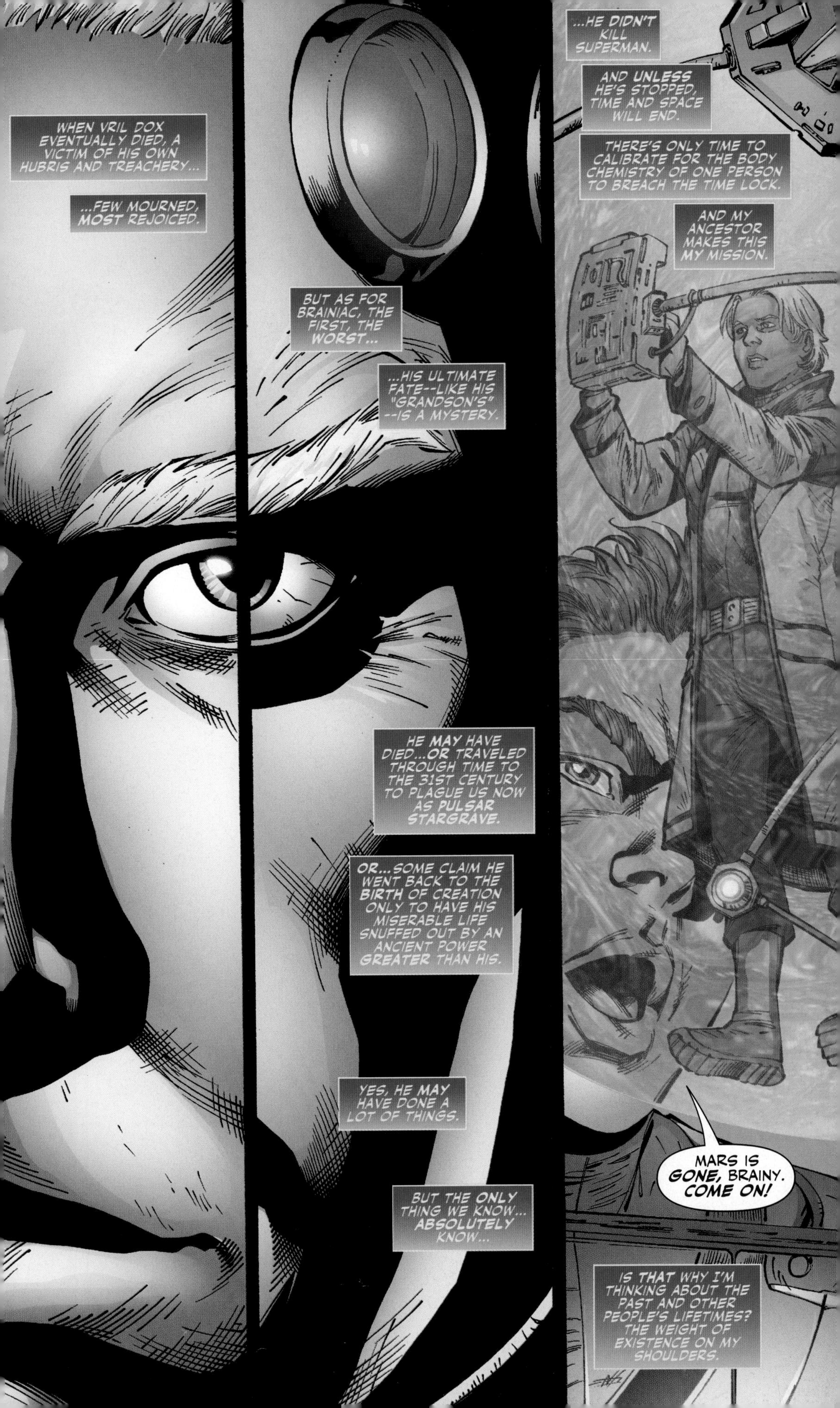
WHEN VRIL DOX EVENTUALLY DIED, A VICTIM OF HIS OWN HUBRIS AND TREACHERY...
...FEW MOURNED, MOST REJOICED.
BUT AS FOR BRAINIAC, THE FIRST, THE WORST...
...HIS ULTIMATE FATE--LIKE HIS "GRANDSON'S" --IS A MYSTERY.
HE MAY HAVE DIED...OR TRAVELED THROUGH TIME TO THE 31ST CENTURY TO PLAGUE US NOW AS PULSAR STARGRAVE.
OR...SOME CLAIM HE WENT BACK TO THE BIRTH OF CREATION ONLY TO HAVE HIS MISERABLE LIFE SNUFFED OUT BY AN ANCIENT POWER GREATER THAN HIS.
YES, HE MAY HAVE DONE A LOT OF THINGS.
BUT THE ONLY THING WE KNOW... ABSOLUTELY KNOW...
...HE DIDN'T KILL SUPERMAN.
AND UNLESS HE'S STOPPED, TIME AND SPACE WILL END.
THERE'S ONLY TIME TO CALIBRATE FOR THE BODY CHEMISTRY OF ONE PERSON TO BREACH THE TIME LOCK.
AND MY ANCESTOR MAKES THIS MY MISSION.
MARS IS GONE, BRAINY. COME ON!
IS THAT WHY I'M THINKING ABOUT THE PAST AND OTHER PEOPLE'S LIFETIMES? THE WEIGHT OF EXISTENCE ON MY SHOULDERS.

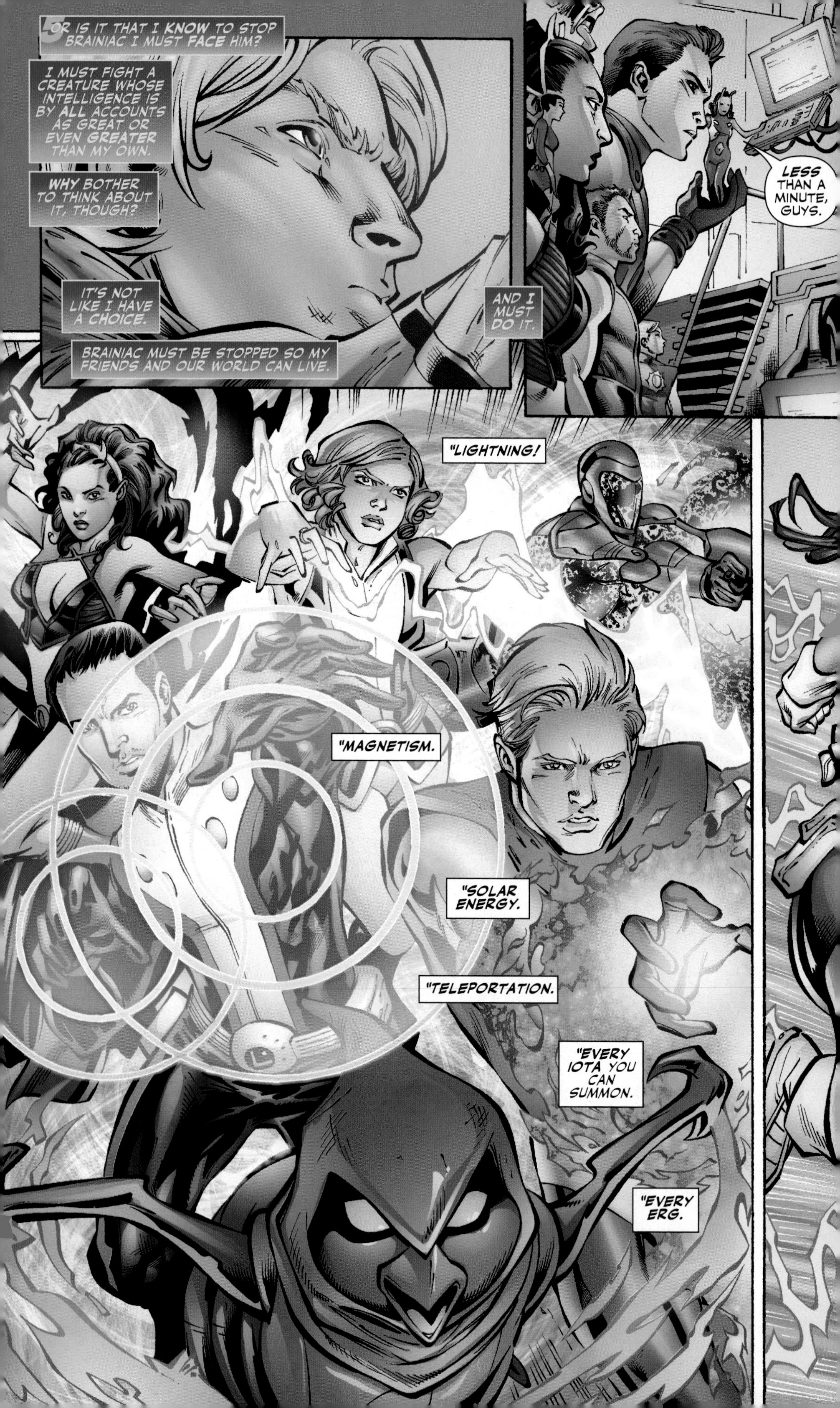

OR IS IT THAT I KNOW TO STOP BRAINIAC I MUST FACE HIM?
I MUST FIGHT A CREATURE WHOSE INTELLIGENCE IS BY ALL ACCOUNTS AS GREAT OR EVEN GREATER THAN MY OWN.
WHY BOTHER TO THINK ABOUT IT, THOUGH?
IT'S NOT LIKE I HAVE A CHOICE.
BRAINIAC MUST BE STOPPED SO MY FRIENDS AND OUR WORLD CAN LIVE.
AND I MUST DO IT.
LESS THAN A MINUTE, GUYS.
"LIGHTNING!
"MAGNETISM.
"SOLAR ENERGY.
"TELEPORTATION.
"EVERY IOTA YOU CAN SUMMON.
"EVERY ERG.

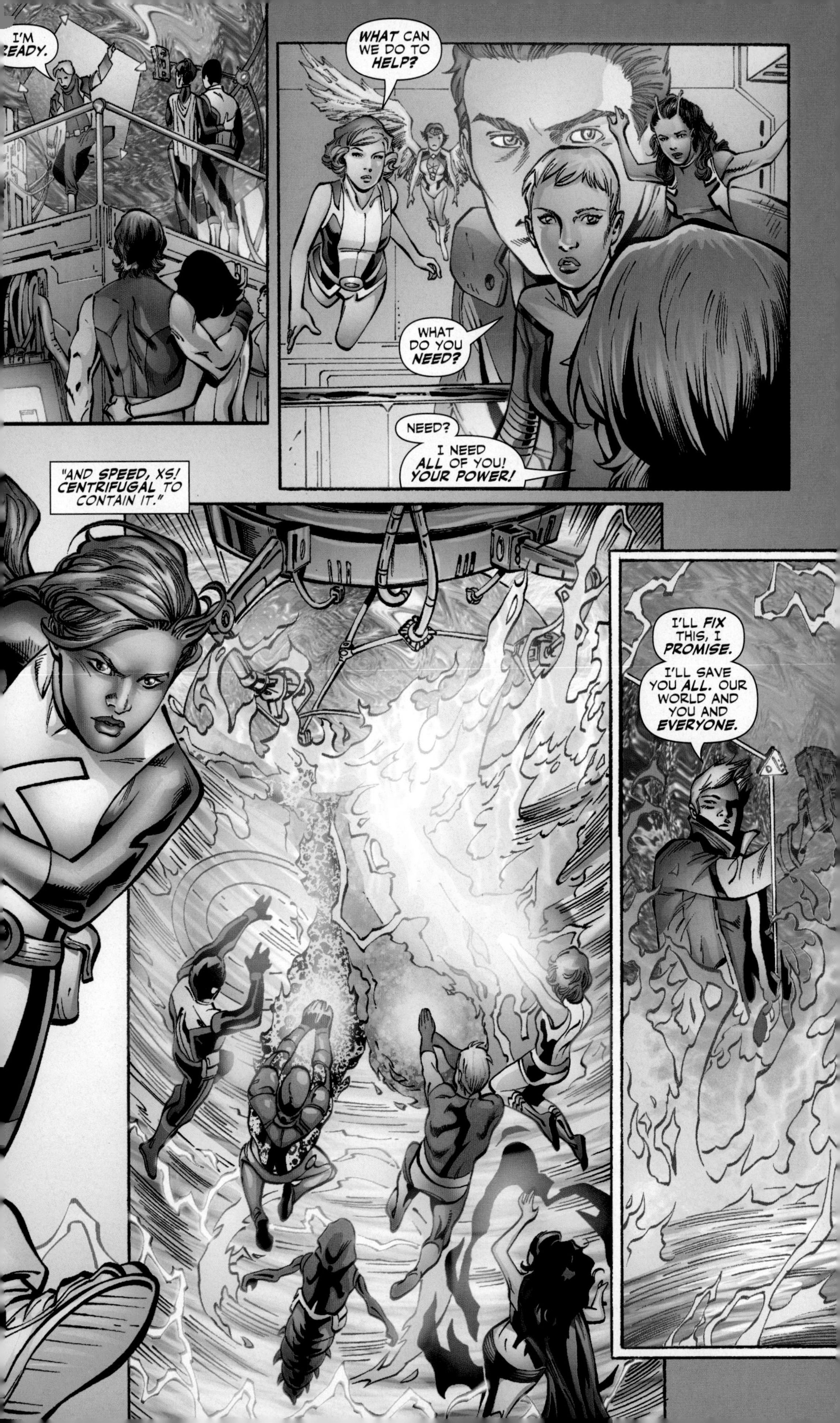

I'M READY.
WHAT CAN WE DO TO HELP?
WHAT DO YOU NEED?
NEED?
I NEED ALL OF YOU! YOUR POWER!
"AND SPEED, XS! CENTRIFUGAL TO CONTAIN IT."
I'LL FIX THIS, I PROMISE.
I'LL SAVE YOU ALL. OUR WORLD AND YOU AND EVERYONE.

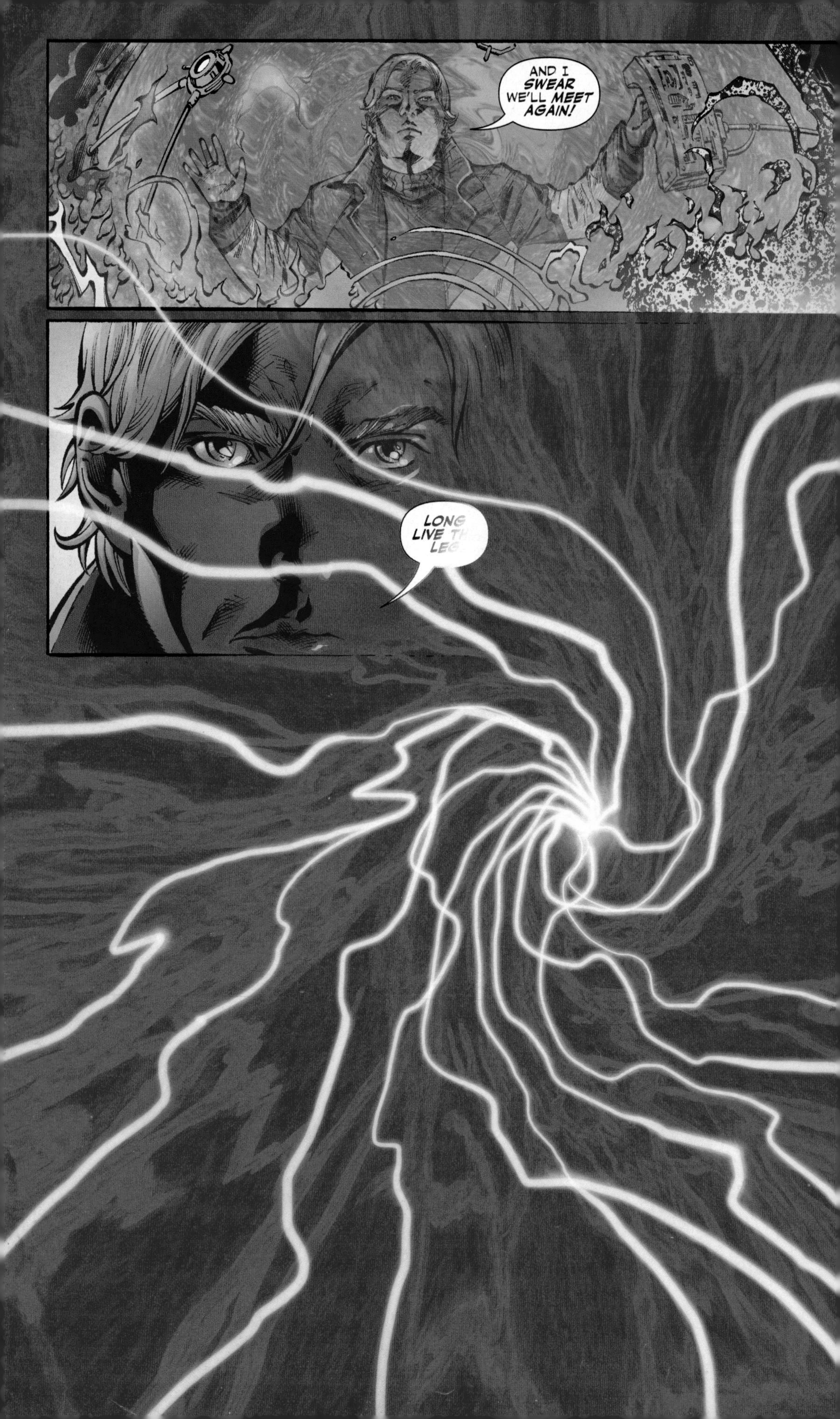
AND I SWEAR WE'LL MEET AGAIN!
LONG LIVE

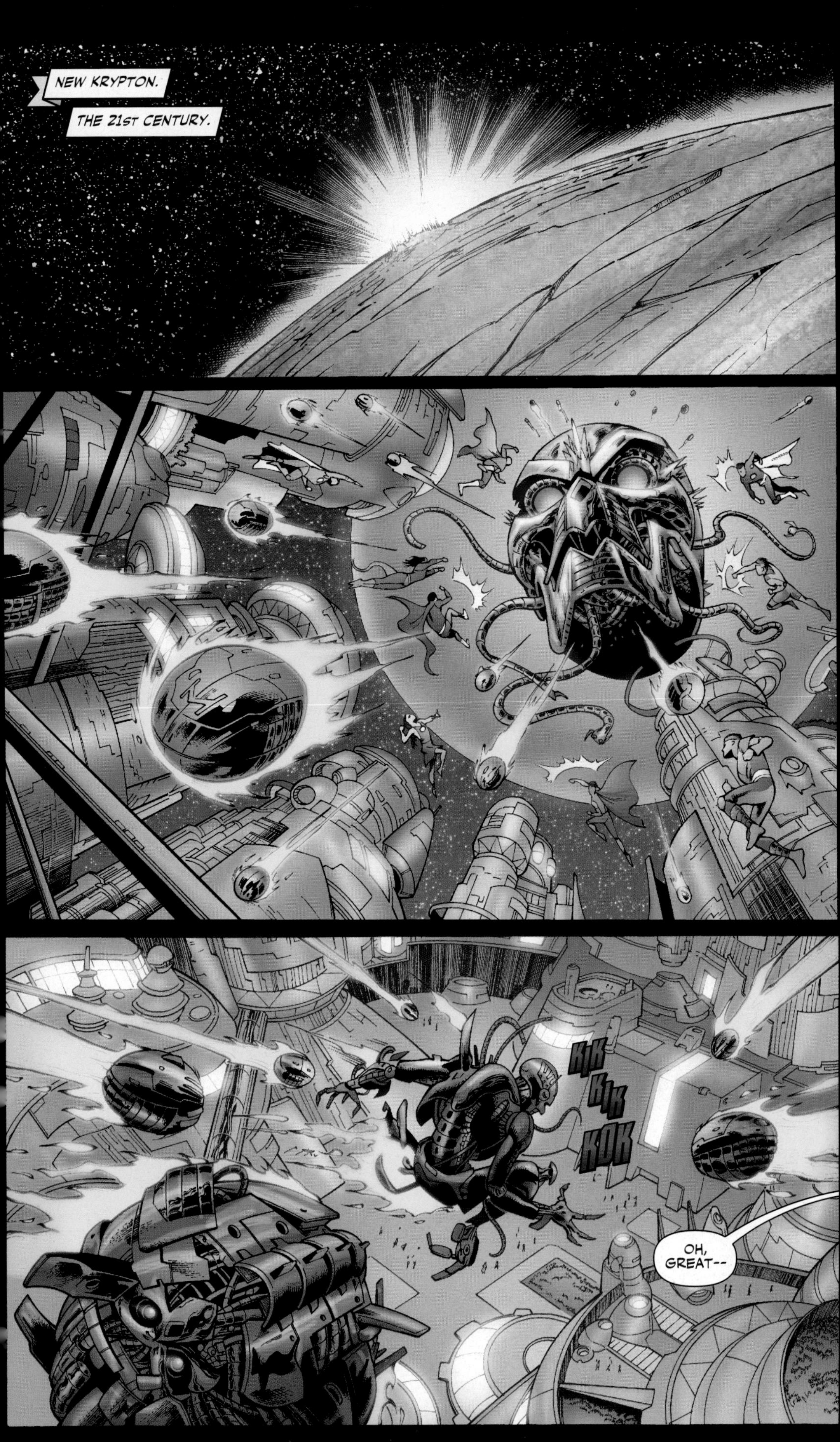
NEW KRYPTON.
THE 21ST CENTURY.
KIK KIK KOK
OH, GREAT--

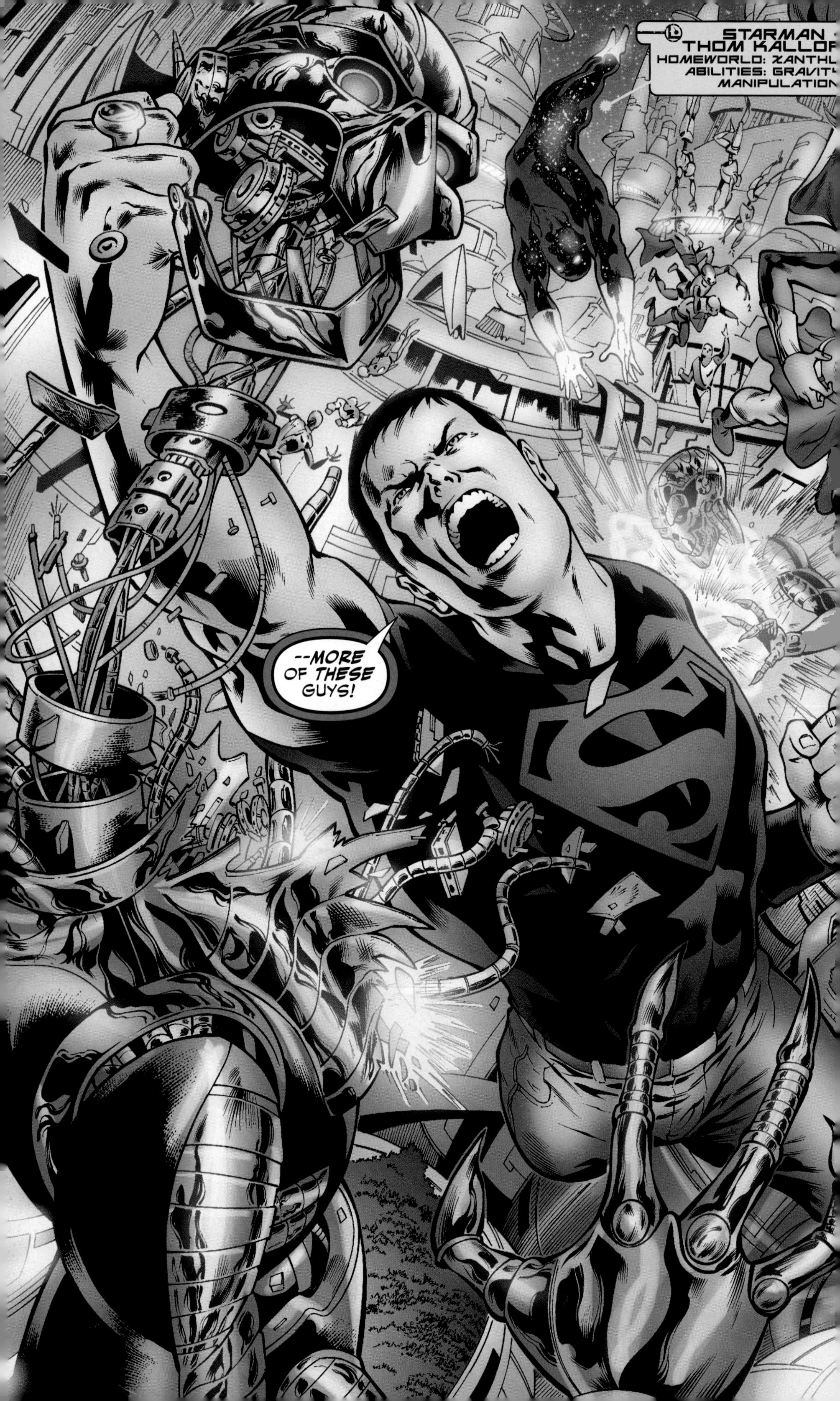
STARMAN
THOM KALLOR
HOMEWORLD: XANTHU
ABILITIES: GRAVITY
MANIPULATION
--MORE OF THESE GUYS!

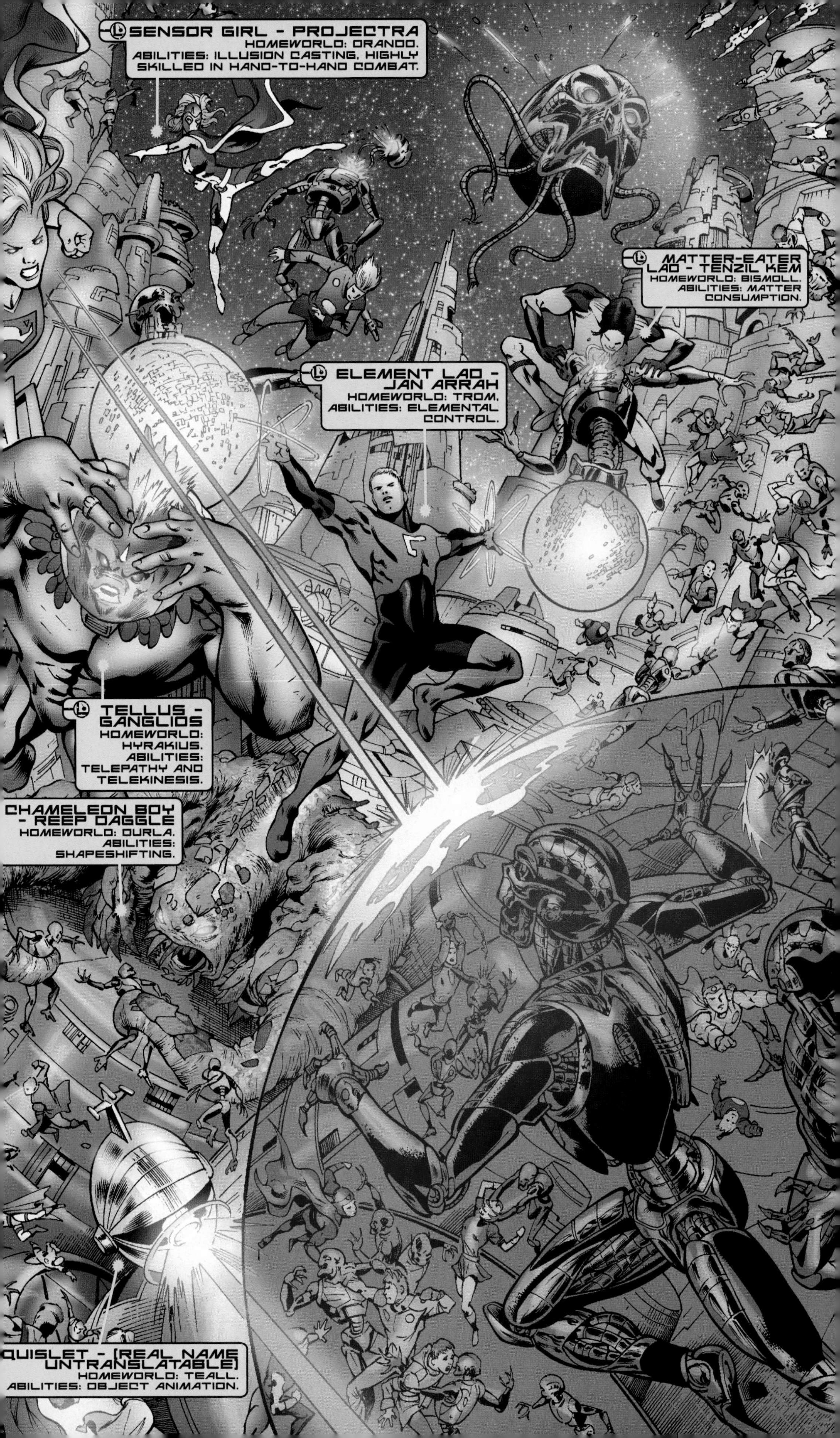
SENSOR GIRL - PROJECTRA
HOMEWORLD: ORANDO.
ABILITIES: ILLUSION CASTING, HIGHLY SKILLED IN HAND-TO-HAND COMBAT.
MATTER-EATER LAD - TENZIL KEM
HOMEWORLD: BISMOLL.
ABILITIES: MATTER CONSUMPTION.
ELEMENT LAD - JAN ARRAH
HOMEWORLD: TROM.
ABILITIES: ELEMENTAL CONTROL.
TELLUS - GANGLIOS
HOMEWORLD: HYRAKIUS.
ABILITIES: TELEPATHY AND TELEKINESIS.
CHAMELEON BOY - REEP DAGGLE
HOMEWORLD: DURLA.
ABILITIES: SHAPESHIFTING.
QUISLET - [REAL NAME UNTRANSLATABLE]
HOMEWORLD: TEALL.
ABILITIES: OBJECT ANIMATION.

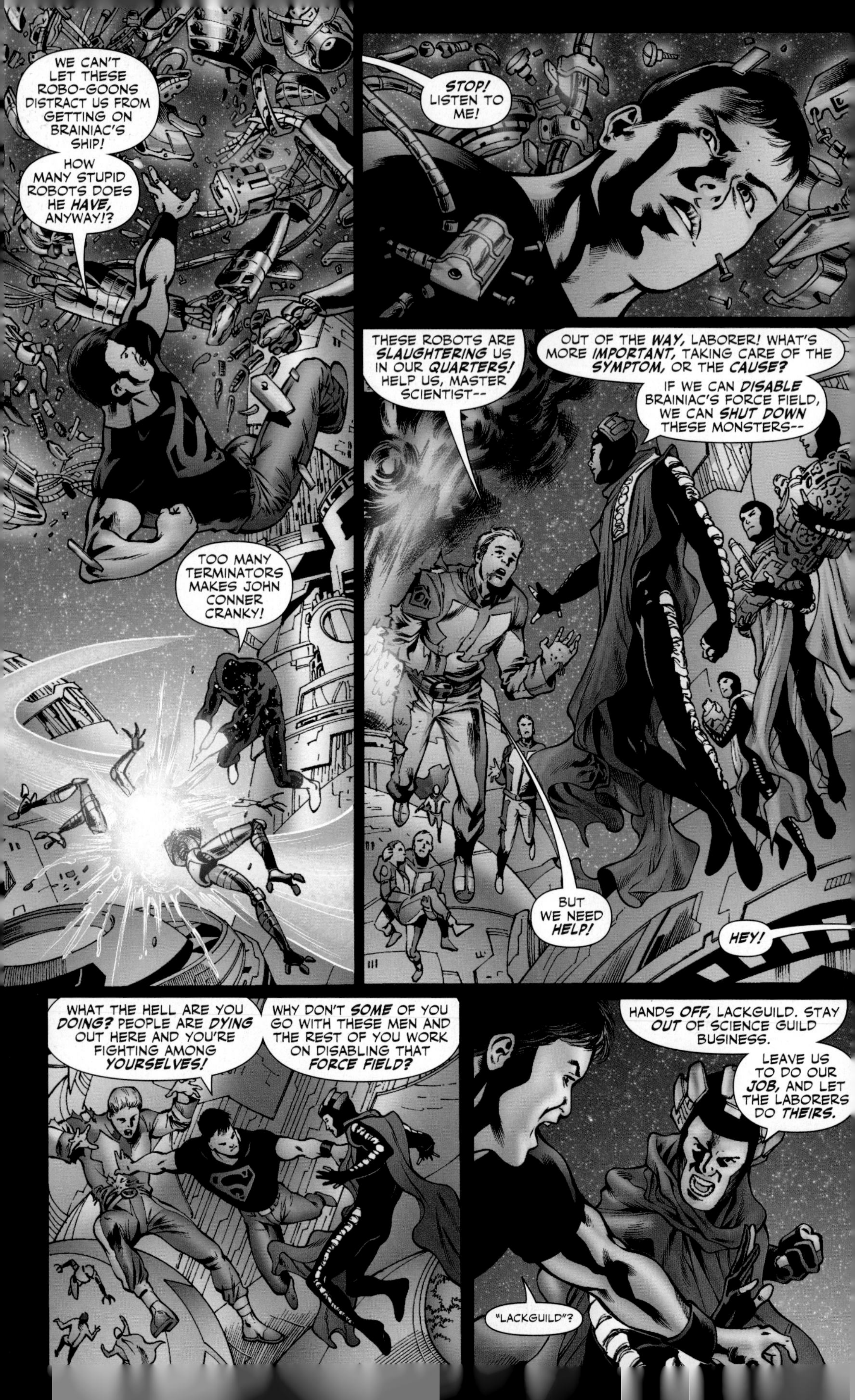

WE CAN'T LET THESE ROBO-GOONS DISTRACT US FROM GETTING ON BRAINIAC'S SHIP!
HOW MANY STUPID ROBOTS DOES HE HAVE, ANYWAY!?
TOO MANY TERMINATORS MAKES JOHN CONNER CRANKY!
STOP! LISTEN TO ME!
THESE ROBOTS ARE SLAUGHTERING US IN OUR QUARTERS! HELP US, MASTER SCIENTIST--
OUT OF THE WAY, LABORER! WHAT'S MORE IMPORTANT, TAKING CARE OF THE SYMPTOM, OR THE CAUSE?
IF WE CAN DISABLE BRAINIAC'S FORCE FIELD, WE CAN SHUT DOWN THESE MONSTERS--
BUT WE NEED HELP!
HEY!
WHAT THE HELL ARE YOU DOING? PEOPLE ARE DYING OUT HERE AND YOU'RE FIGHTING AMONG YOURSELVES!
WHY DON'T SOME OF YOU GO WITH THESE MEN AND THE REST OF YOU WORK ON DISABLING THAT FORCE FIELD?
HANDS OFF, LACKGUILD. STAY OUT OF SCIENCE GUILD BUSINESS.
LEAVE US TO DO OUR JOB, AND LET THE LABORERS DO THEIRS.
"LACKGUILD"?

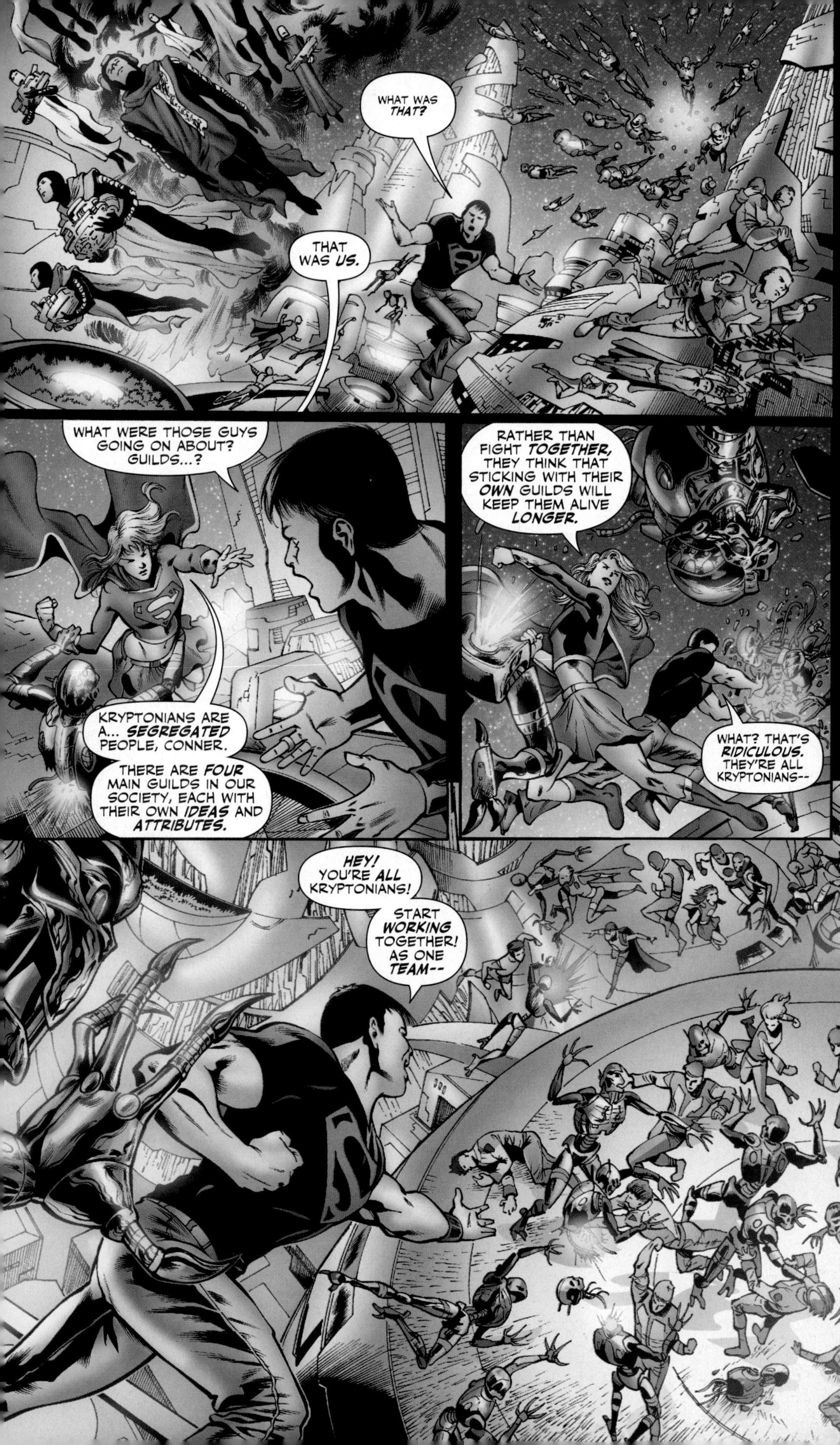

WHAT WAS THAT?
THAT WAS US.
WHAT WERE THOSE GUYS GOING ON ABOUT? GUILDS...?
KRYPTONIANS ARE A... SEGREGATED PEOPLE, CONNER.
THERE ARE FOUR MAIN GUILDS IN OUR SOCIETY, EACH WITH THEIR OWN IDEAS AND ATTRIBUTES.
RATHER THAN FIGHT TOGETHER, THEY THINK THAT STICKING WITH THEIR OWN GUILDS WILL KEEP THEM ALIVE LONGER.
WHAT? THAT'S RIDICULOUS. THEY'RE ALL KRYPTONIANS--
HEY! YOU'RE ALL KRYPTONIANS!
START WORKING TOGETHER! AS ONE TEAM--

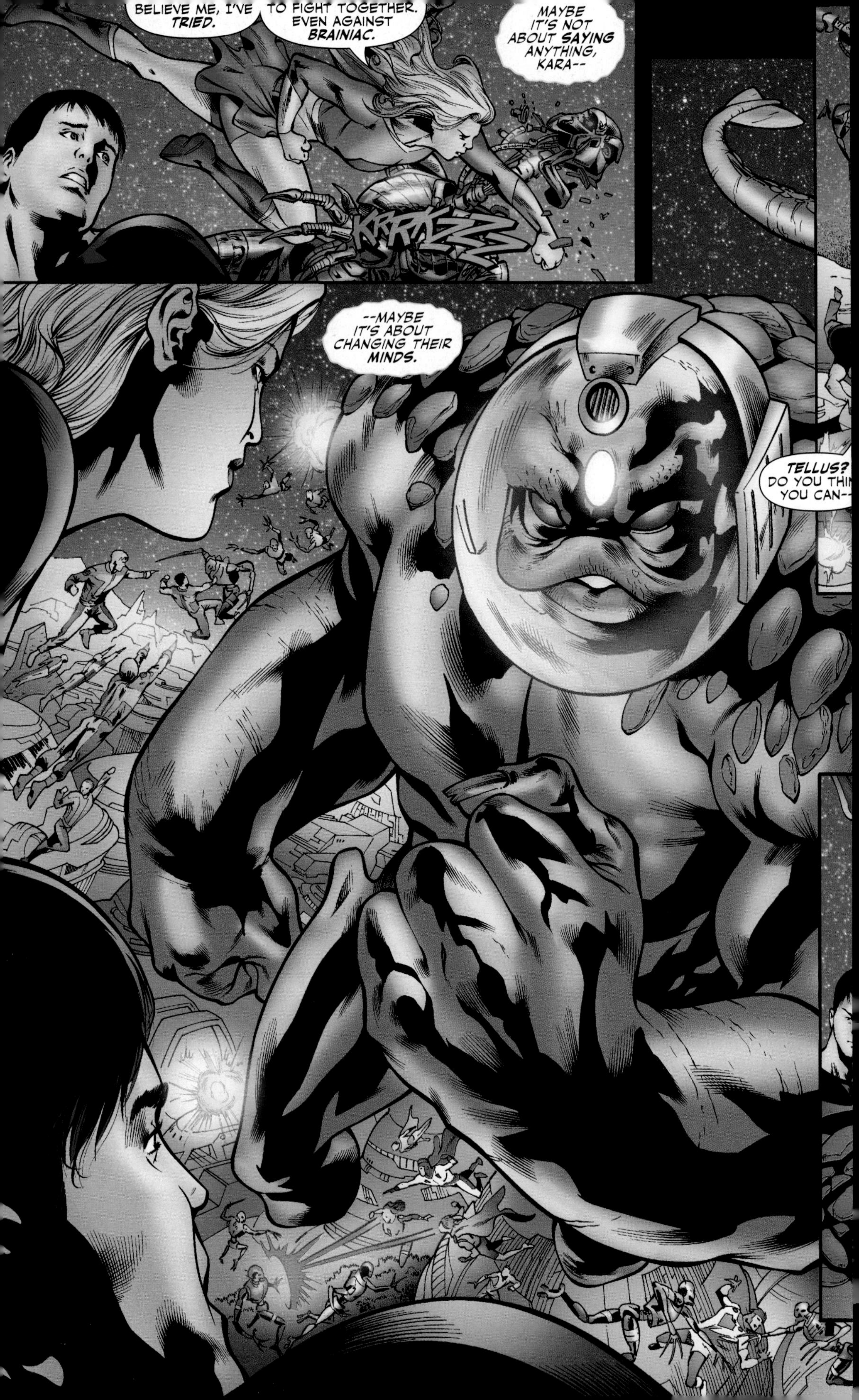
BELIEVE ME, I'VE *TRIED*.
TO FIGHT TOGETHER. EVEN AGAINST *BRAINIAC*.
MAYBE IT'S NOT ABOUT *SAYING* ANYTHING, KARA--
--MAYBE IT'S ABOUT CHANGING THEIR *MINDS*.
TELLUS? DO YOU THI
YOU CAN--

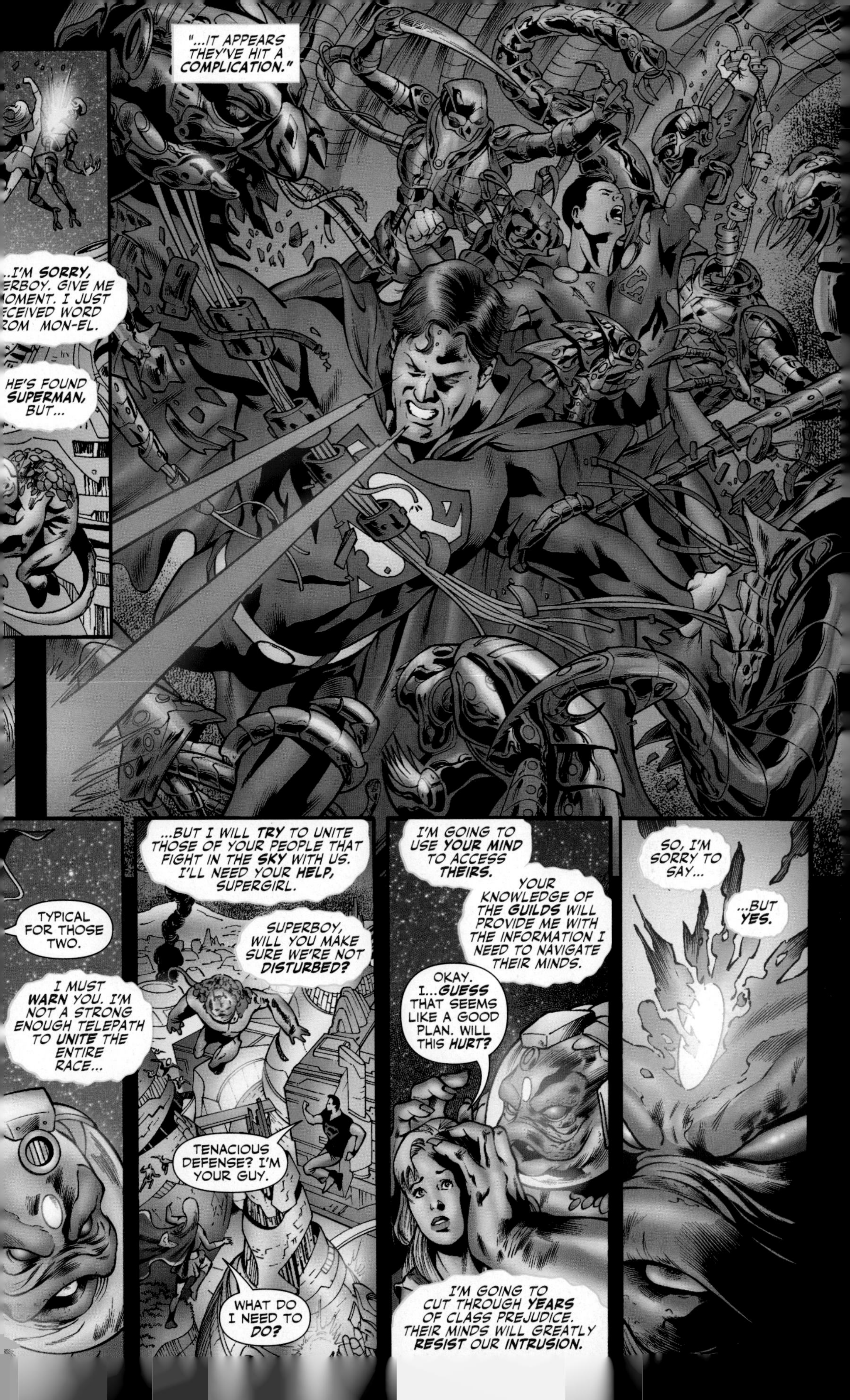
"...IT APPEARS THEY'VE HIT A COMPLICATION."
...I'M SORRY, ERBOY. GIVE ME OMENT. I JUST ECEIVED WORD ROM MON-EL.
HE'S FOUND SUPERMAN, BUT...
TYPICAL FOR THOSE TWO.
I MUST WARN YOU. I'M NOT A STRONG ENOUGH TELEPATH TO UNITE THE ENTIRE RACE...
...BUT I WILL TRY TO UNITE THOSE OF YOUR PEOPLE THAT FIGHT IN THE SKY WITH US. I'LL NEED YOUR HELP, SUPERGIRL.
SUPERBOY, WILL YOU MAKE SURE WE'RE NOT DISTURBED?
TENACIOUS DEFENSE? I'M YOUR GUY.
WHAT DO I NEED TO DO?
I'M GOING TO USE YOUR MIND TO ACCESS THEIRS.
YOUR KNOWLEDGE OF THE GUILDS WILL PROVIDE ME WITH THE INFORMATION I NEED TO NAVIGATE THEIR MINDS.
OKAY. I...GUESS THAT SEEMS LIKE A GOOD PLAN. WILL THIS HURT?
I'M GOING TO CUT THROUGH YEARS OF CLASS PREJUDICE. THEIR MINDS WILL GREATLY RESIST OUR INTRUSION.
SO, I'M SORRY TO SAY...
...BUT YES.

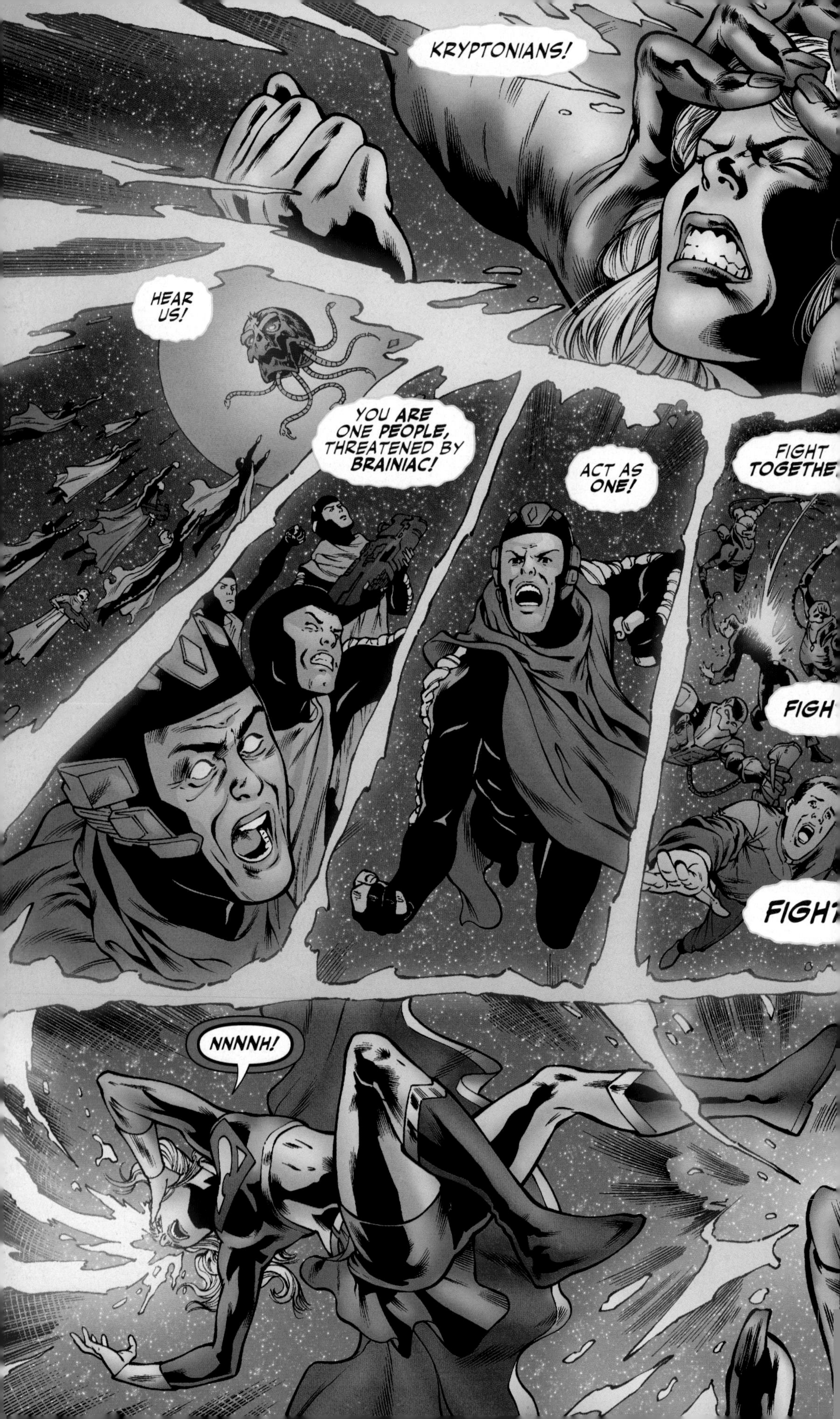
KRYPTONIANS!
HEAR US!
YOU ARE ONE PEOPLE, THREATENED BY BRAINIAC!
ACT AS ONE!
FIGHT TOGETHE
FIGH
FIGH
NNNNH!

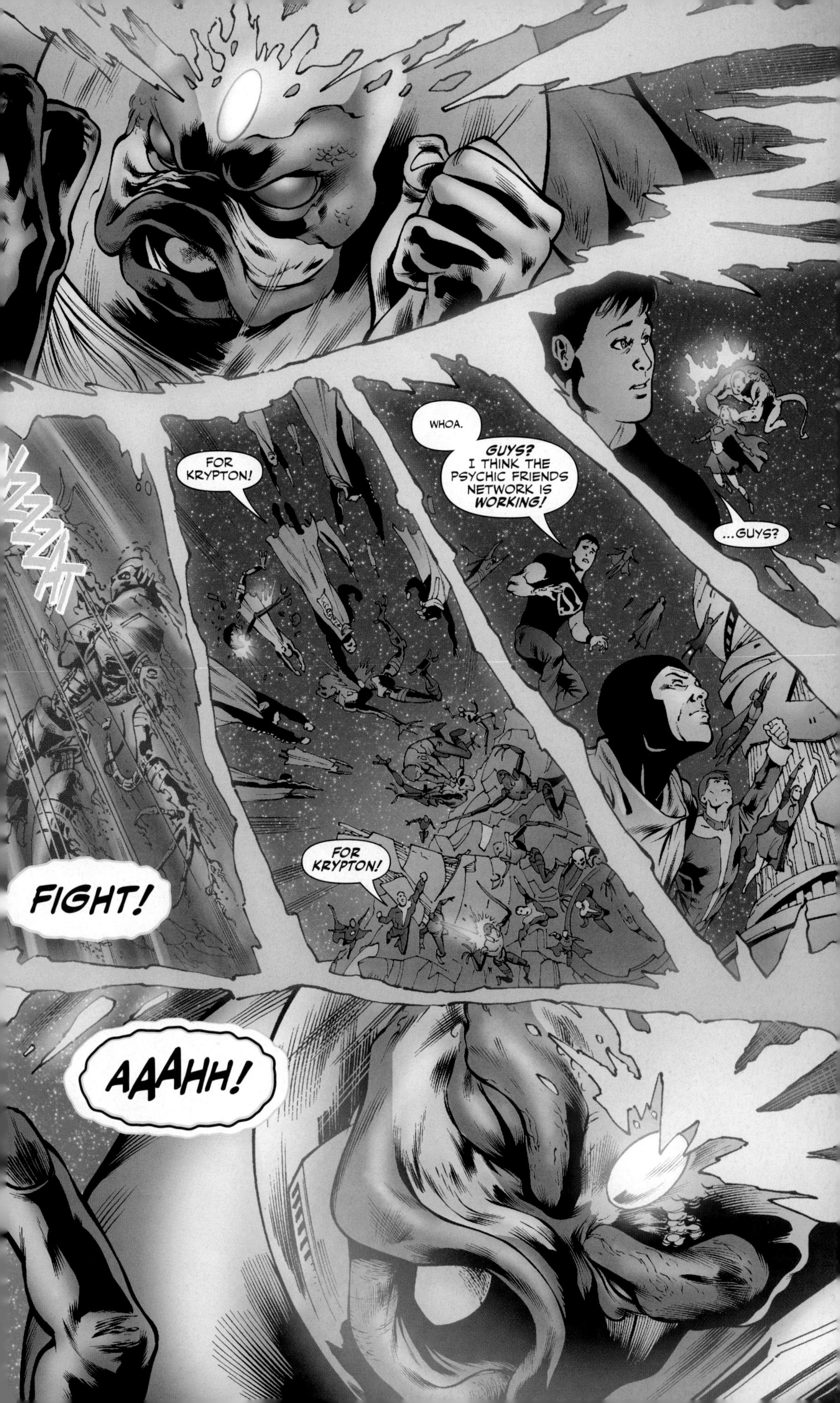
ZZZZAT
FOR KRYPTON!
WHOA.
GUYS? I THINK THE PSYCHIC FRIENDS NETWORK IS WORKING!
...GUYS?
FOR KRYPTON!
FIGHT!
AAAHH!

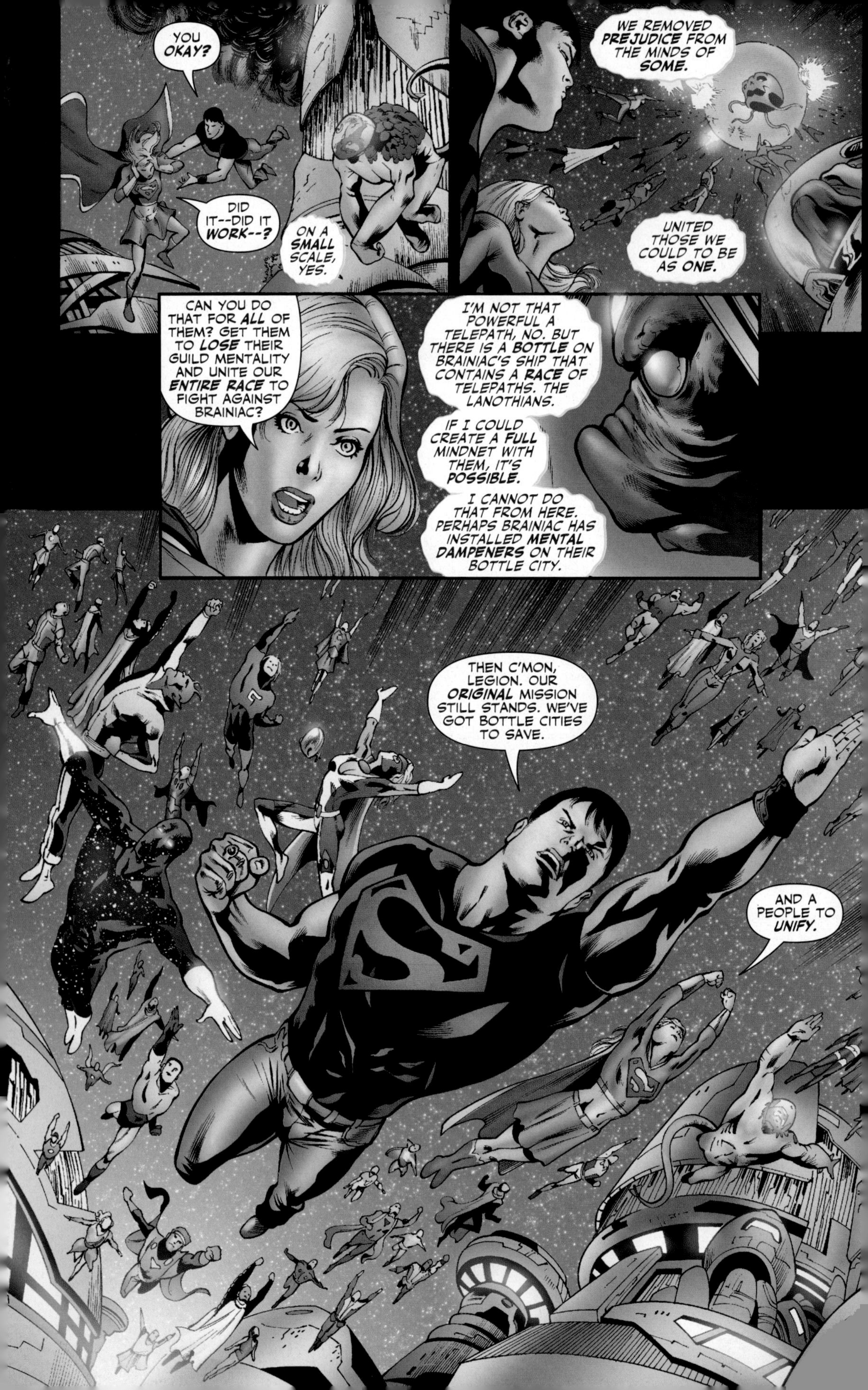
YOU OKAY?
DID IT--DID IT WORK--?
ON A SMALL SCALE, YES.
WE REMOVED PREJUDICE FROM THE MINDS OF SOME.
UNITED THOSE WE COULD TO BE AS ONE.
CAN YOU DO THAT FOR ALL OF THEM? GET THEM TO LOSE THEIR GUILD MENTALITY AND UNITE OUR ENTIRE RACE TO FIGHT AGAINST BRAINIAC?
I'M NOT THAT POWERFUL A TELEPATH, NO. BUT THERE IS A BOTTLE ON BRAINIAC'S SHIP THAT CONTAINS A RACE OF TELEPATHS. THE LANOTHIANS.
IF I COULD CREATE A FULL MINDNET WITH THEM, IT'S POSSIBLE.
I CANNOT DO THAT FROM HERE. PERHAPS BRAINIAC HAS INSTALLED MENTAL DAMPENERS ON THEIR BOTTLE CITY.
THEN C'MON, LEGION. OUR ORIGINAL MISSION STILL STANDS. WE'VE GOT BOTTLE CITIES TO SAVE.
AND A PEOPLE TO UNIFY.

cover by **GEORGE PÉREZ** & **HI-FI**

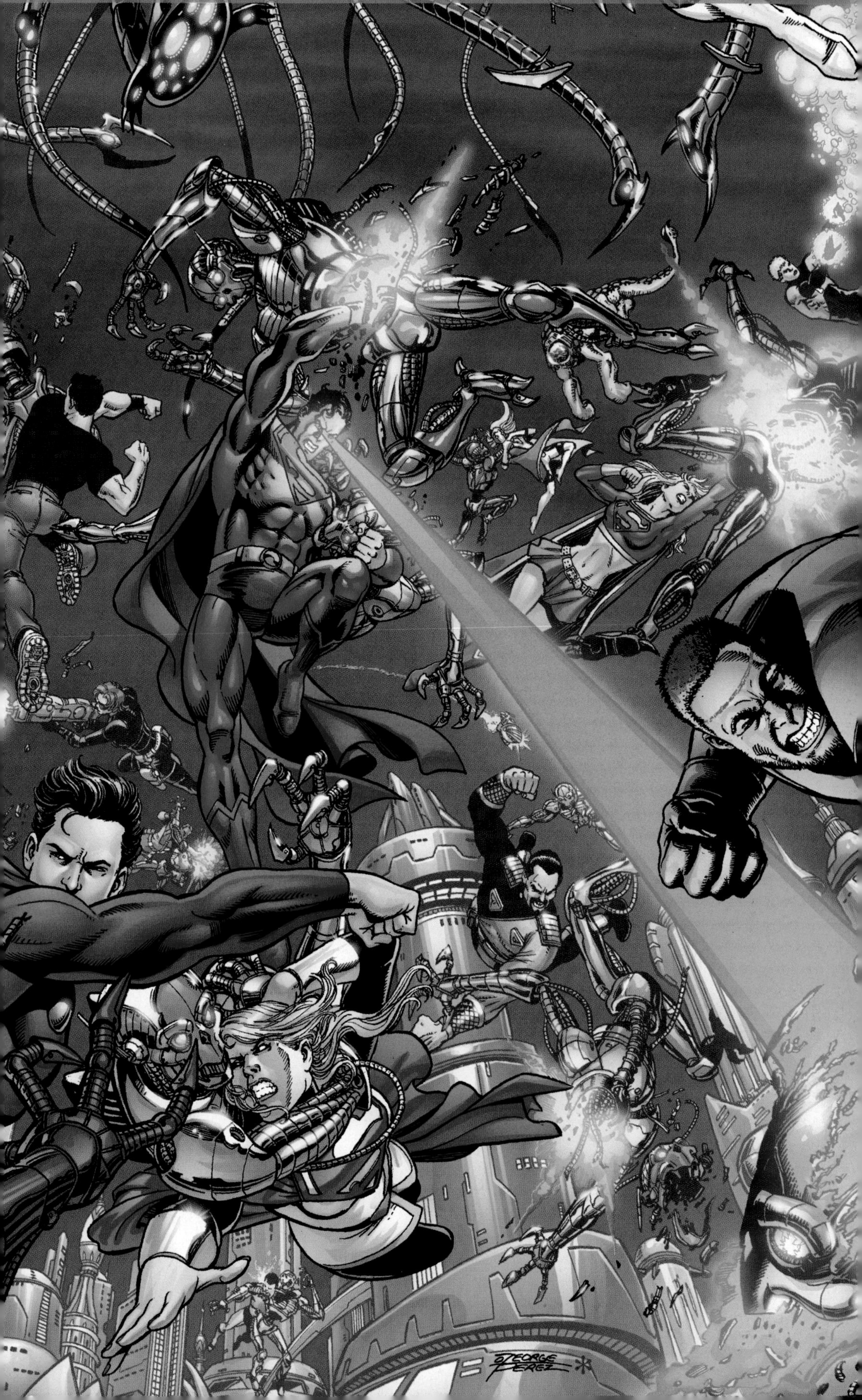

'07 GEORGE PÉREZ

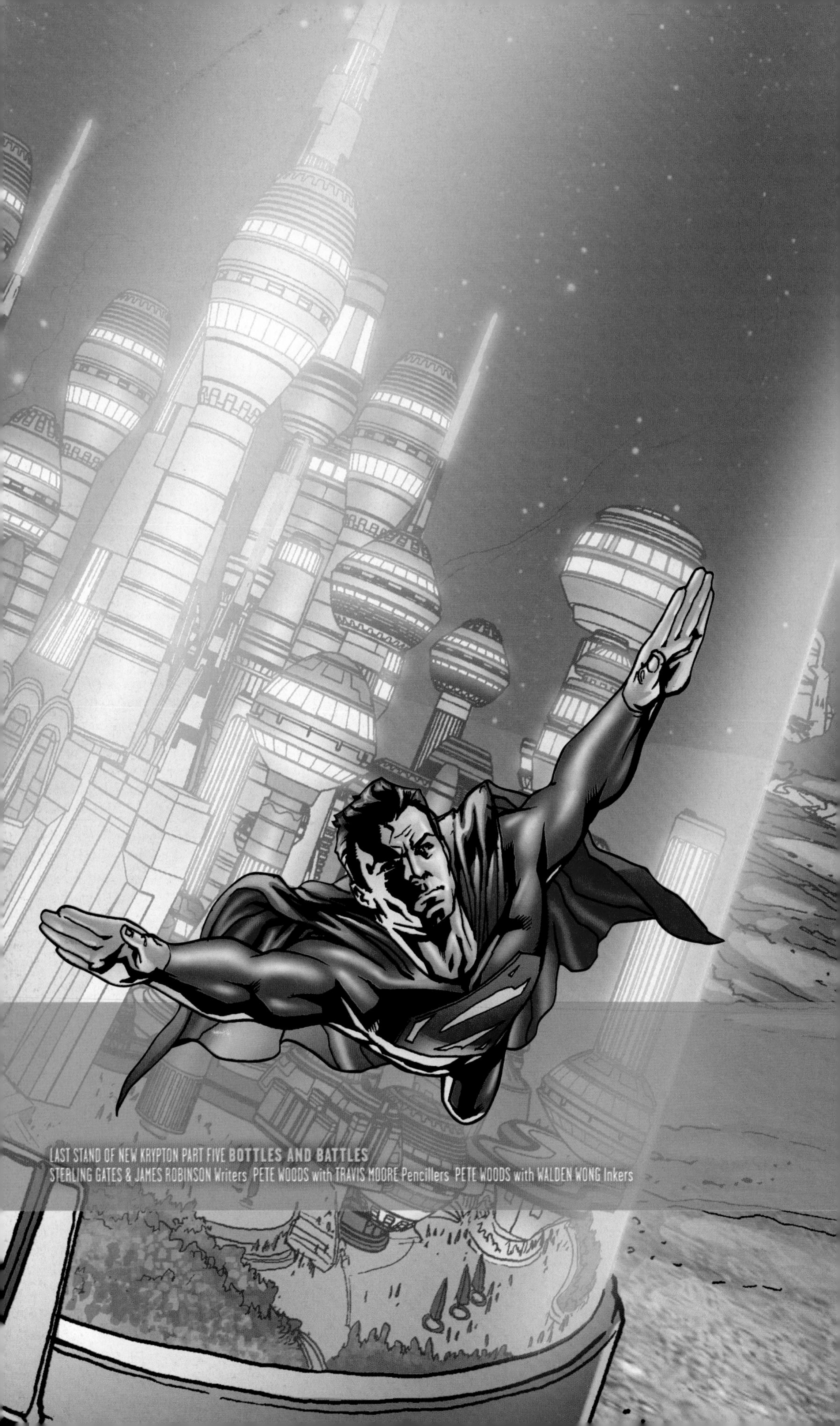
LAST STAND OF NEW KRYPTON PART FIVE BOTTLES AND BATTLES
STERLING GATES & JAMES ROBINSON Writers PETE WOODS with TRAVIS MOORE Pencillers PETE WOODS with WALDEN WONG Inkers

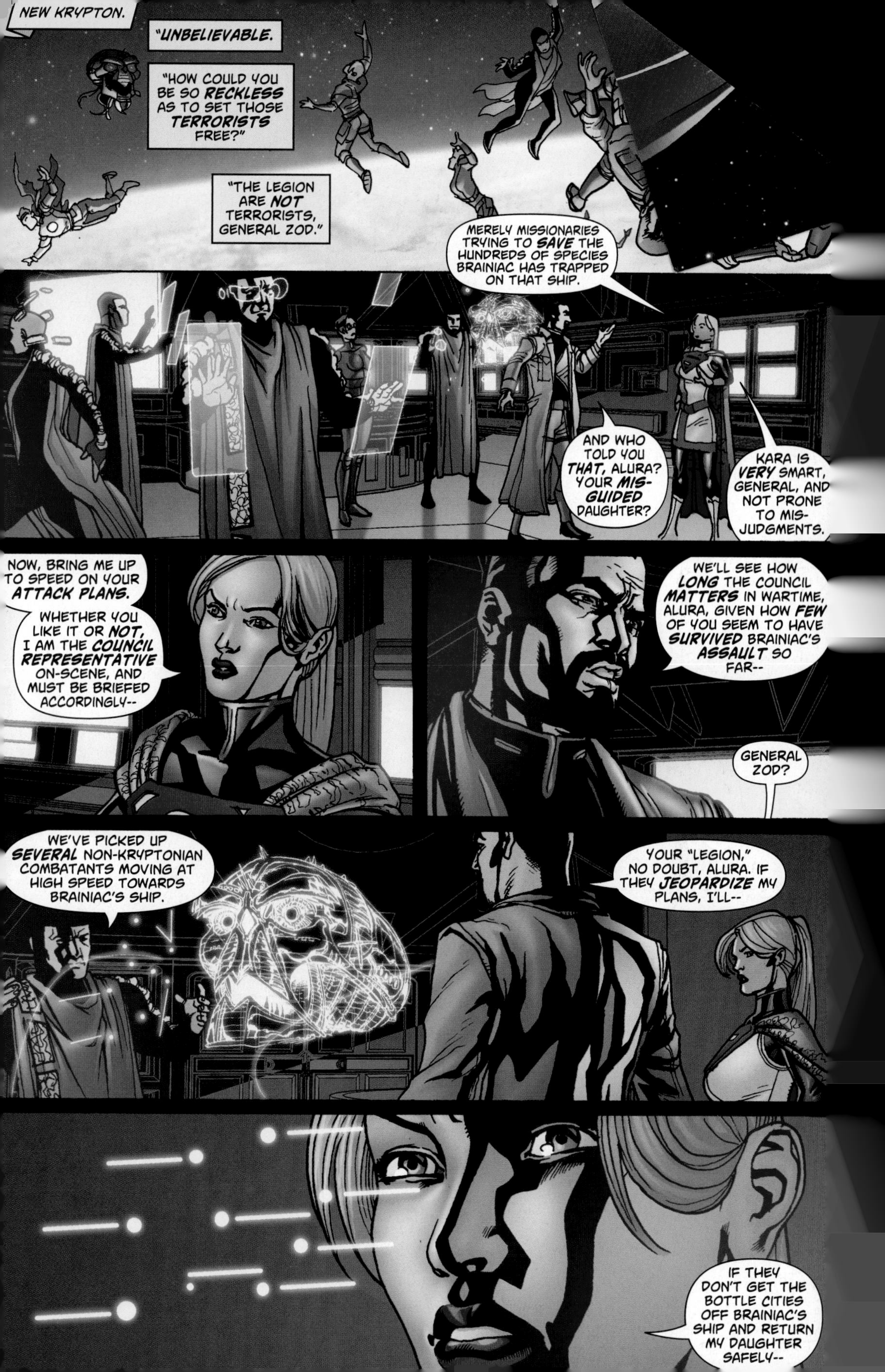
NEW KRYPTON.
"UNBELIEVABLE.
"HOW COULD YOU BE SO RECKLESS AS TO SET THOSE TERRORISTS FREE?"
"THE LEGION ARE NOT TERRORISTS, GENERAL ZOD."
MERELY MISSIONARIES TRYING TO SAVE THE HUNDREDS OF SPECIES BRAINIAC HAS TRAPPED ON THAT SHIP.
AND WHO TOLD YOU THAT, ALURA? YOUR MIS-GUIDED DAUGHTER?
KARA IS VERY SMART, GENERAL, AND NOT PRONE TO MIS-JUDGMENTS.
NOW, BRING ME UP TO SPEED ON YOUR ATTACK PLANS.
WHETHER YOU LIKE IT OR NOT, I AM THE COUNCIL REPRESENTATIVE ON-SCENE, AND MUST BE BRIEFED ACCORDINGLY--
WE'LL SEE HOW LONG THE COUNCIL MATTERS IN WARTIME, ALURA, GIVEN HOW FEW OF YOU SEEM TO HAVE SURVIVED BRAINIAC'S ASSAULT SO FAR--
GENERAL ZOD?
WE'VE PICKED UP SEVERAL NON-KRYPTONIAN COMBATANTS MOVING AT HIGH SPEED TOWARDS BRAINIAC'S SHIP.
YOUR "LEGION," NO DOUBT, ALURA. IF THEY JEOPARDIZE MY PLANS, I'LL--
IF THEY DON'T GET THE BOTTLE CITIES OFF BRAINIAC'S SHIP AND RETURN MY DAUGHTER SAFELY--

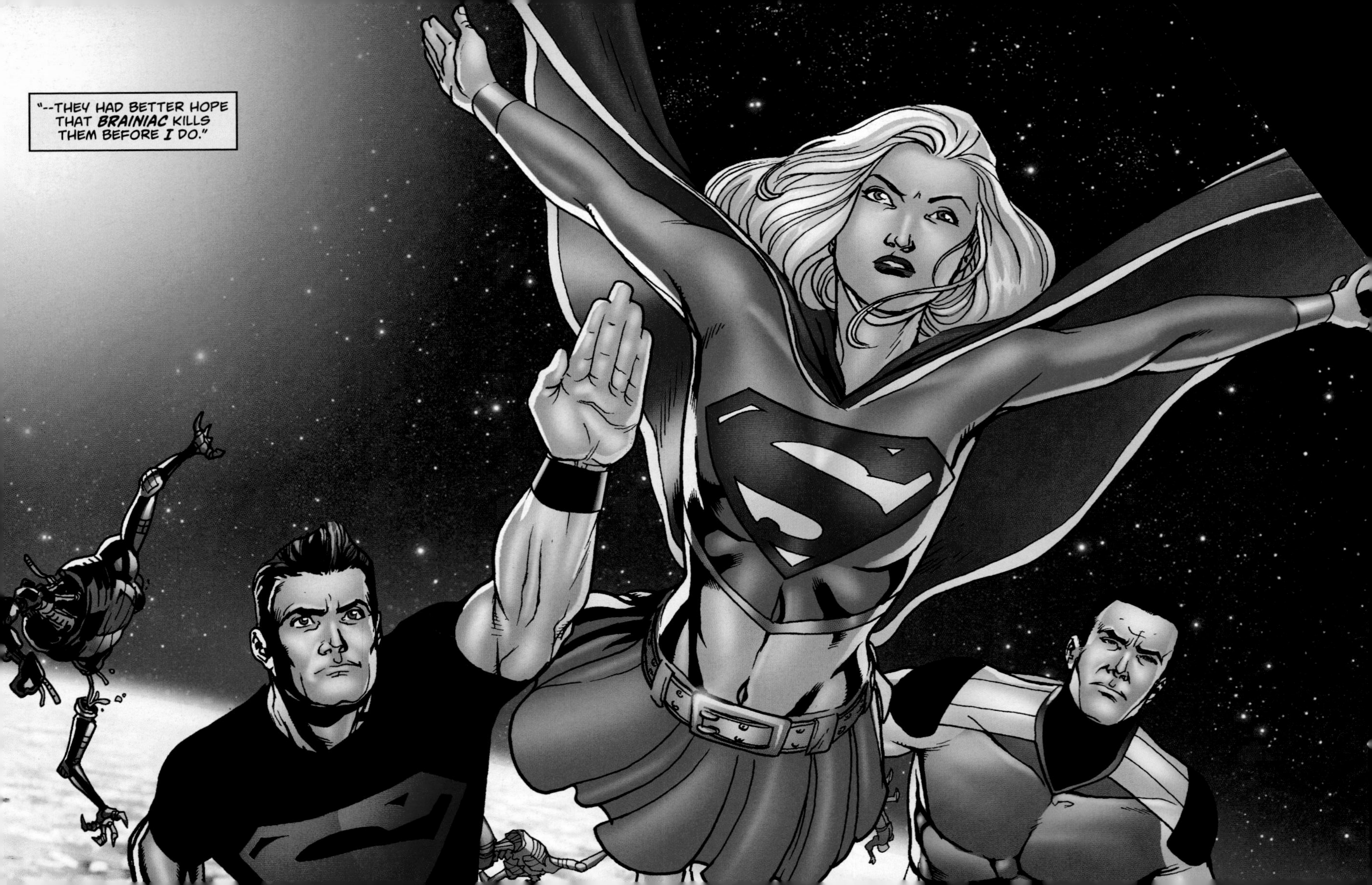
"--THEY HAD BETTER HOPE THAT BRAINIAC KILLS THEM BEFORE I DO."

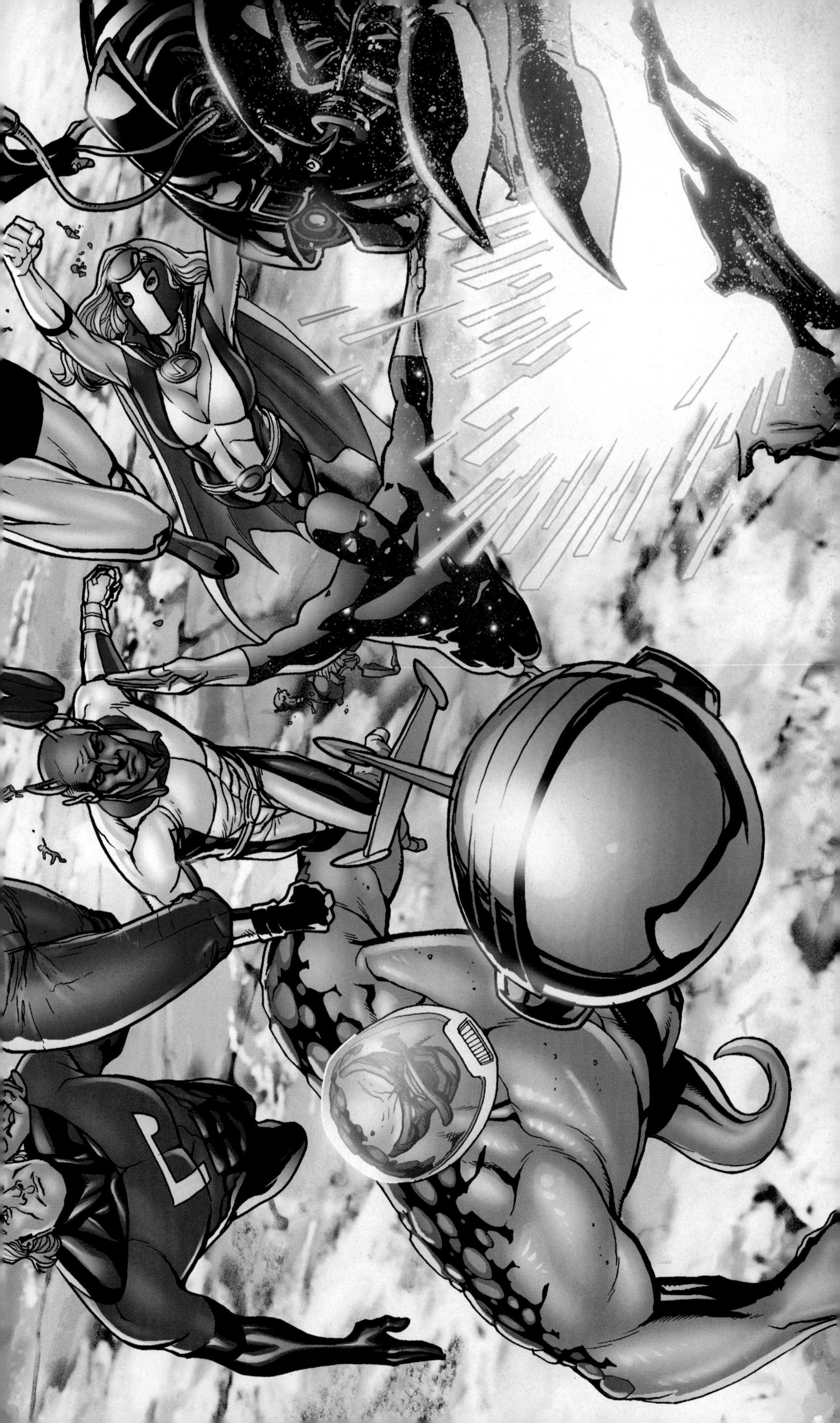

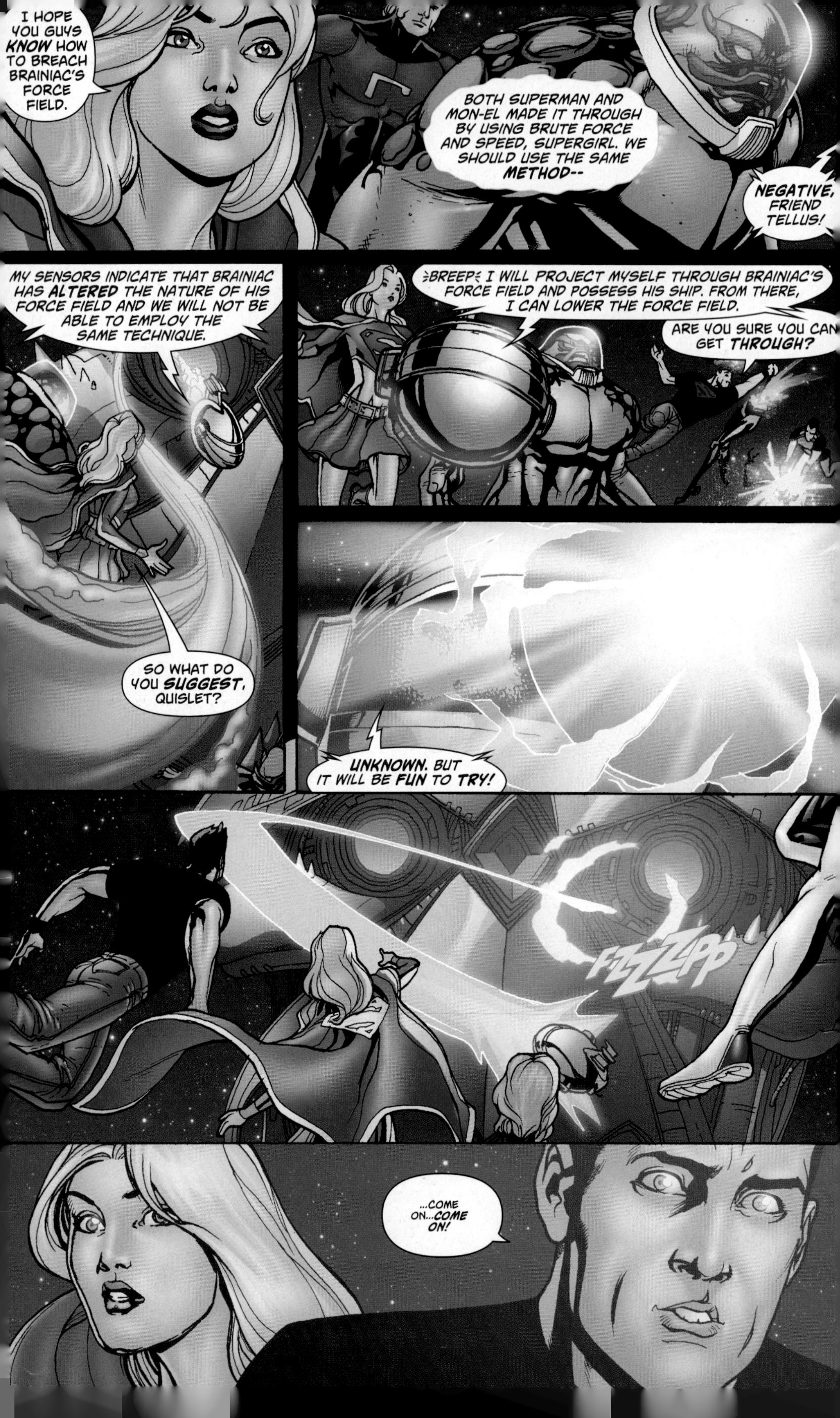
I HOPE YOU GUYS KNOW HOW TO BREACH BRAINIAC'S FORCE FIELD.
BOTH SUPERMAN AND MON-EL MADE IT THROUGH BY USING BRUTE FORCE AND SPEED, SUPERGIRL. WE SHOULD USE THE SAME METHOD--
NEGATIVE, FRIEND TELLUS!
MY SENSORS INDICATE THAT BRAINIAC HAS ALTERED THE NATURE OF HIS FORCE FIELD AND WE WILL NOT BE ABLE TO EMPLOY THE SAME TECHNIQUE.
SO WHAT DO YOU SUGGEST, QUISLET?
BREEP I WILL PROJECT MYSELF THROUGH BRAINIAC'S FORCE FIELD AND POSSESS HIS SHIP. FROM THERE, I CAN LOWER THE FORCE FIELD.
ARE YOU SURE YOU CAN GET THROUGH?
UNKNOWN. BUT IT WILL BE FUN TO TRY!
FZZZAPP
...COME ON...COME ON!

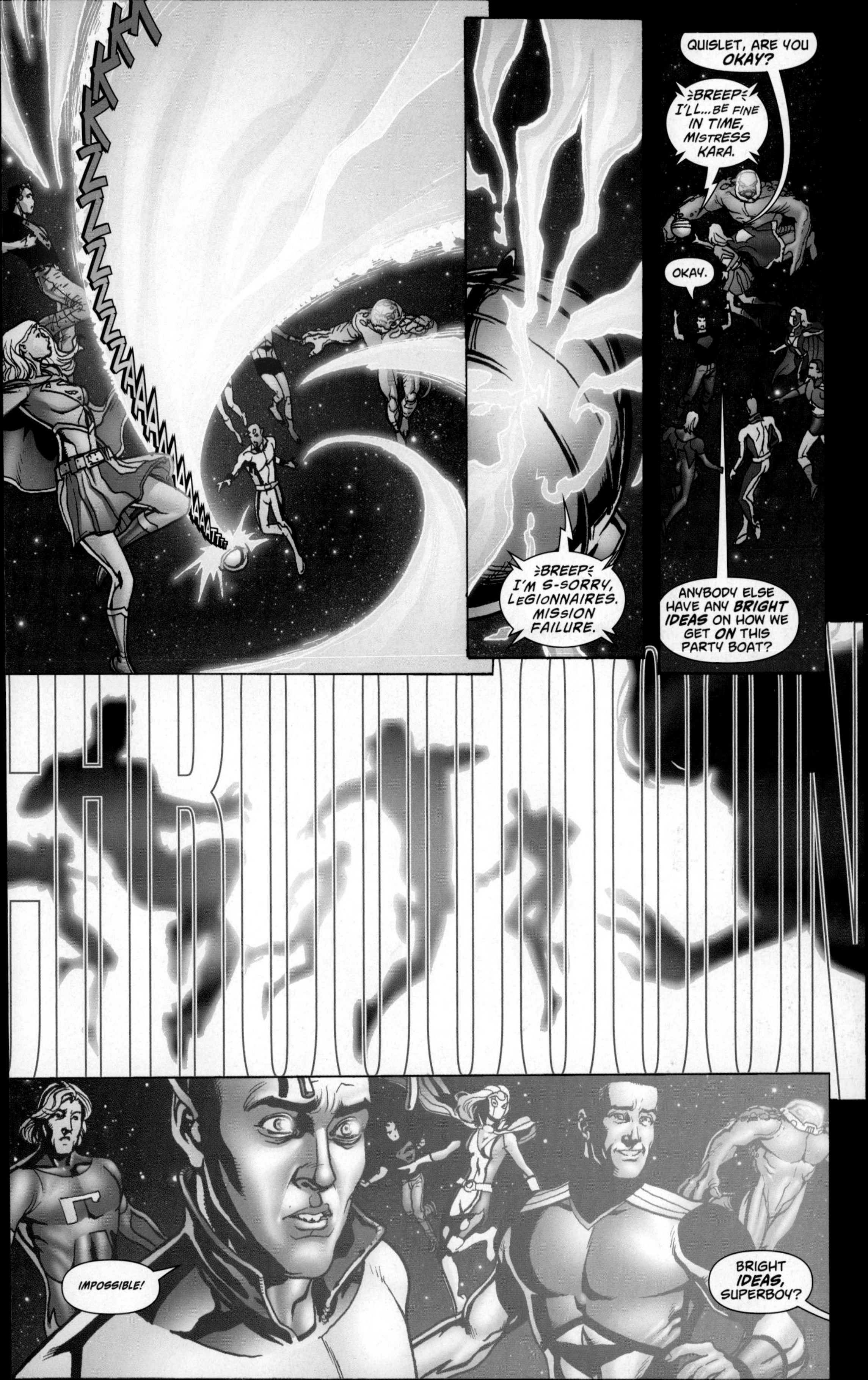
KKKKZZZZZZZZAAAAAAAAAAAAATTT
BREEP I'M S-SORRY, LEGIONNAIRES. MISSION FAILURE.
QUISLET, ARE YOU OKAY?
BREEP I'LL...BE FINE IN TIME, MISTRESS KARA.
OKAY.
ANYBODY ELSE HAVE ANY BRIGHT IDEAS ON HOW WE GET ON THIS PARTY BOAT?
IMPOSSIBLE!
BRIGHT IDEAS, SUPERBOY?

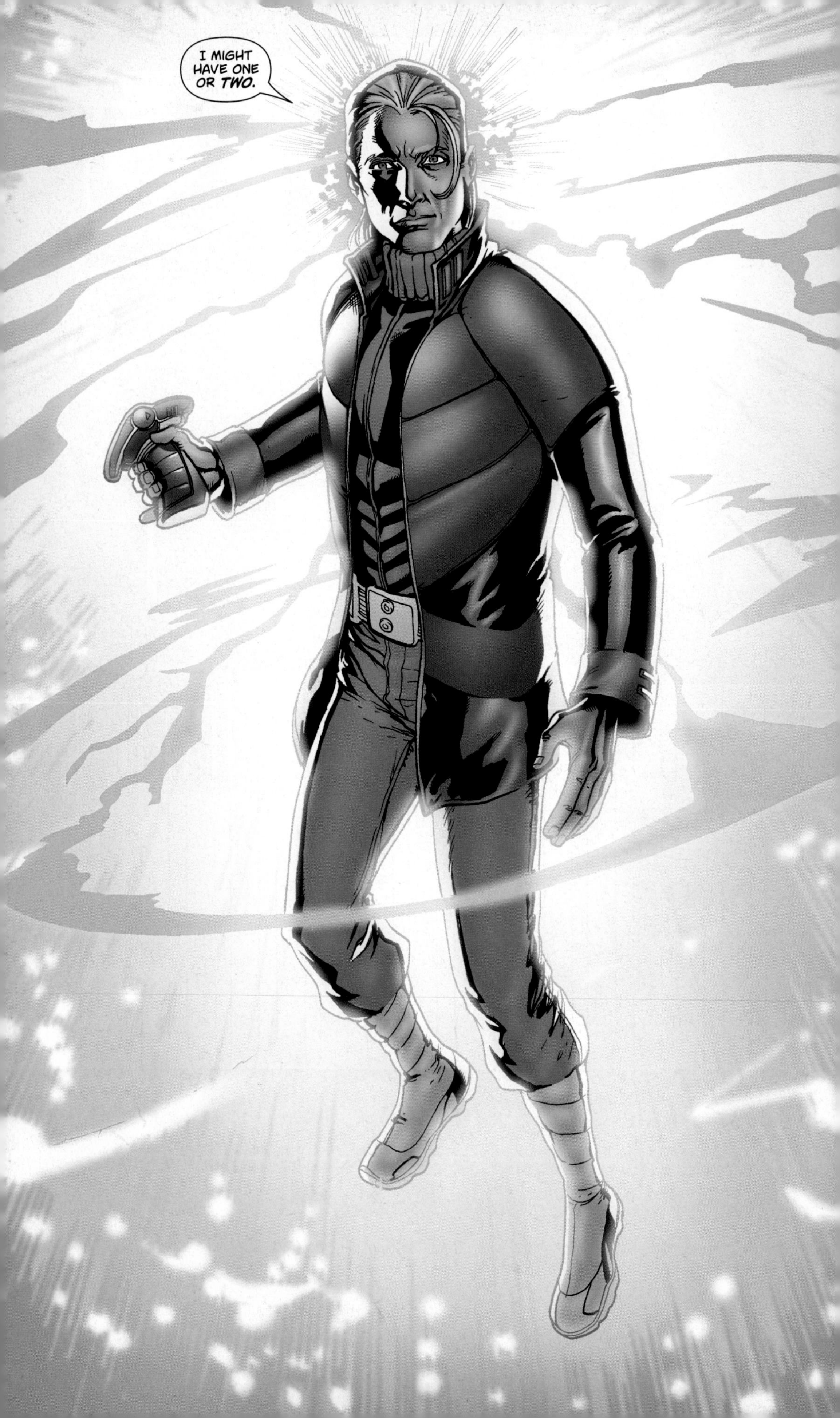
I MIGHT HAVE ONE OR TWO.

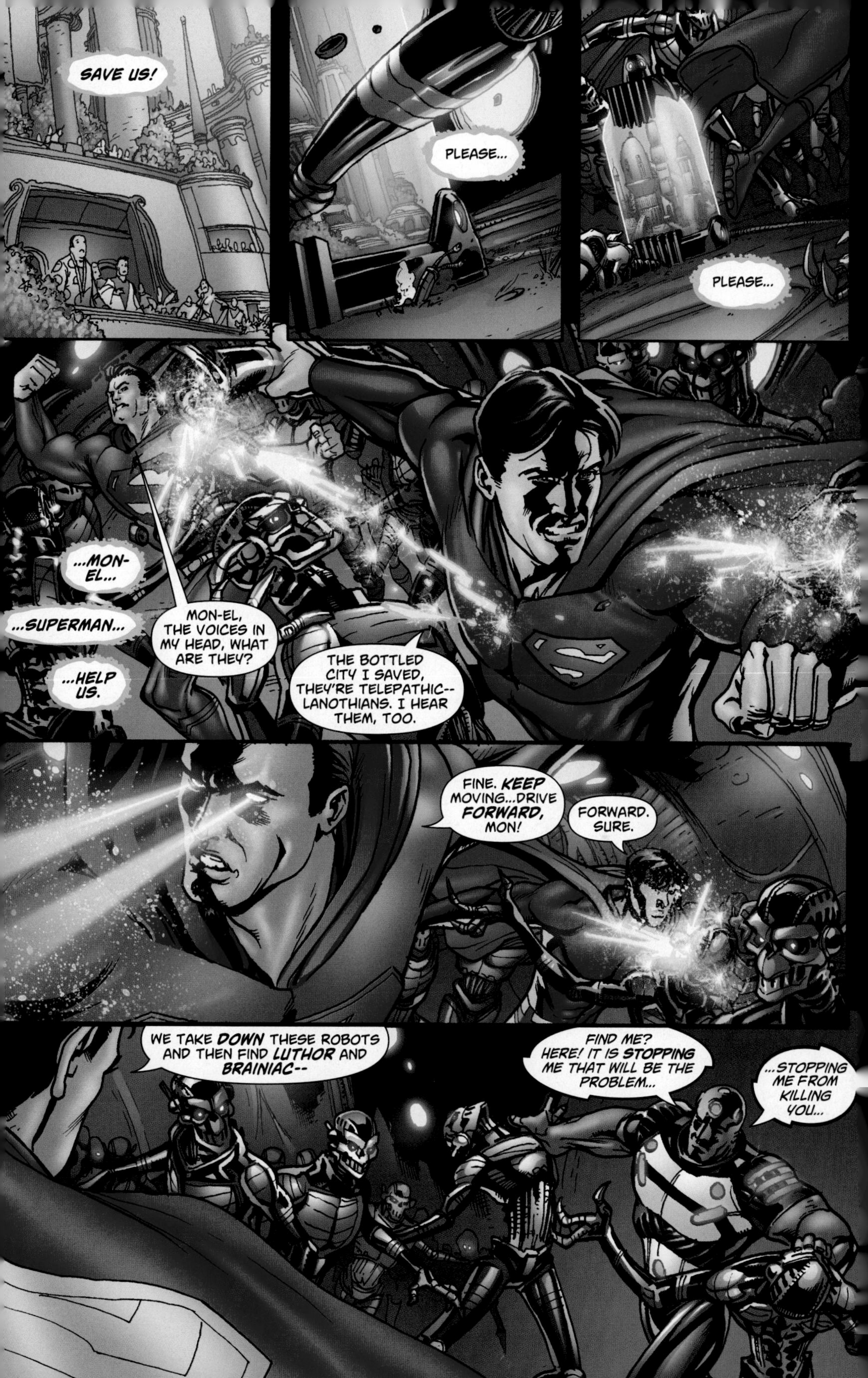
SAVE US!
PLEASE...
PLEASE...
...MON-EL...
...SUPERMAN...
...HELP US.
MON-EL, THE VOICES IN MY HEAD, WHAT ARE THEY?
THE BOTTLED CITY I SAVED, THEY'RE TELEPATHIC--LANOTHIANS. I HEAR THEM, TOO.
FINE. KEEP MOVING...DRIVE FORWARD, MON!
FORWARD. SURE.
WE TAKE DOWN THESE ROBOTS AND THEN FIND LUTHOR AND BRAINIAC--
FIND ME? HERE! IT IS STOPPING ME THAT WILL BE THE PROBLEM...
...STOPPING ME FROM KILLING YOU...

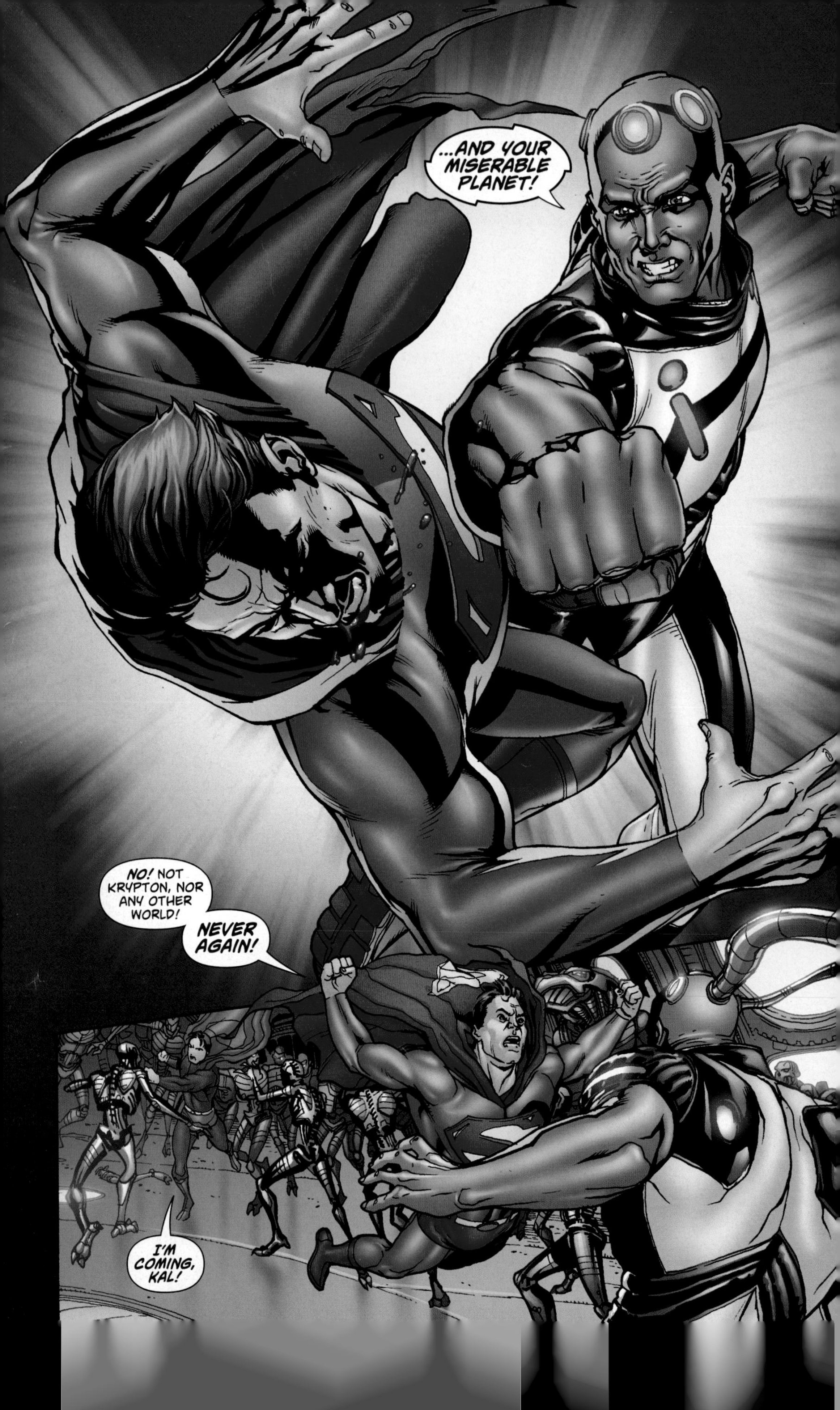
...AND YOUR MISERABLE PLANET!
NO! NOT KRYPTON, NOR ANY OTHER WORLD!
NEVER AGAIN!
I'M COMING, KAL!

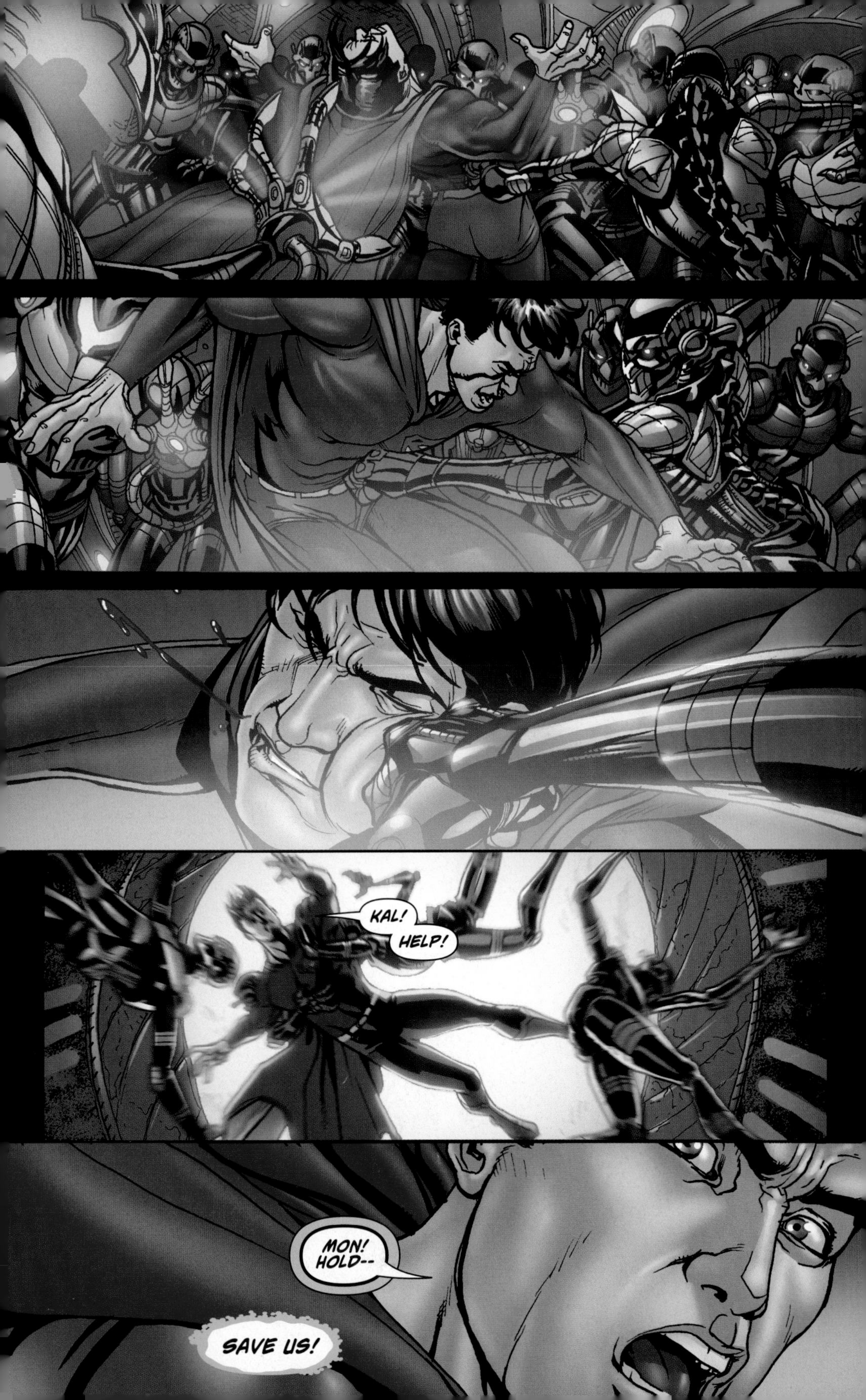
KAL!
HELP!
MON! HOLD--
SAVE US!

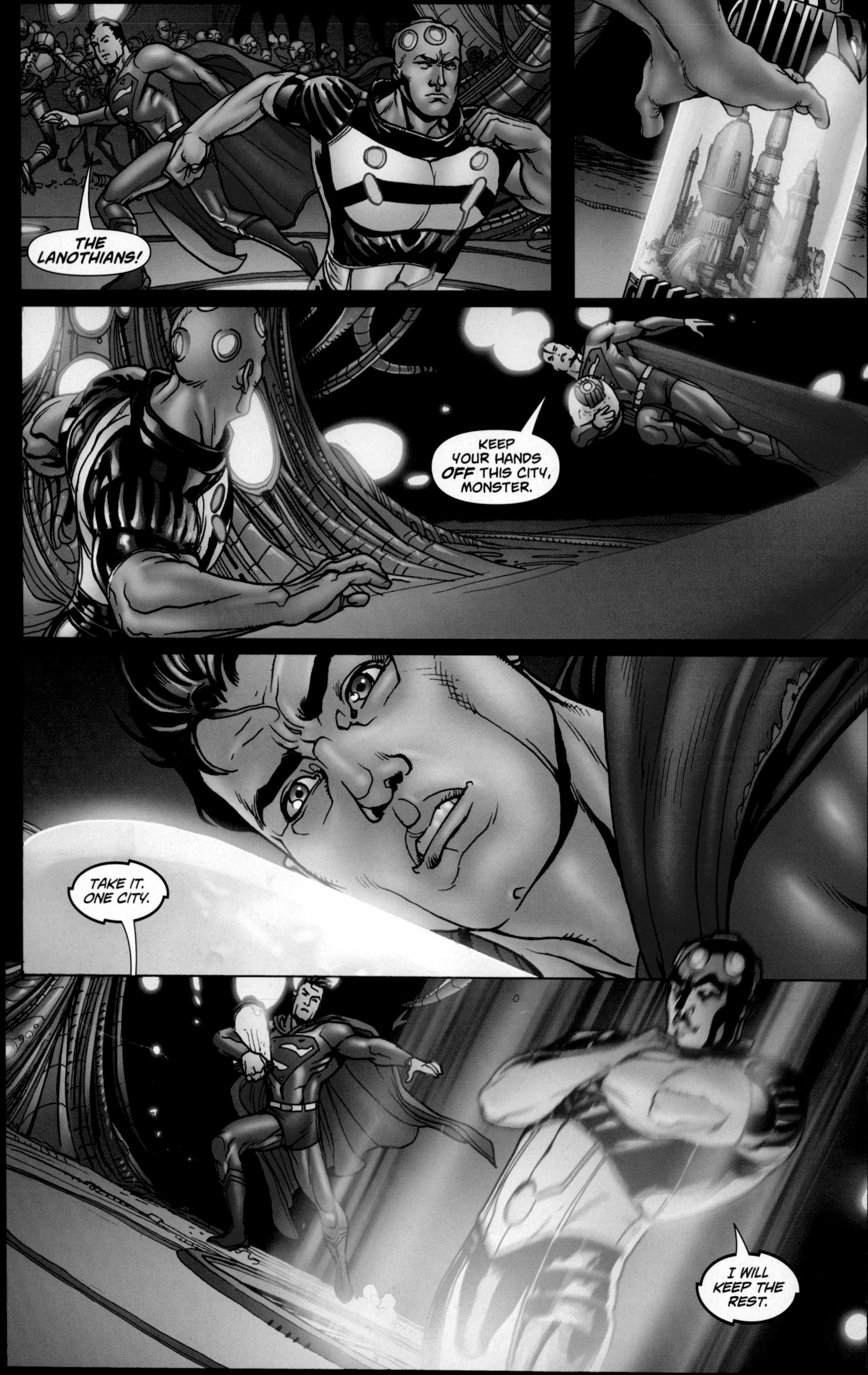
THE LANOTHIANS!
KEEP YOUR HANDS OFF THIS CITY, MONSTER.
TAKE IT. ONE CITY.
I WILL KEEP THE REST.

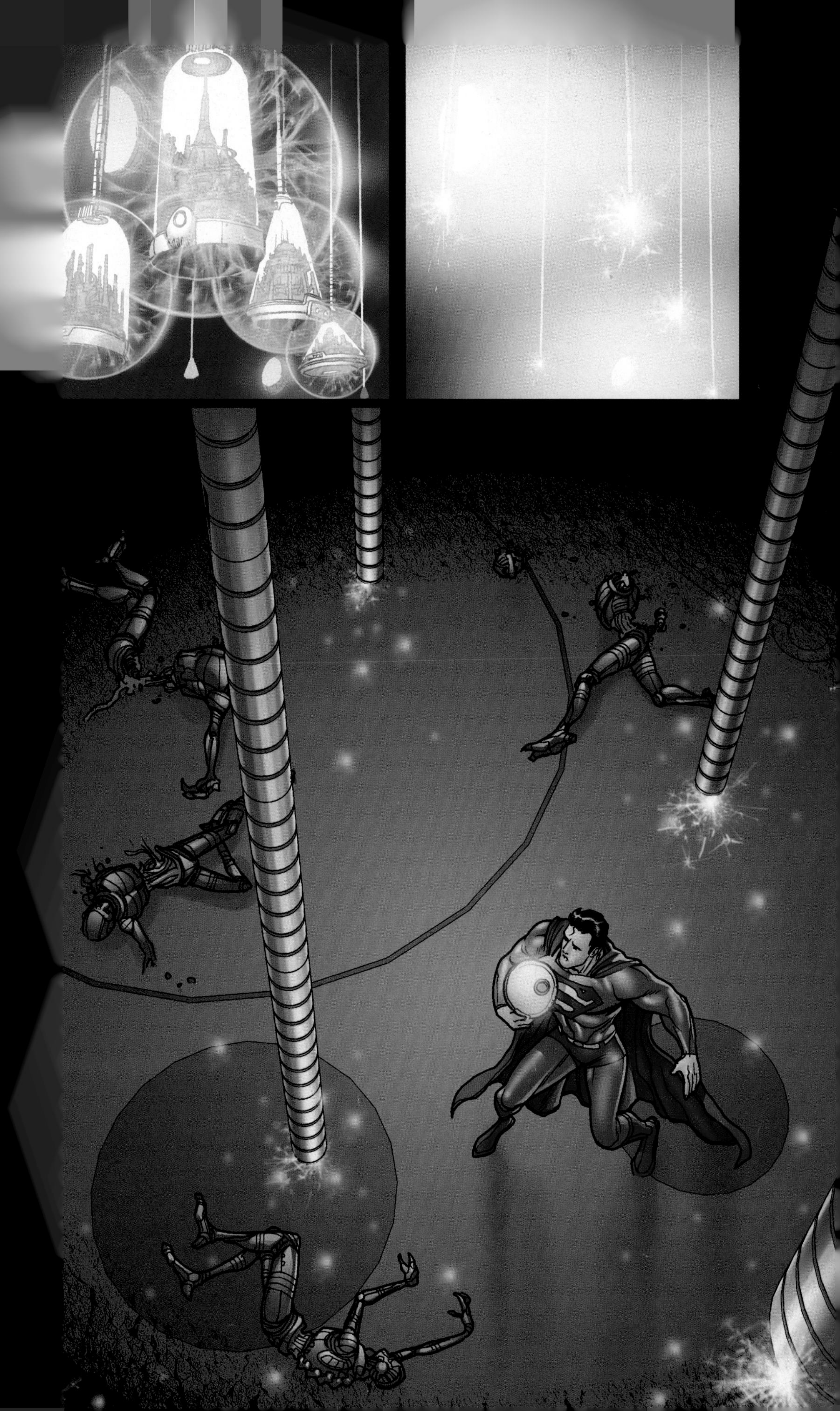

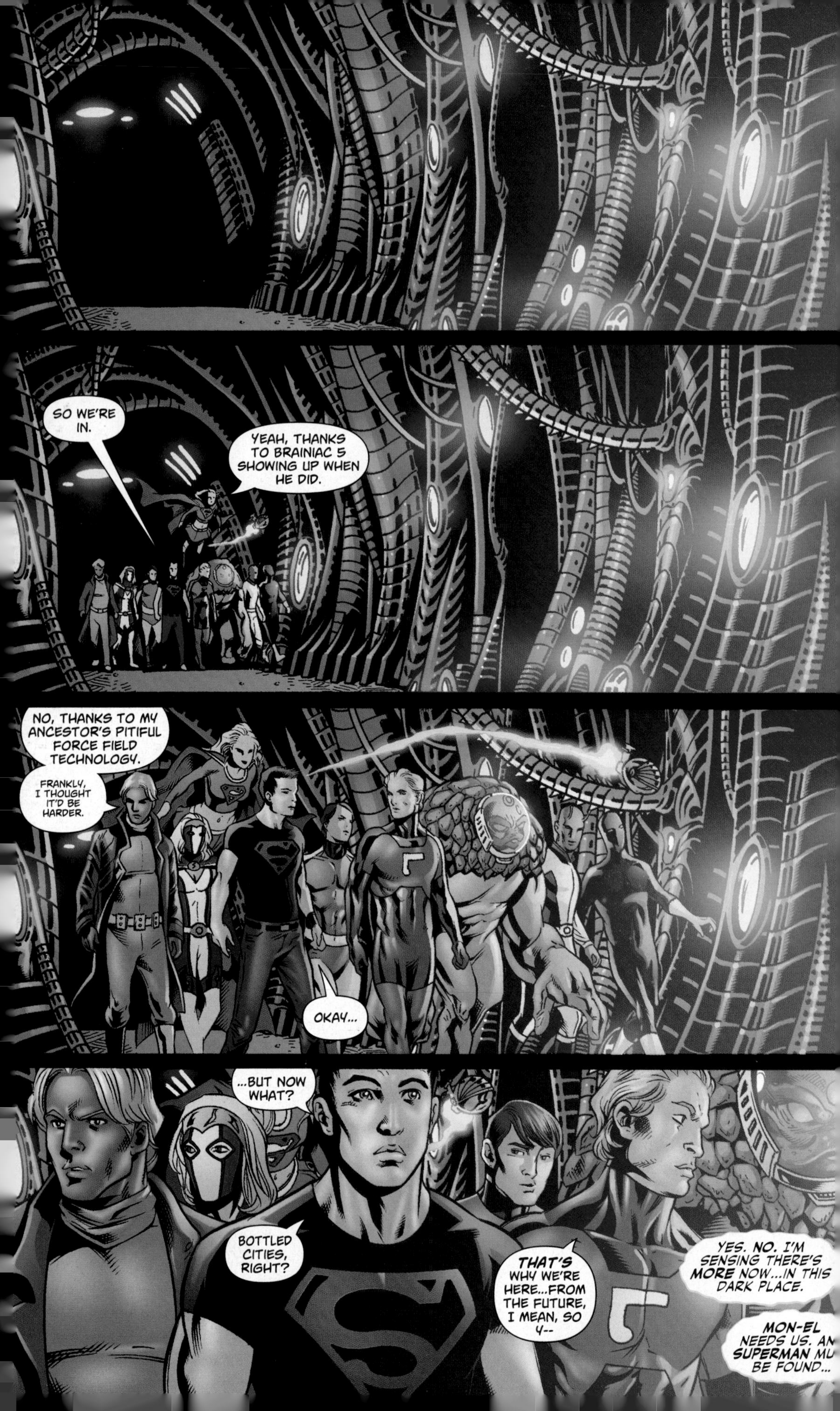

SO WE'RE IN.
YEAH, THANKS TO BRAINIAC 5 SHOWING UP WHEN HE DID.
NO, THANKS TO MY ANCESTOR'S PITIFUL FORCE FIELD TECHNOLOGY.
FRANKLY, I THOUGHT IT'D BE HARDER.
OKAY...
...BUT NOW WHAT?
BOTTLED CITIES, RIGHT?
THAT'S WHY WE'RE HERE...FROM THE FUTURE, I MEAN, SO Y--
YES. NO. I'M SENSING THERE'S MORE NOW...IN THIS DARK PLACE.
MON-EL NEEDS US. AN SUPERMAN MU BE FOUND...

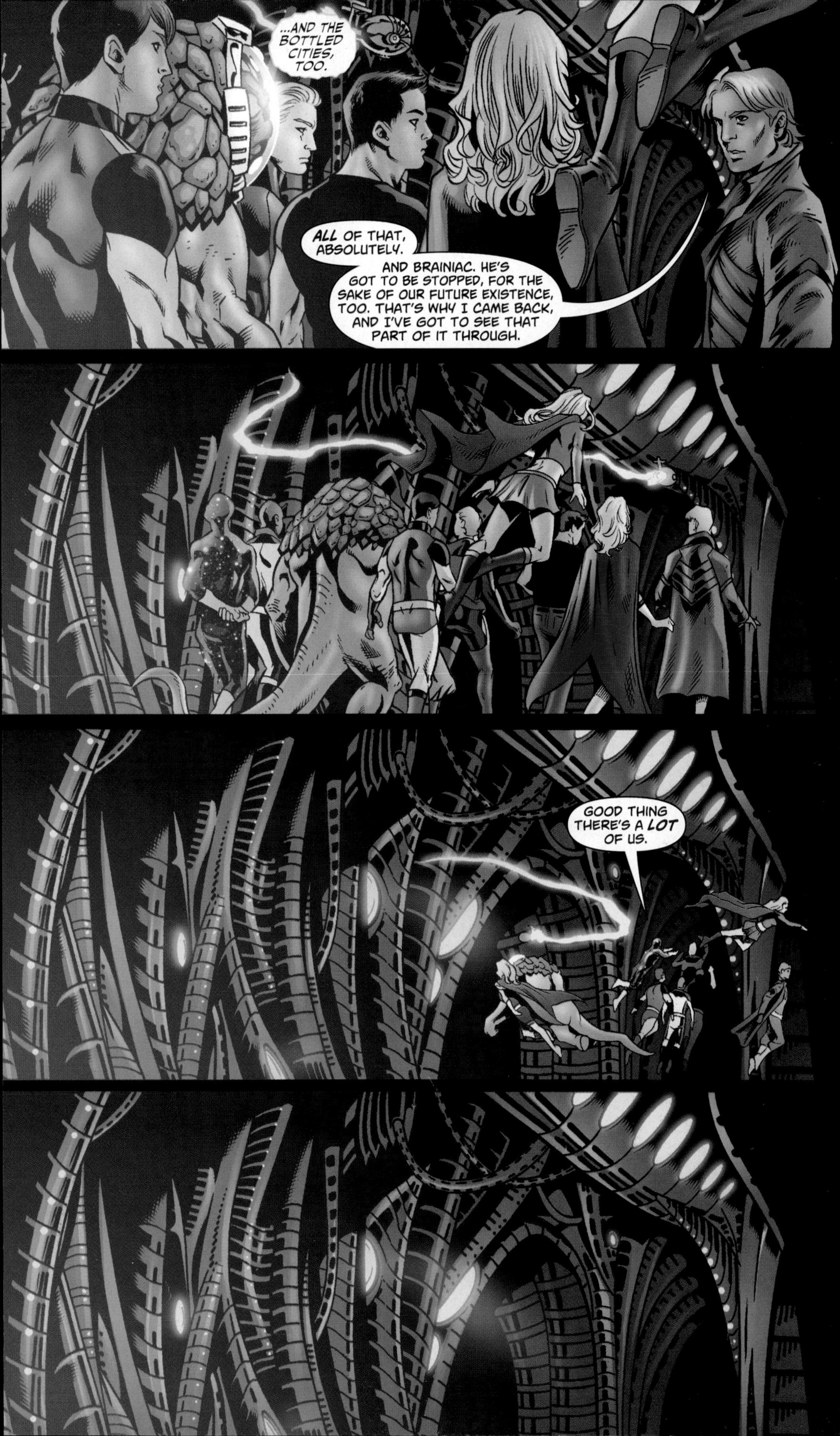
...AND THE BOTTLED CITIES, TOO.
ALL OF THAT, ABSOLUTELY.
AND BRAINIAC. HE'S GOT TO BE STOPPED, FOR THE SAKE OF OUR FUTURE EXISTENCE, TOO. THAT'S WHY I CAME BACK, AND I'VE GOT TO SEE THAT PART OF IT THROUGH.
GOOD THING THERE'S A LOT OF US.

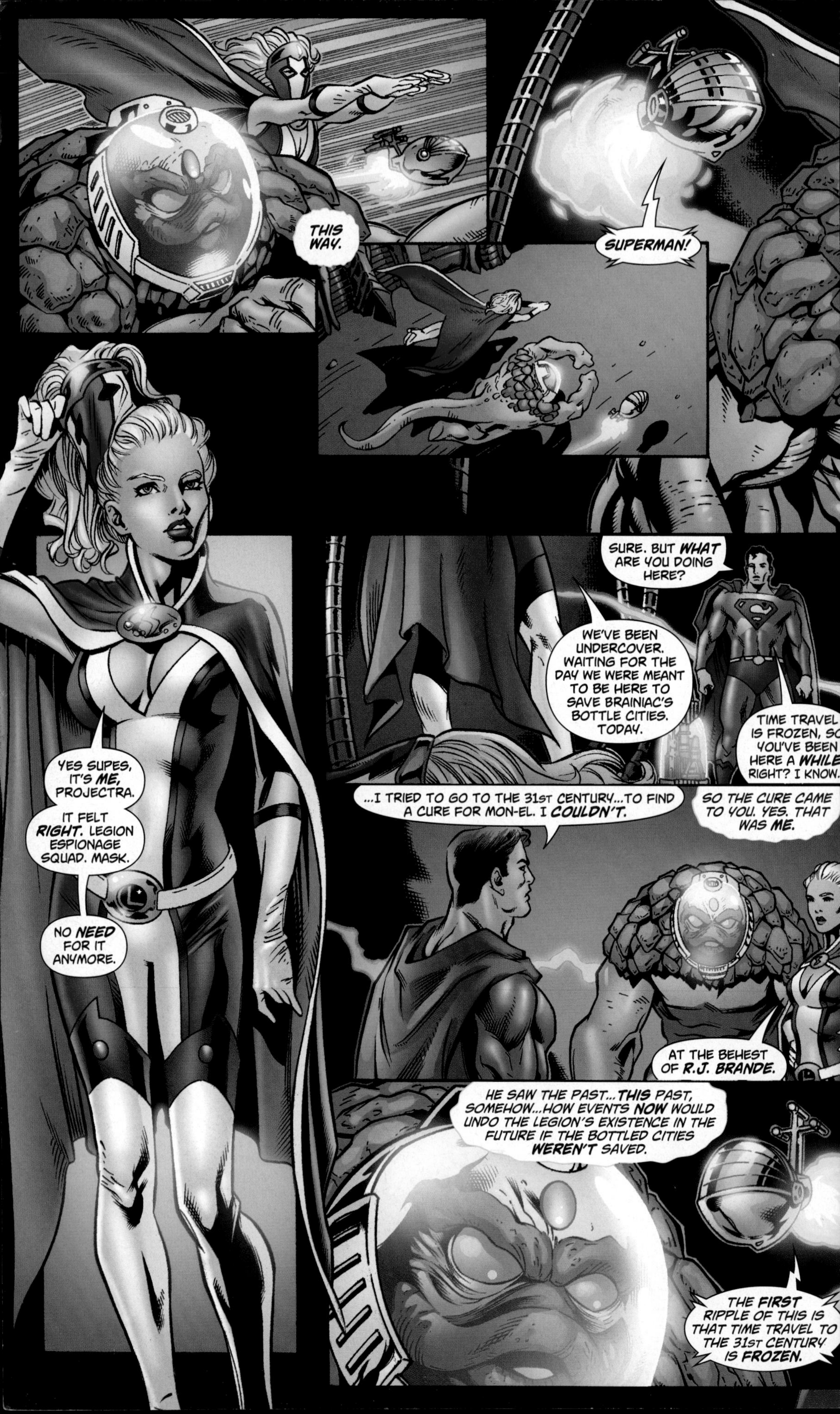
THIS WAY.
SUPERMAN!
YES SUPES, IT'S ME, PROJECTRA.
IT FELT RIGHT. LEGION ESPIONAGE SQUAD. MASK.
NO NEED FOR IT ANYMORE.
SURE. BUT WHAT ARE YOU DOING HERE?
WE'VE BEEN UNDERCOVER. WAITING FOR THE DAY WE WERE MEANT TO BE HERE TO SAVE BRAINIAC'S BOTTLE CITIES. TODAY.
TIME TRAVEL IS FROZEN, SO YOU'VE BEEN HERE A WHILE RIGHT? I KNOW.
...I TRIED TO GO TO THE 31ST CENTURY...TO FIND A CURE FOR MON-EL. I COULDN'T.
SO THE CURE CAME TO YOU. YES. THAT WAS ME.
AT THE BEHEST OF R.J. BRANDE.
HE SAW THE PAST...THIS PAST, SOMEHOW...HOW EVENTS NOW WOULD UNDO THE LEGION'S EXISTENCE IN THE FUTURE IF THE BOTTLED CITIES WEREN'T SAVED.
THE FIRST RIPPLE OF THIS IS THAT TIME TRAVEL TO THE 31ST CENTURY IS FROZEN.

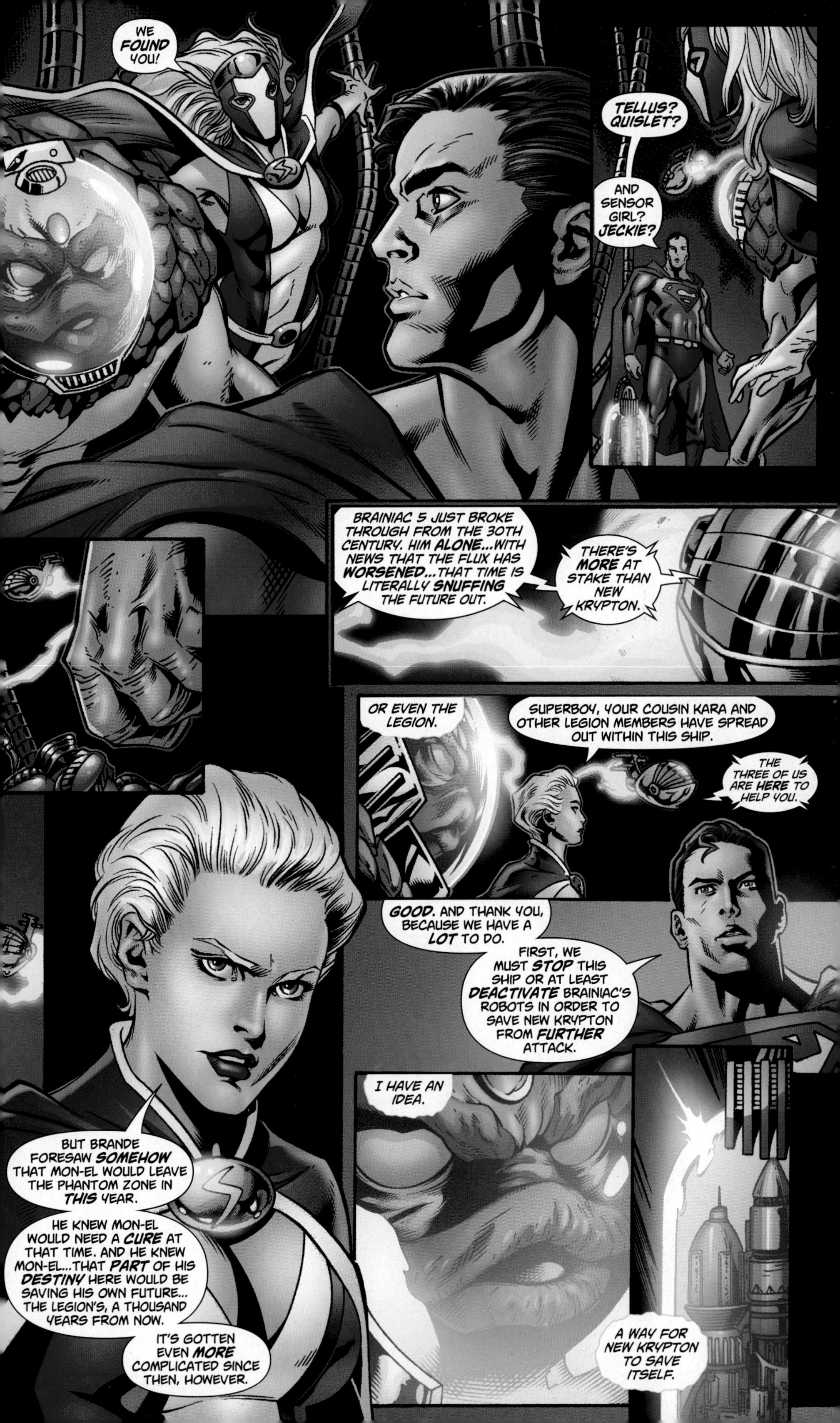

WE FOUND YOU!
TELLUS? QUISLET?
AND SENSOR GIRL? JECKIE?
BRAINIAC 5 JUST BROKE THROUGH FROM THE 30TH CENTURY. HIM ALONE...WITH NEWS THAT THE FLUX HAS WORSENED...THAT TIME IS LITERALLY SNUFFING THE FUTURE OUT.
THERE'S MORE AT STAKE THAN NEW KRYPTON.
OR EVEN THE LEGION.
SUPERBOY, YOUR COUSIN KARA AND OTHER LEGION MEMBERS HAVE SPREAD OUT WITHIN THIS SHIP.
THE THREE OF US ARE HERE TO HELP YOU.
BUT BRANDE FORESAW SOMEHOW THAT MON-EL WOULD LEAVE THE PHANTOM ZONE IN THIS YEAR.
HE KNEW MON-EL WOULD NEED A CURE AT THAT TIME. AND HE KNEW MON-EL...THAT PART OF HIS DESTINY HERE WOULD BE SAVING HIS OWN FUTURE... THE LEGION'S, A THOUSAND YEARS FROM NOW.
IT'S GOTTEN EVEN MORE COMPLICATED SINCE THEN, HOWEVER.
GOOD. AND THANK YOU, BECAUSE WE HAVE A LOT TO DO.
FIRST, WE MUST STOP THIS SHIP OR AT LEAST DEACTIVATE BRAINIAC'S ROBOTS IN ORDER TO SAVE NEW KRYPTON FROM FURTHER ATTACK.
I HAVE AN IDEA.
A WAY FOR NEW KRYPTON TO SAVE ITSELF.

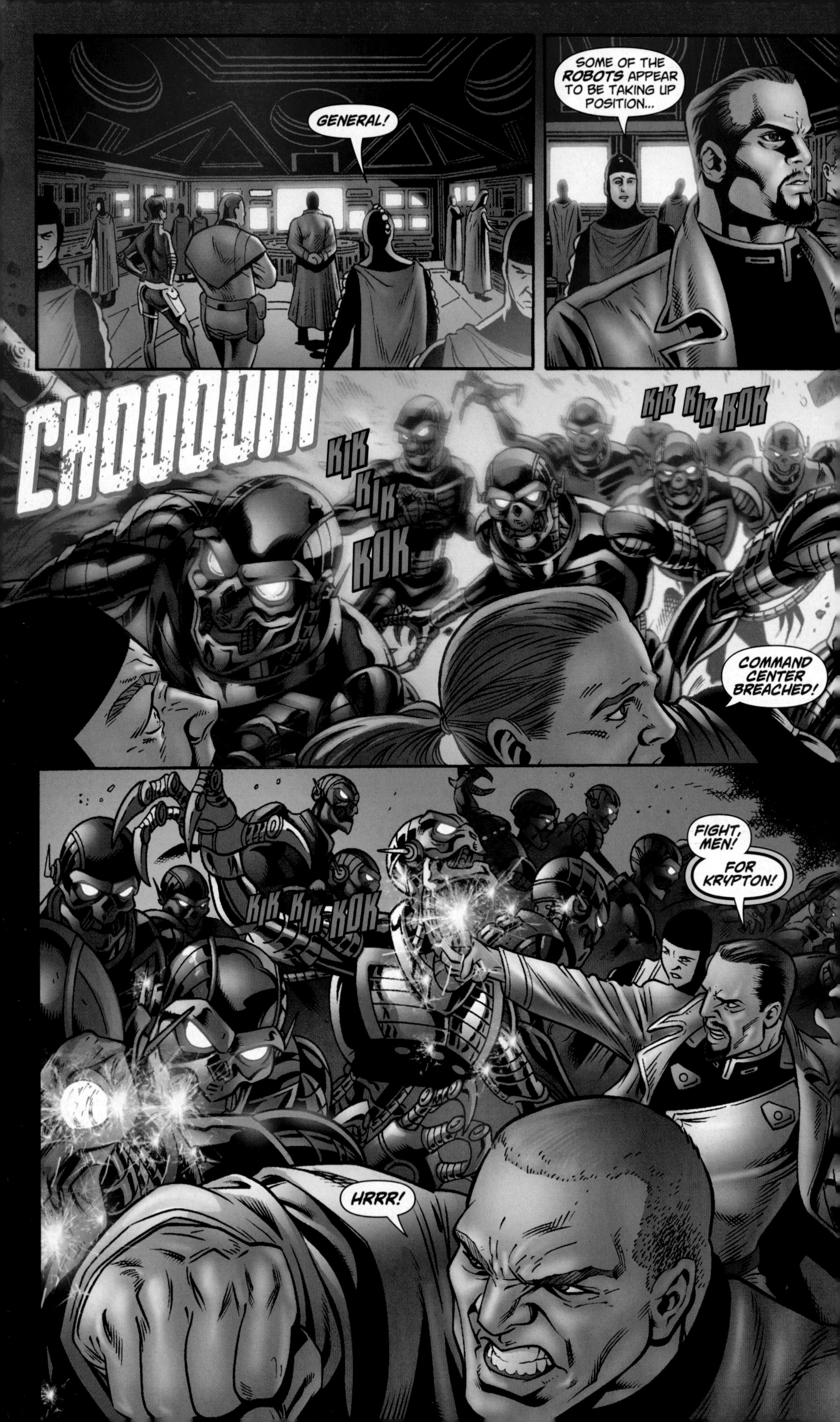
GENERAL!
SOME OF THE ROBOTS APPEAR TO BE TAKING UP POSITION...
CHOOOOM
KIK KIK KOK
KIK KIK KOK
COMMAND CENTER BREACHED!
KIK KIK KOK
FIGHT, MEN!
FOR KRYPTON!
HRRR!

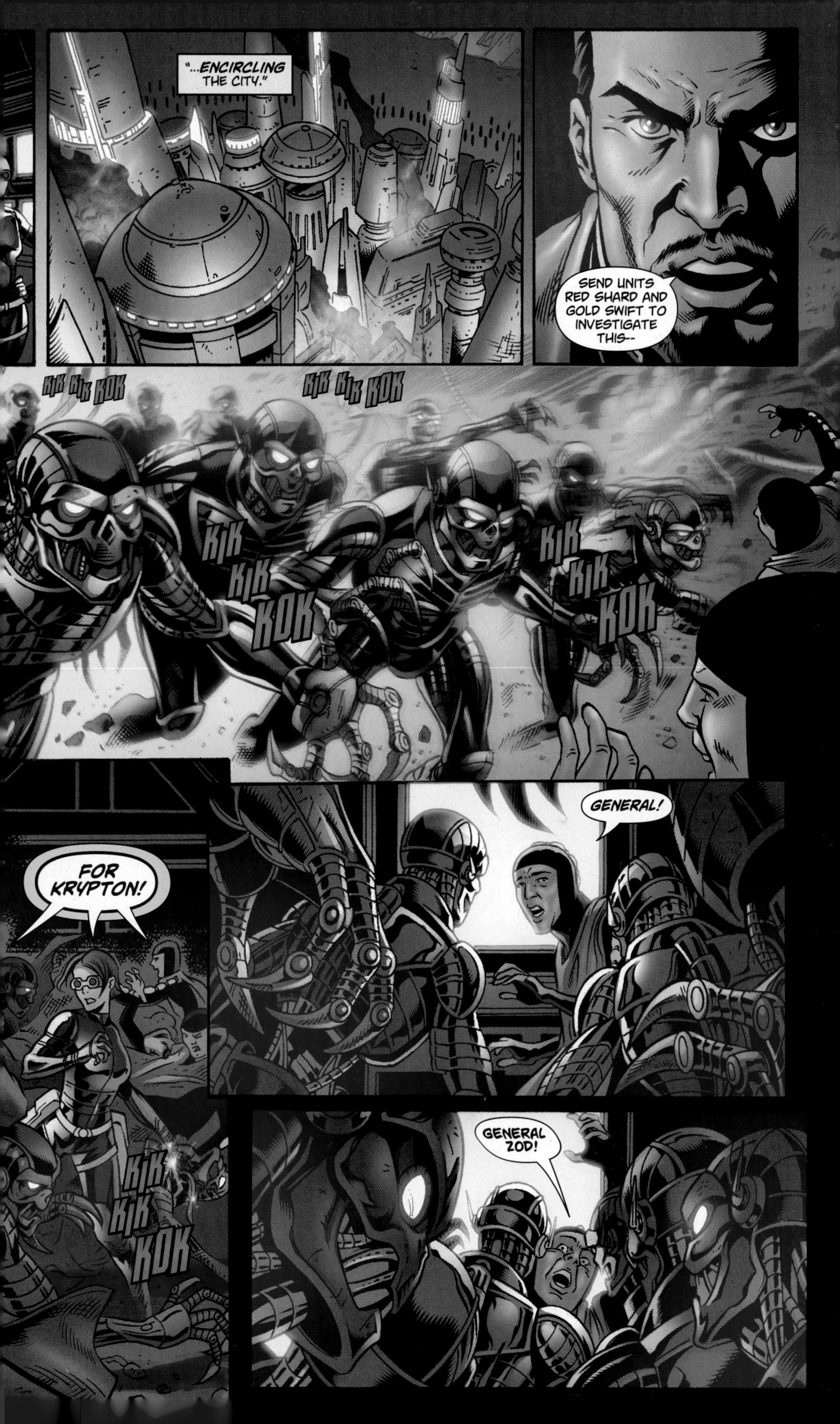
"...ENCIRCLING THE CITY."
SEND UNITS RED SHARD AND GOLD SWIFT TO INVESTIGATE THIS--
KIK KIK KOK
KIK KIK KOK
KIK KIK KOK
KIK KIK KOK
FOR KRYPTON!
GENERAL!
KIK KIK KOK
GENERAL ZOD!

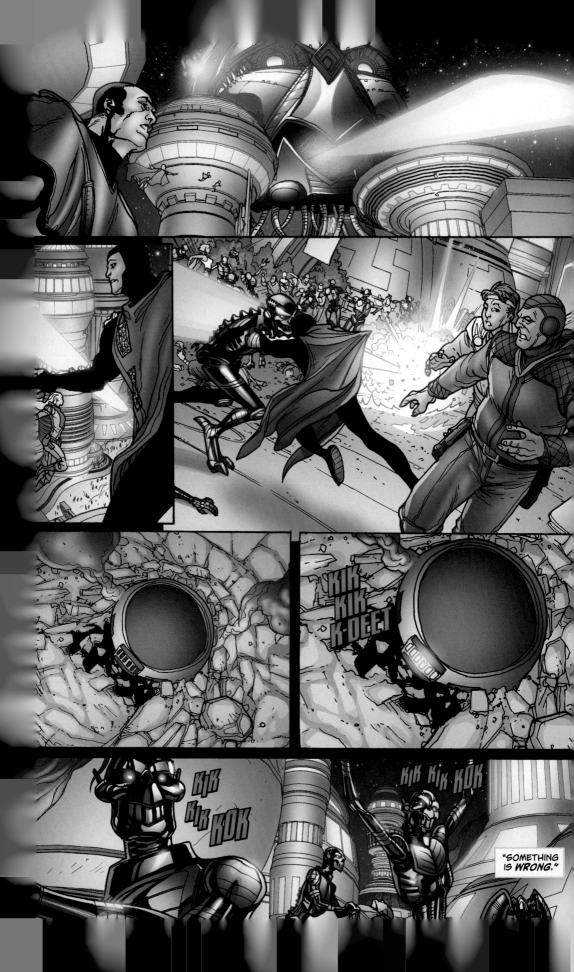

KIK
KIK
K-DEET

KIK
KIK
KOK

KIK KIK KOK

"SOMETHING IS *WRONG*."

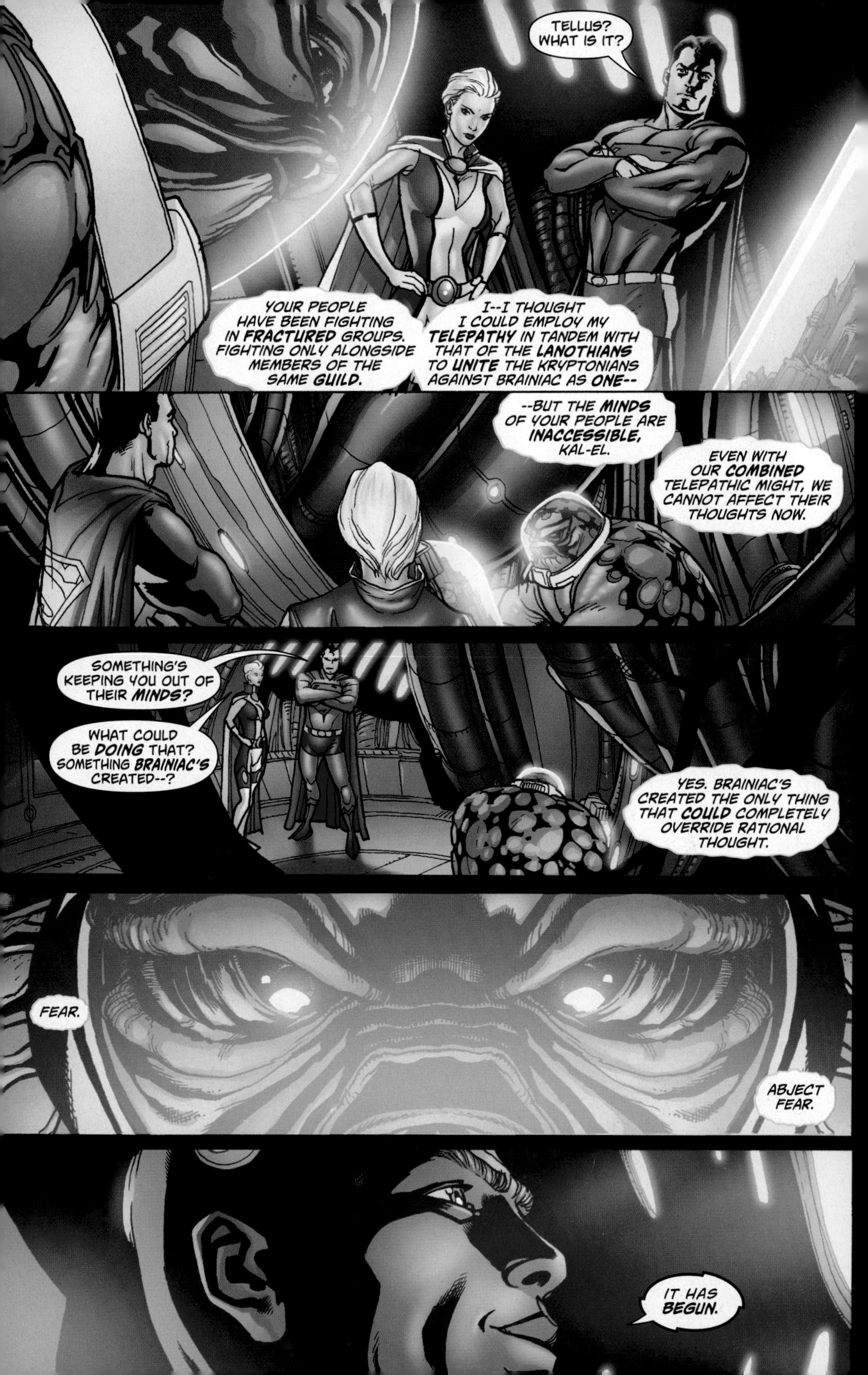
TELLUS? WHAT IS IT?
YOUR PEOPLE HAVE BEEN FIGHTING IN FRACTURED GROUPS. FIGHTING ONLY ALONGSIDE MEMBERS OF THE SAME GUILD.
I--I THOUGHT I COULD EMPLOY MY TELEPATHY IN TANDEM WITH THAT OF THE LANOTHIANS TO UNITE THE KRYPTONIANS AGAINST BRAINIAC AS ONE--
--BUT THE MINDS OF YOUR PEOPLE ARE INACCESSIBLE, KAL-EL.
EVEN WITH OUR COMBINED TELEPATHIC MIGHT, WE CANNOT AFFECT THEIR THOUGHTS NOW.
SOMETHING'S KEEPING YOU OUT OF THEIR MINDS?
WHAT COULD BE DOING THAT? SOMETHING BRAINIAC'S CREATED--?
YES. BRAINIAC'S CREATED THE ONLY THING THAT COULD COMPLETELY OVERRIDE RATIONAL THOUGHT.
FEAR.
ABJECT FEAR.
IT HAS BEGUN.

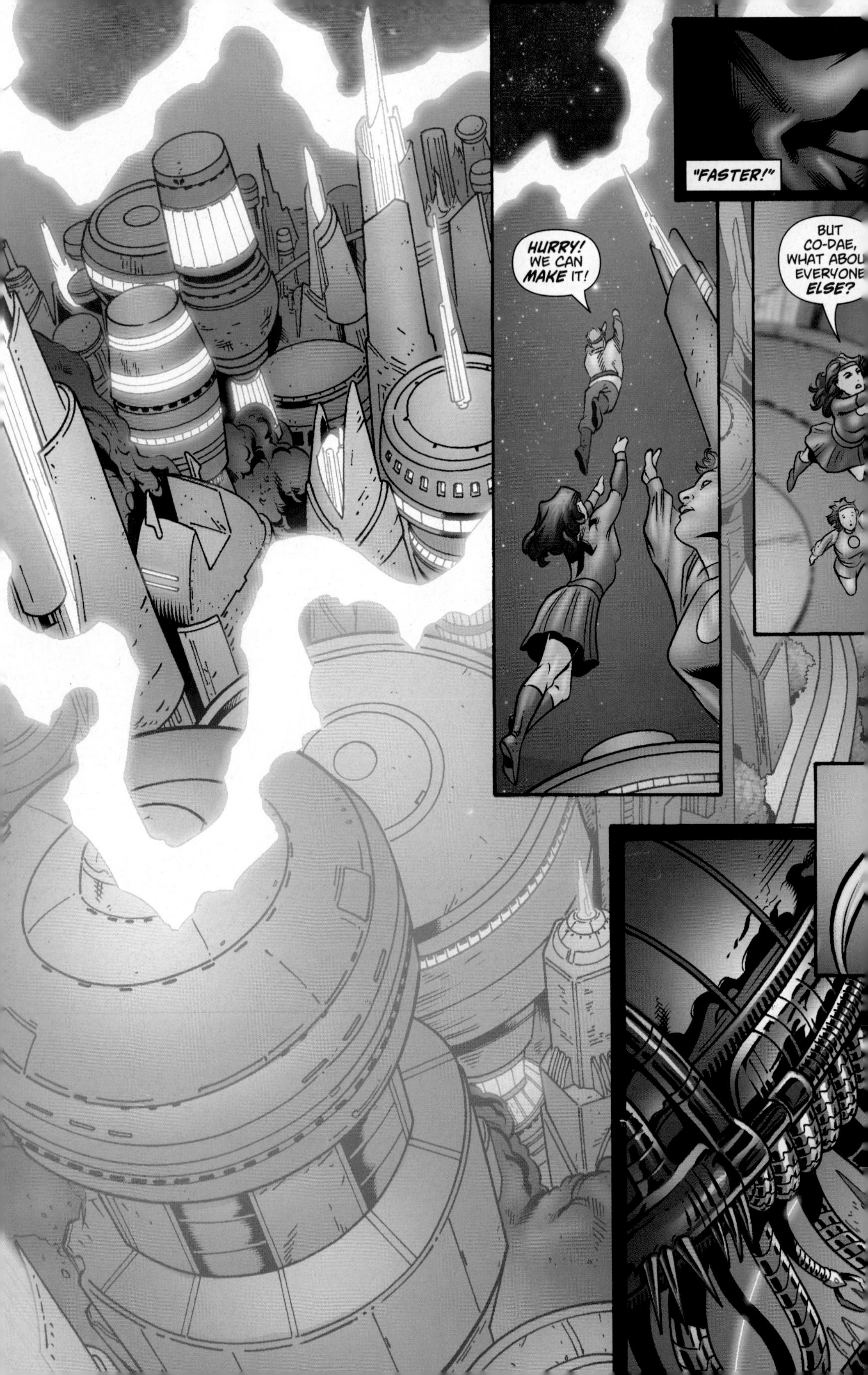
"FASTER!"
HURRY! WE CAN MAKE IT!
BUT CO-DAE, WHAT ABOU EVERYONE ELSE?

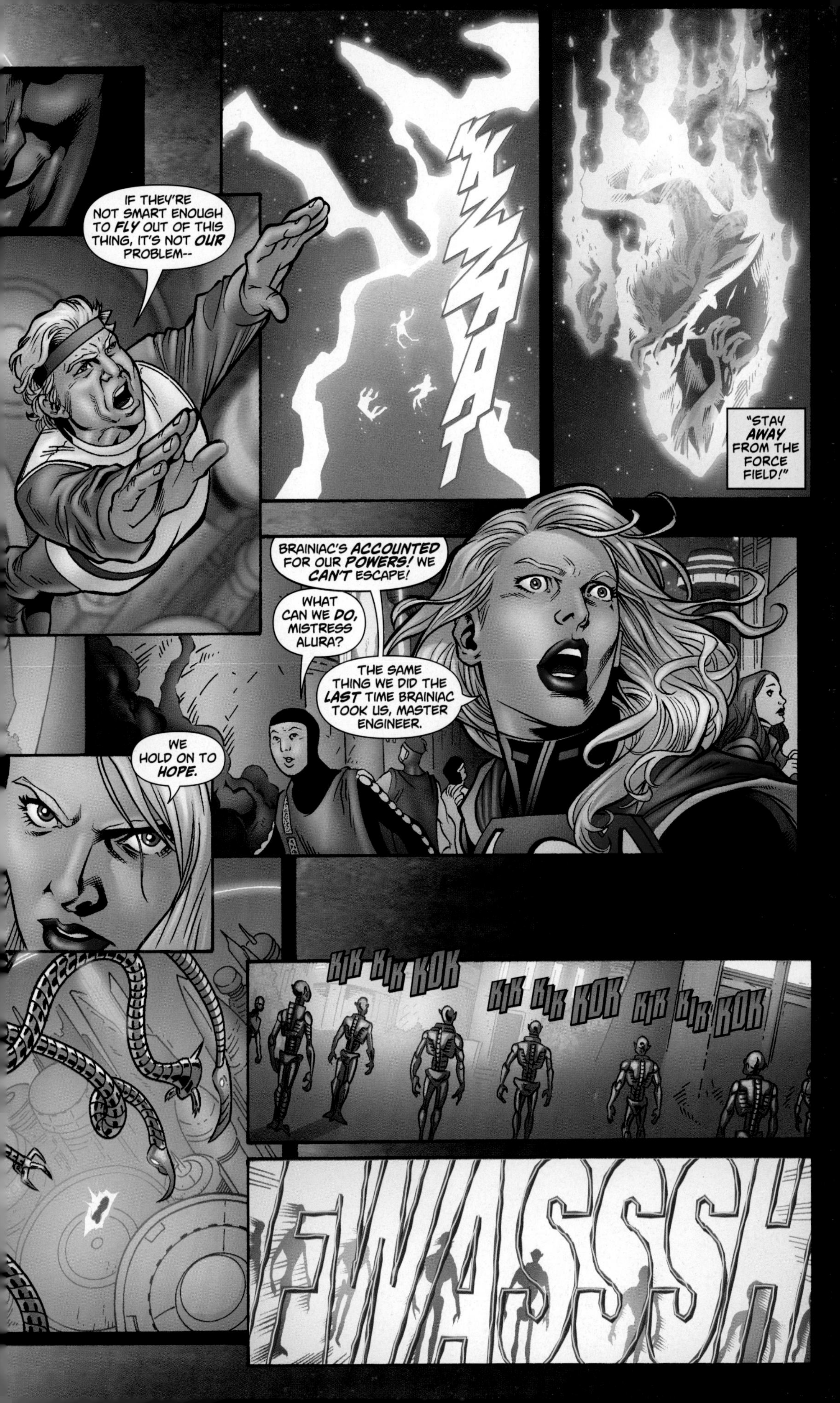

IF THEY'RE NOT SMART ENOUGH TO FLY OUT OF THIS THING, IT'S NOT OUR PROBLEM--
"STAY AWAY FROM THE FORCE FIELD!"
BRAINIAC'S ACCOUNTED FOR OUR POWERS! WE CAN'T ESCAPE!
WHAT CAN WE DO, MISTRESS ALURA?
THE SAME THING WE DID THE LAST TIME BRAINIAC TOOK US, MASTER ENGINEER.
WE HOLD ON TO HOPE.
KIK KIK KOK
KIK KIK KOK
KIK KIK KOK
FWASSSH

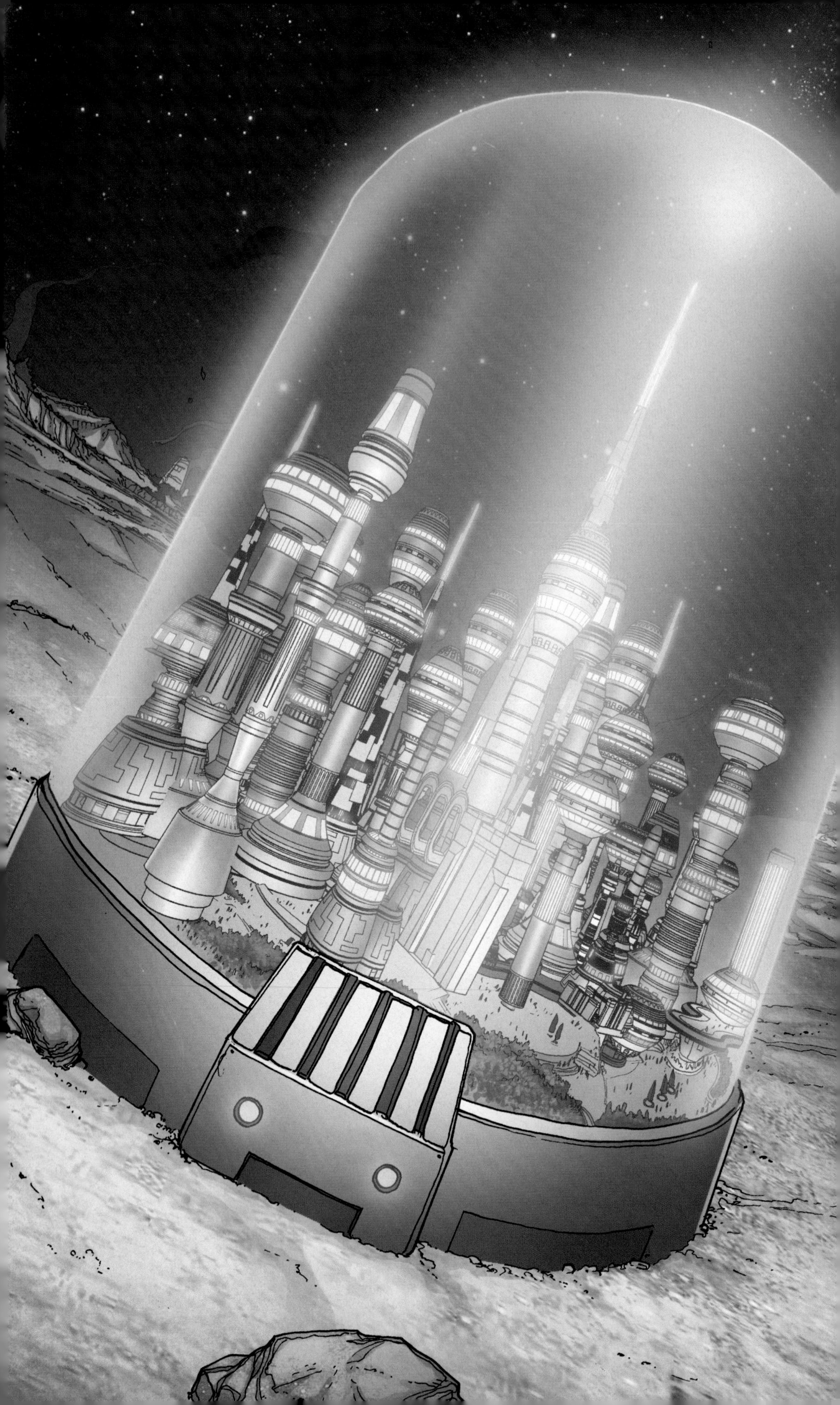

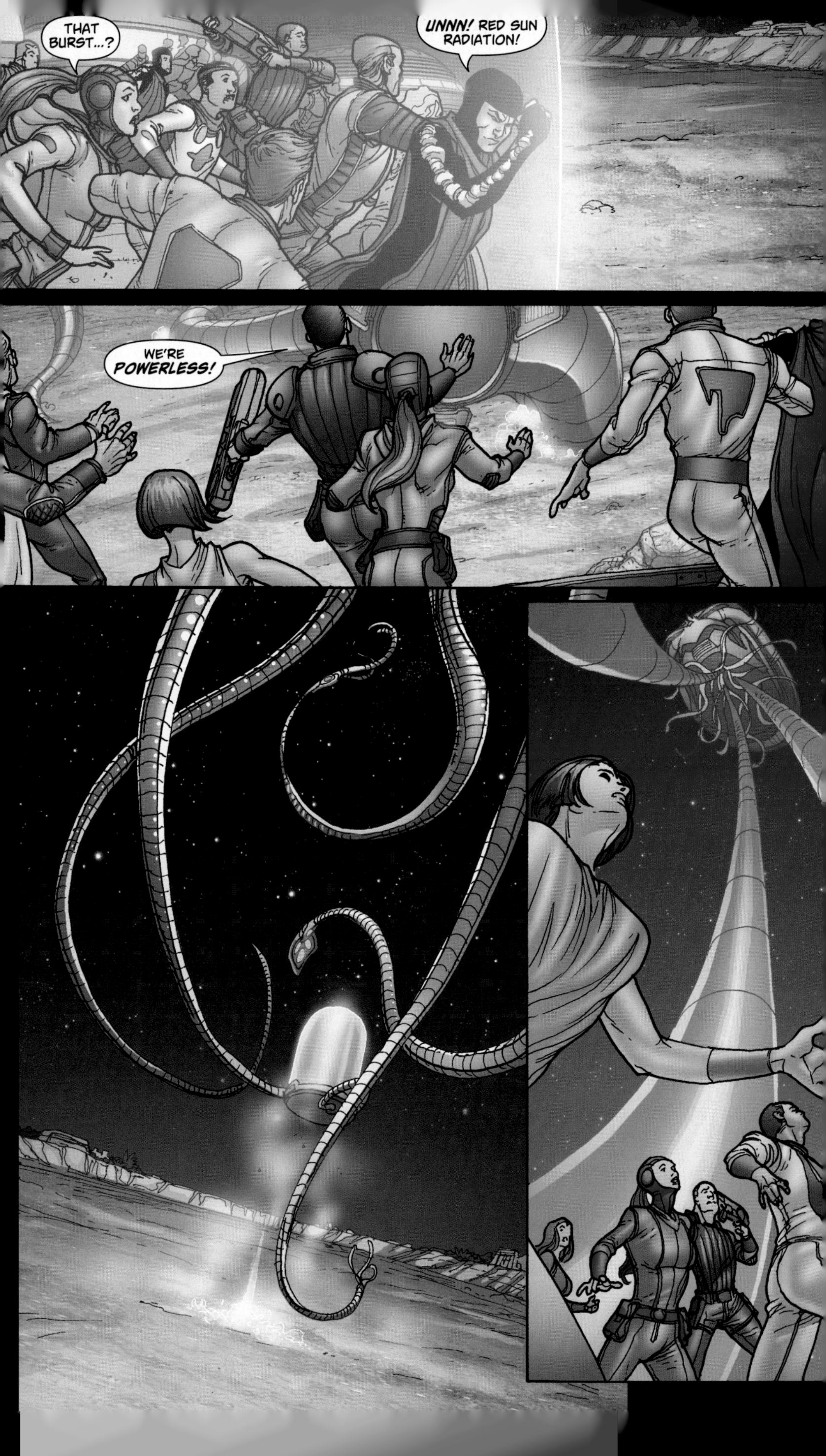
THAT BURST...?
UNNN! RED SUN RADIATION!
WE'RE POWERLESS!

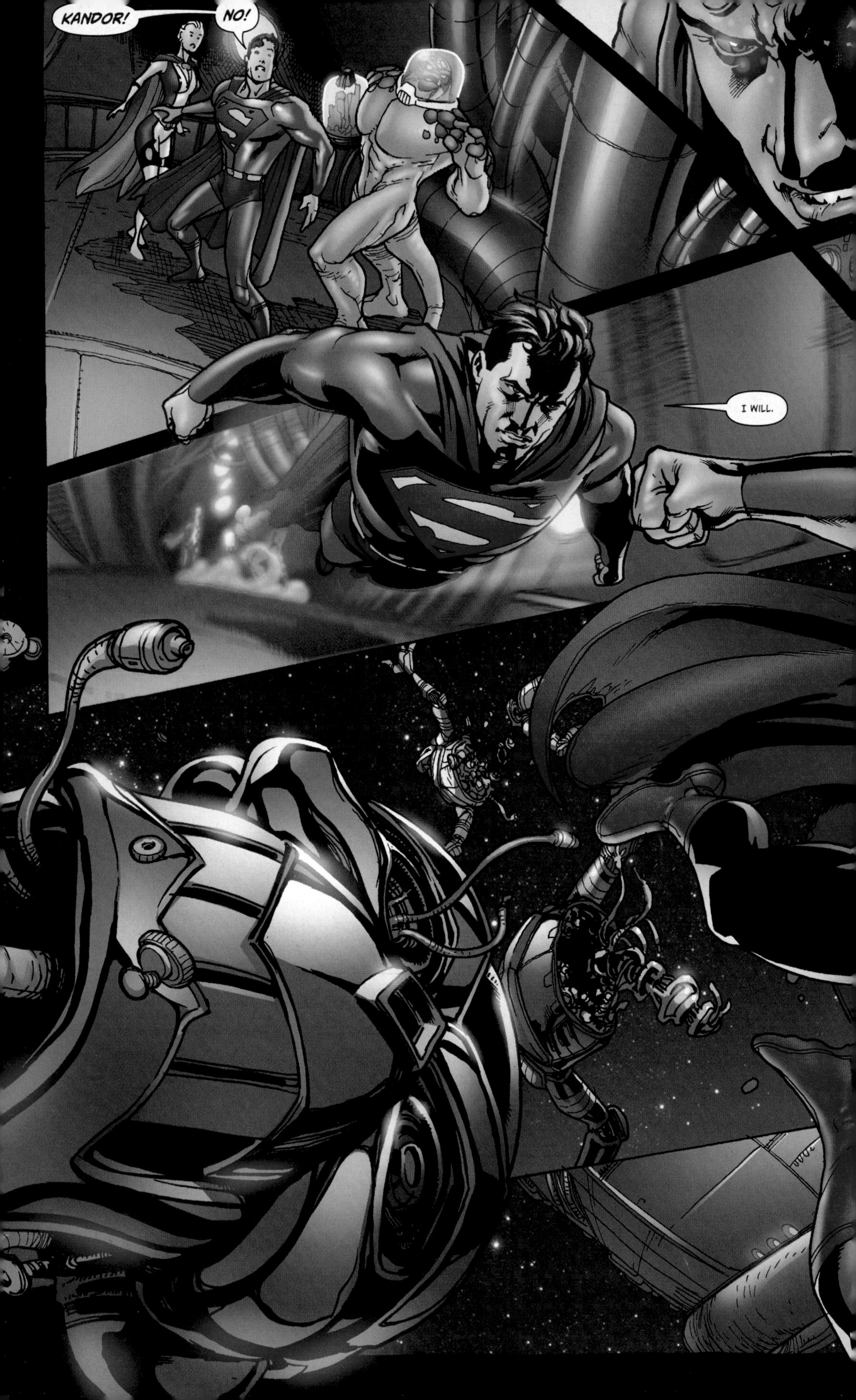
KANDOR!
NO!
I WILL.

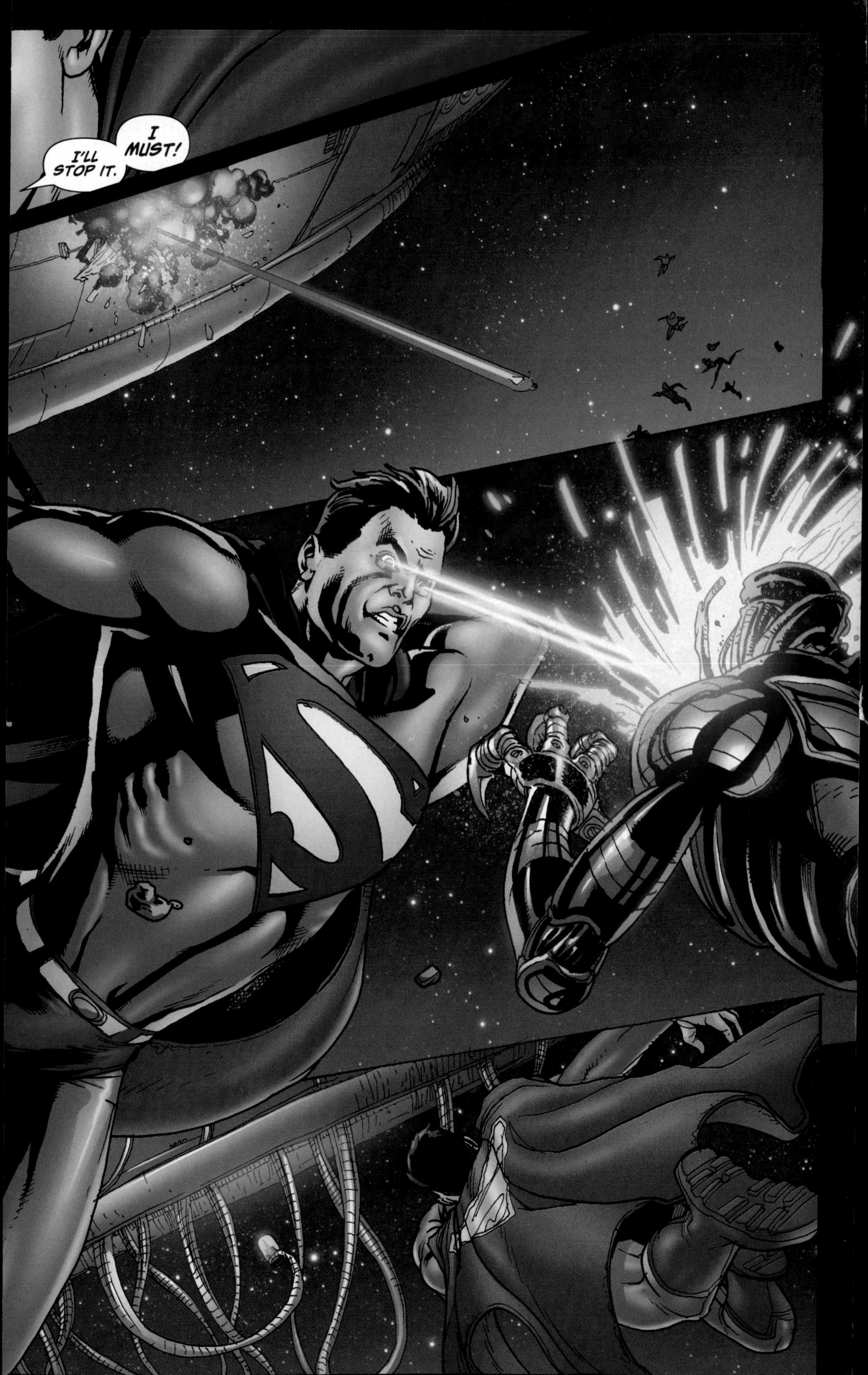
I'LL STOP IT.
I MUST!

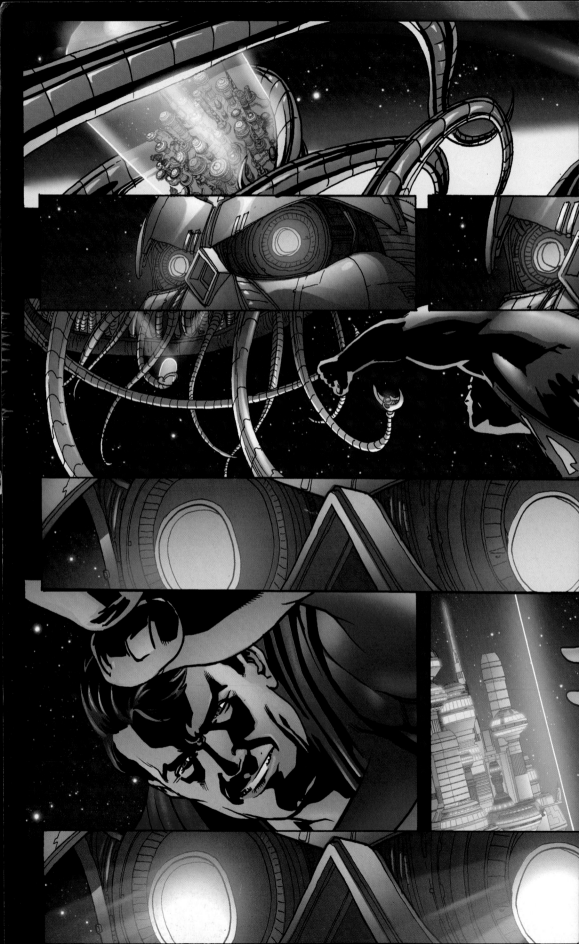

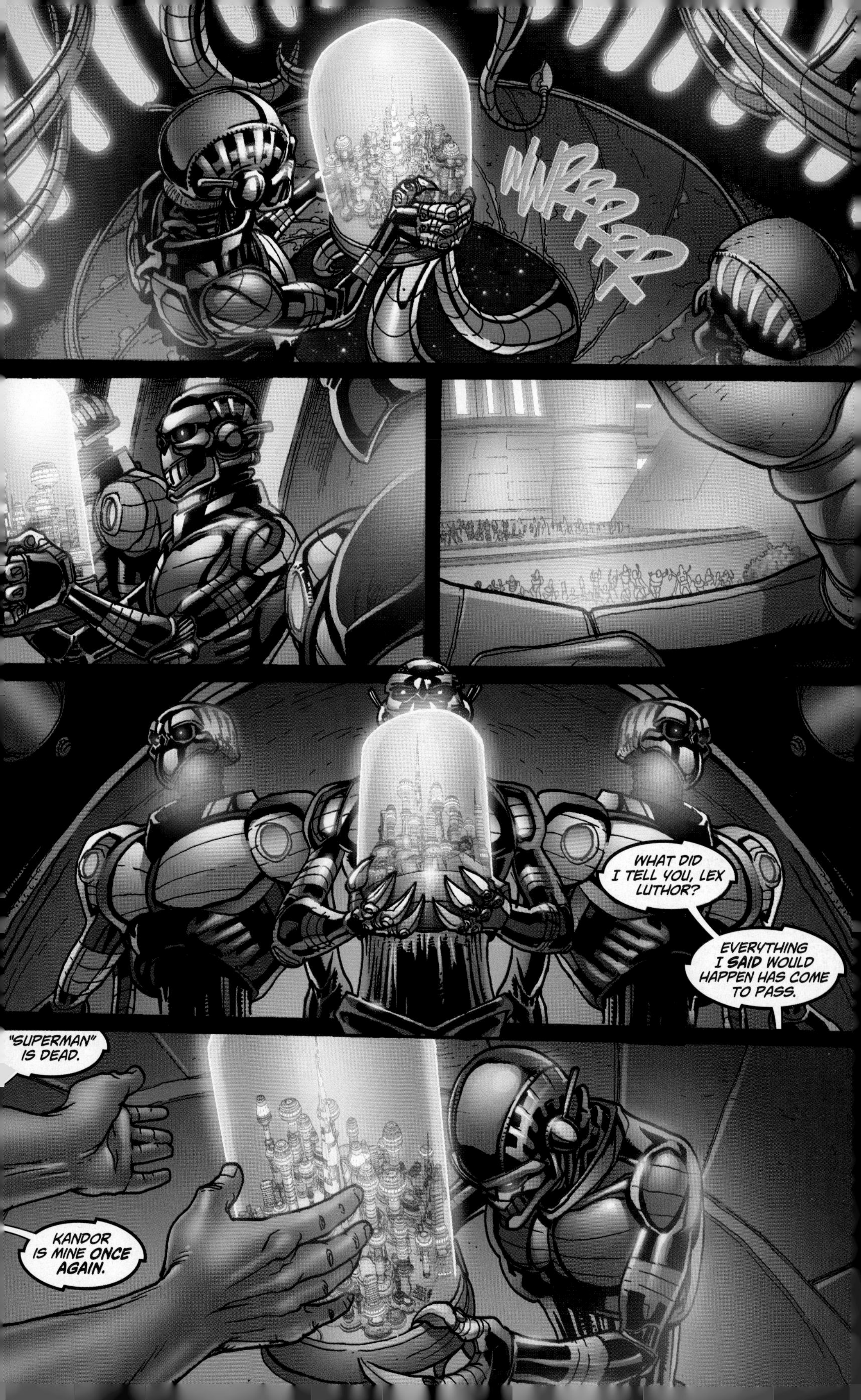

MWRRRRR
WHAT DID I TELL YOU, LEX LUTHOR?
EVERYTHING I SAID WOULD HAPPEN HAS COME TO PASS.
"SUPERMAN" IS DEAD.
KANDOR IS MINE ONCE AGAIN.

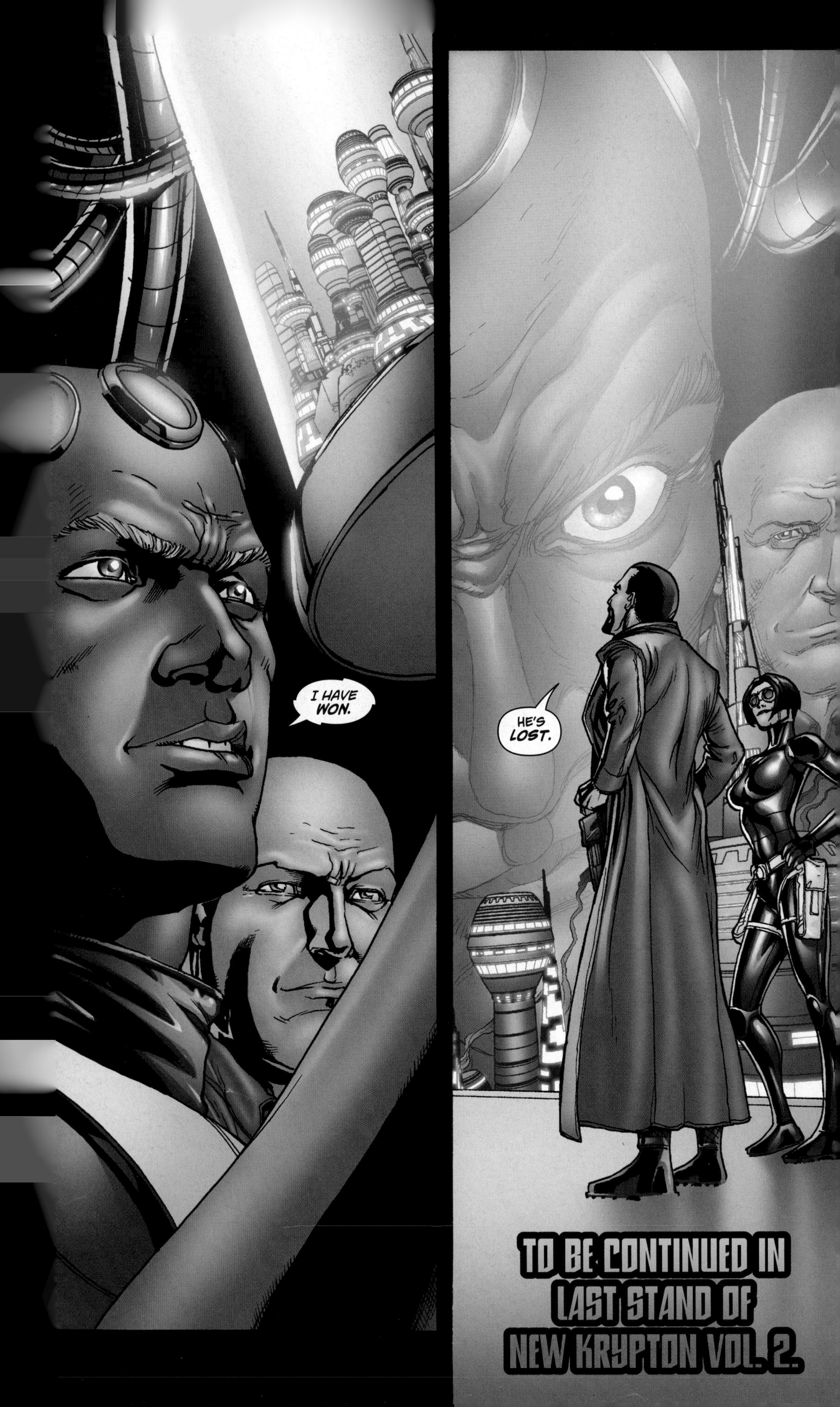
I HAVE WON.
HE'S LOST.
TO BE CONTINUED IN LAST STAND OF NEW KRYPTON VOL. 2.

ADVENTURE COMICS 8 variant by **AARON LOPRESTI** & **HI-FI**

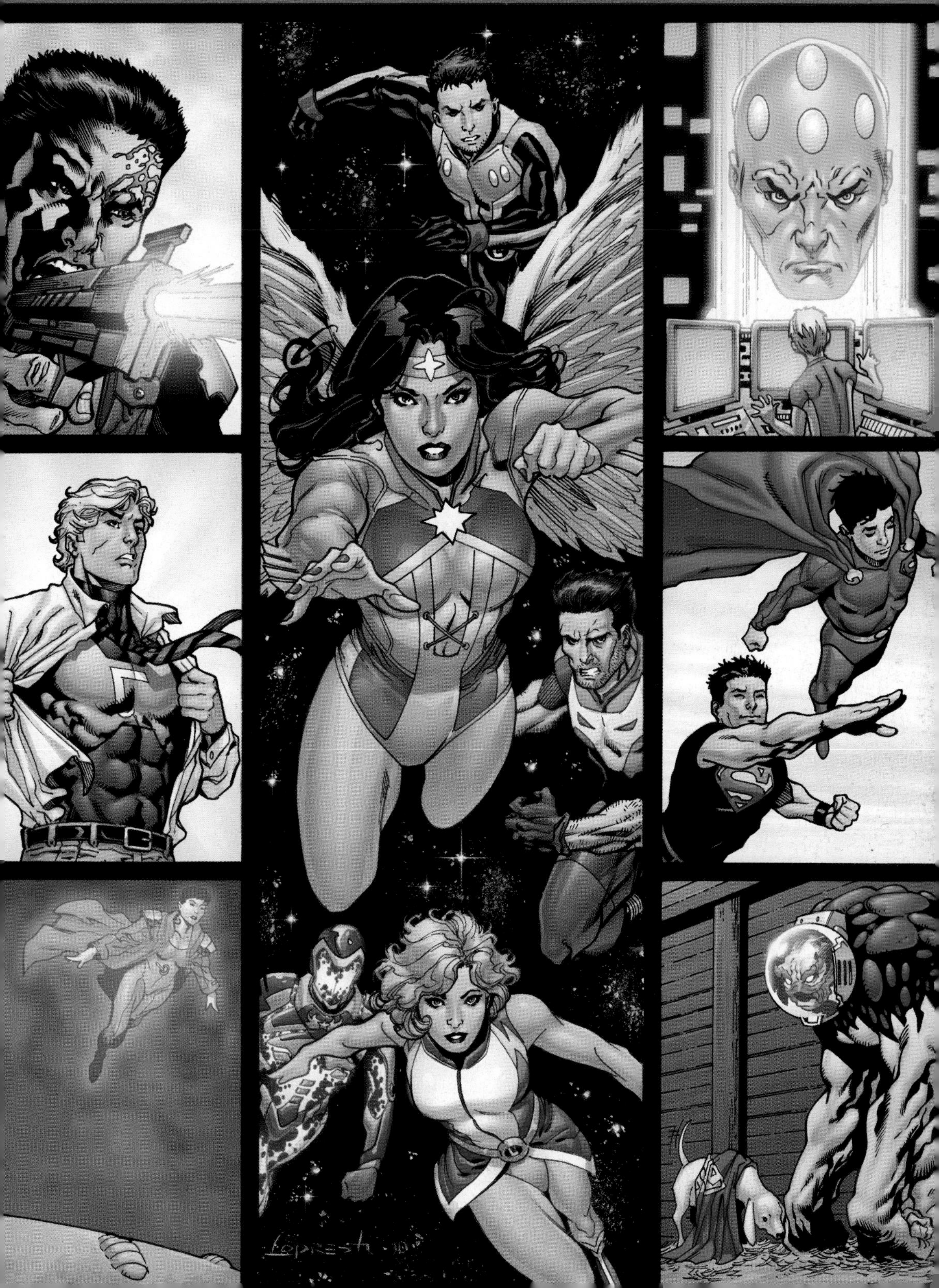

Lopresti '10

ADVENTURE COMICS 9 variant by **RAFAEL ALBUQUERQUE** & **DAVE MCCAIG**

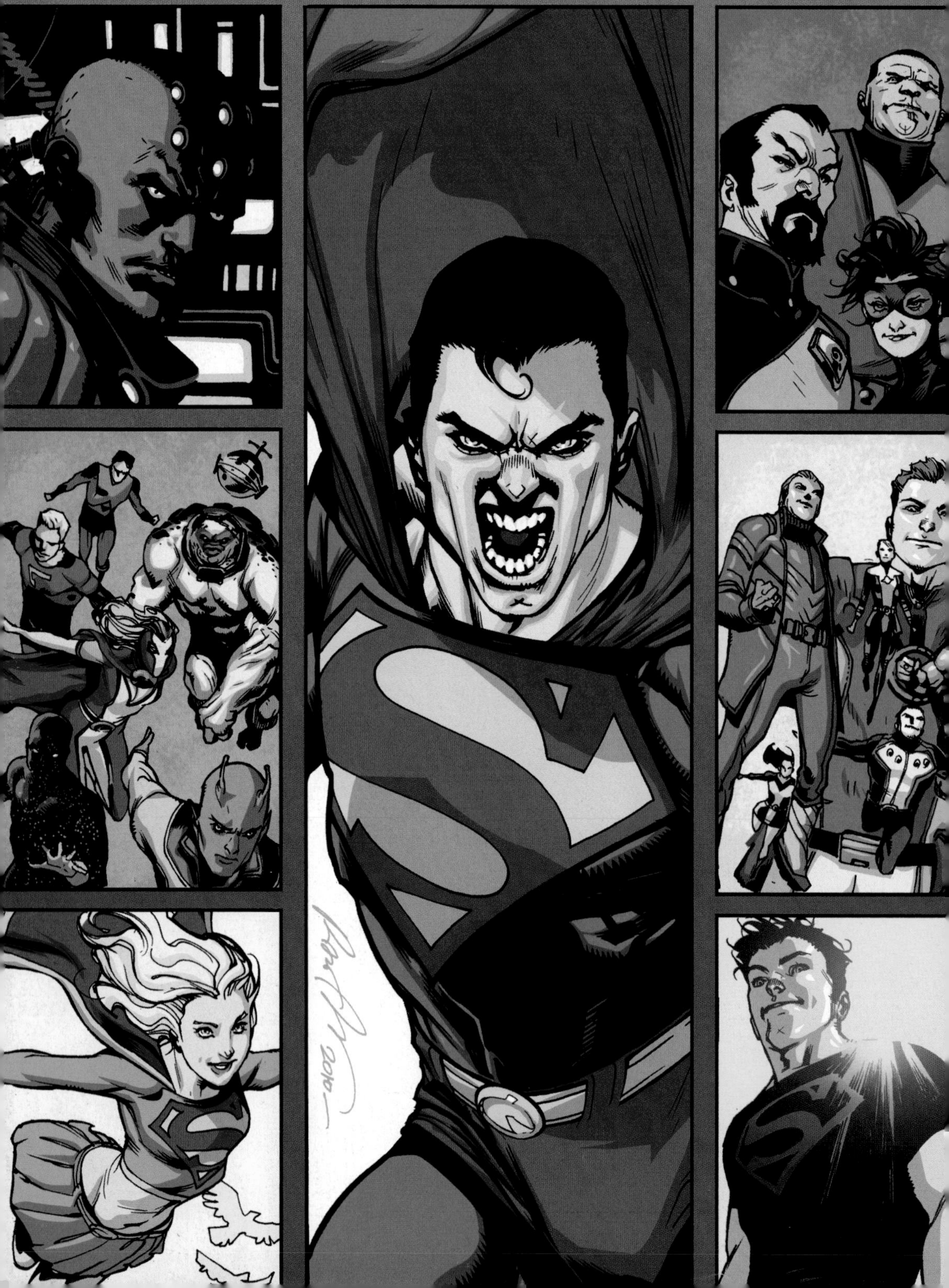

SUPERMAN: LAST STAND OF NEW KRYPTON 1 variant by MARCOS MARZ & ROD REIS

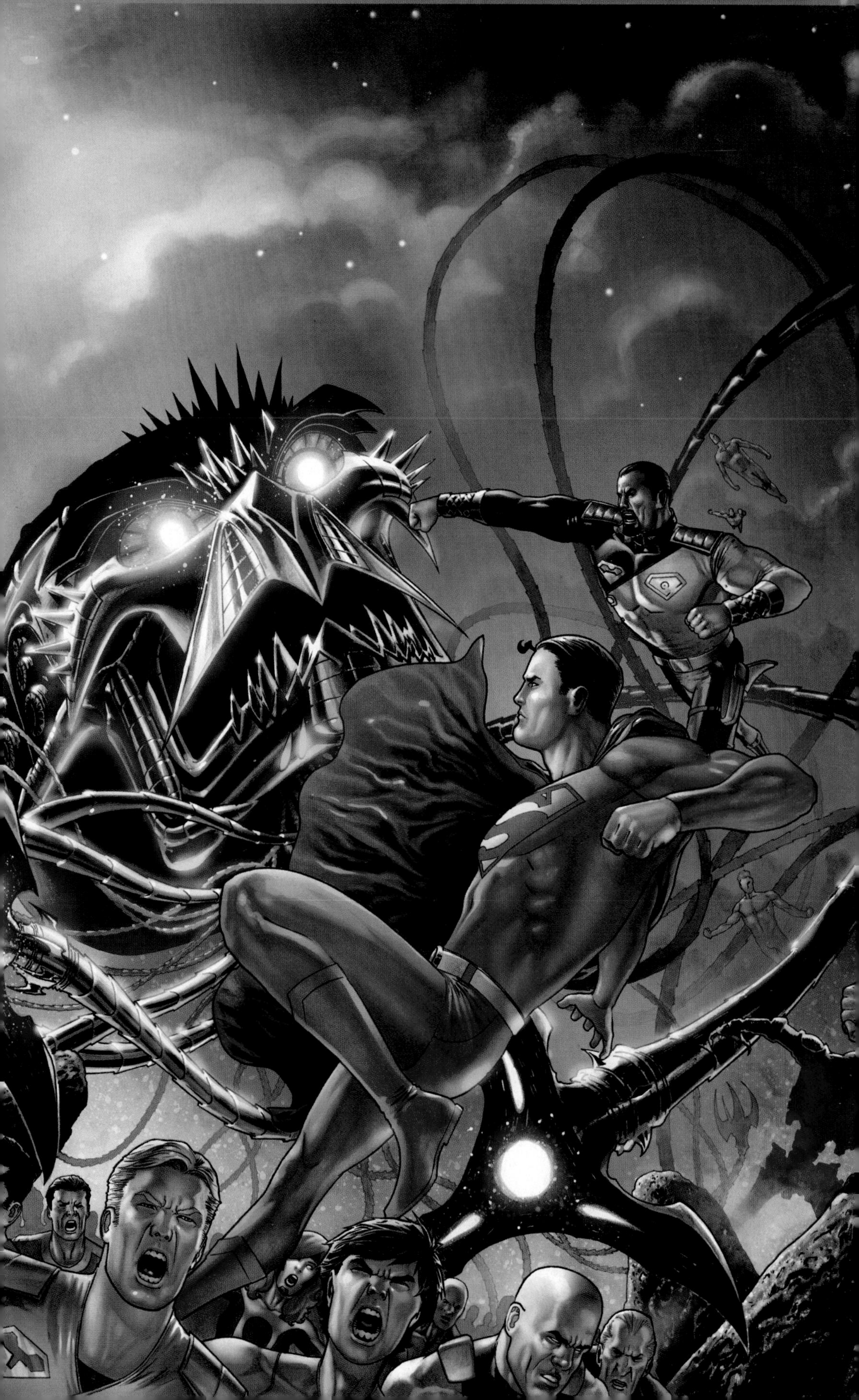

SUPERMAN: LAST STAND OF NEW KRYPTON 2 variant by **JULIAN LÓPEZ, BIT & JAVIER MENA**

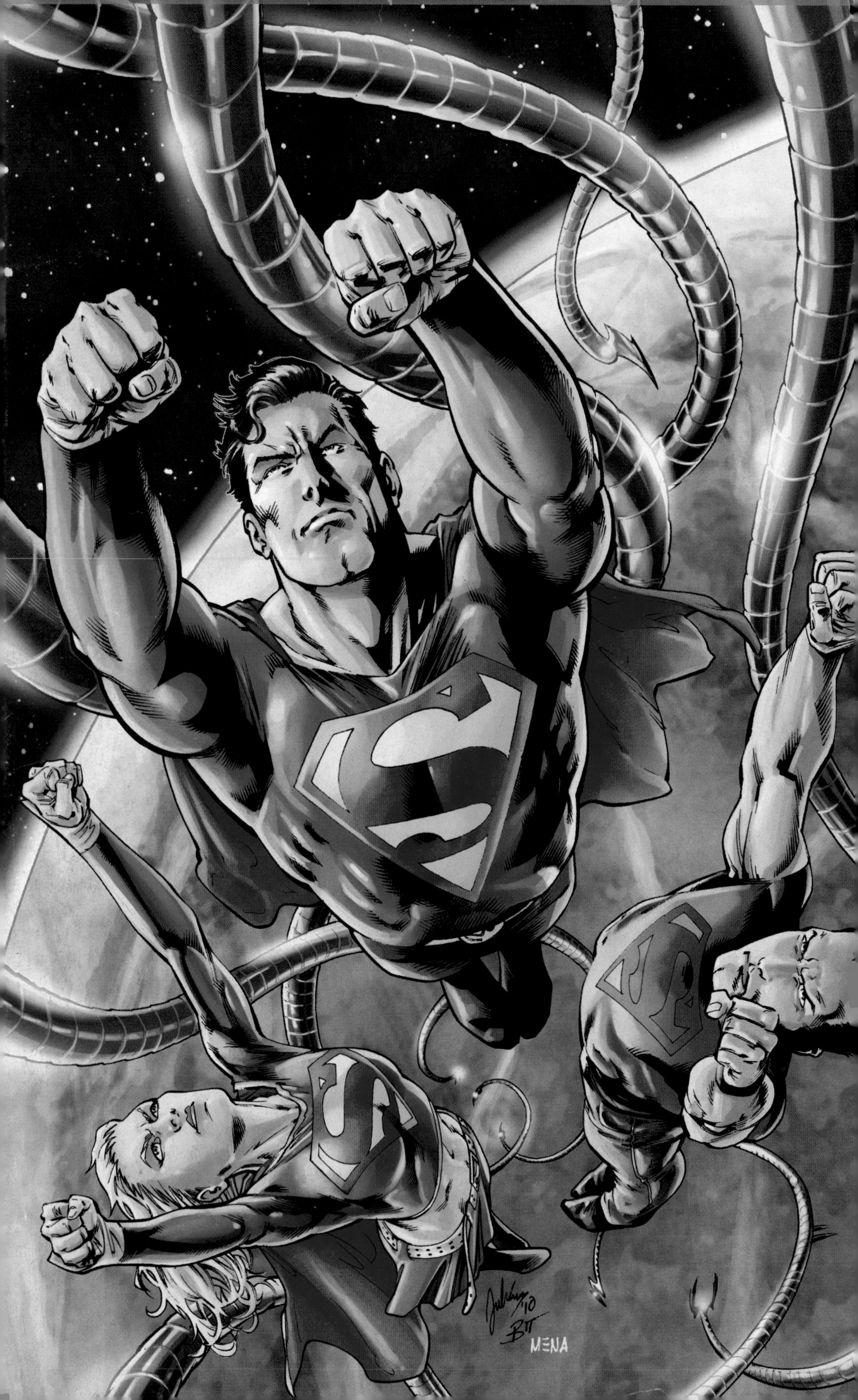
MENA

Andy Kubert's original cover to SUPERMAN: LAST STAND OF NEW KRYPTON 1 features Superman in his New Krypton military uniform.

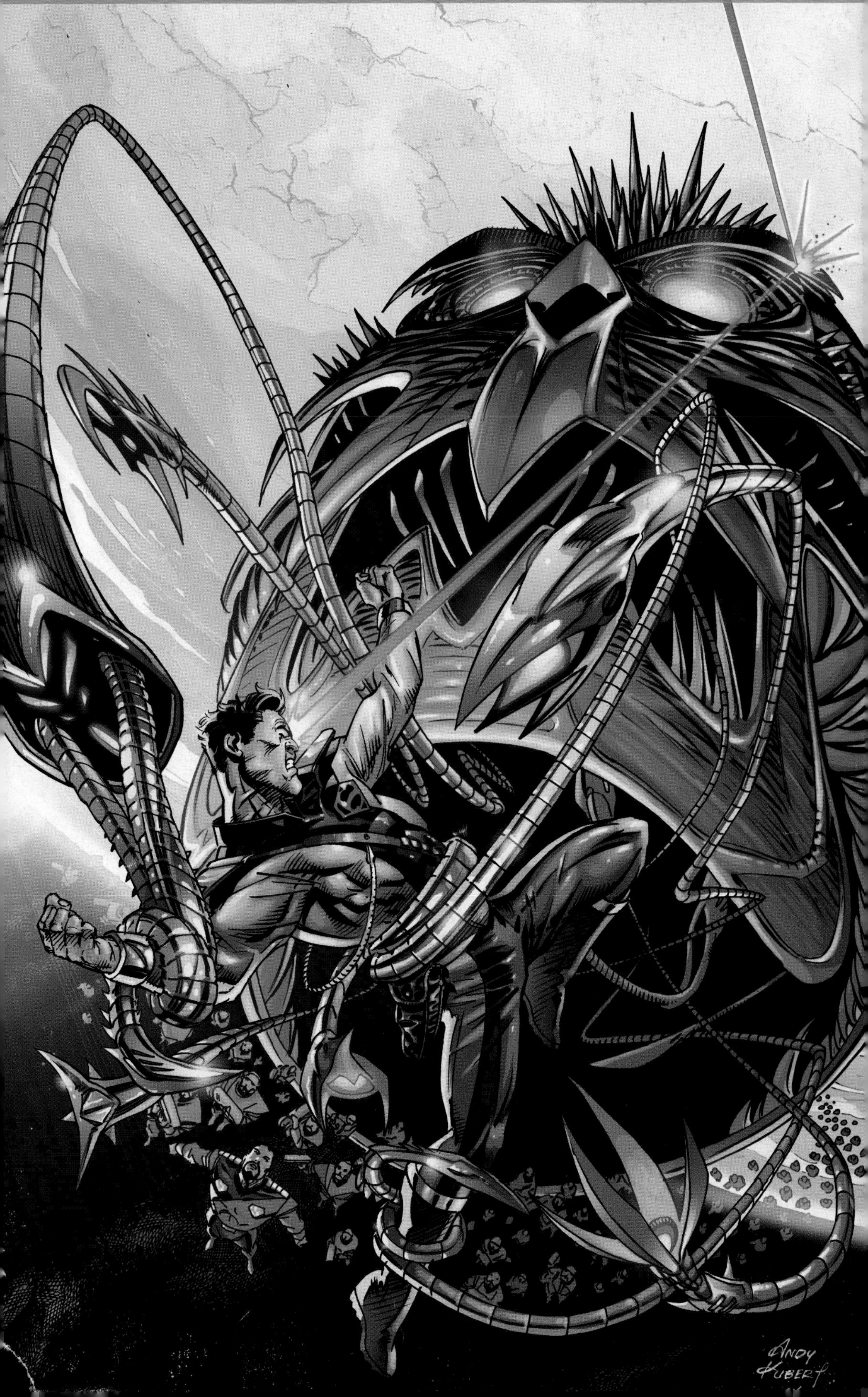
ANDY KUBERT

Brainiac's Red Sun Probot designs by Pete Woods

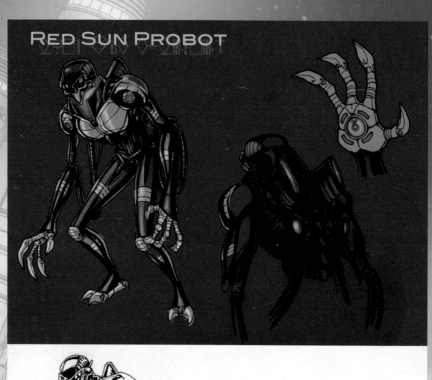

RED SUN PROBOT

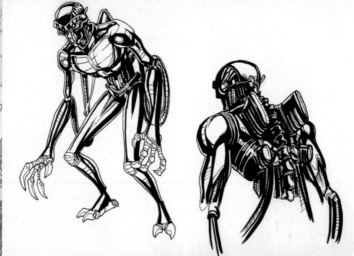